Working with Odoo

Learn how to use Odoo, a resourceful, open source business application platform designed to transform and modernize your business

Greg Moss

[PACKT] PUBLISHING open source community experience distilled

BIRMINGHAM - MUMBAI

Working with Odoo

First published: August 2015

Production reference: 1240815

Published by Packt Publishing Ltd.
Livery Place
35 Livery Street
Birmingham B3 2PB, UK.

ISBN 978-1-78439-455-4

www.packtpub.com

Credits

Author
Greg Moss

Reviewers
Robert Baumgartner
Bruce Letterle
Alan Lord

Commissioning Editor
Amarabha Banerjee

Acquisition Editors
Reshma Raman
Owen Roberts

Content Development Editor
Samantha Gonsalves

Technical Editor
Vivek Arora

Copy Editors
Puja Lalwani
Merilyn Pereira

Project Coordinator
Kinjal Bari

Proofreader
Safis Editing

Indexer
Tejal Soni

Production Coordinator
Aparna Bhagat

Cover Work
Aparna Bhagat

About the Author

Greg Moss has been a business and information systems consultant for over 25 years. Starting in 1988, Greg began to work extensively on financial and accounting-related applications. He wrote his first custom billing system for a rehabilitation facility at the age of 20. He has worked extensively in the healthcare, point of sale, manufacturing, telecommunications, and service sectors.

Greg is a Certified Information Systems Auditor (CISA) and a Certified Six Sigma Black Belt and was the chief information officer for Crownline Boats, Inc. In addition to studying music and computer science at Southern Illinois University, he completed a BS in business administration and information systems at Walden University. Greg also has an information assurance certification from Carnegie Mellon University.

In addition to Odoo, he has experience in a variety of ERP systems and was a Sage Pro partner for several years. Greg is the CEO of First Class Ventures, LLC and the owner of FirstClassComputerConsulting.com (`http://firstclasscomputerconsulting.com/`) and OdooClass.com (`http://www.odooclass.com/`). He is also an Odoo Ready Partner.

In 2014, Greg started a game studio called FirstClassGameStudios.com (`http://firstclassgamestudios.com/`) and designed and developed *NeuroMage*, a game that utilizes an inexpensive research-grade EEG headset to allow you to learn spells in the game using only your mind. *NeuroMage* was first demonstrated at the Neurogaming conference in 2014. As a result, Greg has become a recognized leader in Neurogaming and is humbled to be on an expert panel at the Neurogaming conference in 2015.

Greg is an experienced stock and options trader and has recently started dabbling in currency trading. In his spare time, he enjoys playing trumpet and saxophone with local bands and taking cross-country road trips with his African grey parrot, Bibi.

Acknowledgments

I would like to thank my wonderful wife, Kelly, for all her love and support; my brother, Eric, for his kindness and generosity and for always being there when someone needs him; and my mom, a lifelong public school teacher who never hesitated to support me in anything that involved learning or creativity.

Many thanks to the great team at Silkworm for being the absolute best.

Also, many thanks to all the reviewers, the great people at Packt Publishing, and the Odoo community for all their support.

About the Reviewers

Robert Baumgartner earned a degree in business informatics from Austria, Europe, where he is living today. He began his career in 2002 as a business intelligence consultant working for different service companies. After that, he worked in the paper industry sector as a consultant and project manager for an Enterprise Resource Planning (ERP) system. In 2009, he founded his own company, datenpol gmbh—a service integrator specialist in selected open source software products focusing on ERP and data warehousing. Robert is an open source enthusiast who has given several speeches at open source events. The products he is working on are Odoo, Talend Data Integration, Saiku, and JasperReports. He contributes to the open source community by sharing his knowledge with blog entries on the company website at `http://datenpol.at/`. He commits software to GitHub, such as the OpenERP Talend Connector component, which can be found at `https://github.com/baumgaro`. His Odoo contributions can be found at `https://github.com/datenpol` and the Odoo Community Association at `https://github.com/OCA`. You can follow him on Twitter at `@baumgaro`.

Bruce Letterle is an IT industry veteran with over 30 years of experience running system integration firms and web development agencies. Currently, he is the managing director and founder of Red Lab Media, a digital agency providing web development, hosting, and marketing services.

He has been a reviewer on *trixbox CE 2.6, Kerry Garrison, Packt Publishing*.

Alan Lord has nearly 30 years of experience in the IT industry. He has worked for start-ups that were some of the pioneers of the early Internet (and before!) through to global telecommunication giants.

For the last 15 years or so, Alan has been building and running Linux systems both for business and pleasure. In 2006, he cofounded the open source consulting company Libertus Solutions (`http://libertus.co.uk/`) to offer expertise, help, and advice on free software to businesses, the public sector, and charity organizations alike.

As well as being a business-minded free software evangelist, Alan's areas of expertise include Ubuntu Linux and several popular open source business applications including Odoo and vtiger CRM.

This is the second book that Alan has reviewed for Packt Publishing, the first being *vtiger CRM Beginner's Guide*, published in July 2011.

Alan occasionally writes blogs at `http://www.theopensourcerer.com/` and can easily be found on various social media networks.

www.PacktPub.com

Support files, eBooks, discount offers, and more

For support files and downloads related to your book, please visit `www.PacktPub.com`.

Did you know that Packt offers eBook versions of every book published, with PDF and ePub files available? You can upgrade to the eBook version at `www.PacktPub.com` and as a print book customer, you are entitled to a discount on the eBook copy. Get in touch with us at `service@packtpub.com` for more details.

At `www.PacktPub.com`, you can also read a collection of free technical articles, sign up for a range of free newsletters and receive exclusive discounts and offers on Packt books and eBooks.

`https://www2.packtpub.com/books/subscription/packtlib`

Do you need instant solutions to your IT questions? PacktLib is Packt's online digital book library. Here, you can search, access, and read Packt's entire library of books.

Why subscribe?

- Fully searchable across every book published by Packt
- Copy and paste, print, and bookmark content
- On demand and accessible via a web browser

Free access for Packt account holders

If you have an account with Packt at `www.PacktPub.com`, you can use this to access PacktLib today and view 9 entirely free books. Simply use your login credentials for immediate access.

Table of Contents

Preface

Working with Odoo provides a comprehensive walk-through for installing, configuring, and implementing Odoo in real-world business environments. This book will help you to understand the value of Enterprise Resource Planning (ERP) systems and the best practices and approaches for getting a system up and running in your organization. For those who are new to ERP systems, this book will serve as an introduction so that you will be better prepared to understand more advanced ERP concepts. If you are already experienced in ERP systems, this book will give you an overview of the primary applications for Odoo and how those applications can be used in a real business environment.

Odoo is a very feature-filled business application framework with literally hundreds of applications and modules available. Silkworm, Inc. is a highly respected custom apparel, promotional products, and graphic design company in the Midwest, United States. Silkworm has been serving its customers, team members, and community for more than 30 years. Silkworm has been kind enough to allow us to include some basic aspects of their business processes as a set of real-world examples on implementing Odoo into a manufacturing operation. While the examples in this book are extremely simplified, using real-life examples will assist in understanding how to utilize Odoo to solve real-world business problems.

Although Silkworm is actively implementing Odoo, Silkworm, Inc. does not directly endorse or recommend Odoo for any specific business solution. Every company must carry out their own research to determine if Odoo is a good fit for their operation.

We have done our best in this book to cover the most essential features of the Odoo applications that you are most likely to use in your business. Unfortunately, there are just not enough pages to cover more advanced topics. In *Appendix, Locating Additional Odoo Resources*, we have included additional resources that you can look to for more advanced subjects.

After the book is released, be sure to check for online updates in which we can cover more advanced subjects.

Also, Packt Publishing offers other Odoo books that cover more advanced Odoo topics.

What this book covers

The book is divided into three sections:

- The installation of Odoo and the basics of implementing Odoo in your business (chapters 1 through 5)
- An introduction to accounting and finance setup and modules to help your business run more efficiently (chapters 6 through 8)
- Advanced configuration and customization of Odoo (chapters 9 through 13)

Now, let's discuss in some detail what each chapter will cover:

Chapter 1, Setting Up Odoo, gets you started right away by showing you how to use Odoo online without any setup. Just open your browser and you are ready to get going. Next, the chapter goes on to cover the different installation types and prerequisites for both Windows and Ubuntu. Instructions are provided to find the right download package and set up Odoo on your own server. The chapter then goes into the basics of configuring Odoo. At the end of the chapter is a useful collection of tips on how to troubleshoot your Odoo installation.

Chapter 2, Installing Your First Application, begins by introducing you to the real-world case study that will be used as an example throughout the book. We continue by showing you how to create the company database and configure the basic company settings required to quickly get your first Odoo system up and running. The first module, Sales Management, will be installed, and we will walk through the steps to enter a customer and a product. The chapter concludes by entering a sales order and completing the sale and producing an invoice.

Chapter 3, Exploring Customer Relationship Management in Odoo, starts with a basic overview of CRM systems and their importance in today's modern business environment. After we cover the installation of the CRM application, a lead is entered for our sample company. We will demonstrate the CRM workflow by turning the lead into a customer. Next, a quote is generated for our newly acquired customer, and a call is scheduled for follow-up by using Odoo's meeting functionality. We also cover the OpenChatter feature that is used throughout Odoo to provide notes and messages associated with Odoo documents.

Chapter 4, Purchasing with Odoo, shows us how to install the purchasing application, set up suppliers, and begin purchasing and receiving products in Odoo. Later in the chapter, you learn how to tie purchasing into sales orders to automatically generate draft purchase orders based on your business requirements.

Chapter 5, Making Goods with Manufacturing Resource Planning, begins to explore some of the primary functionalities of ERP systems for manufacturing operations. You will learn how to set up your manufacturing orders and define the bill of materials to specify the raw materials that will go into your final products. Manufacturing operations can then be extended with routing and work centers to give you more control over tracking time and resources.

Chapter 6, Configuring Accounting Finance, discusses the Accounts Receivable and Accounts Payable basic functions. Next, we will introduce the Chart of Accounts and discover how to set up fiscal periods. This chapter will also include the basic accounting reports and how to close a period.

Chapter 7, Administering an Odoo Installation, begins by discussing the overall considerations for implementing Odoo into a business environment. This includes advice on server configurations, documenting your processes, and the importance of considering business continuity. We then go into how to manage users, groups, and set up security roles to manage access to various applications within Odoo. Finally, we look at how to implement Internationalization for multiple languages and currencies.

Chapter 8, Implementing the Human Resources Application, begins by installing the basic HR applications and goes over the employee directory. Other topics in the chapter will include timesheets, the recruitment process, and leave management. At the end of the chapter, we will look at how to create online interviews and hire employees using the tools in Odoo.

Chapter 9, Understanding Project Management, covers the features of the Project Management application in Odoo. We will create a project, see how to enter tasks and tie a project to a specific customer. Next, team members are assigned to the project, and we configure task stages. We then will go over real-world examples of using the Project Management application to more easily manage complex orders and customer needs. Finally, we see how Project Management can be used along with analytic accounting to provide better reporting.

Chapter 10, Creating Advanced Searches and Dashboards, demonstrates how to utilize the advanced search features and configure custom dashboards in Odoo. By the end of the chapter, you will be able to create and save custom searches to reuse later, as well as add search results to dashboards.

Chapter 11, Building a Website with Odoo, is dedicated to exploring Odoo's powerful new website building platform. At the beginning of the chapter, we will look at what a CMS (Content Management System) is and some of the other popular website building platforms. We follow along with Odoo's website building tutorial and then look at the features that can be used to promote your website right from within Odoo.

Chapter 12, Implementing E-Commerce with Odoo, builds on the previous chapter by adding a fully functioning online shopping cart to the website. We see how to publish products to the website and the various options to change their appearance. Midway through the chapter, we cover product variants that add additional flexibility to how you manage your products within Odoo. Finally, we conclude by examining how to set up a payment processor to take payment online through PayPal.

Chapter 13, Customizing Odoo for Your Business, explains how to enter the developer mode for making a variety of custom changes to Odoo. We will walk through the steps to add fields to the sales order form and then include the fields in tree views for sorting and reporting. From here, we will get into advanced configuration topics to better customize Odoo for your specific business requirements.

Chapter 14, Modifying Documents and Reports, goes over the basic reporting mechanisms available in Odoo and weighs up the advantages and disadvantages of the various options. We learn how to use the powerful qWeb template language to modify the default Odoo sales order form.

Chapter 15, Understanding Workflows, introduces the workflow editor and analyzes the basic sales order workflow. Using our case study example, the workflow is modified to improve the flow of information through the business. By the end of the chapter, you should have a basic understanding of modifying workflows to better handle unique business processes.

Chapter 16, Discovering Custom Odoo Modules, introduces the process of developing custom solutions in Odoo. We build on what we learned in *Chapter 13, Customizing Odoo for Your Business* and create a module that will persist our custom field and views within our module. Next, we build on the workflow modifications we made in the previous chapter and upgrade our module to approve art designs for our real-world example.

Appendix, Locating Additional Odoo Resources, covers a list of resources that can extend your knowledge in supporting an Odoo installation.

What you need for this book

You should have Odoo version 8 installed on your system. It can be downloaded from `https://github.com/odoo/odoo`.

Most often, it is installed in VMware or on a cloud such as AWS.

Chapter 1, Setting Up Odoo, provides the basic Odoo installation for both Windows and Ubuntu.

Many people use this guide for a more manual Odoo installation `http://www.theopensourcerer.com/2014/09/how-to-install-openerp-odoo-8-on-ubuntu-server-14-04-lts/`.

Once Odoo is installed, no other software installation is required throughout the book.

To get the most out of this book, you should have an understanding of basic business operations. For example, you should know the purpose of a sales order and a purchase order. You should also have basic computer skills to understand file systems and how to install software. For more advanced customization topics in the book, you should have a basic knowledge of databases and programming concepts.

Who this book is for

This book is for everyone who is interested in implementing an ERP system in a business organization. If you are an IT professional looking to get a functional understanding of Odoo, then this book is for you. This book is also appropriate for business and operations managers who want to get a comprehensive understanding of Odoo and know how it can be used to improve business processes.

Conventions

In this book, you will find a number of text styles that distinguish between different kinds of information. Here are some examples of these styles and an explanation of their meaning.

Code words in text, database table names, folder names, filenames, file extensions, pathnames, dummy URLs, user input, and Twitter handles are shown as follows: "We will then copy the `state` column from `sale.py` and paste it into our module."

A block of code is set as follows:

```
from osv import osv, fields


class silkworm_sale_order(osv.Model):
    _inherit = 'sale.order'

    _columns = {
        'x_daterequired': fields.date('Date Required'),
        'x_rush': fields.boolean('Rush Order'),
       }
```

New terms and **important words** are shown in bold. Words that you see on the screen, for example, in menus or dialog boxes, appear in the text like this: "Click on the **Install** button to begin the installation process."

> Warnings or important notes appear in a box like this.

> Tips and tricks appear like this.

Reader feedback

Feedback from our readers is always welcome. Let us know what you think about this book—what you liked or disliked. Reader feedback is important for us as it helps us develop titles that you will really get the most out of.

To send us general feedback, simply e-mail `feedback@packtpub.com`, and mention the book's title in the subject of your message.

If there is a topic that you have expertise in and you are interested in either writing or contributing to a book, see our author guide at `www.packtpub.com/authors`.

Customer support

Now that you are the proud owner of a Packt book, we have a number of things to help you to get the most from your purchase.

Errata

Although we have taken every care to ensure the accuracy of our content, mistakes do happen. If you find a mistake in one of our books—maybe a mistake in the text or the code—we would be grateful if you could report this to us. By doing so, you can save other readers from frustration and help us improve subsequent versions of this book. If you find any errata, please report them by visiting `http://www.packtpub.com/submit-errata`, selecting your book, clicking on the **Errata Submission Form** link, and entering the details of your errata. Once your errata are verified, your submission will be accepted and the errata will be uploaded to our website or added to any list of existing errata under the Errata section of that title.

To view the previously submitted errata, go to `https://www.packtpub.com/books/content/support` and enter the name of the book in the search field. The required information will appear under the **Errata** section.

Piracy

Piracy of copyrighted material on the Internet is an ongoing problem across all media. At Packt, we take the protection of our copyright and licenses very seriously. If you come across any illegal copies of our works in any form on the Internet, please provide us with the location address or website name immediately so that we can pursue a remedy.

Please contact us at `copyright@packtpub.com` with a link to the suspected pirated material.

We appreciate your help in protecting our authors and our ability to bring you valuable content.

Questions

If you have a problem with any aspect of this book, you can contact us at `questions@packtpub.com`, and we will do our best to address the problem.

1
Setting Up Odoo

Odoo is a powerful set of open source business applications built on the OpenObject framework. When you first install Odoo, the only functionality you will have is limited messaging options between users. From there, Odoo allows you to install the modules you need as you need them. This flexibility makes Odoo much more accessible than many business software solutions.

In this chapter, we will get started working with Odoo by covering the installation and the basics of setting up an Odoo database.

The topics we will cover include:

- Using the free two-user edition of Odoo
- Setting up a trial company
- Installing Odoo on Windows and Ubuntu
- Troubleshooting and configuring your installation

Getting started with Odoo online

Not long ago, nearly all companies kept their primary information systems in-house. This approach requires not only a lot of capital expense in purchasing servers and software licenses, but also creates a lot of responsibility and risk in backing up data and ensuring business continuity. Today, more and more companies are choosing to host their business applications in online networks commonly known as the cloud. Odoo allows you the flexibility of both options—either hosting on your own hardware, or utilizing Odoo's online software services.

Taking advantage of Odoo online

The best thing about accessing Odoo online is that you can jump in and start using the software right away. You don't have to decide what operating system to use. You don't have to install any software at all. Just enter the URL into your web browser and you are ready to get started.

Another added benefit of taking this approach is that you will verify that your web browser is up to date and compatible with the latest version of Odoo. So, even if you intend to install Odoo on your own hardware, it is still worth taking a minute to test out the online trial version of Odoo. Expect to put a great deal of time into determining which Odoo applications are right for your company.

Taking a few hours to use the Odoo online version is time well spent and you can put off installing Odoo until you are more certain it is the right software for your business.

> Use the Odoo free edition to verify browser compatibility with any older machines.

Odoo browser requirements

Odoo is designed to run on a variety of modern web browsers. Supported browsers include:

- Google Chrome (recommended)
- Firefox
- Internet Explorer
- Safari

> Macintosh users will need to make sure they are running Mac OS X or above. Users running older Macintosh systems are currently having difficulties running Odoo version 7. Also, in my experience, Google Chrome tends to offer the best experience in working with Odoo. Firefox is also often recommended by others in the Odoo community.

Odoo mobile phone and tablet support

Beginning with Odoo 8, Odoo has native support for mobile phones and tablets. Menus are designed to flow and format properly. The new website application even includes a preview within the portal administration to emulate how the site would appear on a mobile phone. While you still suffer many of the limitations that come with a small screen size, the applications are functional and make it even easier for developers to create mobile Odoo applications.

Odoo's mobile application support covers both the Android and Apple iOS platforms. Make sure, however, that for any processes you intend to implement for your business, you test all processes thoroughly for both desktop and any mobile solutions. Smaller screen sizes might make some data unreadable or very awkward to work with.

Accessing the Odoo free online trial

Accessing the online trial version of Odoo online could not be simpler. Just open up your browser and navigate to `https://www.odoo.com/start`.

You will then be prompted to choose one of more than 20 business applications, as shown in the following screenshot:

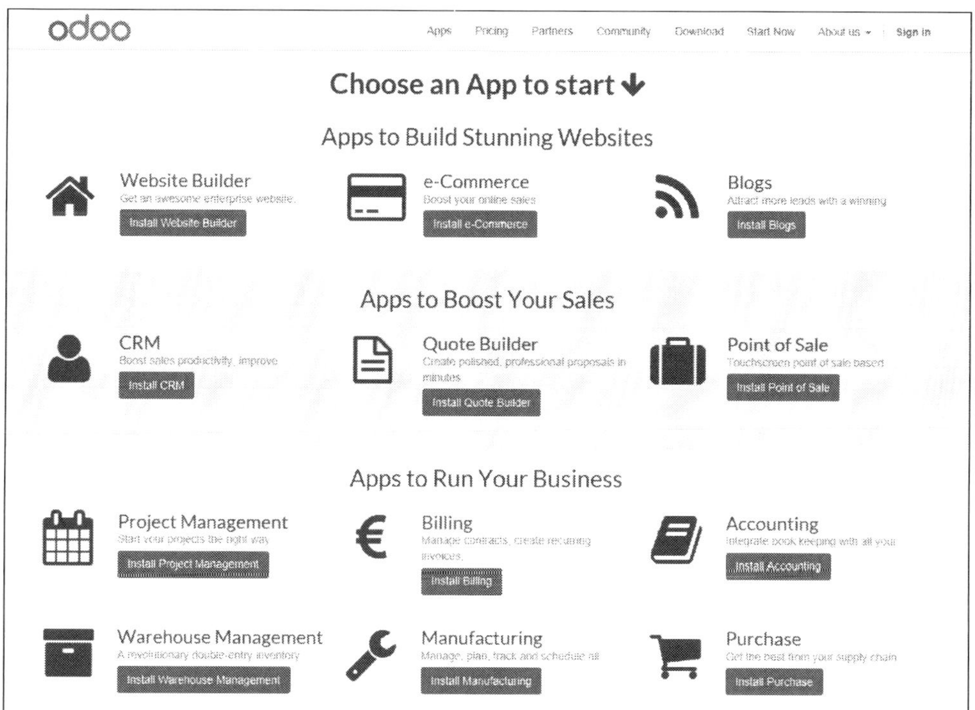

Don't worry, you can add more applications later:

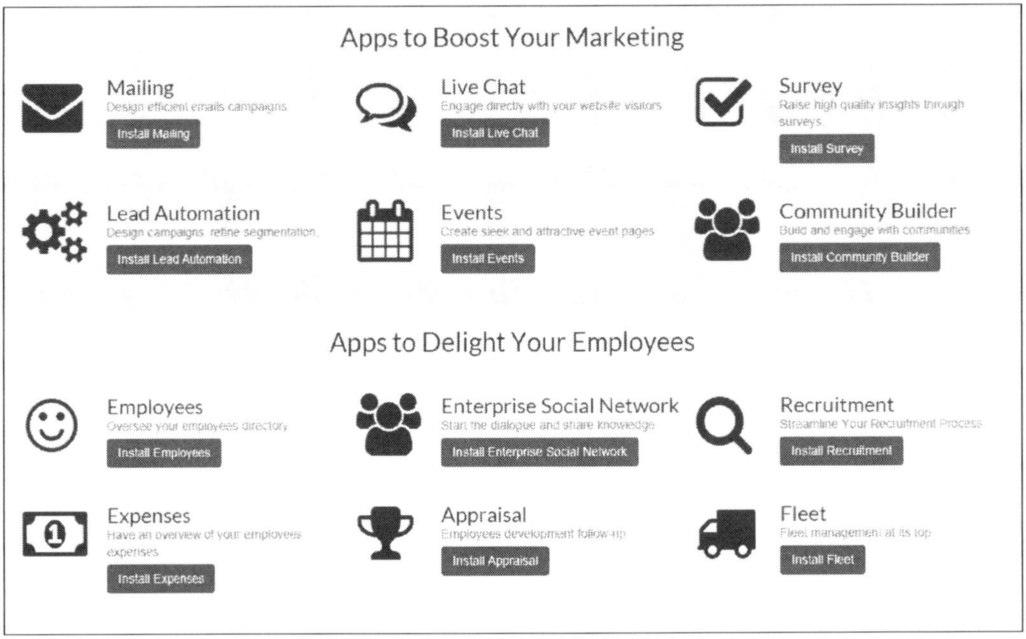

Clicking on the appropriate button for the application immediately begins installing your own unique Odoo instance.

For our example, let's go ahead and install the CRM application by clicking on the **Install CRM** button:

Be patient as it can take thirty seconds or longer for the servers to build the database and bring up the starting page. When the installation is complete, Odoo automatically signs you in so you can begin trying out the software. The goal of this approach is to get users to directly start using the software right away and avoid having to fill out lengthy forms or create logins and passwords to begin using the software. It really is just one click and you have your own version of Odoo to play with.

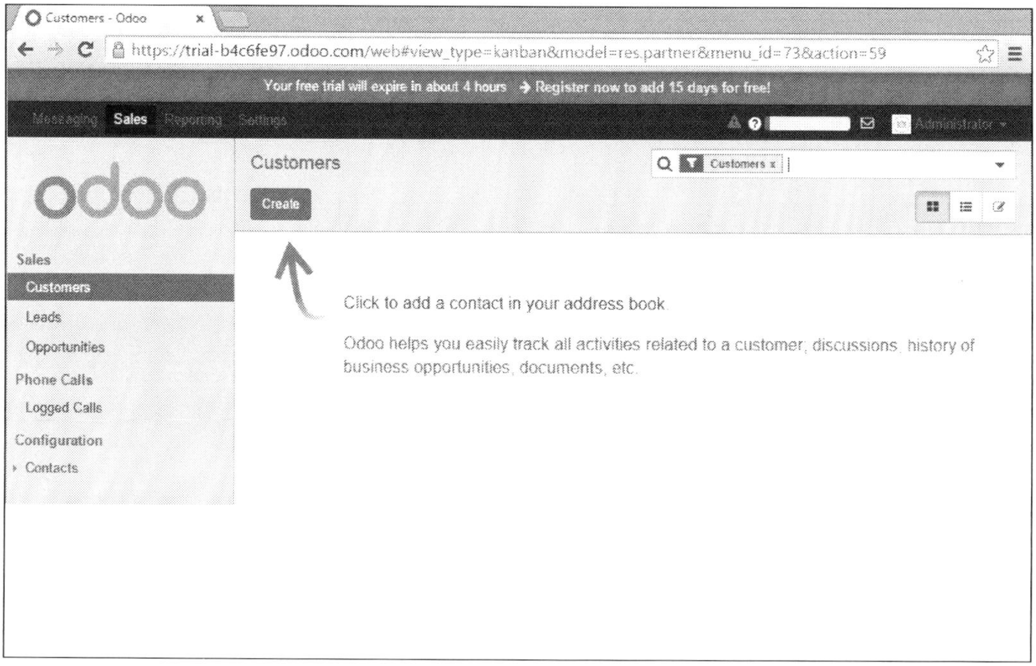

In the preceding screenshot, you can see the screen that appears after installing the CRM application. With it, you can manage your customers, leads, and opportunities. We will discuss the CRM application in detail in *Chapter 3, Exploring Customer Relationship Management in Odoo*.

Take a few minutes to look around in Odoo to get familiar with the interface. You don't have to worry about breaking anything or doing anything wrong. If you run into problems or get confused, just close your web browser and try again.

> This is a demonstration and will only last for one four-hour session. If you close your browser, you will lose your setup and have to start over again.

Continuing to use the trial version of Odoo

At the very top of the Odoo application, just under the address bar in the browser, you will see a message that informs you about how much longer your trial version of Odoo will run before you need to register. Also, remember that it is possible to lose this instance of Odoo before the time runs out.

Clicking on the message will take you to the typical standard signup form to provide your name, e-mail, and other information to register your trial version of Odoo:

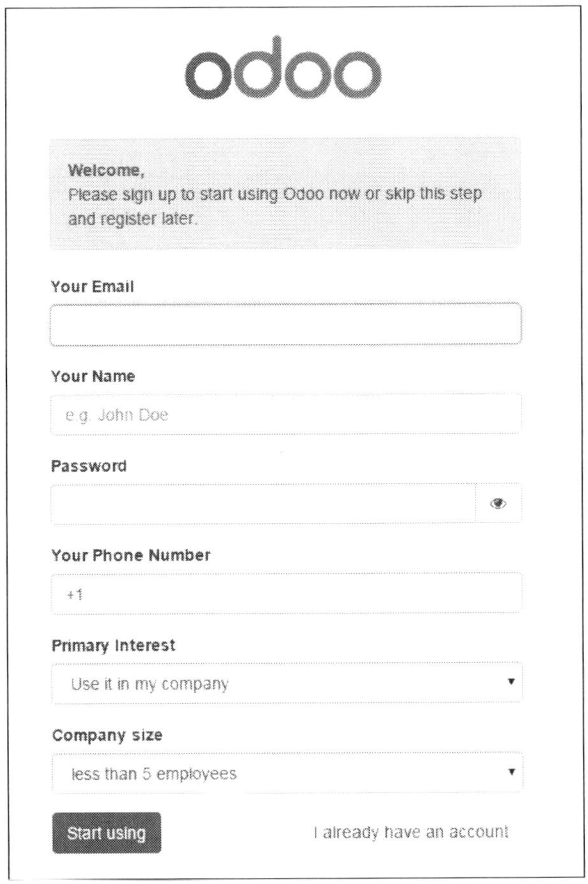

After you have filled out the form and clicked on **Start using**, the Odoo application will once again reload. Now, you will see in the top-right-hand corner that you are logged in under the name you provided in the signup form. Also, you will see at the top, a countdown of how many days are remaining in your trial version.

Subscribing to Odoo

For 15 days, you can use Odoo for free without subscribing. Once your 15 days run out, you must subscribe to Odoo in order to keep using their enterprise cloud-hosted version of the software. The first two users of Odoo are free indefinitely.

This means you can sign up and continue using Odoo with just two users without having to pay any monthly fees. For additional users, the current pricing is $25 per month, per user at the time of writing. Each application that you use also will incur a monthly cost depending upon the specific application.

The following screenshot is the Odoo Online Pricing calculator in July of 2015:

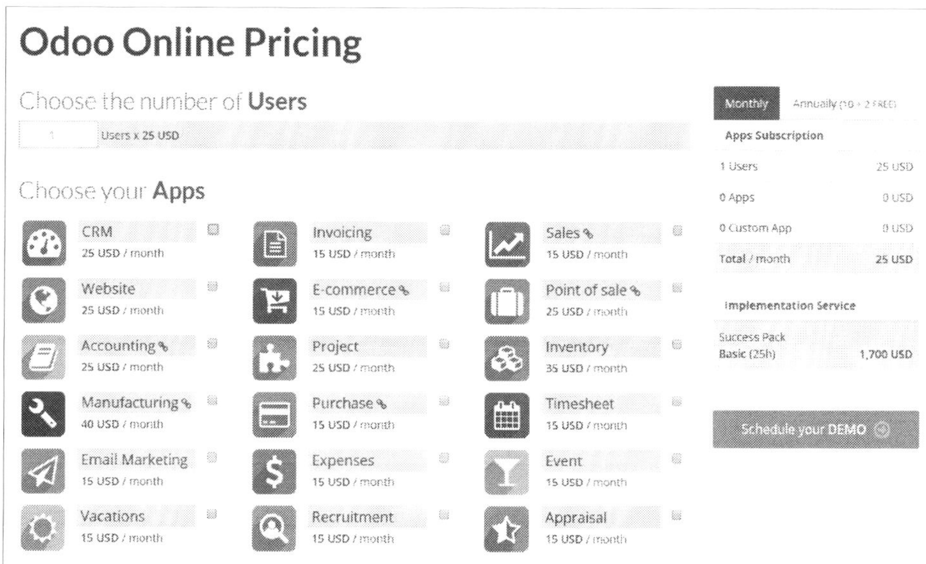

You can locate the Odoo Online Pricing page at `https://www.odoo.com/pricing-online`.

> Odoo Online is priced for employees that use the applications. You are not charged for customers or suppliers that access Odoo through the web portal.

Depending on your requirements, an Odoo subscription might be a good decision. Installing and maintaining an Odoo installation takes a degree of expertise and has risks for production systems. You must maintain adequate disaster recovery procedures in case of server crashes or hard drive failures. There are also complexities in applying bug fixes and migrating to newer versions of Odoo. This book will help you with many of these tasks. Yet, it can be quite convenient to have an Odoo subscription so you can focus on the functional, rather than the technical, aspects of working with Odoo.

To subscribe to Odoo online and continue using Odoo past the 15 day trial period, click on the **Subscribe to keep it running** link at the top of the page:

Using Odoo without subscription fees

If you choose not to pay the subscription fee, do not fear! The remainder of this chapter will assist you with installing Odoo on your own hardware.

Getting to know the Odoo architecture

Setting up and managing an Odoo installation will require a basic understanding of the components that make up Odoo. Every business system has a set of technologies and underlying software platforms that are required for the system to function. Fortunately, unless you plan to customize Odoo, you only need to understand the very basics of the Odoo architecture to complete a successful installation.

> In this book, we provide a basic overview of the Odoo architecture. If you wish to get more detailed documentation on the Odoo architecture, visit `https://doc.Odoo.com/trunk/server/02_architecture/`.

Introducing the PostgreSQL database

Like most ERP systems, Odoo has specific database requirements. In this case, it is PostgreSQL. PostgreSQL is an open source, cross-platform **Object Relational Database Management System** (**ORDMS**). While not popular on the scale of Microsoft SQL Server or MySQL, PostgreSQL is an enterprise-class database server with many advanced features. In fact, PostgreSQL stacks up very well against far more expensive databases such as Microsoft SQL Server and Oracle Database.

PostgreSQL runs on every major operating system. For most Odoo installations, Ubuntu is the operating system of choice. However, PostgreSQL will also run quite well under other versions of Linux, Microsoft Windows, and even Mac OS X.

You can learn more about PostgreSQL at `http://www.postgresql.org/`.

Writing code with Python

The primary programming language of Odoo is Python. Like the other technologies underlying Odoo, the Python language is open source and runs on all the major contemporary operating systems. It is an extremely popular programming language which makes it very easy to find resources to help you get started.

You can learn more about the Python programming language at `http://python.org/`.

Following the Model-View-Controller design

Odoo is built upon a **Model-View-Controller** (**MVC**) architecture. One of the primary goals of this architecture is to separate the visual display of the information from the business rules and management of the underlying data. For example, if you need to change the way data is organized in the model, it is desirable not to have to make dramatic changes to how you view the data. This is true for maintaining flexibility in viewing data. Today, it is common to have many different client applications sharing the same underlying data.

Designing models

The model is essentially the data that makes up your Odoo installation, which is stored in the PostgreSQL database. Odoo is unique, in that, database structures are typically defined by the Odoo modules at the time they are installed. The Odoo framework takes the model definitions and automatically creates the necessary table structures inside the PostgreSQL database. Furthermore, a web interface in Odoo allows administrators to easily extend the Odoo data model in a variety of ways without having to modify the Odoo source code.

Rendering views

Each view in Odoo is defined in XML documents. The Odoo framework is responsible for rendering these view files in a web browser. Alternative views can be built to render Odoo functionality upon other platforms such as mobile devices.

Authoring controllers

The controller component of the architecture is where the business logic and workflow rules of the Odoo application are applied. The controller components in Odoo are written in Python code and stored as objects in Odoo modules.

Choosing your installation operating system

In this section, we will discuss some of the advantages and disadvantages of choosing Ubuntu or Windows for your first Odoo installation.

Choosing a Microsoft Windows Odoo installation

For the most part, Ubuntu has been the platform of choice for most Odoo installations. However, there are some reasons why you might choose to run Odoo under a Windows installation.

Some of you who bought this book might have already jumped ahead and installed Odoo on their Microsoft Windows computer. So, for you go-getters, that working installation of Odoo might function just fine for researching and testing its features. Often, the Windows all-in-one installer provides a simple method to get Odoo up and running instantly on your hardware. Basically, you do not have to install a new operating system.

Learning Ubuntu is not required

If you are familiar with Windows and have no Ubuntu experience, you might get going a little faster by sticking with a Windows install for your first setup. Downloading and installing modules and making changes to configuration files will be much easier if you are familiar with the operating system.

Introducing Ubuntu

While Microsoft Windows does not really need an introduction, it is probably worth giving a brief introduction to Ubuntu. In short, Ubuntu (pronounced *oo-BOON-too*) is a very popular open source operating system based on the Linux kernel. It has enjoyed increasing popularity because it is easy to install and very stable. Ubuntu can be installed either as a server operating system without a graphical interface or as a desktop operating system with a graphical interface that closely resembles Windows.

You can learn more about the Ubuntu operating system and why it is so popular at `http://www.ubuntu.com/`.

Choosing an Ubuntu Odoo installation

It is generally accepted that Ubuntu is the recommended operating system for running a production installation of Odoo. There are several reasons why this is true:

- **Ubuntu is the primary target platform:** While Odoo is released for Windows and still well-supported, the Ubuntu installation continues to be favored. The development team of Odoo works primarily with Ubuntu for bug fixes and platform releases. It can be expected that, for the most part, Odoo development will be optimized around Ubuntu, not Windows or Mac.
- **Ubuntu is open source**: Installing Odoo on any Windows operating system is going to require a license from Microsoft. While using Odoo on your Windows PC or Mac is a viable and perhaps desirable solution for testing and development, it is unlikely you will want to run Odoo on a Windows desktop system for any production environment. Why? Well, this requires Windows Server, which has much higher license costs than desktop editions. With an Ubuntu installation, you get an entirely open source and virtually cost-free solution.
- **Ubuntu has additional scalability options**: It is possible to configure a more scalable solution under Ubuntu than what you can currently configure under Microsoft Windows Server.
- **Ubuntu has strong community support for Odoo**: The fact is that a vast majority of the production installations of Odoo are running under Ubuntu. When you run into trouble or management issues with your Odoo installation, you may find it easier to get assistance if you are running an Ubuntu installation.

Choosing another OS option for Odoo

Although this book will focus on Windows and Ubuntu installations, you do have several other options. In the past, Odoo has been deployed under a variety of Linux distributions and even on the Macintosh OS. There are also many community members actively developing client frontends for mobile platforms such as Google's Android OS.

Understanding Odoo releases

When deploying an Odoo system, it is important to understand the various Odoo versions, as well as the release and upgrade policies. There is currently one major release for versions 6.0, 7.0, and 8.0, as well as a master branch that is the latest development version which will soon become Odoo Version 9.0. The stable versions are the standard support version of Odoo and, typically, the one you should choose to install for most situations. The master version is the development version and will often contain bugs and unfinished features. This is primarily downloaded by developers or those who wish to get a look at the latest features.

Upgrading Odoo

The goal of the Odoo development team is to release two stable version upgrades each year. Odoo further labels some stable versions as **Long Term Support** (**LTS**) versions. These releases are supported by Odoo for those that have an Odoo Enterprise support contract. For any production environment, it is smart to choose an LTS version. Most importantly, installing an LTS release of Odoo will make bug fixes and patches much easier to implement.

> At the time of writing this, the most recent stable LTS version is version 8.0.

Installing Odoo on Windows OS

We begin our installation by locating the packages that are currently available to install. You can find the current list at `http://nightly.odoo.com/`.

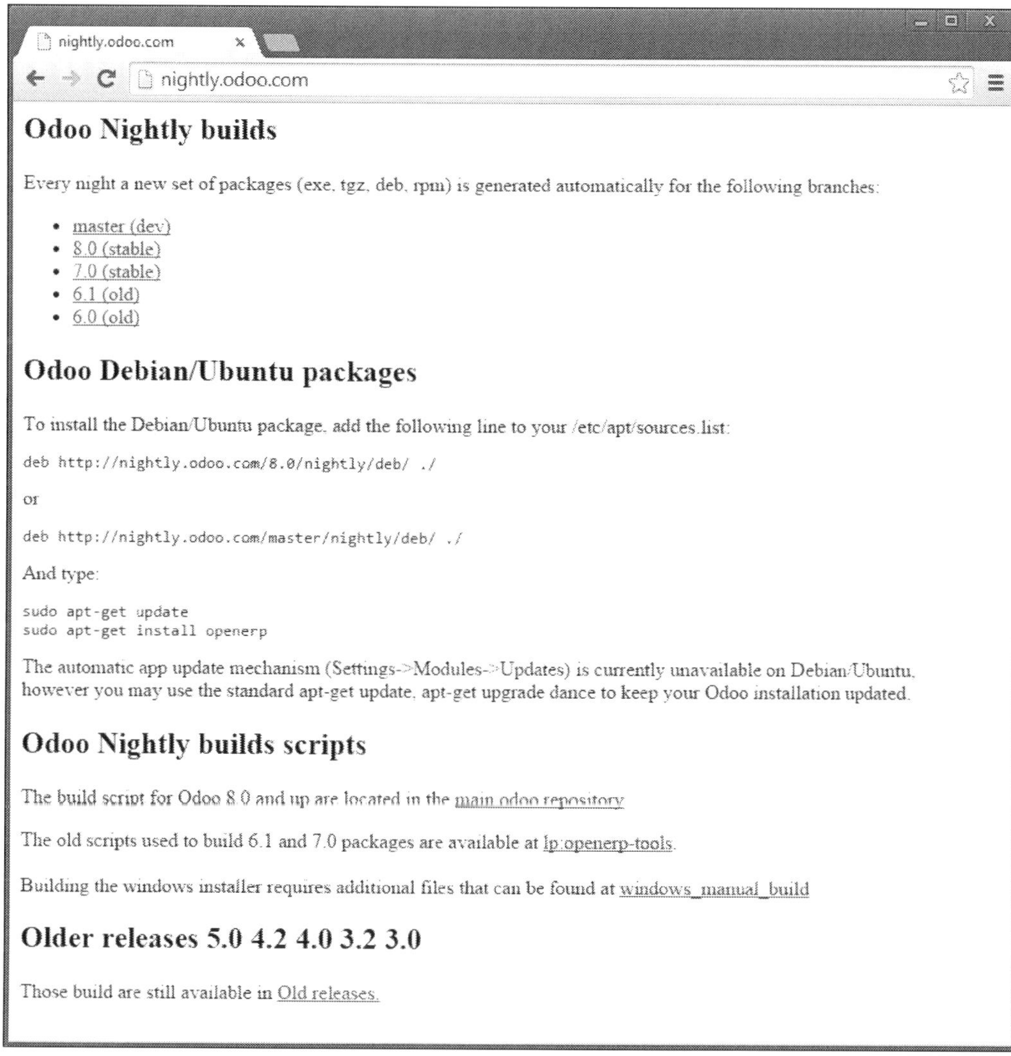

The preceding screenshot is the **Odoo Nightly builds** page that is the jumping off point for downloading the source files for installation.

The examples and case studies in this book use Odoo 8.0. This means you should select the 8.0 LTS (stable) version of Odoo to download. You can navigate directly to the 8.0 Odoo downloads here `http://nightly.odoo.com/8.0/nightly/`.

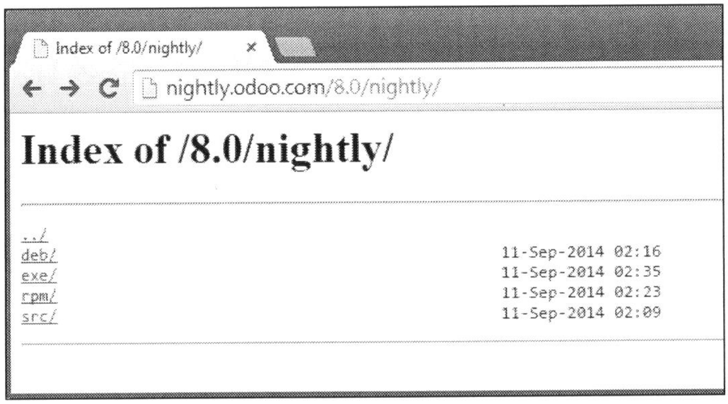

> It is entirely possible that Odoo will change the URL as new versions are released. To best follow the examples in this book, download an 8.x installation of Odoo.

Windows installations use the EXE packages. Click on the **exe** directory to get the list of downloads that are available.

Naturally, the specific download packages are going to change on a nightly basis.

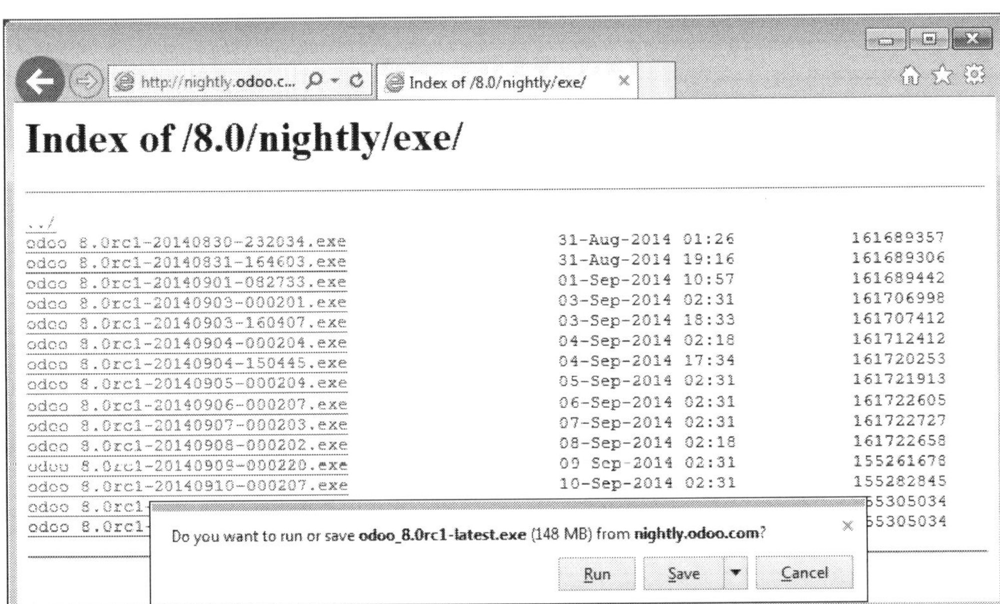

The latest version of the stable LTS release will contain the most current Odoo built with bug fixes included and will appear at the bottom of the list. By the way, the upload dates you'll see are in **Coordinated Universal Time** (**UTC**) and, therefore, might be many hours ahead of your time zone, especially if you live in the Western Hemisphere.

Performing an all-in-one Odoo installation on Windows

Installing Odoo using the all-in-one package is very simple. After the package has finished downloading, double-click on the `.exe` file to begin the installation wizard.

The first screen will prompt you to select the language for your installation.

After you have selected the language and clicked on **OK**, the wizard will continue with the installation. From here, everything will continue like a normal Windows installation.

> I highly recommend that you choose the **Custom** install, so you can select the directory for installation. The default directory name contains the lengthy build number making it rather difficult to work with in the command prompt.

Configuring Postgres on Windows

During the installation, you will be asked to provide information for the PostgreSQL connection.

It is recommended that you change the username and password for security purposes. These values will be written into the Odoo configuration file. The username and password provided will be the administration credentials for the PostgreSQL database, so be sure to remember them.

After the wizard is complete, if you leave **Start Odoo** checked and then click on **Finish**, Odoo should open up in your default browser.

If Odoo fails to launch, you can look at the *Troubleshooting Odoo Installations* section later in this chapter for solutions to some of the problems commonly encountered during installation.

Installing Odoo on Ubuntu

This book will walk you through the installation procedure for Odoo on Ubuntu using the latest all-in-one nightly package. Depending on your Ubuntu installation and how you want to work with Odoo, there are alternative installation methods.

At the time of this writing, Odoo is most commonly installed on Ubuntu Version 14.04.

Modifying the sources.list file

Installing Odoo on Ubuntu is easy when you use the Debian repository. You can use any standard text editor, such as Nano, to modify the `/etc/apt/sources.list` file and add the following line:

```
deb http://nightly.Odoo.com/8.0/nightly/deb/ ./
```

This installs the package.

After saving `sources.list`, you can start the installation process by entering these commands into a terminal window:

```
sudo apt-get update
sudo apt-get install openerp
```

The Odoo packages will be first downloaded and then installed. This is an all-in-one installation and should set up all the necessary packages, PostgreSQL, and library dependencies required to run Odoo.

> Take note that the installation itself still uses `openerp`, instead of the new `odoo` brand name.

Testing your Odoo installation

Point your browser to `http://localhost:8069` and you should see the Odoo login page appear.

Troubleshooting and Odoo management tips

As far as ERP installations go, Odoo is typically very easy to install. Unfortunately, it is possible for an installation to fail for a variety of reasons. In this next section, we will discuss some of the most common installation issues and provide some troubleshooting tips for diagnosis problems with an Odoo installation.

Checking your browser destination

If you have followed the default installation, then your Odoo installation should be accessing Odoo at `http://localhost:8069`.

Make sure the URL is exactly as you can see it above. If you did change the port number during installation, make sure you change the port in the URL.

Verifying that the Odoo service is running

If you are unable to pull up Odoo in the browser, it can be good to verify that the Odoo services are running.

Checking for Odoo services running in Windows

Pull up the **Task Manager** and go to the **Services** tab, then look for **Odoo-server8.0**. The status should be running, as shown in the following screenshot:

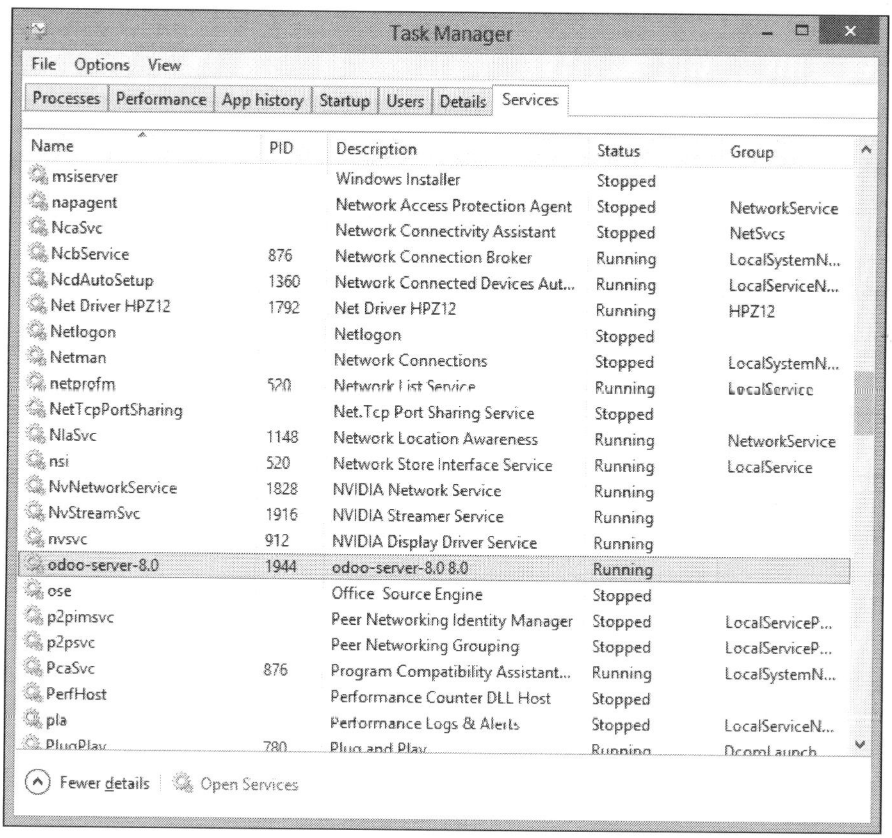

Here is an example of the Odoo-server-8.0 service successfully running on Windows.

Additional Odoo troubleshooting steps for Windows can be found at `https://doc.odoo.com/install/windows/server/complementary_install_information/`.

Checking for Odoo services running in Ubuntu

In Ubuntu, you can locate the Odoo services by running the following command in a terminal window:

```
ps aux | grep Odoo
```

You will then see the Odoo service listed if it is running.

Starting and stopping Odoo services in Ubuntu

When managing an Odoo server, one of the most common tasks you will find yourself performing is starting and stopping the Odoo services. Odoo allows you to start and stop the services with a command switch.

To start the services, use:

```
sudo /etc/init.d/Odoo-server start
```

To stop the services, use:

```
sudo /etc/init.d/Odoo-server stop
```

Finding the primary Odoo log file

Odoo writes many messages, warnings, and error messages to a log. Often, when troubleshooting problems, this log file is valuable in determining what action you should take. In a default installation, the log file is located at `{install directory}/server/server/Odoo-server.log`.

The log is especially valuable to locate problems you may have when installing new modules.

Modifying the Odoo configuration file

The Odoo framework allows you to specify a configuration file for your installation. By default, this file is located at `/etc/Odoo/Odoo-server.conf`.

Using this file, you can change many of the attributes of Odoo.

Changing port numbers

By default, Odoo runs on port `8069`. For many installations, the default port will work fine. There are situations, however, where it can be useful to change this default port. One common scenario would be the need to run more than one version of Odoo. Multiple installations cannot run on port `8069`, so you will need to modify the port. Sometimes there are security reasons behind changing ports, as many hackers are aware of the default ports that people use.

Fortunately, changing the default port number is easy.

Simply specify:

```
Port=[port]
```

For example, `Port=8059` will change the default port for the web client to port 8059.

Accessing the database management tools

Odoo offers database management tools that can be accessed easily through your web browser. This makes it easy to create, backup, and even delete database, all through a web interface. While there are sometimes links available on the login page that will take you to these tools, it is possible that when installing some applications, such as the website builder, you will not find a link easily.

To access the database management tools, use the following path:

```
[ServerAddress]:[port]/web/database/manager
```

Changing the admin password

As mentioned earlier, by default, Odoo sets the password for these operations to `admin`. To secure your server, it is necessary to change this password in your configuration file:

```
Admin_password=[your password]
```

Also, be careful while starting up your Odoo server from the command line without specifying an alternative password or the path to the configuration file. If you do, you leave the instance open with the default password.

Finding additional resources for installing Odoo

Installing and configuring Odoo can quickly become a very complex task that is outside the scope of this book. In *Appendix, Locating Additional Odoo Resources*, you will find links to additional resources that can assist you with installing Odoo.

Summary

In this chapter, we saw how easy it was to get started using Odoo online. We discussed how to set up a trial company and the basics of creating a database and installing your first module. If you choose not to use the online services, you likely found the topics on installing Odoo on Windows or Ubuntu helpful. Finally, we discussed various methods of troubleshooting and configuring Odoo.

In the next chapter, we will begin to jump into our first real business applications in Odoo. You will get introduced to our real world case study and set up the basic configuration of the company. We will walk you through setting up your first product and, finally, creating and printing your first sales order.

2
Installing Your First Application

You have learned about the various applications that Odoo has to offer and how you can install Odoo on your own system. Before the release of Odoo 8, most users were focused on ERP- and financial-related applications. Now, Odoo 8 has added several important applications that allow companies to use Odoo in much greater scope than ever before. For example, the website builder can be installed to quickly launch a simple website for your business. A task that typically would have been accomplished with a content management system such as WordPress.

Despite all these new options that are available in Odoo 8, the overall process is the same. We begin by looking at the overall business requirements and decide on the first set of applications we wish to implement. After understanding our basic objectives, we will create an Odoo database and configure the required company information.

Next, we begin exploring the Odoo interface to create and view information. We will see just how easy Odoo is to use by completing an entire sales order workflow. We will finish up the chapter by reviewing some of the more advanced sales order configuration options.

The topics we will cover include:

- Adding a password-protected database to our installation
- Installing and configuring the Sales Management module
- Using interface features to view, edit, and find information
- Entering a new customer
- Adding our first product to sell
- Writing an order and confirming it for invoicing

Gathering requirements

Setting up an Odoo system is no easy task. Many companies get into trouble by believing that they can just install the software and throw in some data. Inevitably, the scope of the project grows and what was supposed to be a simple system ends up becoming a confusing mess. Fortunately, Odoo's modular design will allow you to take a systematic approach to implement Odoo for your business.

Implementing Odoo using a modular approach

The bare bones installation of Odoo simply provides a limited messaging system. To manage your Odoo implementation, you must begin with the planning of the applications with which you will work first. Odoo allows you to install just what you need now and then install additional Odoo applications as you better define your requirements. It can be valuable to take this approach when you are considering how to implement Odoo for your own business.

> Don't try and install all the applications and get everything running all at once. Instead, break down the implementation into smaller phases.

Introducing Silkworm – our real-world case study

To best understand how to work with Odoo, we will build our exercises around a real-world case study. Silkworm is a custom apparel, promotional products, and graphic design company that provides unparalleled customer service. Using Odoo's modular design, we will begin by implementing the sales management application to set up the selling of basic products. In this specific case, we will be selling t-shirts. As we proceed through the book, we will continue to expand the system by installing additional applications.

> When implementing Odoo for your organization, you will also want to create a basic requirements document. This information is important for the configuration of the company settings in Odoo and should be considered essential documentation when implementing an ERP system.

Using Odoo online – installing your first application

When you use Odoo's online trial on enterprise services, they will handle all the details, not only for installation of the Odoo software but also for creating the database. All you have to do is select the first application you wish install from the list provided on Odoo's setup page.

For our purposes, we are going to begin by implementing the sales order application. In Odoo's trial version, the sales order application is bundled inside the Quote Builder on their installation page.

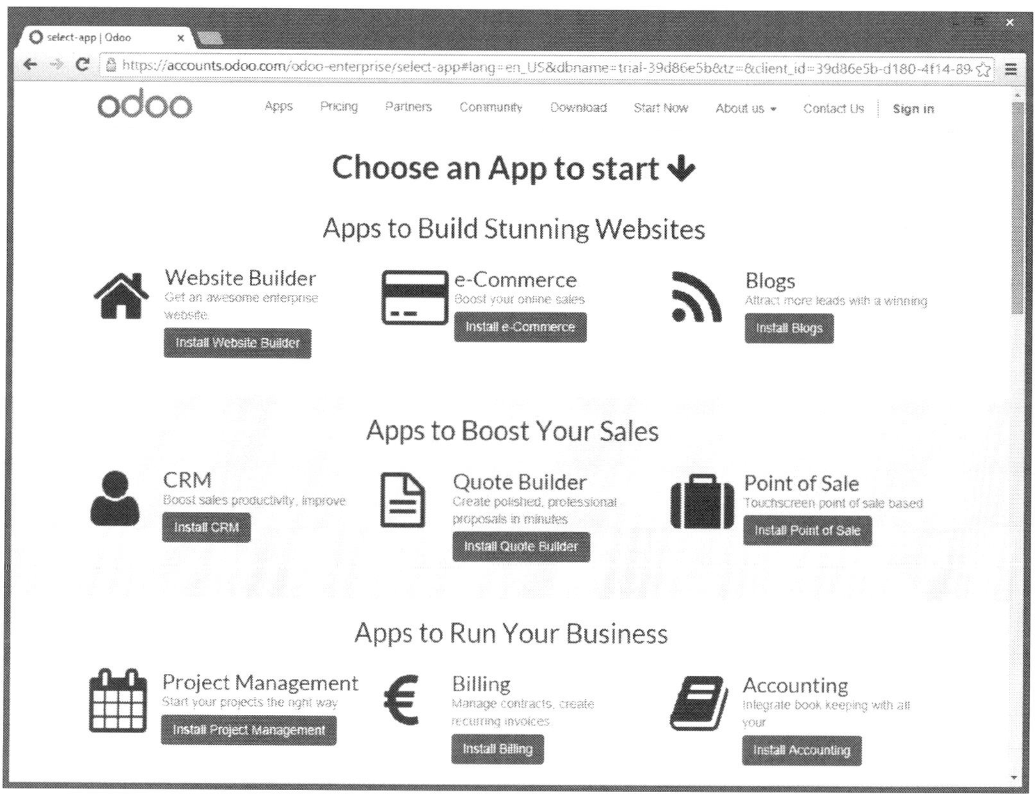

Creating a new database in Odoo

If you have installed Odoo on your own server, you will first need to create a database. As you add additional applications to Odoo, the necessary tables and fields will be added to the database you specify.

> **Odoo online**
>
> If you are using Odoo online, you will not have access to create a new database and instead will use Odoo's one click application installer to manage your Odoo installation.

If you have just installed a fresh copy of Odoo, you will be prompted automatically to create a new Odoo database:

In the preceding screenshot, you can see the Odoo form to create a new database.

Odoo provides basic instructions for creating your database. Let's quickly review the fields and how they are used.

Specifying the master password

The master password is set in the Odoo configuration file. In this form, you are not setting the master password. Instead, you are supplying the master password so that Odoo can be sure you are authorized to create databases. If you enter an incorrect master password or do not enter a master password, you will get an access denied message when you try to create the database.

> By default, the master password for Odoo is `admin`.

For security reasons, it is essential that you change the default master password. Refer to the installation in *Chapter 1, Setting Up Odoo*, to see how you can change the configuration file to specify an alternative master password.

Selecting a database name

When selecting a database name, choose a name that describes the system and will make the purpose of the database clear. There are a few rules:

- Your database name cannot contain spaces and must start with a number or letter
- Also, you will need to avoid commas, periods, and quotes
- Underscores and hyphens are allowed if they are not the first character in the name

It can also be a good idea to specify in the name whether the database is for development, testing, or production purposes.

For the purposes of our real-world case study, we will use the database name `SILKWORM-DEV`.

We have chosen the `-DEV` suffix as we will consider this to be a *development* database that will not be used for production or even for testing.

> Take the time to consider what you will name your databases. It can be useful to have standard prefixes or suffixes, depending on the purpose of your database. For example, you might use `-PROD` for your production database or `-TEST` for the database that you are using for testing.

Loading demonstration data

You will see the **Check this box to evaluate Odoo** box. If you mark this checkbox when you create a database, Odoo will preload your tables with a host of sample data for each module that is installed. This may include fake customers, suppliers, sales orders, invoices, inbox messages, stock moves, and products. The purpose of the demonstration data is to allow you to run modules through their paces without having to key in a ton of test data.

For the purposes of our real-world case study in this book, *do not* load any demonstration data.

Specifying our default language

Odoo offers a variety of language translation features with support for more than 20 languages. All of the examples in this book will use the English (US) language option. Be aware that depending on the language you select in Odoo, you might need to have that language also installed in your base operating system.

Choosing a password

Each Odoo database is created with an administrator account, named `admin`. This is also known as the superuser account. The password you choose during the creation of the database will be the password for the admin account.

> Choose any password you wish and click on **Create Database** to create the `SILKWORM-DEV` database.

Managing databases in Odoo

The database management interface allows you to perform basic database management tasks, such as backing up or restoring a database. Often with Odoo, it is possible to manage your databases without ever having to go directly into the Postgres database server. It is also possible to set up multiple databases under the same installation of Odoo. For instance, in the future, you might want to install another database, which will load demonstration data and might be used to install applications simply for testing purposes.

> If you have trouble getting to the interface to manage databases, you can access the database management interface directly by going to the path `/web/database/manager`.

Installing the Sales Management application

After clicking on **Create Database**, it can take a little time depending on your system before you are shown a page that lists the available applications.

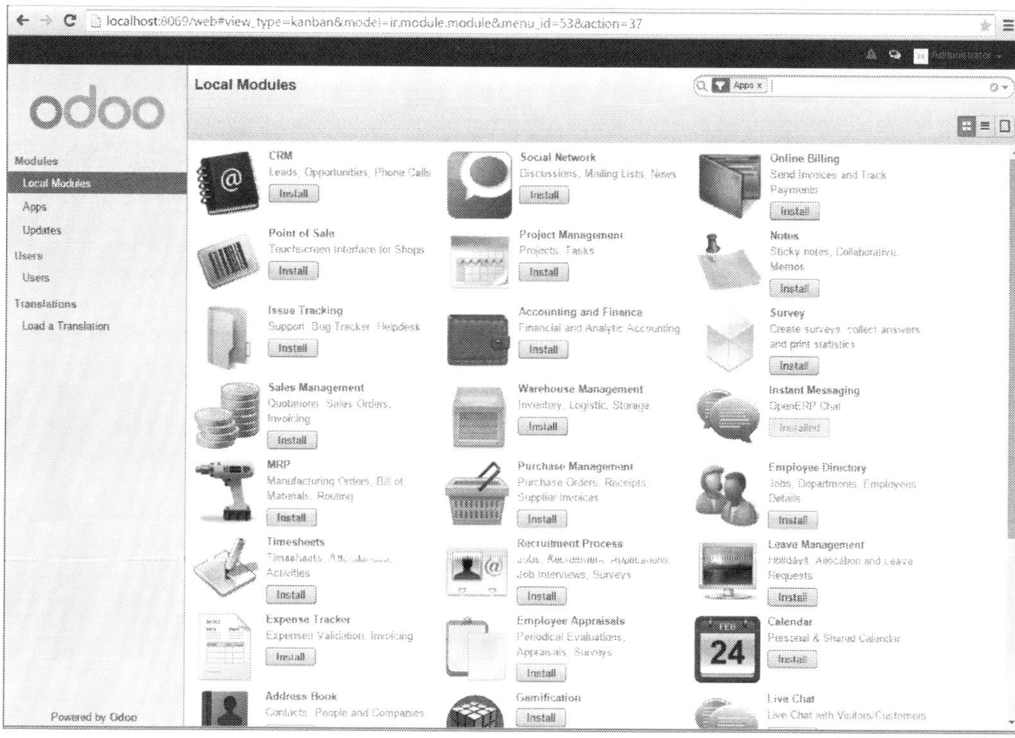

This screen lets you select from a list of the most common Odoo applications to install.

There is very little you can do with just an Odoo database, without any applications installed. Now, we will install the **Sales Management** application so we can begin setting up our business selling t-shirts.

[Click on the **Install** button to install the Sales Management application.]

During installation of applications and other long operations, you will often see a **Loading...** icon at the center of your screen.

Configuring accounting data

With the installation of the Sales Management application, Odoo prompts you to configure the accounting package you will use with your company. For our example, we will be using the United States chart of accounts. As we have only installed one company in this installation, you will leave the company field as **Your Company**. We will see how to change the name of our company later in the chapter.

The following screenshot is the screen you will see during the installation of the Sales Management application:

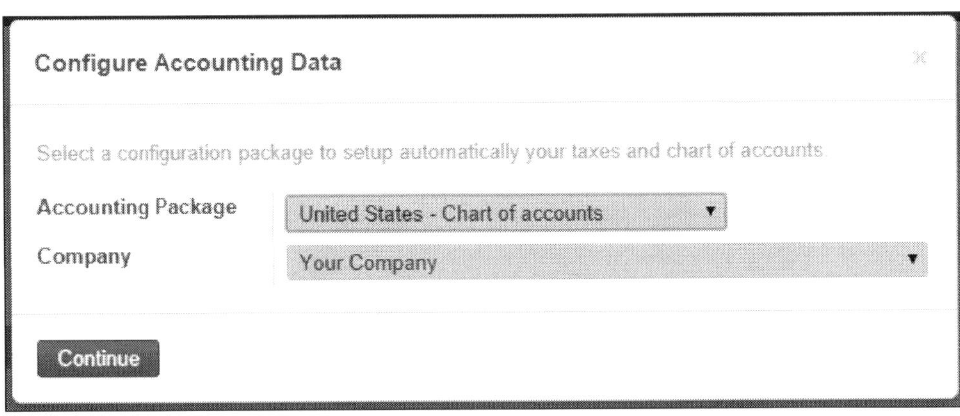

Setting your accounting options

There are several basic chart templates that are included with Odoo. These templates include:

- Advertising
- Agriculture
- Construction trades
- Financial services
- General Service-based business
- Legal Services
- General Product-based business

> Odoo allows you customize your chart of accounts later. Most businesses will probably need to spend some time organizing their chart of accounts according to their requirements. We will cover how to manage accounts in Odoo in *Chapter 8, Implementing the Human Resources Application*.

The following screenshot is presented during the setup of the Sales Management application:

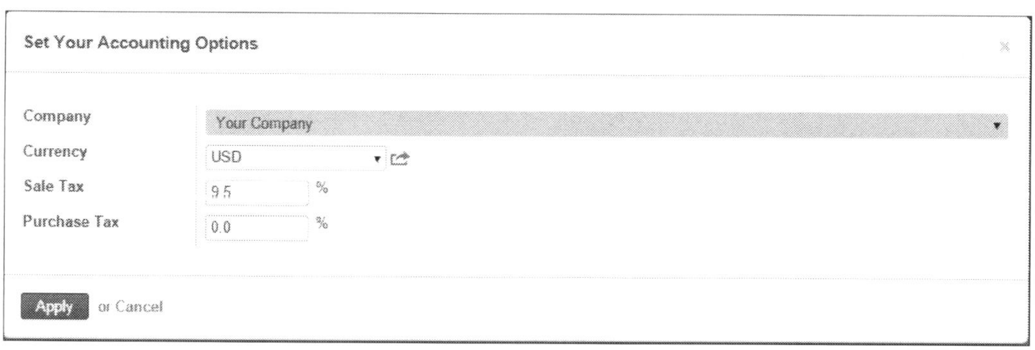

You are welcome to experiment with the currency and sales/purchase tax settings. For the purpose of our case study, we have selected the **General Product-Based Business** chart template and the **USD** currency. Once again, we have left the company field as **Your Company**. Click on **Apply** to finish installing the Sales Order Management application.

Knowing the basics of the Odoo interface

After the installation of the sales order application, Odoo takes you directly to the customers form. Let's take a moment to look at the screen elements that will appear consistently throughout Odoo. In the top left of the main form, you can clearly see that we are in the **Customers** section.

Using the search box

In the top-right corner of our form, we have a search box:

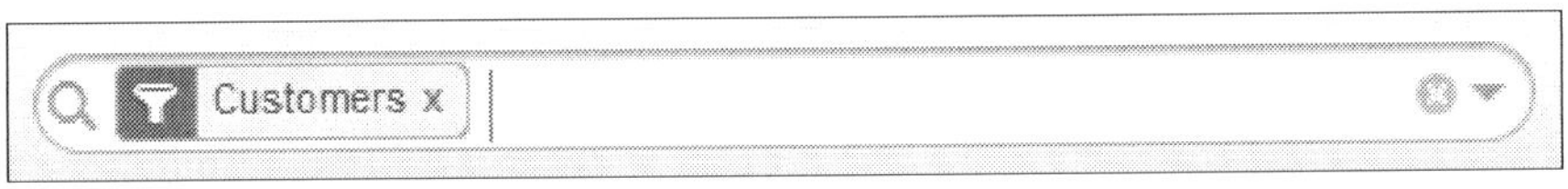

The search box allows you to quickly search for records in the Odoo application. If you are in the customer section, naturally, the search will be looking for customer records. Likewise, if you are looking at the product view, the search box will allow you to search the product records that you have entered into the system.

Picking different views

Odoo also offers a standard interface to switch between a list view, form view, or other views such as Kanban or graph views. You can see the icon selections under the search box in the right corner of the form:

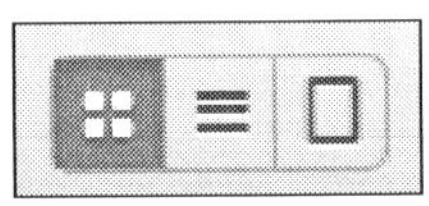

The currently selected view is highlighted in black. If you hover over the icon, you will get a tooltip that shows you the description of the view. As we have no records in our system currently, let's add a record so that we can further explore the Odoo interface.

Creating your first customer

Helpful instructions prompt you to begin entering your first customer into Odoo by clicking on the **Create** button:

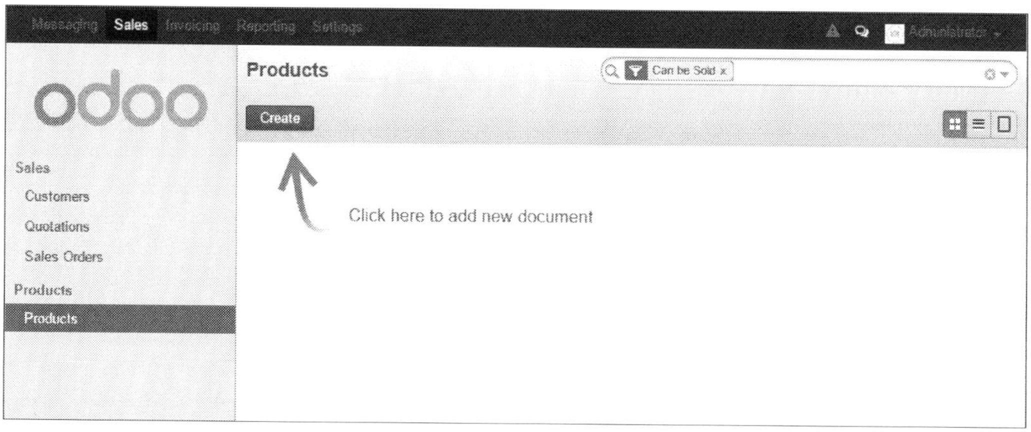

This is the Odoo Customers form. Clicking on **Create** will generate a customer record.

Silkworm sells t-shirts to both businesses and retail customers. For this example, we will use a fictional customer named `Mike Smith`, who wishes to purchase several t-shirts. Odoo offers flexibility in collecting customer information, and by default, most fields are not required. Three main fields are required in a default installation of Odoo sales management:

- Customer name
- Accounts receivable account
- Accounts payable account

The rest of the fields are optional. Later in the chapter, you will learn how to configure Odoo to make additional fields required.

In this example, we have filled out some of the basic fields for our fictional customer `Mike Smith`:

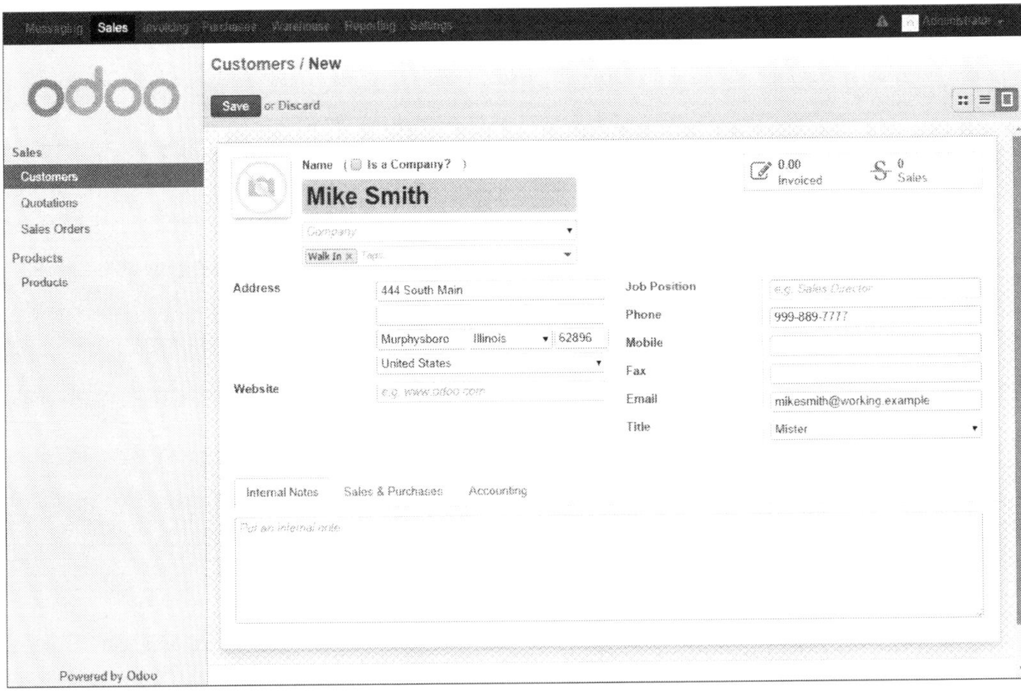

Is this customer a company?

At the very top of the form is a check box to inform Odoo whether this customer is a company. For our example, we are using a walk-in retail customer. If you were doing a business-to-business type operation, then often your customers would have the **Is a Company** checkbox selected.

> When you set up a customer as a company, you will have the option to have multiple contacts available for that customer. If, however, you leave this option unchecked, as we have in our example, you will not have the option to have contacts associated with that customer.

Entering data into an Odoo form

Odoo utilizes a consistent interface to enter data throughout the application. Once you have learned how to enter data into one form, you should have no problem entering data into other forms in Odoo.

The required fields will always be in purple. If you see a purple field, you must fill in that data or you will not be able to save the record. You can move between fields by using your mouse or the *Tab* key. *Shift* + *Tab* will take you back to the previous field. Unlike some systems, you cannot move between fields in Odoo by using the arrow keys.

In many forms, you will have to select lists that allow you to choose from a list to populate the field. You can use your keyboard to type and limit the items that are displayed in a select list. By using the tab key and your keyboard to find the appropriate item in the list, it is possible to enter data into a form with limited use of the mouse.

Many select lists have two options at the bottom that will allow you to use additional search options, or to create an item that is not in the list.

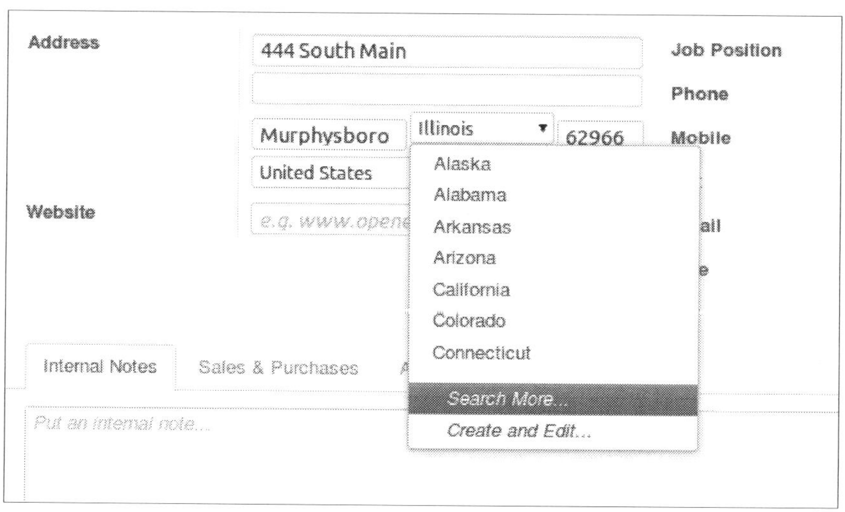

In this example, we see a list of states with the option for additional searching or to create a new state that is not in the list.

Use the **Internal Notes** area to enter any additional notes that you wish to keep on the customer.

Editing a customer – Sales & Purchases

The bottom area of the customer screen is divided into a series of tabs or pages that assist in organizing customer information. In the **Sales & Purchases** tab, we can assign such options as a salesperson and various e-mail options:

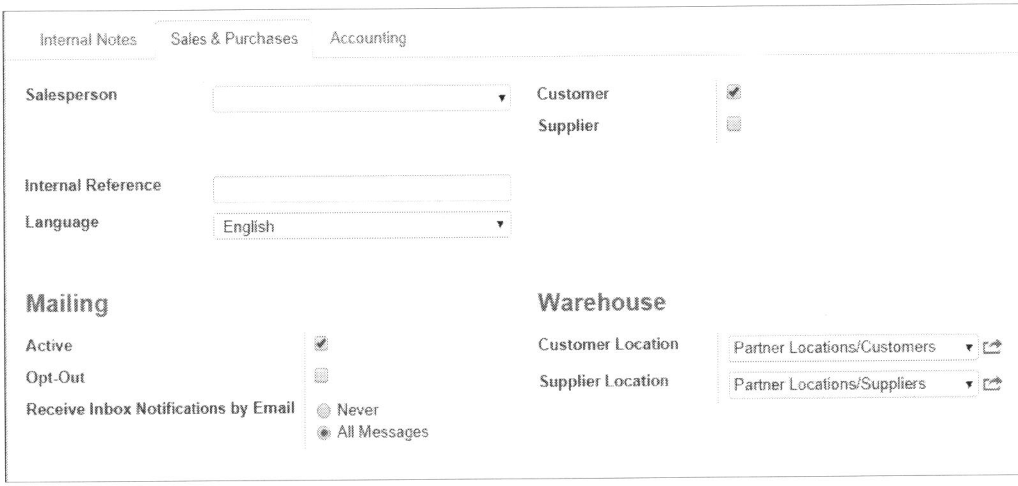

The following are the available options in the customer's **Sales & Purchases** tab.

Salesperson

The **Salesperson** field allows you to select who the direct salesperson will be for this customer. While this field is not required, it is often populated if you are integrating your sales management system with the **Customer Relationship Management** (**CRM**) application. We will use this field in the chapter on CRM; for now, we can leave the field blank.

Reference

Often when implementing Odoo, a company already has an existing customer numbering system in place. The **Internal Reference** field is the perfect field to populate with an existing customer number. Otherwise, this field can be left blank or used for another purpose. For our example, we are going to leave this field blank.

Language

Odoo has the ability to work with customers in a variety of languages. For our example, we will leave this as **English**. If, however, you were working with a company that preferred their documents in other languages, you could specify that language and Odoo will manage the translation.

Date

The **Date** field does not specify exactly what date this refers to for the customer. In most implementations, the business would define this date to be the date on which the customer was acquired. Depending on your needs, you could define the customer date to have an alternative definition. It is also perfectly acceptable to leave this field blank, as we will in our example.

Customer

The **Customer** checkbox is known in Odoo as a Boolean field. It is marked as either yes or no or on or off. Odoo has a unique method of storing data related to people in the system. All individuals are stored in the same table (`res_partner`), regardless of whether they are a customer or supplier. The customer flag tells Odoo that this is in fact a customer record. This field MUST be checked for Odoo to recognize `Mike Smith` as a customer.

Supplier

Because Odoo stores customer and supplier data in the same table, it is possible to be both a customer and a supplier. In this example, we will leave `Mike Smith` as a customer.

> Odoo uses a common table to store customer and supplier records. This makes it easier to manage data, as customers and suppliers are designated by simple checkboxes in the **Sales & Purchases** tab on the customer screen.

Active

Turning off the **Active** flag allows you to hide a customer from the customer list, without deleting them from the database. A sample use for the active field would be to uncheck it if a customer has not made a purchase in a few years. For our example, we will leave this checked.

> Odoo provides an **Active** field for most records in the system. This allows you to easily make a record inactive, without having to remove the record from the database.

Receiving messages by e-mail and opting out

The **Receive Inbox Notifications by Email** option allows you to decide the communication level that you wish to have with your customer and under what conditions they should receive e-mails. The available options include:

- **Never**
- **Incoming Emails only**
- **Incoming Emails and Discussions**
- **All Messages** (discussions, emails, followed system notifications)

The **Opt-Out** flag will allow you to prevent any automatic or campaign e-mails from being sent to the e-mail address in the customer record. It is worth noting that the **Opt-Out** setting will even prevent the customer from receiving e-mail messages sent manually via OpenChatter. For the purposes of our example, we will maintain the default settings.

Editing a customer – Accounting

At first, the accounting page on the customer screen can feel a bit intimidating, but in order to enter a new customer, we must provide some essential information. Fortunately, there are only two required fields on this page: the accounts payable and the accounts receivable fields. We will leave the more complex accounting configuration for a later chapter.

The AR and AP options available in the select lists will vary if you chose to install a chart of accounts other than United States:

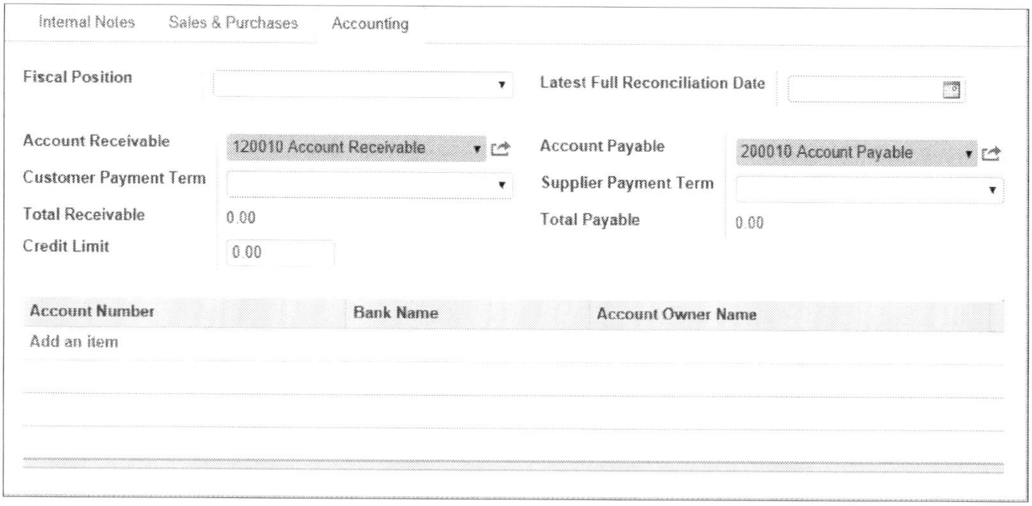

Here are the available options in the customer accounting page.

Fiscal Position

The **Fiscal Position** field is sometimes also known as the tax status and in some systems, it is represented simply as taxable. In Odoo, you have two options for fiscal position:

- **Normal Taxes**
- **Tax Exempt**

Tax exempt is common in business-to-business situations in which taxes are waived because the customer is purchasing the product for resale. Customers might also be exempted from tax if they represent a nonprofit business. This field is not required, and it is possible to override this selection when producing a sales order.

Account Receivable

This field specifies the default accounts as receivable account for the customer. It is a required field, and the account will be automatically debited when a customer is invoiced. When the invoice is paid, the account's receivable account will be credited.

Customer Payment Term

It is common in many businesses for different customers to have different payment terms. Perhaps for a lifelong customer, you would extend 30 or even 60 day net terms for them to pay their invoice. For a new customer, you might require immediate payment. Additional terms can be configured in Odoo, depending on your needs. The default payment terms included are:

- **Immediate Payment**
- **15 Days**
- **30 Net Days**

For our example, we will set the payment term to **Immediate Payment**.

Total Receivable

This is a computed field and is currently **0.00** dollars, because this is a new customer. As customers are invoiced, this field will change to reflect how much they currently owe.

Credit Limit

The **Credit Limit** field allows you to establish credit limits for your customer. The system can then configure warnings to alert you if a sales order would push a customer beyond their credit limit. For our example, we have immediate payment required, so we will leave the credit limit at **0.00** dollars.

Latest Full Reconciliation Date

This is the date on which the accounting entries for the customer were last reconciled. As there have been no automatic or reconciliation operations performed, this field is blank.

Account Payable

While this account is required, it is unlikely to be utilized by customers in Odoo. If, however, the **Supplier** field on the **Sales & Purchases** tab is checked, then this would be the accounts payable account that will be used in supplier-related transactions. Still, you will need to specify an accounts payable account to finish entering the customer.

Supplier Payment Term

Much like the customer payment term, this field will determine the payment terms for the supplier. Because a partner can be both a customer and supplier, we have separate terms for each.

Bank accounts

At the very bottom of our **Accounting** tab, we can set up optional bank accounts for our customer. Clicking **Add an item** will bring up a bank account screen to collect information that would be valuable in sending payment data or issuing ACH drafts against a customer's bank account. For our example, we will not enter a bank account.

Saving the customer record

With the basic customer information entered, we can now hit the **Save** button to commit our changes to the record.

Entering a product in Odoo

Now that we have a customer, it is time we enter some products to sell to our new customer. For our example, we are going to enter a medium white cotton t-shirt. Click on the **Products** item in the menu, on the left:

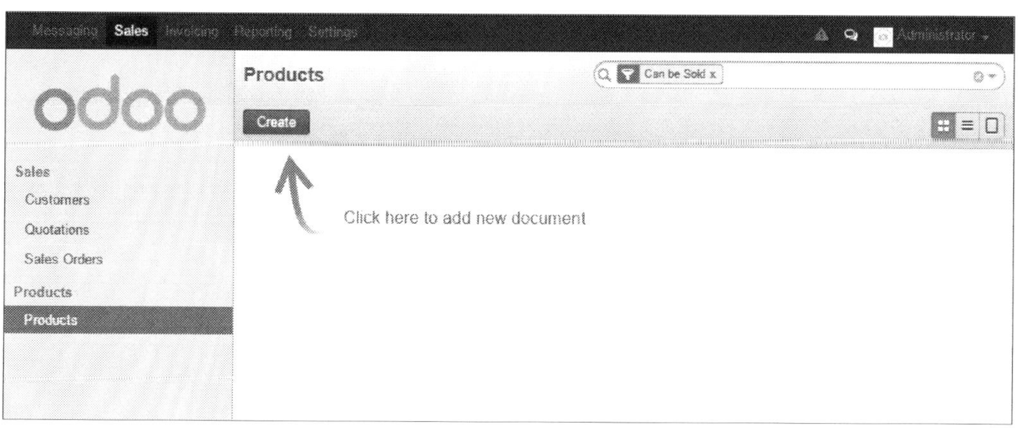

Creating products in Odoo

Create a new product by clicking on the **Create** button.

The following is the form to enter a product record into Odoo:

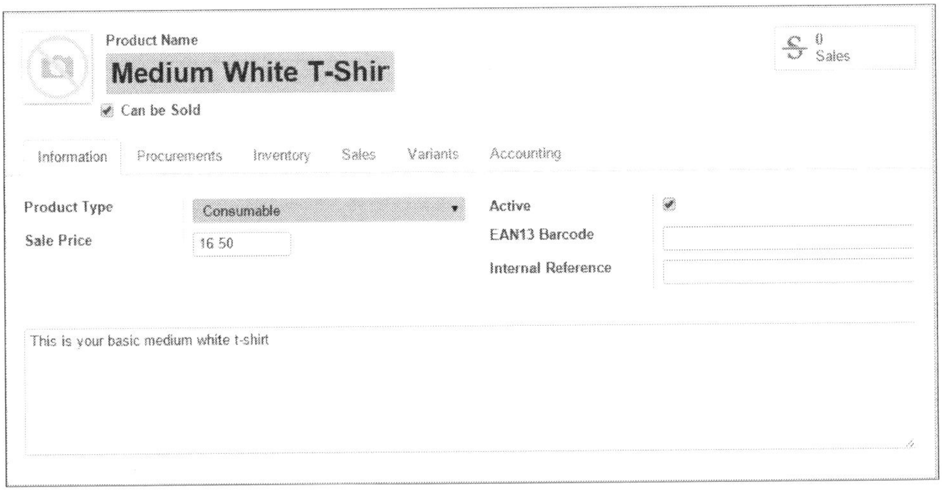

Product name

The product name is what will be displayed on the sales orders, invoices and in all other screens that refer to this specific product. For our example, we are selling a **Medium White T-Shirt**.

Can be Sold

Much like the customer **Active** flag, you can use **Can be Sold** to remove products from showing up on product lists by unchecking **Can be Sold**. For our example, we want to sell this t-shirt to `Mike Smith`, so we will leave the option checked.

Product Type

Product Type is the first option on the **Information** tab on the product screen. There are two available product types:

- **Consumable**
- **Service**

Service product types will not create procurements in purchase orders. Consumables are products that you actually sell and can be configured to generate purchase orders. For our example, we will set the product type to **Consumable**.

Sale Price

This field sets the sales price of the item as it will appear on the sales order. For our example, we are setting the sales price of the t-shirt to $`16.50`.

Internal Reference

For the most part, Odoo utilizes the name field and the description when displaying product information. It is very common for a company to have a coding system for their products. The internal reference field is useful to enter an alternative product code or number for the product. In this example, we will leave the **Internal Reference** field blank.

EAN13 Barcode

Odoo provides the **EAN13 Barcode** field, so that product records can be easily integrated with scanning solutions. For now, we will be leaving this field blank.

Entering a product – the Procurements tab

The second tab on the product screen collects any information related to procurements.

The following is the **Procurements** tab on the product screen:

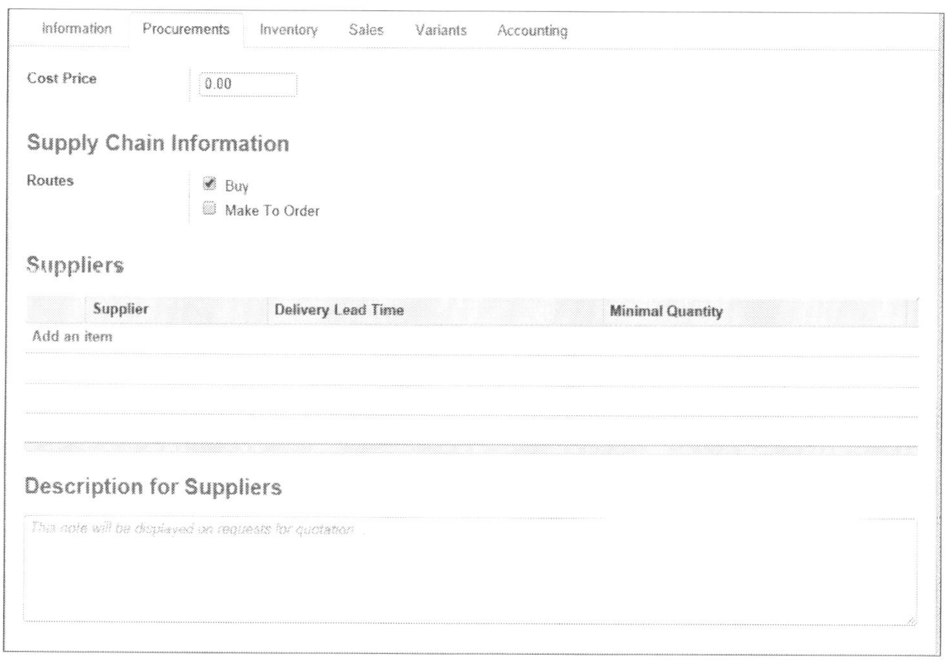

Cost Price

This number will be used for standard stock valuation in accounting and will also serve as the base price on purchase orders once the purchasing application is installed. In fact, because much of this information can be ignore until we install the purchase application, we are just going to leave the cost at **$0.00**.

Supply Chain Information

Beginning in Odoo 8, Odoo now provides great flexibility in routing products. Fortunately, for our purposes, Odoo provides the basic route—**Buy** that is required for us to purchase this product. Leave the **Buy** checkbox set to true.

Suppliers

In the suppliers list, you can specify which suppliers you use to purchase the product. For now, we are focusing on selling the product and will wait until the later chapter on purchasing to learn more about suppliers.

Description for Suppliers

It is not uncommon in business to use different names for the same products, depending on whether you are talking to a supplier or the customer. This field allows you to specify the product description for the supplier. Some industries will find this essential for communicating product information to the supplier. For our example, we will leave this field blank.

Entering a product – the Inventory tab

The **Inventory** information tab lets you collect information on the current status of the product and to assign a product manager.

The following is the **Inventory** tab from the product form:

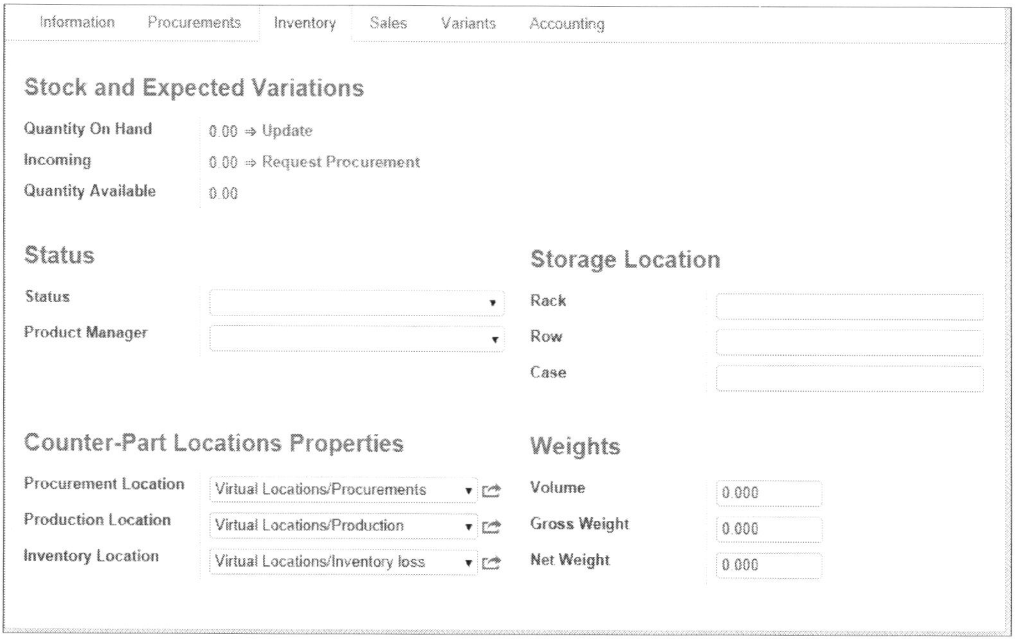

Stock and Expected Variations

In this section, you see the quantity on hand, the quantity that is incoming, as well as the quantity that is available. Quantity available, for example, would exclude products that may still be in inventory but have been allocated to delivery orders. Naturally, as we are just setting up this project, all these values are zero.

Status

The status field allows you to specify the various product stages and provides an additional level of classification in the inventory. The default status values are:

- **In Development**
- **Normal**
- **End of Lifecycle**
- **Obsolete**

For our example, we will select the **Normal** status. This is not a required field and the product can be still entered on a sales order if this field is left blank.

Product Manager

Each product can be assigned a dedicated product manager. This can be useful for reporting purposes and creating intelligent dashboards. For example, an engineer could have their dashboard configured to only show them the products in which they are the product manager. For our example, we will leave this field blank.

Entering a product – the Sales tab

The **Sales** tab on the product form allows you to specify optional information on the product, as it relates to sales and quotations. If there is a warranty on the product, you can specify the warranty duration in months. You can also specify a description that will show up just on quotations. This would be used, for example, if you wanted a different description on the quotation than you have on the invoice. We will leave these fields as their defaults for our case study.

The following is the **Sales** tab, located on the product form:

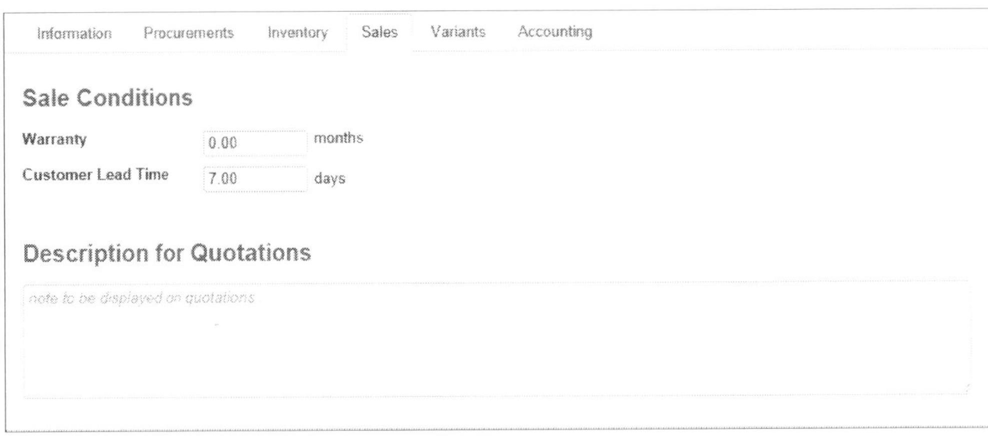

Entering a product – the Accounting tab

The **Internal Category** field for now can just be left as **All**. Categories can be used to group products and organize them in a way that makes sense for your internal requirements. Beginning with Odoo 8, you can now have alternative categories defined for the products on your website.

We set up a default tax of **9.5%** when we installed the sales management application. However, there will be times when you have a product that has a specific tax. In the United States, one example is that cigarettes often have a more substantial tax than other items, such as food. Odoo allows you to specify additional tax options for a given product in the accounting page. Taxes can be specified for both the customer and the supplier separately.

The following is the **Accounting** tab that is located in the product form:

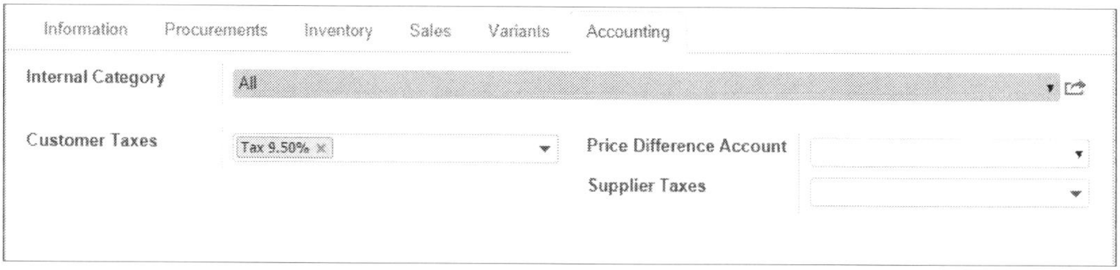

For our example, we will set the customer taxes to the **9.50%** rate that we defined in the sales order accounting setup.

Saving the product

Clicking on the **Save** button stores the product record in Odoo. If you click on **Discard**, you will get prompted with a warning message that you will lose your changes.

Setting the company information

We have entered both a customer and a product. However, before we create a sales order, we still have some work to do in setting up our company. Currently, Odoo does not even know the name of our company and has used **Your Company** as the name, by default.

We can locate the company information by choosing **Settings** from the top menu and then choosing **Companies** from the submenu on the left.

The following is a list of the companies in the current Odoo database:

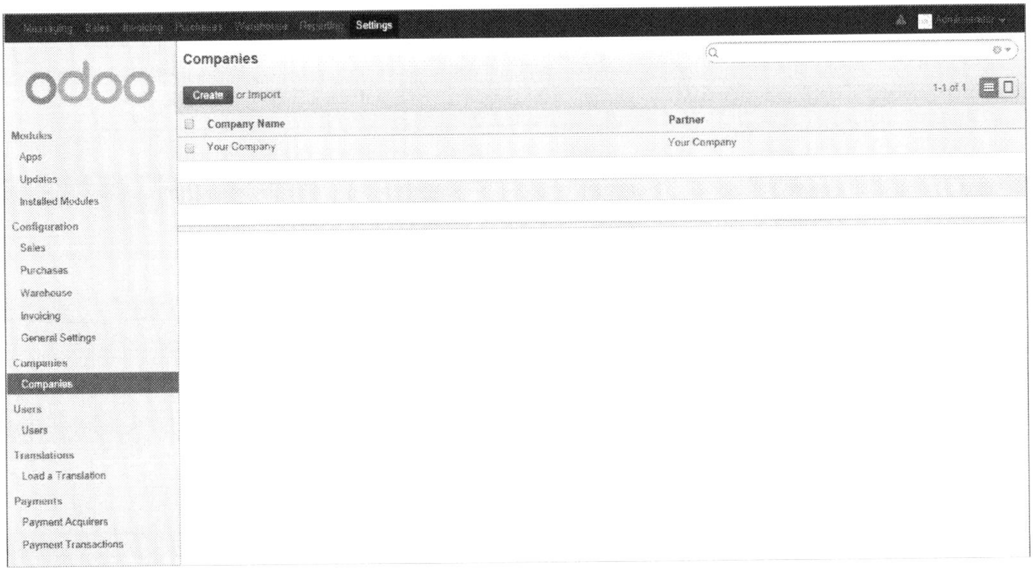

You can now click once on **Your Company** to open up the company information screen. Click on the **Edit** button so that we can enter edit mode and update the company information.

The following is a company record, filled in with the data for our sample case study:

Here, we have supplied the company name, along with address, e-mail, phone, website, and the company slogan. It is also possible to click on the photo icon at the top left to assign a logo to the company. At the bottom of the screen, you can add bank accounts for the company. We will wait to configure bank accounts for a later chapter.

The Configuration tab

The **Configuration** tab simply allows you to set the default currency for the company. This field was set to USD (US Dollars) during the sales order management setup.

Overdue Payments

The **Overdue Payments** tab will allow you to change the statement that will appear to customers who are flagged for being late with their payments. For our example, we will keep the default.

Saving company information

Click on **Save** to update the company information. We are now ready to enter our first sales order.

Entering your first sales order

Now, for the moment we have all been waiting for. We finally get to sell our products by entering a sales order. To get to the sales order entry screen, click on **Sales** in the top menu and then choose **Sales Order** from the submenu on the left.

The following screen lists existing sales orders and allows users to create a new sales order:

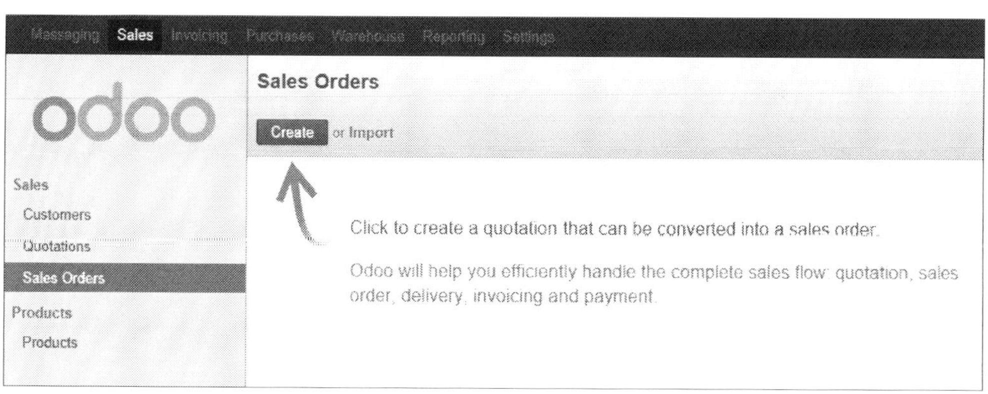

Click on the **Create** button to create a new sales order. Every brand new sales order begins as a quotation and stays in that state until you confirm the sale. Only after confirming the quotation will your sale be referred to as a sales order.

The following is a new sales order form, with the cursor set on the **Customer** field:

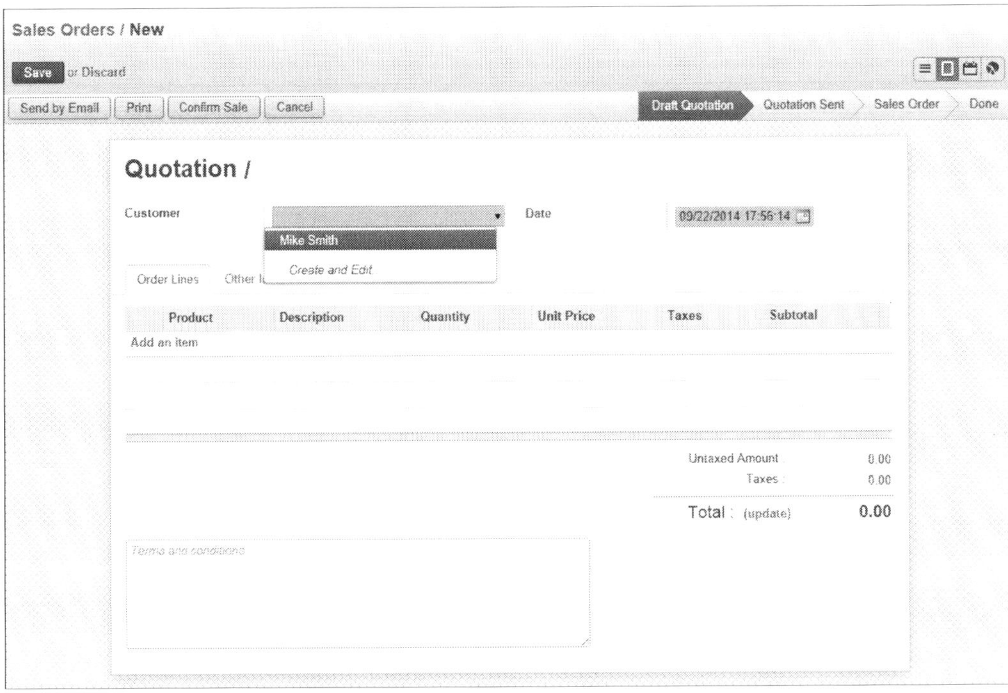

Selecting the customer

When you create a new quotation sales order, you are prompted to first select the customer from the select list. As you add customers, you will have the option to search and locate customers for the sales order. For now, we will be selecting the customer we entered early in the chapter, **Mike Smith**.

> You will not be able to begin entering line items until you have specified the customer for the sales order.

Date

By default, the current date is populated into the **Date** field. If necessary, you can modify this date:

Selecting a date in Odoo

If you click on the little clock at the bottom of the date, you get a selector that allows you to set the time:

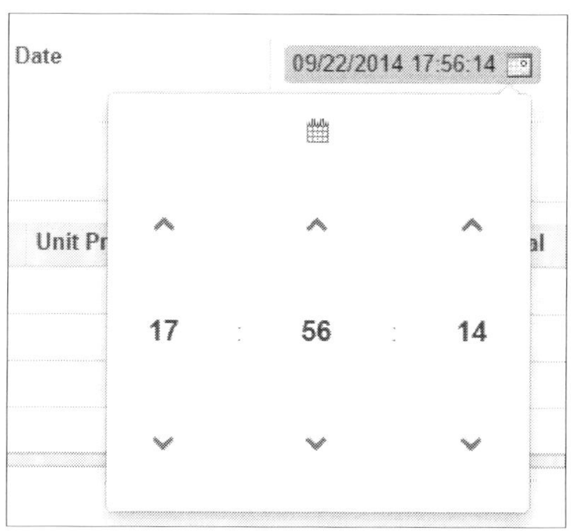

Customer Reference

The **Customer Reference** field can be used to collect information that you might wish to associate with the sale. For example, you might wish to store a reference to how the customer was acquired. We are leaving this field blank for our example.

Entering line items on a quotation sales order

Now, we are ready to begin specifying the product we wish to sell. Click on **Add an item** in the line item area to add a line to the grid. The first field will be **Product**. Select **Medium White T-shirt** from the list box. Your line item fields should populate and look like this:

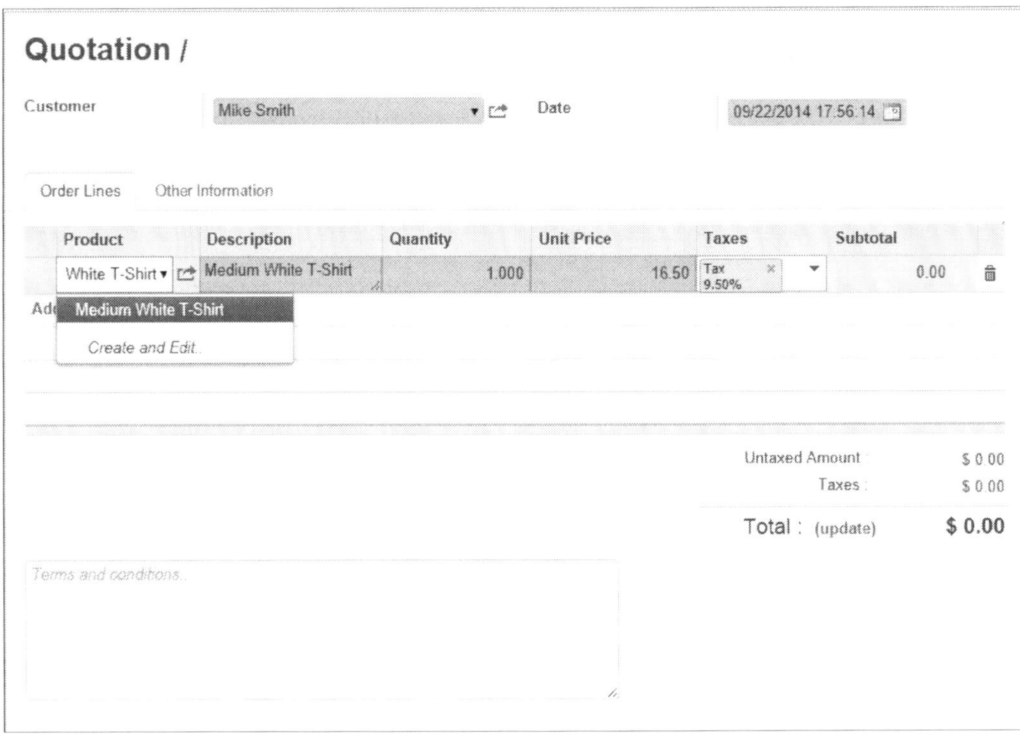

The Product field

Each line item starts out by selecting the product. You can add products on-the-fly by choosing **Create and Edit...** from the bottom of the list. Once there are more products in the list, you can also bring up a product search window using the **search more...** option. After you select the product field, Odoo retrieves the tax and pricing information from the server to display it in the line item.

Odoo does not automatically refresh the total. If you wish to see the total before clicking on the save button, click on the **(update)** link that is located next to the **Total** at the bottom of the form.

Description

Odoo will pull over the description from the product record to populate the description field on the line item. It is possible to override the description on the quotation sales order. For this example, we will leave the description as it pulled over from the product record.

Quantity

Product quantity will default to 1. Naturally, you will change this field to the quantity of products you have sold. We will just leave quantity as 1 for this example.

Taxes

Odoo supports taxes by line item and will automatically pull over the **9.5%** tax rate that we have defined in the product record. Additional taxes can be added or removed from the line item. For this example, we will leave the tax at **9.5%**.

Unit price

Odoo pulls the sale price from the product record to populate the unit price in the line item. It is possible to override the price in the line item. For this example, we will leave the unit price at **$16.50**.

Be careful while changing prices in the line items of Odoo. It is possible that if you click back on the **Product** field or tab through other fields in the line item that the unit price will flip back to the price in the product record. If you are changing prices in the line items, make sure to double-check your unit prices before you confirm your sales order.

Saving the quotation sales order

Click on **Save** to save the quotation. The form will refresh, displaying the full customer address, as well as updating the tax and final total of the quotation sales order.

The following is a screenshot of our first quotation in Odoo:

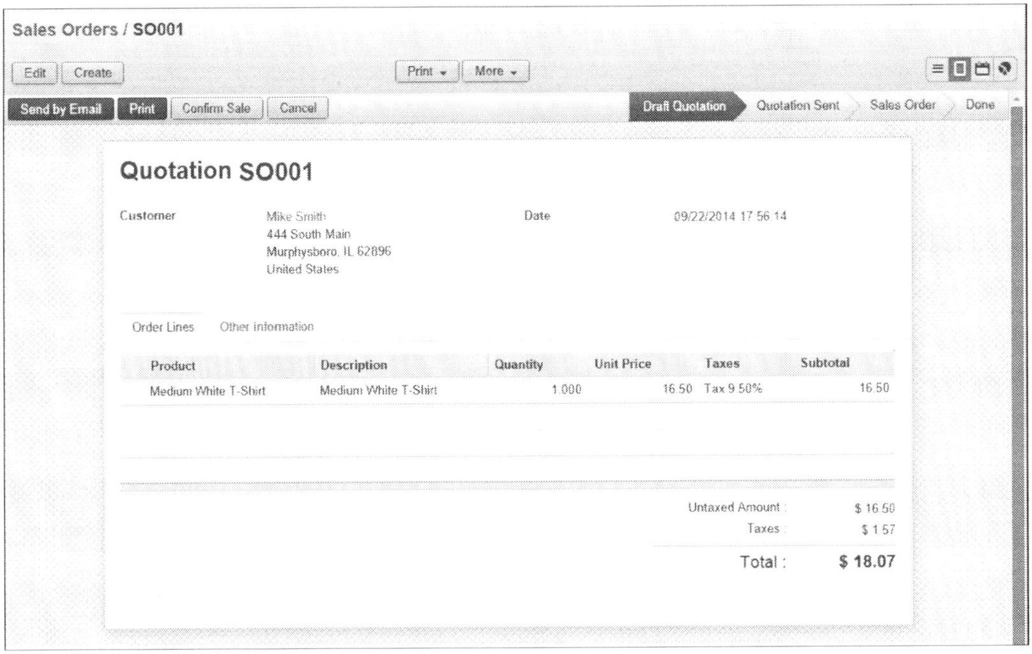

Understanding the sales order workflow

Although we started out entering a sales order, the current state of this order is a **Draft Quotation**. Odoo 8 displays the current state of transactions in the top-right corner of the form.

This indicator makes it very easy to see the current stage of a transaction throughout the Odoo workflow. In this example, we can see that this is currently a **Draft Quotation** status. We can also see that the quotation would first need to be sent and/or be confirmed as a sales order, before the quotation can finally be considered 'Done'.

The available actions you can take on this quotation are displayed at the top-left corner of the form.

The following is a list of available actions for an Odoo quotation:

Send by Email

Clicking on the **Send by Email** button will send a copy of the quotation to the e-mail address in the customer's file.

Print

Even in the digital age, it is still very common to need a printed copy of a quotation or sales order. Clicking on the **Print** button will generate a PDF document containing your quotation.

Confirm Sale

The confirm sale button will convert the quotation into a sales order and push the transaction further down the sales workflow.

Cancel Quotation

Clicking on the **Cancel Quotation** button will prompt you to cancel this quotation. The quotation is not deleted and can still be viewed. Canceling the quotation ends the sales order workflow, and the quotation will only be kept in the system for archive purposes.

Click on the **Confirm Sale** button to convert this quotation into a sales order.

Invoicing the sale

Depending on the workflow of the business, a lot of different things can happen after you have confirmed a sales order. In manufacturing companies, you might need to both purchase products and create a manufacturing order to produce the final product before you invoice the customer. In our example, we are going to go ahead and invoice the customer for the t-shirt they have ordered. Click on the **Create Invoice** button to generate an invoice for the sales order.

An Odoo **Invoice Order** wizard pops up to walk you through the invoice creation process.

The following is the **Invoice Order** wizard:

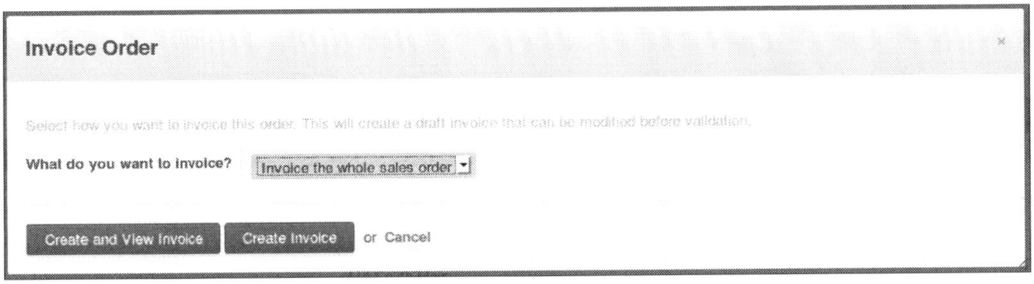

What do you want to invoice?

Odoo provides a variety of options for invoicing the entire sales order or, instead, invoicing based on other methods. The available choices are:

- **Invoice the whole sales order**: If this option is selected then the invoice will be created for the whole sales order.
- **Percentage**: If this option is selected, you are prompted to specify what percent of the total sale you wish to invoice in advance.
- **Fixed Price (deposit)**: Choose this option if you have received a deposit on a product. You will be prompted to enter the amount of the deposit, as well as the opportunity to designate an advance product.
- **Some Order Lines**: This option will prompt you to select specific line items you wish to invoice.

Creating the invoice

For our example, we will be invoicing the whole sales order. Click on **Create Invoice** to generate the invoice. Initially, the invoice is created in a draft state. Clicking on **Validate** will confirm the invoice and post the transaction.

If you have followed along and everything worked as it should, then you will see an invoice similar to the following screenshot:

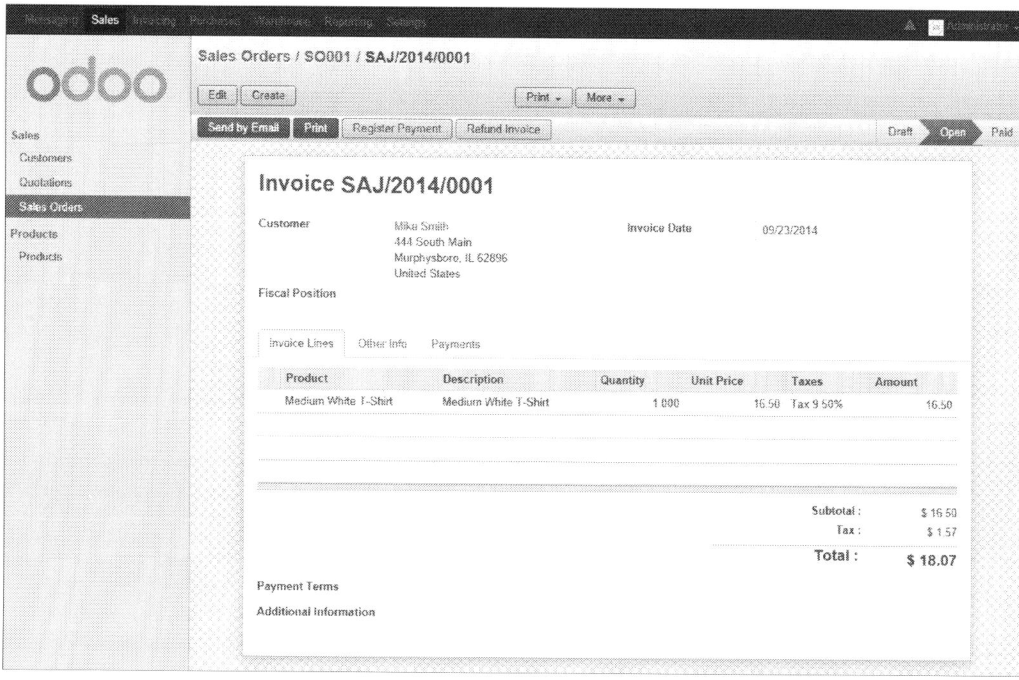

At this time, it is worth noting Odoo's use of an interface feature called **breadcrumbs**. These links, which appear on form views just below the topmost menu, allow you to traverse from your invoice back to the relevant sales order from which it derived. The use of these links is the preferred method of backtracking to prior screens, as opposed to using your browser's back button.

Summary

In this chapter, we started by creating an Odoo database. We then installed the Sales Management application and created our first customer. With our customer created, we turned our attention to setting up a product in Odoo and entering our basic company information. Next, we created a quotation and followed the workflow all the way through to confirming the sales order and generating an invoice.

In the next chapter, let's look our sales strategy and what we want to achieve via the CRM software.

3

Exploring Customer Relationship Management in Odoo

Until recently, most business and financial systems had product-focused designs while records and fields maintained basic customer information; processes and reporting typically revolved around product-related transactions. Earlier, businesses were centered on specific products, but now the focus has shifted to the customer. Customer Relationship Management (CRM) systems provide the tools and reporting necessary to manage customer information and interactions.

In this chapter, we will begin by covering the following topics:

- Looking at what it takes to implement a CRM system as part of an overall business strategy
- Installing the CRM application, and setting up salespersons that can be assigned to our customers
- Learning how to create and manage leads
- Creating opportunities and schedule events in Odoo
- Discovering the Odoo OpenChatter feature
- Managing multiple sales teams

Using CRM as a business strategy

Before jumping into the specific CRM features of Odoo, it is important to discuss briefly the importance of a comprehensive approach to implementing a CRM system in your business. The fact is that successfully implementing a CRM system requires much more planning than just installing software and asking employees to fill in the data. CRM software systems are only a technical tool in assisting your sales and marketing department in acquiring and keeping customers. Certainly the software will play an important role, but to obtain real benefits from a CRM system, you must perform research to understand your customer and how exactly you wish to shape the customer experience.

It is critical that salespeople share account knowledge and completely understand the features and capabilities of the system. They often have existing tools that they have relied on for many years. Without clear objectives and goals for the entire sales team, it is likely they will not use the tool. A plan must be implemented to spend time training and encouraging the sharing of knowledge to successfully implement a CRM system.

Managing the customer experience

Today, customers face a wide range of choices when it comes to purchasing products and services. At the most fundamental level, customers often build great loyalty to brands that give them a positive customer experience. Companies such as Apple and Harley Davidson are successful largely because of fierce brand loyalty based on positive customer experiences. Making the most of a CRM system requires you to put yourself in the role of your customer and develop a consistent strategy to improve their overall customer experience.

Treating your customer like a real person

As computers became more common, it wasn't long until people began to feel as if they were treated *like a number* by many companies. In many ways, CRM systems turn the tables around. Instead of treating customers like cattle, a smart account manager, using a CRM system, can greatly personalize the customer experience. With a CRM system, you treat your customer like an individual, and they will reward you with their loyalty.

Because you are looking to create a personalized customer experience, it is important to thoroughly look at your customer's interactions with the company when designing your own CRM system. A company that sells high-end security systems to government institutions will need to provide drastically different customer experiences than a company that provides a pool maintenance service.

Using your mission statements and company goals to drive the design of your CRM system

A good CRM system will be built around the core goals and mission of your company. If your company does not have customer-focused goals or a mission statement, then you should address that before you begin designing a CRM system. Most critically, a focus must be placed on concerns and interactions that have a direct impact on customer experience. A good CRM system will not just manage the sales process but the entire customer experience and interactions before and after the sale.

The real-world case study – improving customer experience

Now we will take a detailed look at how a real-world CRM system can be implemented to improve customer experience. We begin by looking at a company slogan. *We make great first impressions last.*

Here, we have a slogan that most certainly speaks of the value of customer experience. To make that great first impression and keep it, there are several critical service expectations:

- Orders must be accurate and easy for customers to place
- Orders must be delivered on time
- Quality must be excellent

While listing these customer service goals may seem obvious, explicitly enlisting your objectives is important when building a CRM system. In the building process, there is often a natural tendency to focus almost exclusively on customer acquisition and pre-sale activities. We must take care to remember that a CRM system must also support processes that manage the entire customer experience. How are problem orders handled? How is the customer contacted if there is a product back order? If the customer calls, can the service representative easily provide delivery-tracking information? These are the kind of scenarios to consider when building your own CRM system.

Installing the CRM application

If you have not installed the CRM application, log in as the administrator and then click on the **Settings** menu. In a few seconds, the list of available apps will appear. The CRM will likely be in the top-left corner:

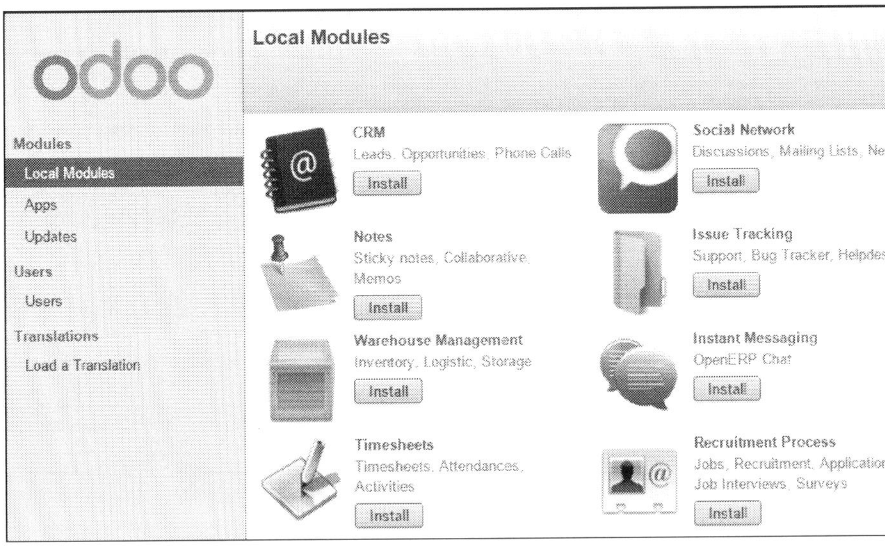

Click on **Install** to set up the CRM application.

Assigning the sales representative or account manager

In Odoo, like in most CRM systems, the sales representative or account manager plays an important role. Typically, this person will ultimately be responsible for the customer account and a satisfactory customer experience.

> While most often a company will use real people as their salespeople, it is certainly possible to instead have a salesperson record refer to a group or even a sub-contracted support service.

We will begin by creating a salesperson who will handle standard customer accounts. Note that a sales representative is also a user in the Odoo system.

Create a new salesperson by going to the **Settings** menu, selecting **Users**, and then clicking on the **Create** button. The new user form will appear. We have filled in the form with values for a fictional salesperson, `Mike Zeigler`. The following is a screenshot of the user **Access Rights** tab:

Email Address

Beginning in Odoo 8, the user and login form prompts for e-mail as opposed to a username. It is still possible to use a username instead of an e-mail address, but given the strong encouragement to use an e-mail address in Odoo 8, it is possible that in future versions of Odoo, the requirement to provide an e-mail address will be more strictly enforced.

Access Rights

The **Access Rights** tab lets you control which applications the user will be able to access. There is no need to give Mr. Zeigler access to the **Sharing** or **Administration** privileges. By default, Odoo will specify Mr. Ziegler as an employee, so we will accept that default.

> Depending on the applications you may have already installed or the dependencies Odoo may have had in various releases, it is possible you will have other access rights listed.

Sales application settings

When setting up your salespeople in Odoo, you have three different options on how much access an individual user has to the sales system:

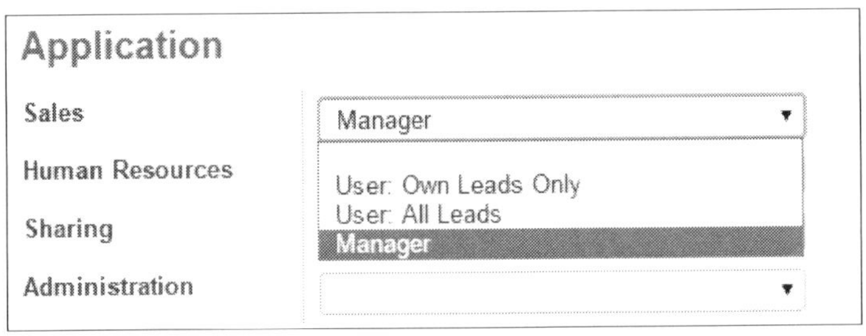

User : Own Leads Only

This is the most restrictive access to the sales application. With this access level, the user is only allowed to see the leads they have entered themselves or those that have been assigned to them. They will not be able to see leads assigned to other salespeople in the system.

User : All Leads

With this setting, the user will have access to all leads within the system.

Manager

The **Manager** setting is the highest access level in the Odoo sales system. With this access level, the user can see all leads, as well as access the configuration options of the sales application. The **Manager** setting also allows the user to access statistical reports.

For the purposes of our example, we are going to assign Mike Zeigler the role of manager. The following form is to enter a new user into Odoo:

Language and Timezone

Odoo allows you to select the language for each user. Currently, Odoo supports more than 20 language translations. Specifying the **Timezone** field allows Odoo to coordinate the display of the date and time on messages.

> Make sure you specify a timezone when creating a user record. Leaving timezone blank for a user may sometimes lead to unpredictable behavior in the Odoo software. Check the customization chapter to find out how you can make timezone a required field!

Receive Inbox Notifications by Email

In Odoo 7, messaging became a central component of the Odoo system. In version 8, the support has been improved, and it is now even easier to communicate important sales information between colleagues. Therefore, determining the appropriate handling of email along with the circumstances in which a user will receive an e-mail is very important. The **Receive Inbox Notifications by Email** option lets you determine when you will receive e-mail messages from notifications that come into your Odoo inbox.

For our example, we have chosen to receive **All Messages**. This is now the new default setting in Odoo 8. However, since we have not yet configured an e-mail server, no e-mails will be sent or received at this stage.

Let's review the user options that are available in communicating by e-mail.

Never

Selecting **Never** suppresses all e-mail messaging for the user. Naturally, you will wish to use this setting if you do not have an e-mail server configured. This is also a useful option for users to use Odoo's built-in inbox to retrieve their messages.

All Messages – discussions, e-mails, and followed system notifications

This option sends an e-mail notification for any action that would create an entry in your Odoo inbox. Unlike the other options, this action could include system notifications or other automated communication.

Default Sales Team

In Odoo, sales teams allow you to organize salespeople. For example, you could have sales teams organized by region or by product category. Even if you do not load demo data during an Odoo installation, the system will have one sales team record named **Direct Sales**. In version 7 of Odoo, this default team was called the Sales Department.

Signature

The **Signature** section allows you to customize a signature that will automatically be appended to Odoo-generated messages and e-mails.

Manually setting the user password

You may have noticed that there is no visible password field in the user record. That is because the default method is to send the user an account verification email that they can use to set their password. However, if you do not have an email server configured, there is an alternative method to set the user password.

After saving the user record, use the **More** menu at the top of the form and select **Change Password**, as shown in the following screenshot:

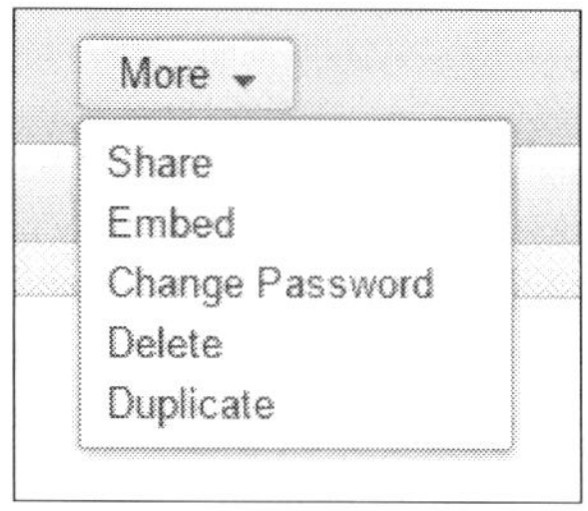

A form will then appear allowing you to set the password for the user.

Assigning a salesperson to a customer

Now that we have set up our salesperson, it is time to assign him his first customer. Previously, no salesperson was assigned to our one and only customer, Mike Smith. So let's go to the sales menu and then click on **Mike Smith** to pull up his customer record and assign Mr. Ziegler as his salesperson. The following is a screenshot of the customer screen opened to assign the salesperson:

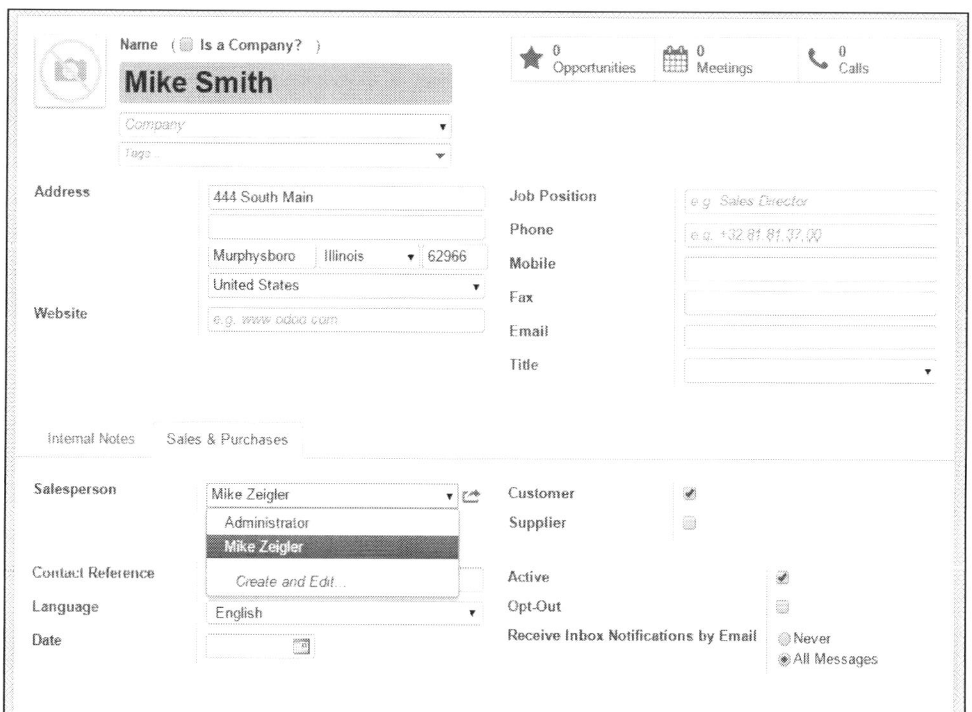

Here, we have set the salesperson as **Mike Zeigler**. By assigning your customers a salesperson, you can better organize your customers for additional statistical analysis and report development.

> In Odoo 7, you were required to supply both the salesperson and the department. Now in Odoo 8, you specify only the salesperson.

Leads and opportunities

Odoo provides two primary documents to manage interactions with your customers or potential customers. You can think of leads as less critical—and perhaps less likely to turn into a real sales situation—than an opportunity. A good example of leads would be the few dozen business cards you get from people you met at a conference. You could add each of them as a lead for further follow-up. An example of an opportunity would be meeting someone at the conference and having a detailed conversation on how your company provides appropriate services.

Many people get confused between when to use leads and when to use opportunities. The best way to remember the difference is that leads are intangible and are essentially potential contacts. Opportunities should be more clearly defined, have some sort of expected income if successful, and provide significant project details and scope compared to a simple lead.

Creating leads in Odoo

Many a time, it can take quite a bit of work to uncover an opportunity. Use Odoo to create leads when you need a qualification step before creating an opportunity or a customer. For example, you may receive a business card or an unqualified lead from your website. Another common situation is that leads are purchased, perhaps from a mailing list, and then imported into Odoo.

Let's create a new lead for a potential customer we met at a local event. Under the **Sales** menu, click on **Leads** and then on the **Create** button to open a new lead. The following is the screenshot of the form used to create a new lead:

As you will see, the form is very similar to the standard customer screen. There is a good reason for this, as Odoo uses a standard structure to hold address information for leads, customers, suppliers, and users/employees. In our example, we have filled out the basic contact and address information as well as assigned our sales representative to this lead.

For this example, we are not yet creating a customer. Notice, however, that there is a customer field available in the form. It is possible that you come across a lead that perhaps is tied to an existing customer you already have in the system. In this case, you could select the customer and the rest of the information would be filled in.

Converting a lead into an opportunity

Leads will stay leads indefinitely until you take some action to either turn them into opportunities or mark them as lost/dead. You will notice a button labeled **Convert to Opportunity** at the top-left corner of your form. At any point, you can convert a lead into an opportunity simply by clicking on this button.

Once you click on **Convert to Opportunity**, you will be presented with an Odoo wizard that will allow you to choose how you wish to handle the conversion of the lead into an opportunity.

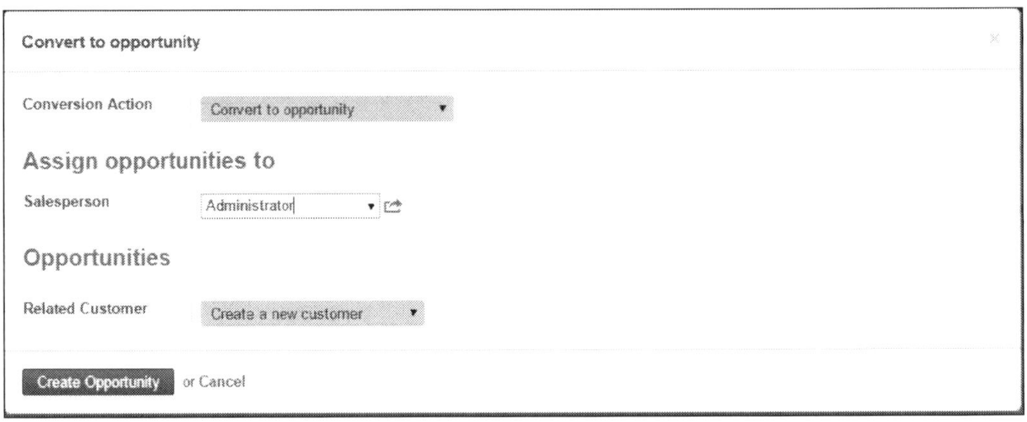

Each of the options presented are pretty self-explanatory. The **Conversion Action** field determines if you will create a new opportunity or merge this lead with an existing opportunity. You also have the option of assigning the opportunity to a specific salesperson. Finally, you get to tell Odoo if you wish to create a new customer for this opportunity or if instead you wish to assign this opportunity to an existing customer.

Marking a lead as lost or dead

Sometimes, a lead cannot be converted into an opportunity, and you must mark it as lost. To do so, identify the lead you wish to mark as lost. You can mark a lead as lost by choosing Mark as Lost from the **More** menu at the top of the page or by clicking on the **More** status on the far right of the form and choosing **Dead**. There is no difference between the two methods. Lost and Dead mean the same thing. Odoo just names them differently in the interface.

Creating a new opportunity

In Odoo, a potential sale is defined by creating a new opportunity. An opportunity allows you to begin collecting information about the scope and potential outcomes of a sale. Opportunities can be created from new leads or originate from an existing customer.

For our real-world example, let's assume Mike Smith has called and was so happy with his first order that he now wants to discuss using Silkworm for his local sports team. After a short conversation, we decide to create an opportunity. To do so, we click on the **Opportunities** button. This is a screenshot of a new opportunity:

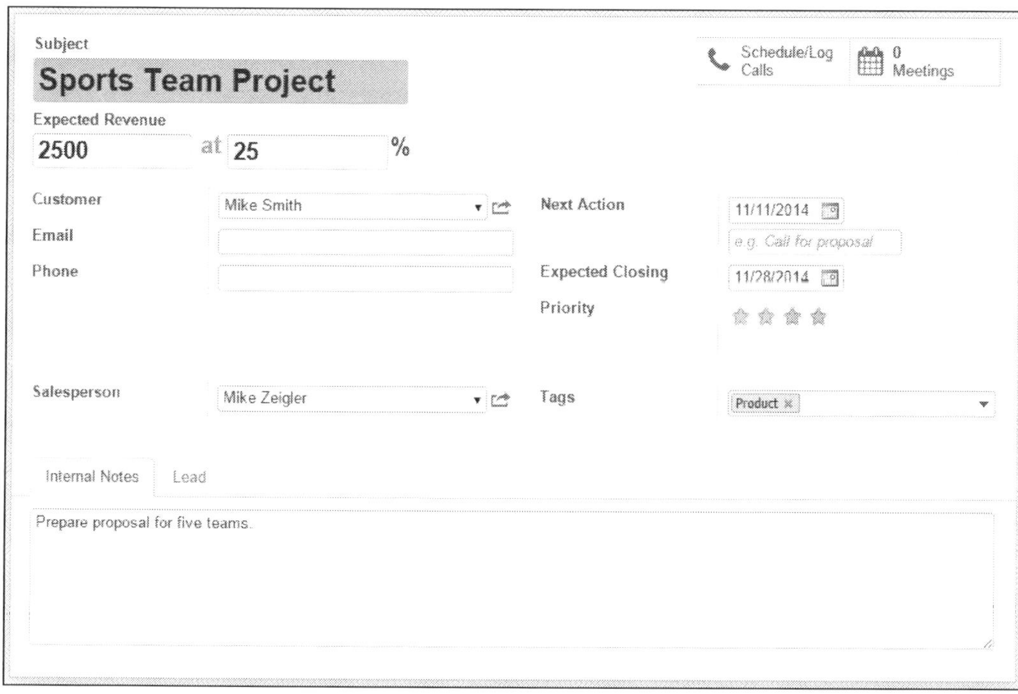

Subject

The subject used for your opportunity can be anything you wish. It is naturally important to choose a subject that makes it easy to identify the opportunity in a list. This is the only field required to create an opportunity in Odoo.

Expected Revenue and percentage

Here, you specify the amount of revenue you can expect from the opportunity if you are successful and then the percentage likelihood that this opportunity will result in a sale. These values are useful in many statistical reports, although they are not required to create an opportunity.

> An increasingly number of reports looks to the expected revenue and percentage of opportunity completions. Therefore, depending on your reporting requirements, you may wish to encourage salespeople to set target goals for each opportunity to track conversion better.

Customer

This field is automatically populated if you create an opportunity from the customer form. However, you can assign a different customer if you like. This is not a required field, so if you have an opportunity that you do not wish to associate with a customer, that is perfectly fine. For example, you may leave this field blank if you are attending a trade show and expect to have revenue but do not yet have any specific customers to attribute to the opportunity.

Next Action

When following up on your opportunities, one of the most important triggers will be the **Next Action** date. Here, you decide when you should next take some sort of action on the opportunity. You are provided a small note field to remind you of the action that you should be taking. This could be anything from placing a phone call to sending an email to performing a presentation. For our example, we intend to present a proposal on the action date.

Expected Closing

When managing your opportunities, it is important to establish a goal for when you wish to close the sale. Providing an expected closing date is handy for managing opportunities and running reports identifying which opportunities are due to be closed. The priority setting ranges from lowest to highest, with three settings in between. In defining your CRM system, you should identify business rules to determine under what conditions an opportunity will receive the highest priority.

Tags

Odoo allows you to assign multiple tags to an opportunity. For example, you could choose 'trade show' and 'sports' as tags to designate an opportunity that is sports-related and will take place at a trade show.

Email and Phone

The **Email** and **Phone** fields allow you to specify the primary contact methods you will likely use to communicate with your opportunity.

Internal Notes

The **Internal Notes** area is where you provide all the details of the opportunity. For our example, we kept the notes brief. However, when you are working with real opportunities, make sure you take advantage of the **Internal Notes** area to document anything that will help you close the sale.

The Lead tab

When you create an opportunity from either a customer or a lead, the information is automatically brought over into the **Lead** tab in the opportunity. The following is a screenshot of the **Lead** tab of an opportunity:

Lead address and contact information

The top half of the **Lead** tab contains the standard fields for an address and other contact information. This information is automatically populated but can be overwritten for the opportunity if you desire. The **Function** field is used to provide a bit of detail on the event that triggered the opportunity.

> Odoo does not provide separate fields for first and last names like many other accounting systems. Consider this as you plan how to organize customers in your system.

Mailings

The **Opt-Out** checkbox prevents the lead or customer associated with this opportunity from receiving mass mailings.

Active

This field is useful if you have an opportunity that perhaps has gone cold. Instead of deleting the opportunity, you can make it inactive by unchecking the box. Later if the opportunity becomes viable again, you can make it active once again.

Referred By

This is a simple text field that is not tied to any other data. It is just a field where you can make a note of who may have referred this opportunity to you.

References

The two places to specify references at the bottom of the screen have a great deal of flexibility in tying other information in Odoo to the opportunity. Not only can you select the type of reference, you can tie the opportunity directly to many records in the system. The list includes:

- Partner
- Product
- Invoice
- Voucher
- Sales Order

- Event
- Meeting

Save the **Opportunity** by clicking on the **Save** button at the top of the form.

Looking at your opportunities in the Kanban view

When you navigate to the **Sales** menu and choose **Opportunities**, you will see your opportunities displayed in the Kanban view. Here, we see our brand new $2,500 opportunity along with the customer and the next action we need to take. The following is a screenshot of the Kanban view for opportunities:

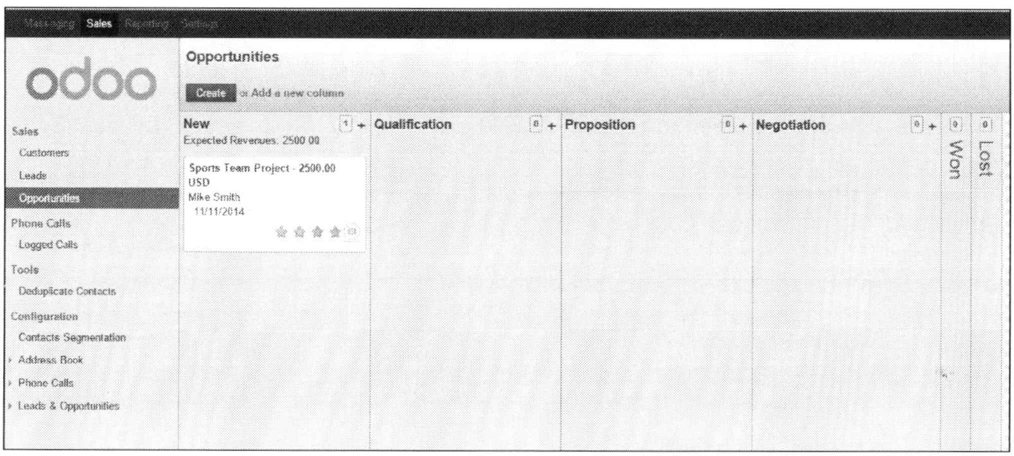

Clicking on the small arrow on the Kanban card will bring up a small menu allowing you to perform actions related to the opportunity.

An introduction to sales stages

At the top of the Kanban view, you can see the default stages that are provided by the Odoo CRM installation. In this case, we see **New**, **Qualification**, **Proposition**, **Negotiation**, **Won**, and **Lost**. Notice that **Won** and **Lost** are currently collapsed and you can use the + icon to expand them.

As an opportunity moves between stages, the Kanban view will update to show you where each opportunity currently stands. Here, we can see that because **Sports Team Project** has just been entered, it is in the **New** column.

View the details of an opportunity

If you click the small arrow at the top right of the opportunity card in the Kanban view, you will see a pop-up menu with your available options. The following is a screenshot of the actions available on an opportunity:

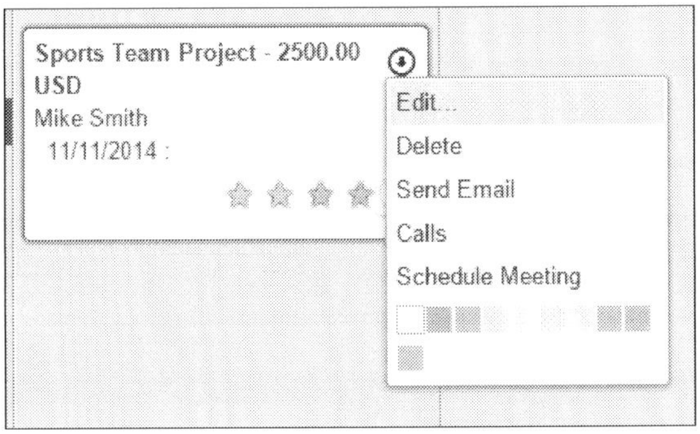

Actions you can take on an opportunity

Selecting the **Edit...** option takes you to the opportunity record and into edit mode for you to change any of the information. In addition, you can delete the record, send an email to the contact associated with the opportunity, and schedule a call or meeting. The color palette at the bottom lets you color code your opportunities in the Kanban view. The small star on the opportunity card allows you to highlight opportunities for special consideration. You can also easily drag and drop the opportunity into other columns as you work through the various stages of the sale.

Using Odoo's OpenChatter feature

One of the biggest enhancements brought about in Odoo 7 was the new OpenChatter feature that provides social networking style communication to business documents and transactions. This feature has been improved in Odoo 8 and is more important than ever to create clear communication processes within an organization.

As we work on our brand new opportunity, we will utilize the OpenChatter feature to demonstrate how to communicate details between team members and generate log entries to document our progress.

The best thing about the OpenChatter feature is that it is available for nearly all business documents in Odoo. It also allows you to see a running set of logs of the transactions or operations that have affected the document.

Changing the status of an opportunity

For our example, let's assume that we have prepared our proposal and made the presentation. Bring up the opportunity by using the right-click menu in the Kanban view or by going into the list view and clicking the opportunity in the list.

It is time to update the status of our opportunity by clicking on the **Proposition** tab at the top of the form.

Notice that you do not have to edit the record to change the status of the opportunity.

At the bottom of the opportunity, you will now see a logged note generated by Odoo that documents the change of the opportunity from a **New** opportunity to a **Proposition**. The following is a screenshot of OpenChatter displaying the changed stage of the opportunity:

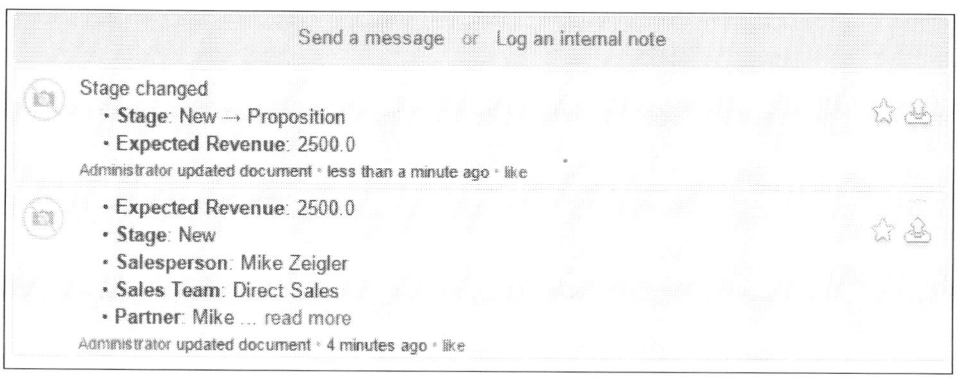

Notice how Odoo is logging the events automatically as they take place.

Managing the opportunity

With the proposal presented, let's take down some details from what we have seen so far, which may help us later when we come back to this opportunity. One method of collecting this information could be to add the details to the **Internal Notes** field in the opportunity form. There is value, however, in using the OpenChatter feature in Odoo to document our new details.

Most importantly, using OpenChatter to log notes gives you a running transcript with automatically generated date and time stamps. With the generic notes field, it can be very difficult to manage multiple entries. Another major advantage is that the OpenChatter feature can automatically send messages to team members' inboxes, thus updating them on the progress. Let's see it in action!

Click on the **Log a Note** link to attach a note to the opportunity. Here's a screenshot showing how to create a note:

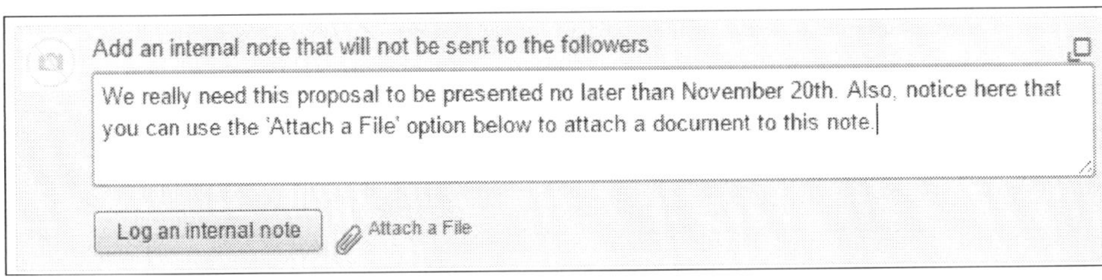

When you create a note, it is attached to the business document; but no message will be sent to followers. You can even attach a document to the note by using the **Attach a File** feature. Clicking on the **Log an internal note** button saves the note and makes it part of the OpenChatter log for that document.

Following a business document

Odoo brings social networking concepts into your business communications. Fundamental to this implementation is that you can get automatic updates on a business document by following the document. Then, whenever a note, action, or a message is created related to a document you follow, you will receive a message in your Odoo inbox. In the bottom right-hand corner of the form, you are presented with notification options and the option to add or remove followers from the document. The following is a screenshot of the OpenChatter **Following** options:

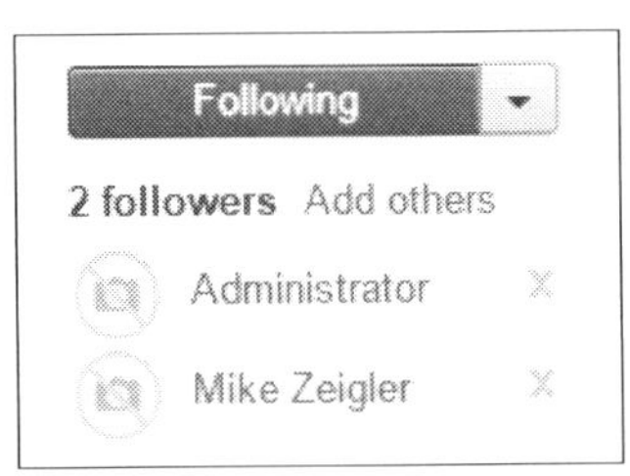

In this case, we can see that both **Mike Zeigler** and **Administrator** are set as followers for this opportunity. The blue **Following** button at the top indicates that I am following this document. Using the **Add others** link, you can add additional users to follow the document.

Now in Odoo 8, the items that followers are notified of can be viewed by clicking on the arrow to the right of the **Following** button. This brings up a list of the actions that will generate notifications to the followers:

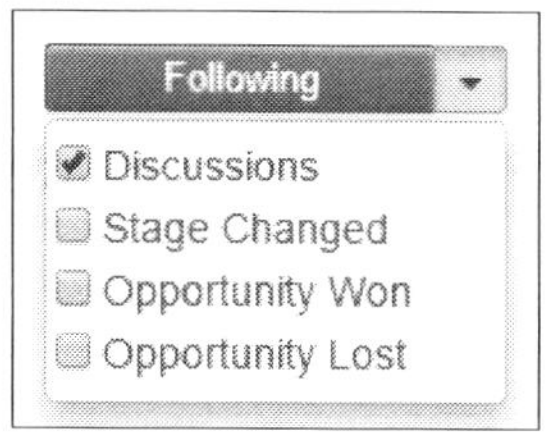

The checkbox next to **Discussions** indicates that I will be notified of any discussions related to this document. However, I will not be notified, for example, if the stage changes.

> When you send a message, by default, the customer will become a follower of the document. Thus, whenever the status of the document changes, the customer will receive an email. Test out all your processes before integrating with an e-mail server. For additional resources on community modules that help manage the OpenChatter features, refer to *Appendix, Locating Additional Odoo Resources*.

Modifying the stages of the sale

We have seen that Odoo provides a default set of sales stages. Many times, however, you will want to customize the stages to best deliver an outstanding customer experience. Moving an opportunity through stages should trigger actions that create a relationship with the customer and demonstrate your understanding of their needs. A customer in the qualification stage of a sale will have significantly different needs and expectations than a customer in the negotiation phase.

In terms of our case study, there are sometimes printing jobs that are technically complex to accomplish. With different jerseys for a variety of teams, the final details need to go through a final technical review and approval process before the order can be entered and verified.

From a business perspective, the goal is not just to document the stage of the sales cycle; the primary goal is to use this information to drive customer interactions and improve the overall customer experience.

To add a stage to the sales process, switch to the Kanban view, then click on the **Add column** link in the top-left corner of the form.

You can find the Kanban button in the top-right corner of the form. This is what the Kanban button looks like:

The **Add column** form is in the following screenshot:

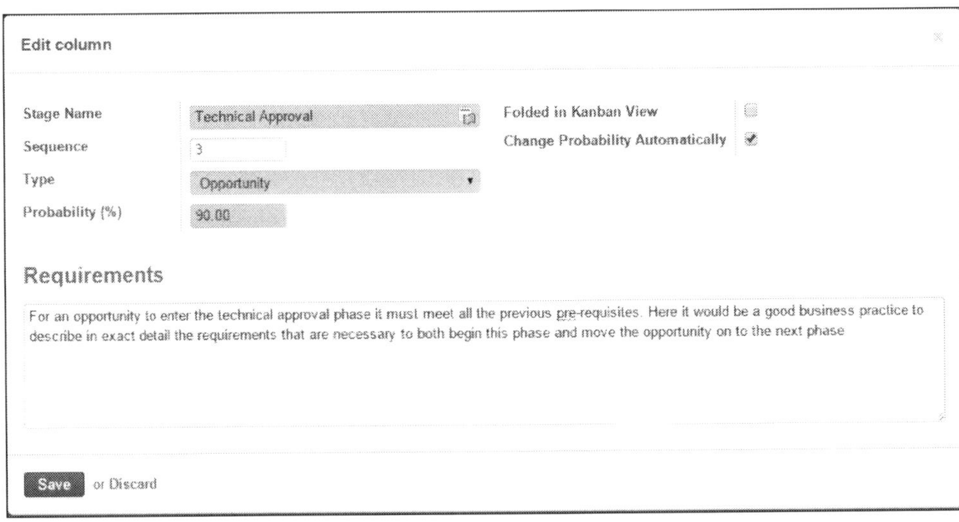

After you have added the column to the sales process, you can use your mouse to drag and drop the columns in the order you wish them to appear. We are now ready to begin the **Technical Approval** stage of this opportunity.

> In Odoo 7, there was also a **Status** property that was confusing for many users. Therefore, **Status** has been removed in Odoo 8.

Drag and drop the Sports Team Project opportunity over to the **Technical Approval** column in the Kanban view, as seen in the following screenshot:

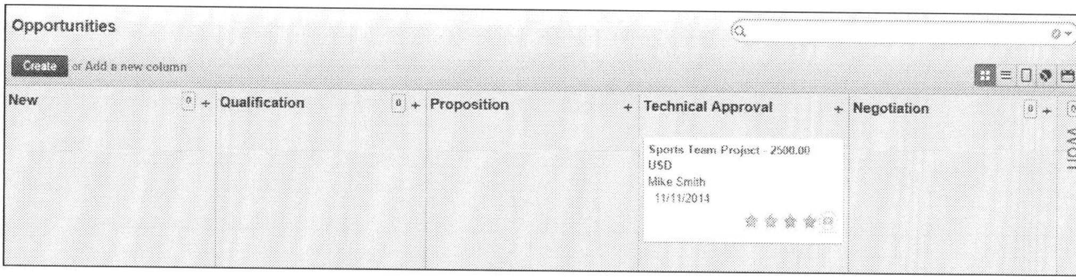

We have now moved the opportunity over to the Technical Approval column in our Kanban. You will also notice that any time you change the stage of an opportunity, an entry is created in the OpenChatter section at the bottom of the form. In addition to the ability to drag and drop an opportunity into a new stage, you also have the ability to change the stage of an opportunity by going into the form view.

Closing the sale

After a lot of hard work, we have finally won the opportunity, and it is time to turn this opportunity into a quotation. At this point, Odoo makes it easy to take that opportunity and turn it into an actual quotation.

Open up the opportunity and click on the **Convert to Quotation** button at the top of the opportunity form:

Taking this action will bring you to the **Make Quotation** screen, where you can confirm the customer and mark the opportunity as **Won**. Since we definitely want to update our opportunity and get credit for the win, we make sure that the **Mark Won** box is checked. Notice that it is also possible to create a quotation for other customers as well by simply selecting them from the list. The following is a screenshot of the **Make Quotation** action for an opportunity:

Clicking on the **Create** button will move your opportunity to the **Won** stage and automatically populate the reference field in the opportunity with a link to your newly created quotation.

Your opportunity converted to a quotation

The workflow in Odoo handles moving over all the required information from your opportunity to your quotation document. At this point, you are ready to begin adding line items and creating a quotation just as we did in *Chapter 2, Installing Your First Application*.

Managing multiple sales teams

Like most Odoo applications, by default, most settings are pre-configured to provide a simple out-of-the-box solution. Many companies, however, may have multiple sales teams that handle different customer types, perhaps by product line or by geographical territory. When your company has those requirements, you will want to turn on the option to handle multiple sales teams within Odoo.

You can access these settings through the **Sales** application under the **Configuration** options:

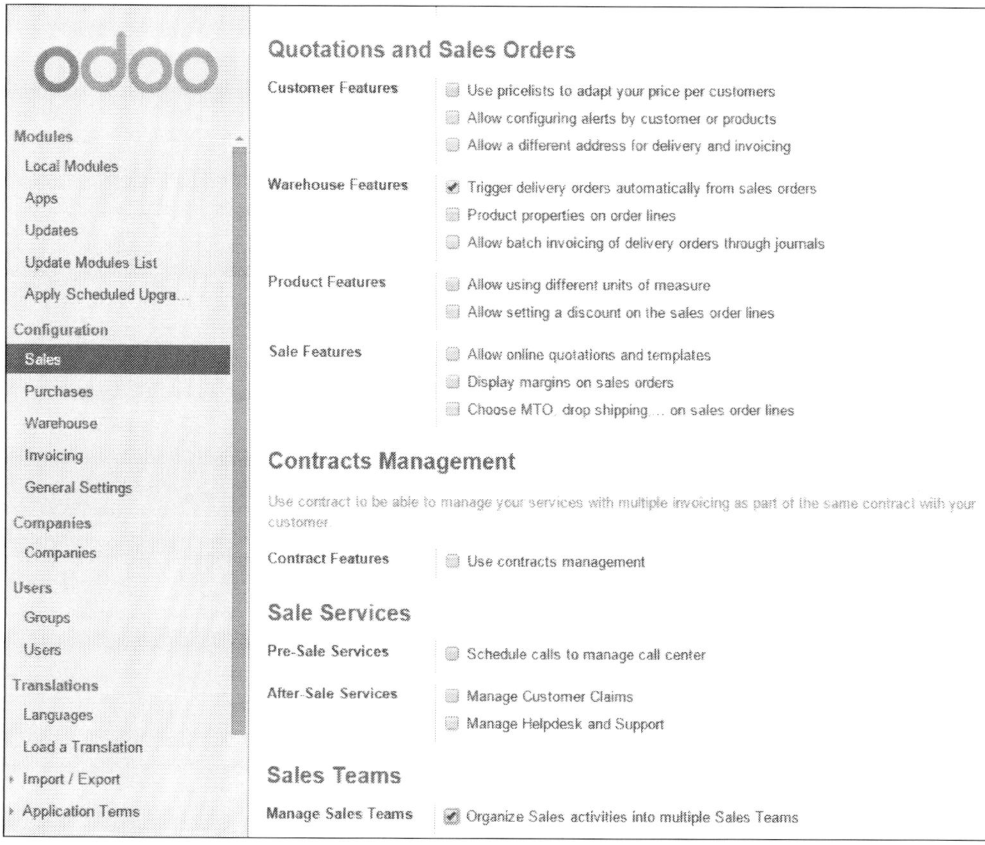

Clicking on the checkbox under **Sales Teams** | **Manage Sales Teams**, allows you to organize sales activities into multiple sales teams. You will also notice that when you now click on the **Sales** menu, you will get a new default view that breaks operations down by sales team.

Creating custom stages through Sales Teams

For many sales operations, a company may use the same stages for all their sales. However, depending on the complexity of your company's product line, it may be better to create custom stages for different sales teams. For our case study, Silkworm provides creative design services that require a different set of stages when managing the sales process. As we have discussed, the primary purpose of stages in a CRM system is to support a positive customer experience.

To configure the stages of a sales team, click on the small arrow in the Kanban view or switch to the row view and double-click on the row. Click on the appropriate sales team and then the **Stages** tab to see the current stages assigned to the sales team, as seen in the following screenshot:

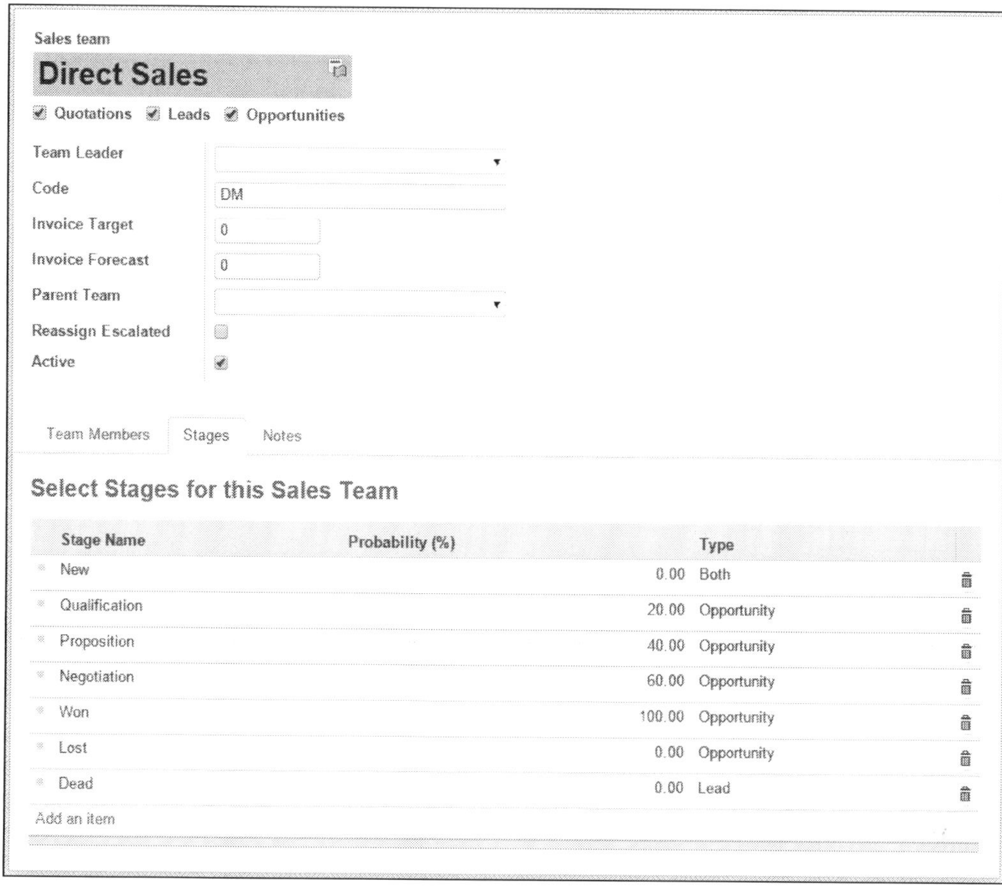

On the far left of the list, you can click and drag the little dot to reorder the stages. The far right of the grid has a small trash icon that can be used to delete a stage.

Each stage is assigned to a related status, and you can determine whether a stage is applicable to a lead or an opportunity, or to both.

Creating a new sales team

We can create a new sales team to handle creative designs and more artistic projects that require extra customer service. Click on **Create** in the **Sales Team** view to create a new sales team.

For our new **Creative Designs** team, we have added a few stages to better represent the sales cycle for this service category:

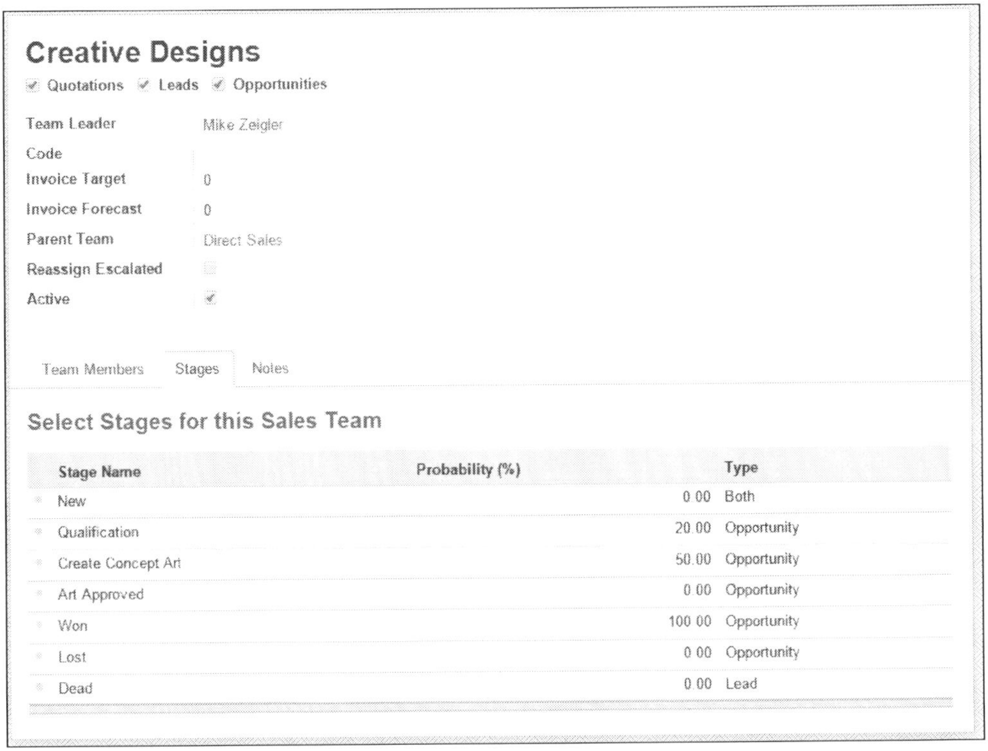

Using Odoo to schedule calls, meetings, and events

Often when working with leads and opportunities, you will find it beneficial to schedule meetings and calls. Odoo provides a built-in meeting scheduler you can use specifically to manage your schedule and relate those events to customers within Odoo. Let's take a look at how we can schedule an event in Odoo. Meeting scheduling is handled in the messaging menu of Odoo. Begin by going to the messaging menu and choosing **Calendar**.

Odoo will then display your personal calendar and bring up the current month.

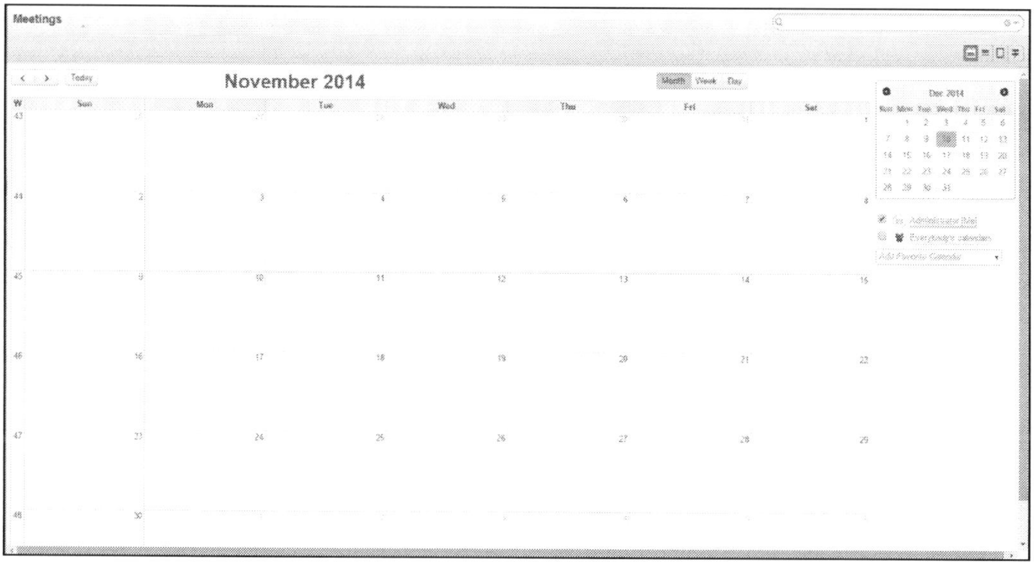

The arrows at the top left of the form allow you to quickly navigate to the previous and next month respectively. To the right of the title is the option to look at the calendar by month, week, or day. This can be particularly valuable to see more information when you have many meetings scheduled.

On the far right, you have a small calendar for the next month. This small calendar is interactive, and you can use it to quickly jump to that month and even a specific day.

Scheduling an event

Scheduling an event is very easy. Simply click on the day you wish to schedule an event. You will then be prompted to name the event.

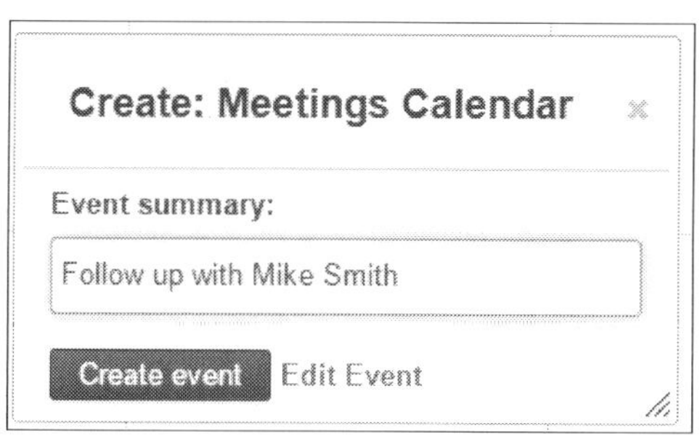

After entering the event summary, you will have two options. You can directly create the event, or you can choose **Edit Event** to provide additional details about the event.

Depending on how you want to organize and manage your meetings, it may work for you just fine to create the event; provided the event summary is enough information for you to take the action you require. Typically, however, it will be a better practice to edit this event and provide some more details.

Click on **Edit Event** to create an event and automatically bring it up for editing:

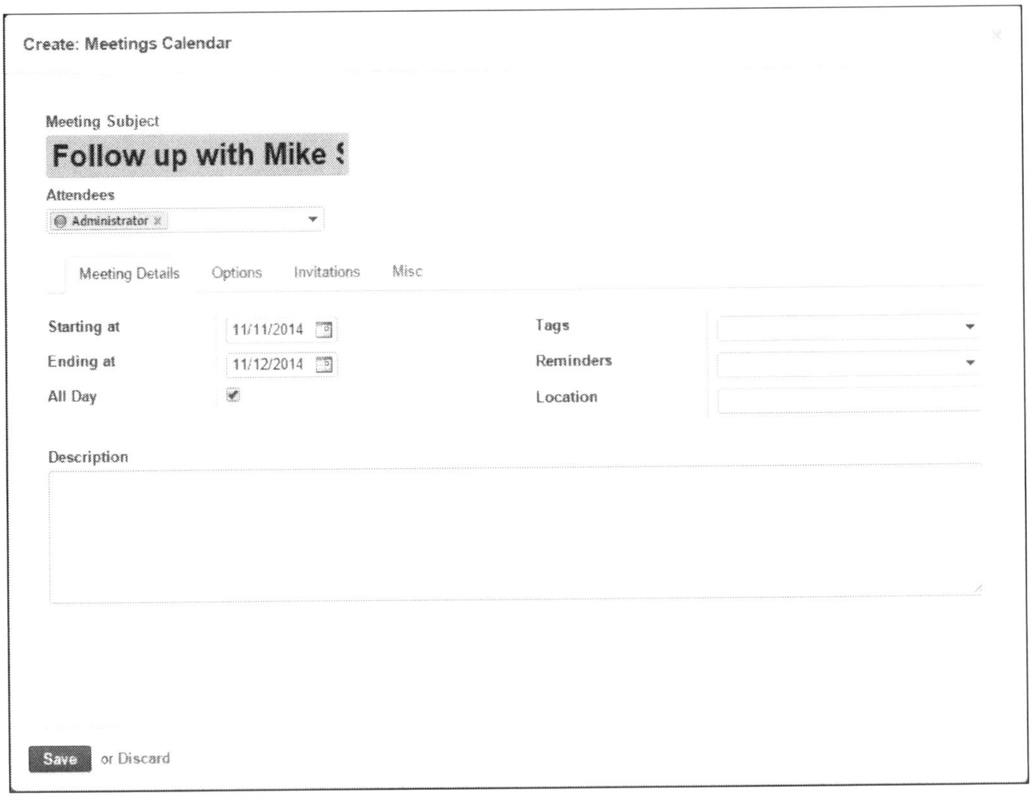

Odoo will automatically bring over the event summary that you filled in after clicking on the day. Notice, however, that instead of **Event summary**, the title is now **Meeting Subject**. Perhaps Odoo will modify this in the future for greater consistency. Make sure that the **Ending at** date is one day after the **Starting at** date and the **All Day** option is checked.

Adding attendees to your meeting

By default, you are the only person attending this meeting. When you are meeting with a client, customer, or vendor, it is largely up to you to add the attendee here in the list. For our purpose, we will add **Mike Smith** to the list of attendees. Odoo will automatically search in real time as you type out the name.

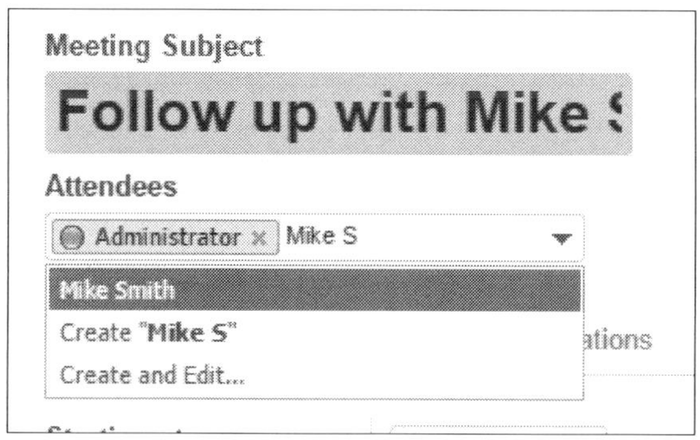

Odoo will then add the attendee to the attendees list. For internal communications, this can be used to make sure all of the necessary team members are notified of the meeting if they are also using the Odoo schedules.

> Odoo will give you a warning if you add an attendee that does not have an email address. In this case, Odoo will still add the attendee, but naturally, any automated notifications will not be delivered to the attendee.

Specifying the meeting details

Odoo's meeting scheduler offers quite a few different options that assist you in customizing the meeting. One of the first things to notice is that, by default, Odoo schedules a meeting for the full day. If you wish to schedule for a specific time, uncheck the **All Day** option. After you have unchecked the option, the **Starting at** and **Ending at** fields will expand to allow you to specify the time.

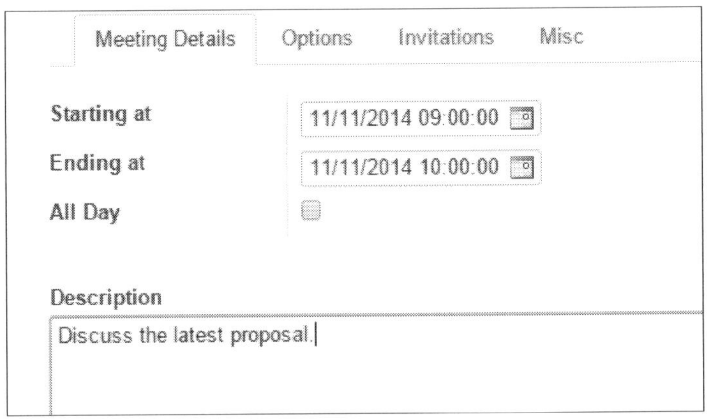

One other important thing to notice is that even after you uncheck the **All Day** option, Odoo will leave the ending date as the next day. Therefore, at least with this version of Odoo, you will have to go back and adjust the end date to be the same as the start date. In this example, we have also added a simple description to show how you can specify details of the event.

Specifying tags for your meeting

Odoo provides a set of default meeting tags that quickly tell you the overall scope of the meeting. You can specify multiple tags as well as create new tags to organize your meeting schedules.

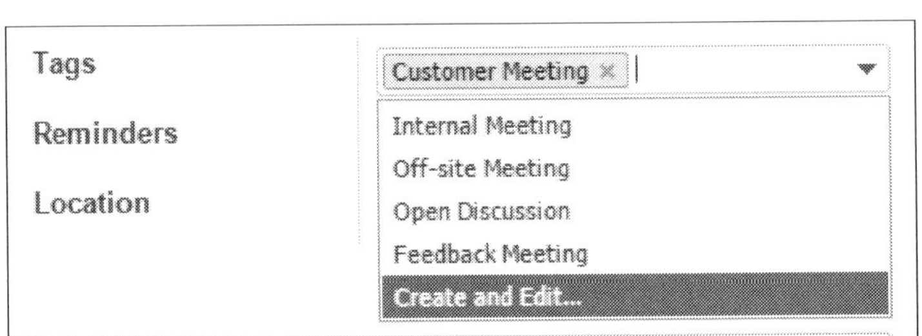

Setting up reminders for your meeting

Oftentimes, you might like to have a reminder or notification a little while before your meeting. Setting reminders can possibly help prevent you from missing an important meeting. Odoo offers two kinds of basic reminders: notifications and email reminders.

Notifications will prompt you visually on screen in the top-right corner of your window at a specified time before the meeting. Email reminders will send you an e-mail.

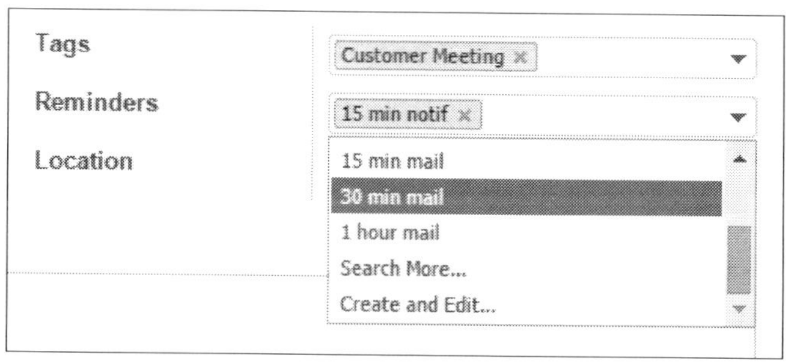

In addition to tags and reminders, you also have the option to specify the location of the meeting. This location is a simple text field and is just some extra information you can use to keep your team members informed.

Specifying additional meeting options

Under the options page, Odoo allows you to specify several additional options for meetings. One of the most powerful features is the ability to configure recurring meetings. When you select the **Recurrent** option, additional options will become available in which you can select the interval.

Depending on the interval you select, the form will refresh with the appropriate options for that interval. In the following screenshot, we have selected a weekly interval. Odoo then allows us to select which day(s) of the week the meeting will repeat.

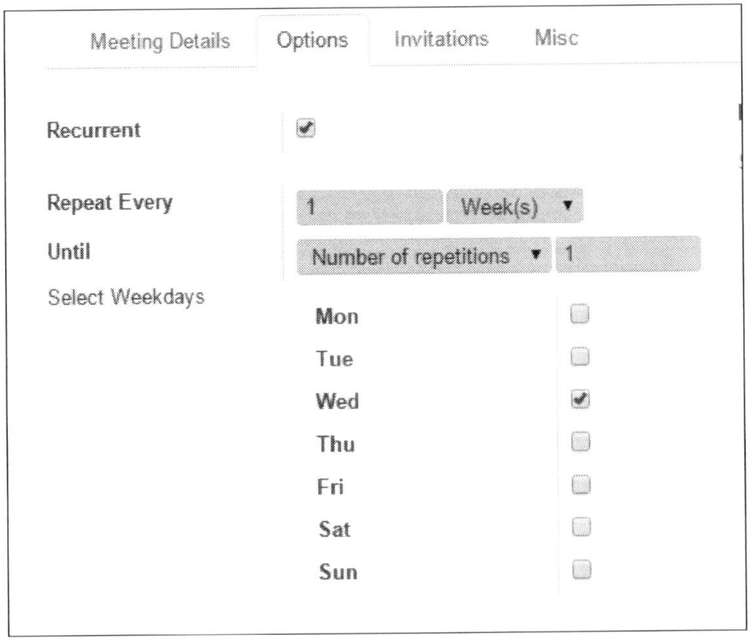

In addition to selecting the specific days, you can also specify how long before the recurring meeting will end by using the **Until** option. The preceding example demonstrates how you can specify a meeting to end based on the number of repetitions. If you choose, you can select an end date to stop the recurring meeting.

Summary

In this chapter, we started by discussing the role of a CRM system in a modern-day business. We installed the CRM application, created salespeople, and then proceeded to develop a system to manage the sales process. In our example, we walked an opportunity through the various stages in the sales process. Finally, we saw how to modify stages in the sales cycle and turn the opportunity directly into a quotation.

In the next chapter, we will turn our attention to install the purchasing application to set up suppliers, create purchase orders, and receive goods into our warehouse.

4

Purchasing with Odoo

In this chapter, we start getting into what could be considered the core functionality of most ERP systems. We will begin by setting up a supplier and then purchasing raw material components. After the products arrive, we then receive the products in the inventory and pay the invoice to complete the purchasing cycle.

The topics we will cover in this chapter include:

- Examining a typical purchasing process for a business
- Setting up your suppliers and warehouse locations
- Entering a quote and turning it into a purchase order
- Receiving products from your suppliers
- Paying invoices

Understanding the overall purchasing process

> Let's begin with a 30,000 foot view of the purchasing process. Putting together a purchasing system requires several steps, and initially, it can be confusing for people new to ERP systems. However, when you break the steps down and look at them individually, the process becomes much easier to understand.

Setting up a supplier

When you set up a supplier, you are determining the individuals or companies that are providing you with products. Sometimes suppliers are also referred to as vendors. In Odoo, it is perfectly possible to create a product and sell it without implementing a purchasing system. However, to begin using your system for purchasing, you will need to configure the suppliers.

The steps you take for setting up a supplier are much the same as setting up a customer. In fact, now is as good a time as any to tell you that Odoo maintains core customer, employee, and supplier records all in the same model (or table) named `res.partner`. Odoo distinguishes between customers, suppliers, and those who are both with the **Is a Customer** and **Is a Supplier** checkboxes.

Setting up warehouse locations

Once you have decided to start using Odoo to purchase your products, you will need to set up locations to receive them. In a simple operation, you might only have one location, but other companies might have literally hundreds of warehouse locations. In Odoo, each location can maintain its own address, and it is possible to create nested sublocations for better management and the reporting of inventory.

Generating quotations and purchase orders

To acquire the raw product, you will need to create **Request for Quotations** (**RFQ**) and/or purchase orders to send to your suppliers. In purchasing, these are the documents you create that tell the suppliers which products you want, the quantity in which you want them, and what you expect to pay for those products. Often this process is referred to as procurement. Depending on the industry and the specific location of the company, it is possible that there can be a variety of methods to manage quotations and approvals when purchasing products.

Receiving the product

In a simple purchasing workflow, once your purchase order has been received by the supplier, you will be waiting for them to fulfill the order. At some point, you will receive the product. Depending on your industry, this could be the same day or it could even stretch up to months. When the delivery is complete, you will receive the products, and they will move into the location you select.

Settling the invoice

Once you have received the product, it is just a matter of time before you must pay for it. Invoicing can happen at the time you order the product, before the product is shipped to you, or after you have received the product. Regardless of when you get an invoice, you can be sure that if you are receiving products, you will eventually be invoiced for them.

When an invoice is received, it is essential to compare it to the purchase order for accuracy. Any discrepancies between the purchase order and invoice must be resolved before the invoice is paid. Essentially, this is your way of ensuring that you are only paying for the products you have authorized for purchase. Finally, it is a good practice to match the receiving or delivery order to the purchase order and invoice as well. This *three-way match* ensures that you got exactly what you ordered and that the invoice reflects exactly what you are required to pay.

Installing the purchasing application

Odoo is a modular set of applications in which you only install the applications you need. Therefore, we must install the **Purchase Management** application to continue. By this point, you should be familiar with the process of installing a new application into Odoo. The following is a screenshot of the **Purchase Management** application in the **Apps** list:

When you install the purchasing application, you will get two new menus:

- Purchases
- Warehouse

> It is possible that these menus might already exist or that purchasing might already be installed if you have installed another application such as e-commerce that requires Purchase Management as a dependency.

The **Purchases** menu is where you can create quotations and purchase orders for the products you purchase from your suppliers. In the **Warehouse** menu, you can manage physical inventories. If you take a few moments to look through the menus, you will notice you can access some of the same features from both menus. For example, you can get to the **Incoming Shipments** view from either menu.

Setting up your first supplier

To begin setting up your first supplier, you will select **Invoicing** | **Suppliers** and click on **Create**.

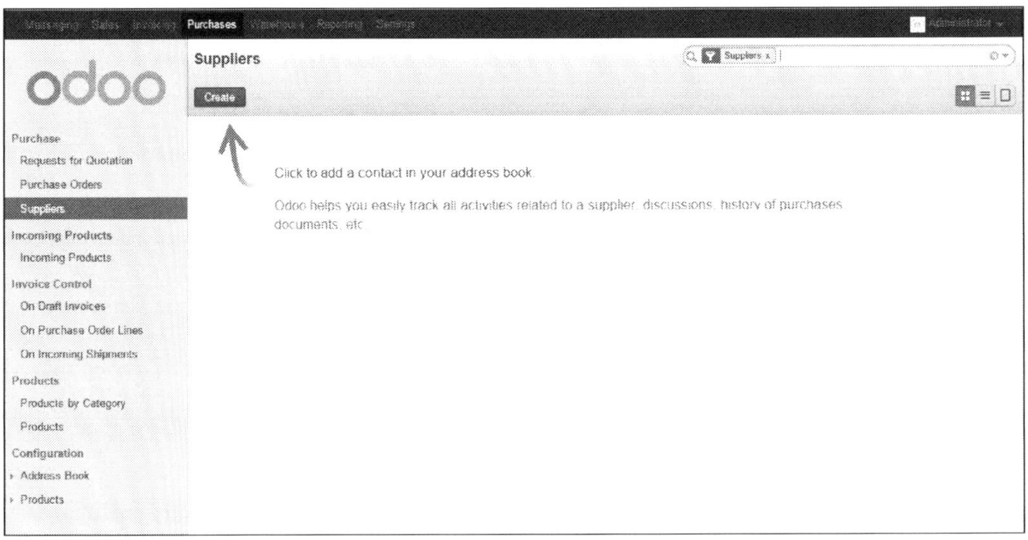

This is the **Suppliers** listing, but as it is empty, you will see instructions on how you can add a new supplier. Odoo also lists a few of the features that you can expect from supplier management such as tracking discussions, a history of purchases, and documents associated with a supplier.

After clicking on **Create**, Odoo will bring up the supplier form for you to fill out.

This form is very much like the customer form because it is based on the same basic structure. In fact, it is perfectly acceptable for a customer to also be a supplier. When you create a new supplier record, a supplier checkbox is automatically marked for you under the **Sales & Purchases** page on the form. Sometimes this can get a little confusing for people new to Odoo. This chapter will start to make the relationships between companies, contacts, customers, and suppliers in Odoo clearer.

Designating supplier companies versus individuals

Much like when you set up a customer, the **Is a Company** checkbox at the very top of the form is where you inform Odoo about the relationship you have with this supplier. Typically, you will be purchasing products from a company. When this box is checked, the **Contacts** tab appears in the section at the bottom of the **Suppliers** form. This allows you to specify contacts for the supplier. If the **Is a Company** checkbox is not checked, then you are specifying that this supplier is an individual, and you will not see a tab for adding contacts.

For our example, we will check the **Is a Company** checkbox.

> Suppliers require accounting configuration such as customer records. By default, Odoo will supply an accounts payable and accounts receivable account under the **Accounting** tab. It is important to verify these accounts when you are entering a supplier into a production system.

Once you've filled in the supplier's name, address, and other contact information, as well as the required accounting information, click on **Save** at the top of the form.

Configuring your product for procurement

When we set up our first product, we were only concerned with selling the product to a customer. We essentially named the product and set the price at which we wished to sell it. To purchase the product from our supplier, we must provide a little more information. To do this, we will edit the product and change the information under the **Procurement** tab.

Go to **Purchases** | **Product**, then double-click on **White T-Shirt** to bring up the product form. Then click on **Edit** to enter the edit mode.

The following is a screenshot of the procurement section of the product form:

At the top of the form, check **Can be Purchased** so that the purchasing system knows that it has to include this product in the list of products when you make a purchase order.

Once you are in the edit mode, click on the **Procurements** tab.

Supply chain information

Now in Odoo 8, you have far more options to manage your purchasing supply chain using routes. Fortunately, by default, Odoo sets up two of the most common routes. These routes are **Buy** and **Make to Order**. For purchasing, we must check the **Buy** checkbox so that Odoo can properly route the products we purchase from our supplier to our internal warehouse location.

Using buy routes

When you configure a buy route, you can purchase products in one of two ways. One of the ways to purchase this product would be to create a purchase order and add the product to the purchase order manually. This is the typical manual purchasing system where a purchase agent uses, perhaps, other events outside Odoo or examining reports in Odoo to create purchase orders.

In addition to creating manual purchase orders, you can also create reordering rules that would automatically create draft purchase orders when the stock of the product dips below a set minimum. This method works well on products that are ordered frequently and frees up your purchasing managers from having to manually create purchase orders for some or even most of your inventory.

Using make to order

When you configure a make to order route, you are telling Odoo that you wish for draft purchase orders to be created when a sales order includes that specific product regardless of the stock you have on hand. For example, even if you had 2,000 units of a product in stock and a customer orders 10 of that product, Odoo will create a draft purchase order for 10 units if you have the **Make To Order** route checked.

Often, a business would use the **Make To Order** option when they do not need to keep stock on a product and instead will either manufacture or purchase the product for reselling once a sales order is confirmed. It is certainly possible to use a combination of **Buy** and **Make to Order** with reordering limits to set up a system in which you always keep a minimum quantity in stock; however, a draft purchase order is created for sales orders that include that product. Remember, draft orders can always be cancelled; so depending on the processes in your purchasing department, it may be desirable for them to get make to order purchase drafts even if they wish to maintain their own minimum and maximum limits within Odoo.

Setting the cost price of the product

Most often you will wish to assign a cost to the product. This will be the cost that will appear on your purchase quotations, though it can be overwritten at any time to reflect a supplier's new pricing. If your supplier happens to give you a one-time discount, you will want to reflect that change on the actual purchase order, rather than here in the base product record. For our example, we have set the cost price of the shirt to $9.50.

Purchasing information

In addition to the changes under the **Procurement** tab, there are also a few changes we need to make under the **Information** page on the product form.

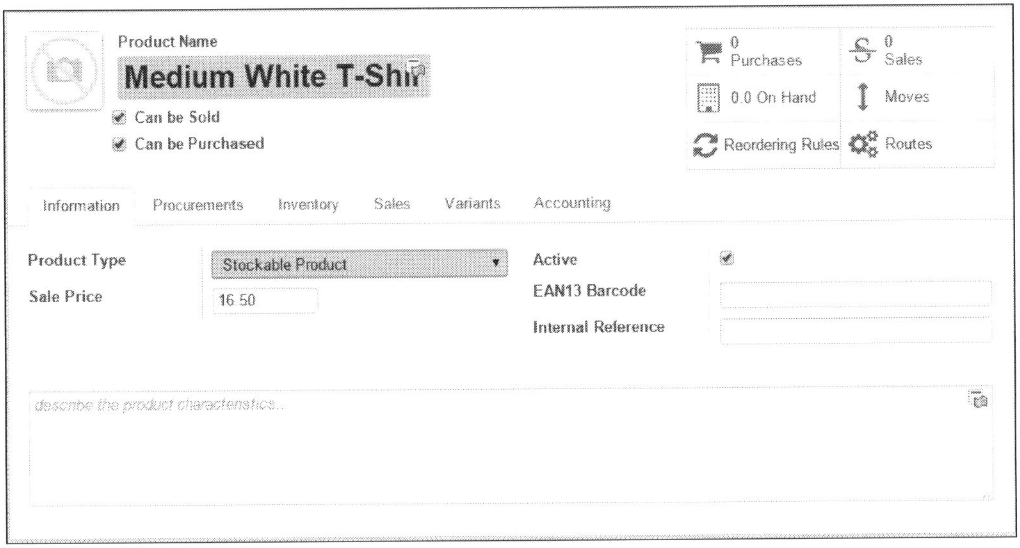

Product type

When you configure purchasing, you will want to pay special attention to product type. For this example, we have chosen **Stockable Product** because we wish to manage the inventory of the product and perhaps sell it directly out to the customer. Alternatively, you can choose a product type of consumable. This would be a good choice for products you don't wish to manage in inventory and just plan to purchase and use, such as office supplies or coffee filters for the breakroom.

Setting records to active

Like most records in Odoo, you can set a product to **Inactive** so that it will no longer be available when creating new sales orders or purchase orders. You can do this from the **Information** tab on the product page.

> Once you have any transactions associated with a product, you will not be allowed to delete that product from the system. Instead, set active to false so that the product will no longer appear in the active lists. To view these inactive records, you can use the advanced search feature to create a filter to show records where the active flag is false.

Assigning suppliers to the product

At the bottom of the **Procurement** tab is the option to add suppliers. It is very common that a company might have multiple suppliers that offer the same product.

Click on **Add an Item** in the suppliers grid to add the supplier to the product:

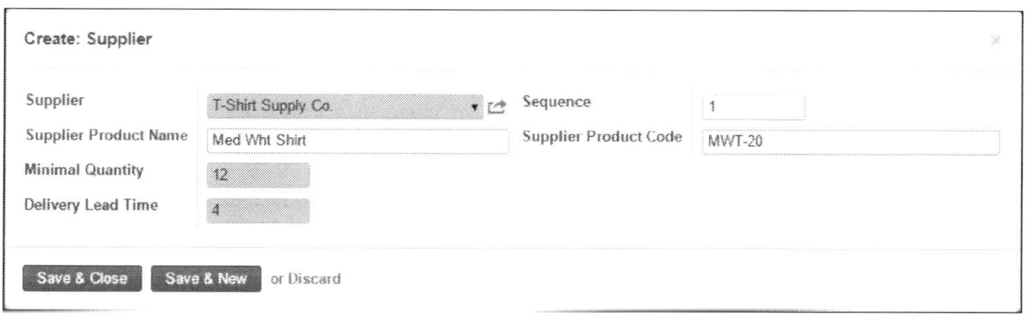

Establishing the supplier

You have the choice in the pop-down list to search for suppliers, as well as to create and edit a new supplier on the fly. To the far right of the dropdown, you can use the small icon to edit the current supplier. In the dropdown, we have selected **T-Shirt Supply Co**. as the company to provide our blank medium white t-shirts.

Designating supplier product name and product code

Because a supplier might use different product codes or product names than your company does to describe a given product, here you have the option to specify how the supplier identifies the product. This information will appear on the purchase quotations and purchase orders you create to make sure you get the right product from the supplier.

Setting minimal quantity

Suppliers will often have a minimum order quantity for a product. Sometimes, suppliers might actually sell you a lower quantity but the cost per unit is dramatically higher. Setting a minimal quantity in this form allows you to prevent those problems by forcing purchase quantities to be at least the minimal quantity value. For our example, we will set the minimal quantity to **12**.

Calculating delivery time

Depending on the supplier, a product might take less or more time to obtain. Often, this can make a difference when you are putting together a time-sensitive purchase quotation. A product might be cheaper, but if the delay is too long and will put the delivery time for the order in jeopardy, you might need to buy the product at a higher price from another supplier who can deliver the product faster. Setting the delivery time in days for the supplier to deliver the product provides your purchasing agents with the information they require to make decisions based on price and availability. For our example, we have set the delivery time to **4** days.

Creating your first purchase quotation

Now that we have our supplier entered and the product associated with the supplier, we are ready to create our first request for quotation to purchase. This is typically the document you will create when requesting pricing from a supplier (sometimes called a vendor) prior to actually ordering the product. For our example, we are going to create a request for the quotation for one dozen Medium White T-Shirts.

Go to **Purchases** | **Requests for Quotation** and click on **Create** to make a new RFQ.

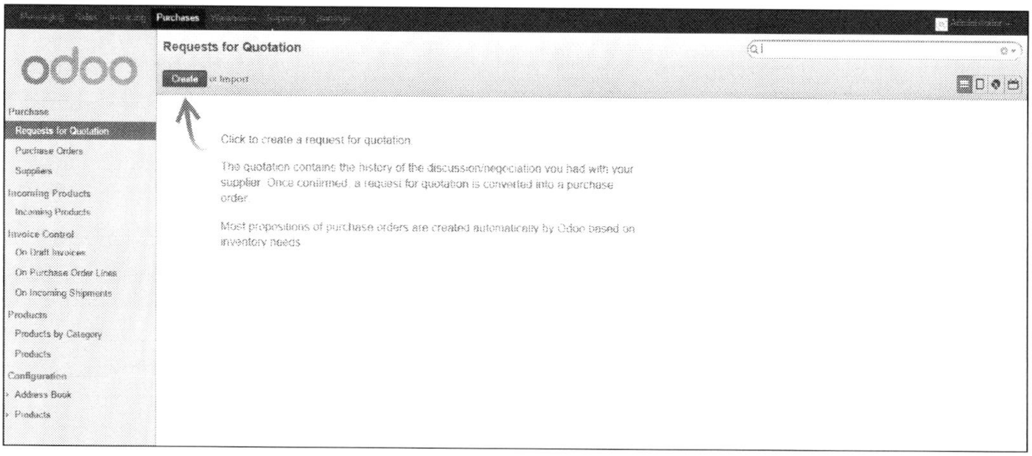

After you click on **Create**, the RFQ will appear for you to enter the required information.

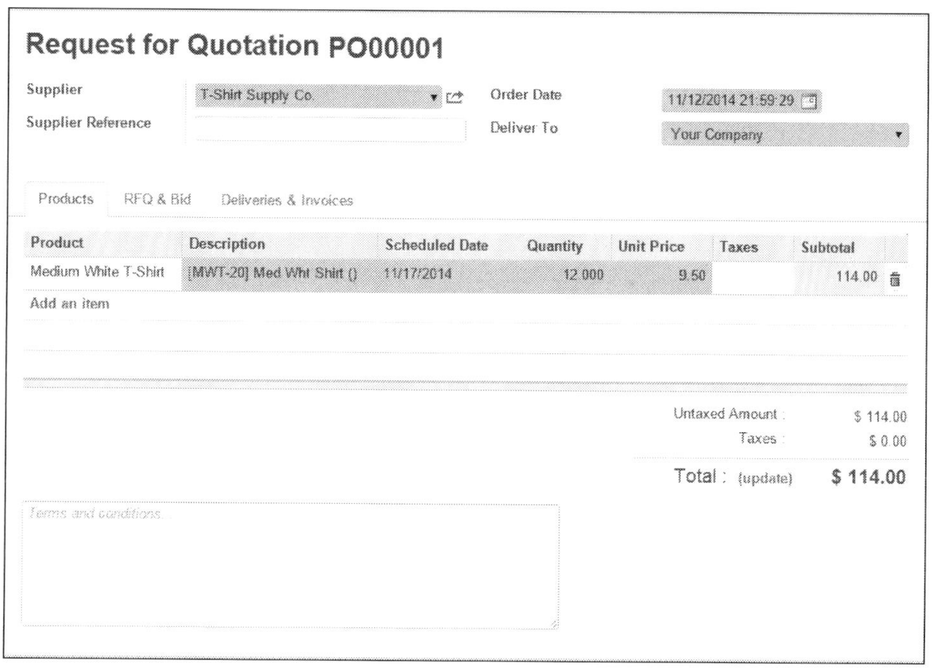

When you first create the request for quotation, the order date will be automatically populated with the current date. You can then select the supplier you wish for the RFQ as well as include an optional supplier reference and source document. An example of a source document would be a sales order number that triggered the purchase order process.

Adding products to your request for quotation

After you click on **Add an Item**, you can select the product from the drop-down list on the far left. The description will automatically be filled in. The scheduled date will be determined based on the delivery delay from the supplier. We also find the minimum order quantity from the supplier has been pulled to the RFQ. Finally, the unit cost is populated from the unit price on the **Procurements** tab of the product.

Printing RFQs and updating the status

For now, we will skip Incoming Shipments & Invoices and go right to printing our RFQ. By default, Odoo will print to a PDF file. This file can easily be attached to e-mails. Once you have configured an e-mail server, you can configure Odoo to automatically send the purchase order by e-mail.

The status is then updated to show that the RFQ has been sent.

Promoting the status to RFQ sent

At this point, the RFQ would be considered in the hands of the supplier. The supplier could agree to it as is, or perhaps, the pricing or other attributes of the purchase order will change. In this stage of the transaction, the RFQ can be edited as needed. You can add additional items or remove line items that you do not need.

In the Odoo 8 default workflow, you must now confirm that you have received the bid back from the supplier.

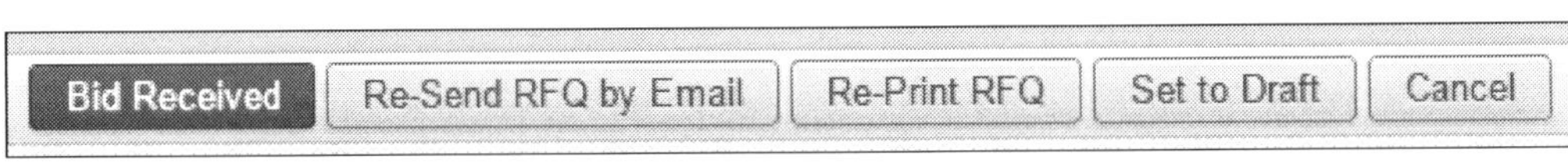

Click on the **Bid Received** button to let Odoo know that the bid has been received and the purchase order can now move on to the next step in the workflow. Also, in this stage, you have the option to resend the RFQ, reprint the RFQ, set it back to draft, or cancel the draft purchase order altogether.

After the bid has been received, you will now see the status updated on the right to **Bid Received** and you will see the **Confirm Order** button in the top-left corner along with the option to cancel the quotation.

Notice that in this state the **Edit** button is still available and you can make changes to the quotation as required before you confirm the order.

Confirming a purchase order

Once you have a final quotation, you are ready to confirm the purchase order. It is very important to understand that once you have confirmed the quotation, it becomes a purchase order and it can no longer be modified. Once you are sure that you wish to finalize the quotation, click on the **Confirm Order** button. Any modifications that need to be made at this stage would require you to duplicate and cancel the original order. This is necessary so that Odoo can maintain an audit trail.

> If you happen to receive an error message reading **No Expense Account** when you attempt to confirm the order, check your settings for your chart of accounts. You must have an expense account designated for the products contained on the PO.

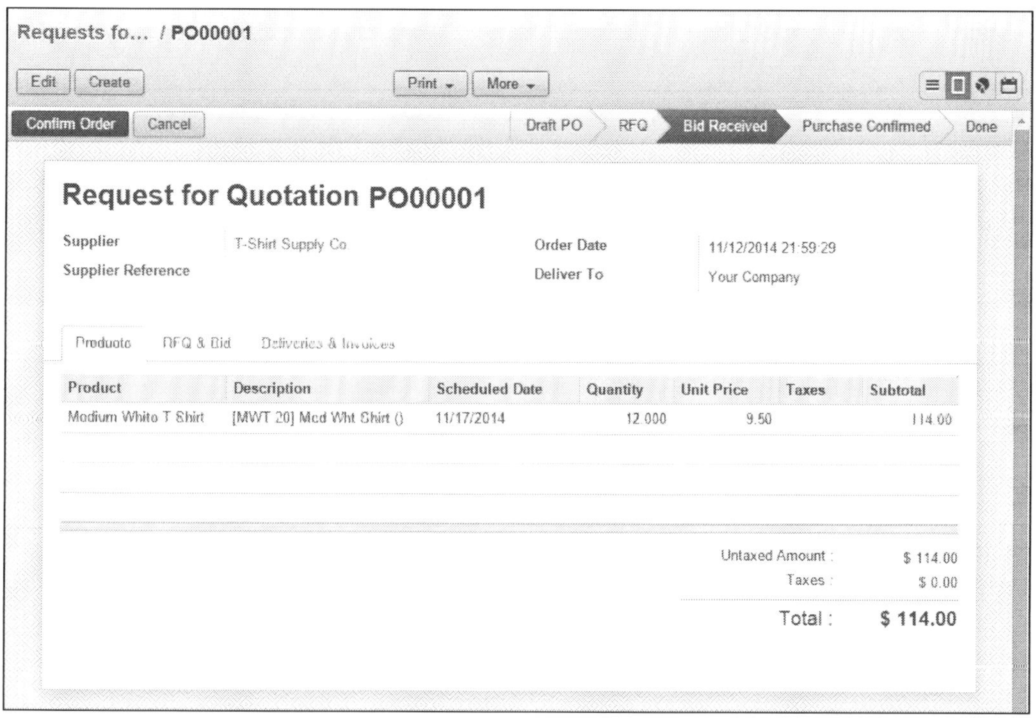

Once you have confirmed the order, the form will refresh to show the new status of the purchase order. At this point, you are waiting for the supplier to deliver the products and send you an invoice. The status is updated to **Purchase Order** and is now just one step from the **Done** condition.

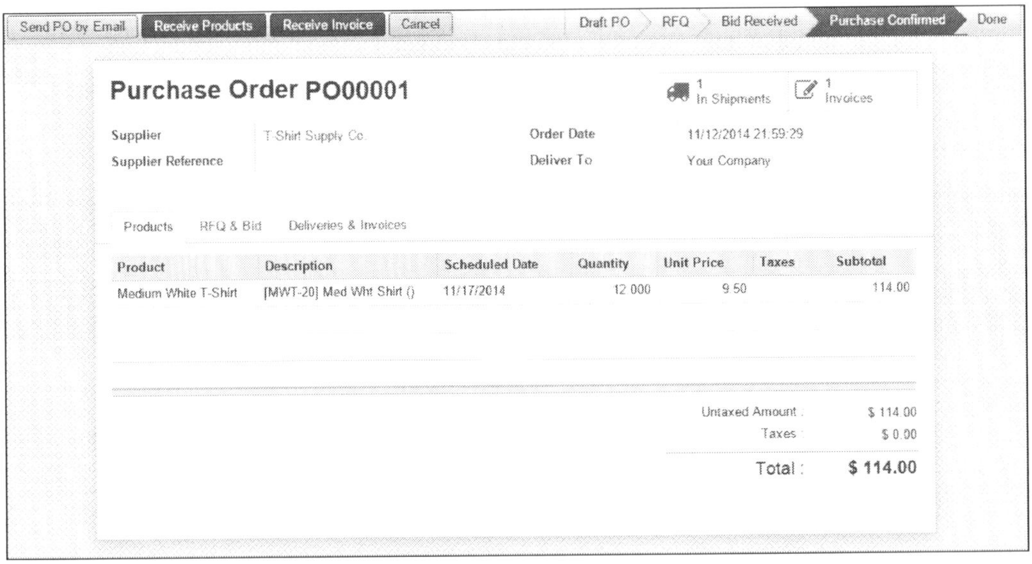

After clicking on **Confirm**, you will notice in the upper right corner that we can see there is one incoming shipment and one invoice to go along with it. Each of these is an active button that you can click on to see the corresponding shipments or invoices associated with this purchase order.

Receiving products

If everything goes as planned, the products we have ordered will be arriving within four days. Once the products have arrived, we must receive our products into the inventory.

Click on **Receive Products** to bring up the **Receiving** form.

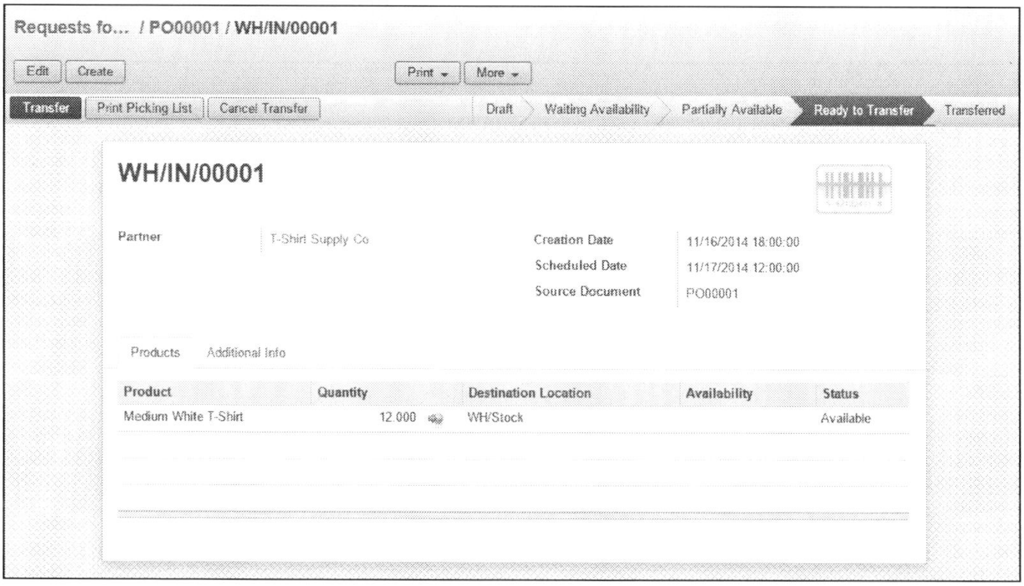

Getting ready to receive

At this point, we have not actually received the product yet. This is just showing us the details about the product that we are ready to receive. The **WH/IN/00001** transaction name is sequentially assigned for each transaction.

> Be aware that it is possible that the transaction name **WH/IN/000001** might be different in your installation as Odoo has changed the sequences that are defined in a default installation from time to time. These names can be user-configured by going to **Settings** | **Sequences** and **Identifiers** | **Sequences**. You could even change the default prefix from **PO** to whatever you desire, as long as it does not conflict with the prefix of another application.

The **WH** initials in the transaction name are short for warehouse and **IN** is for incoming goods. When we are receiving products into the inventory, we are creating an inventory transaction. You can see the associated purchase order under the **Source Document** field on the right side of the form. We can also see the actual time the order was received compared to the scheduled time of the order. In this case, we can see we received the order in plenty of time.

Receiving our goods

When you click on the **Transfer** button near the top of the form, you will get a final screen that pulls the default quantities from the purchase order.

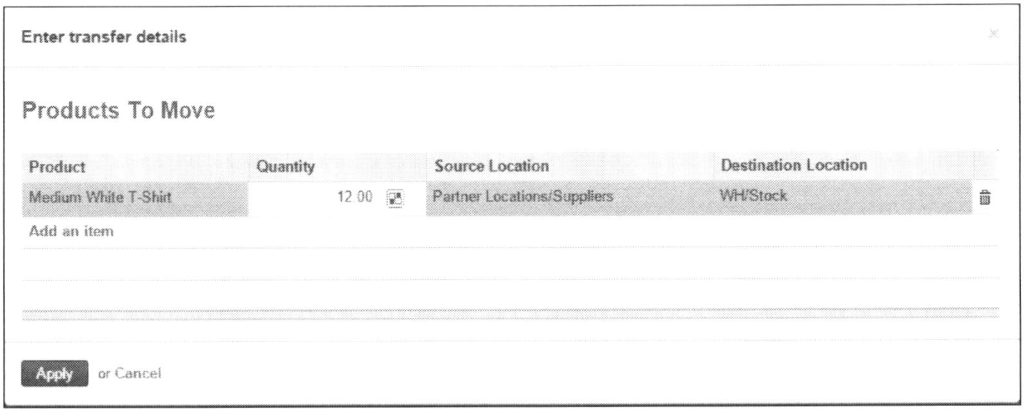

Once you click on **Apply**, the status on the product line item is set to **Done**; the product is now in the inventory. Since all of the products in this purchase order have been received, the purchase order status at the top right is set to **Transferred**. Finally, you will notice the **Reverse Transfer** button that is available for instances in which you need to manage product returns.

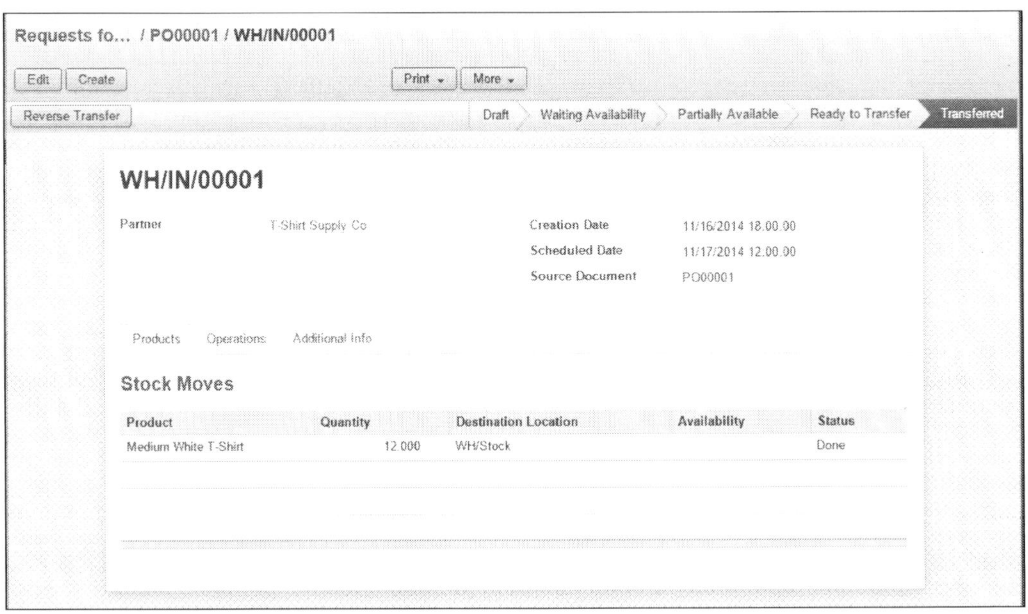

If you would like to verify that your goods have been received into the inventory, look up **Medium White T-Shirt** under **Products** and click on the **Inventory** tab. You should notice its quantity on hand increased by 12 units. Odoo automatically adjusts stock levels as products are received into your company's inventory. Likewise, stock levels are decremented if products are returned to their supplier.

Paying supplier invoices

Once you have received your product, sooner or later you should receive an invoice. It is, of course, possible to receive an invoice before you receive products. Each business will have to decide the exact workflow for when they pay invoices and under what conditions.

Once you confirm a purchase order, Odoo will create a draft invoice. You can view this invoice in **Supplier Invoices** under the **Invoicing** menu:

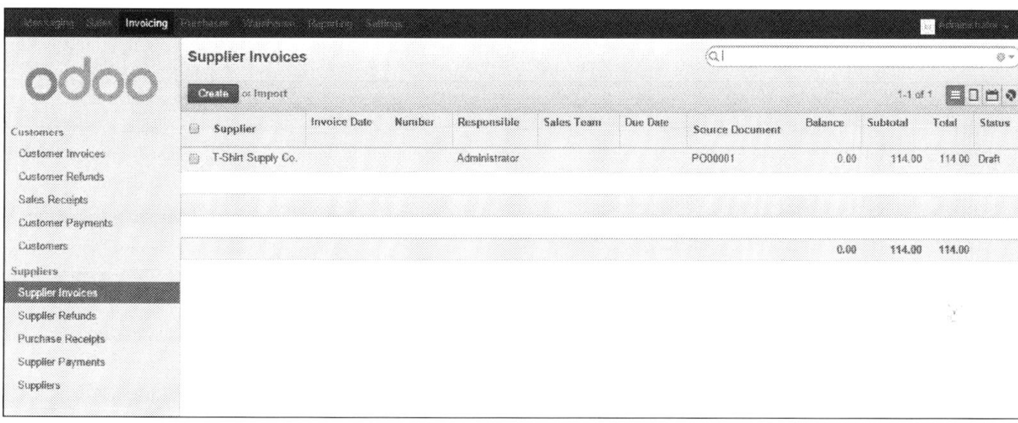

Here you can see the draft invoice for the t-shirts we received. We have the products. Let's go ahead and pay for them.

Click on the line item to bring up the supplier's invoice and then validate it. Validating is an important step that will create accounting entries for both the supplier's accounts payable and your products' expense accounts.

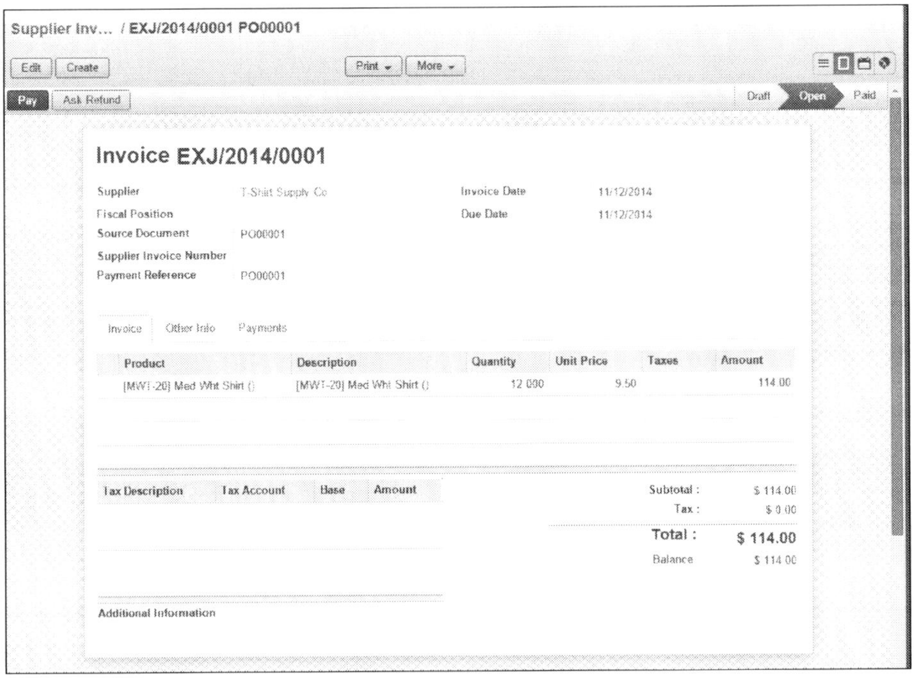

Now that we have validated the invoice, our remaining options are to pay the invoice or ask for a refund. For our example, we will pay the invoice.

Click on **Pay**:

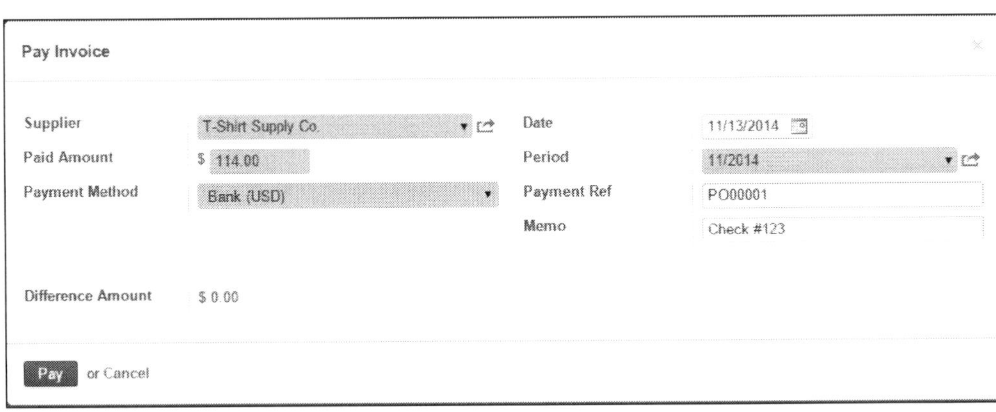

Most of the information will automatically be filled out. The **Payment Ref** field is your tie back to the original purchase order for the product. Also, you can use the **Memo** field to specify the check number you use to pay your supplier.

> When implementing a purchase order system, it is critical to train users thoroughly on how transactions are tied together. While many forms allow you to click on a link to view a related record, fields such as **Payment Ref** store the data just as text. Train and encourage users to quickly use copy and paste rather than re-entering data into search fields.

Odoo will allow you to configure multiple payment methods. For now, choose **Bank** and click on **Pay** to complete the transaction.

You have now completed the entire purchase cycle from purchasing, to receiving, to finally paying for the product.

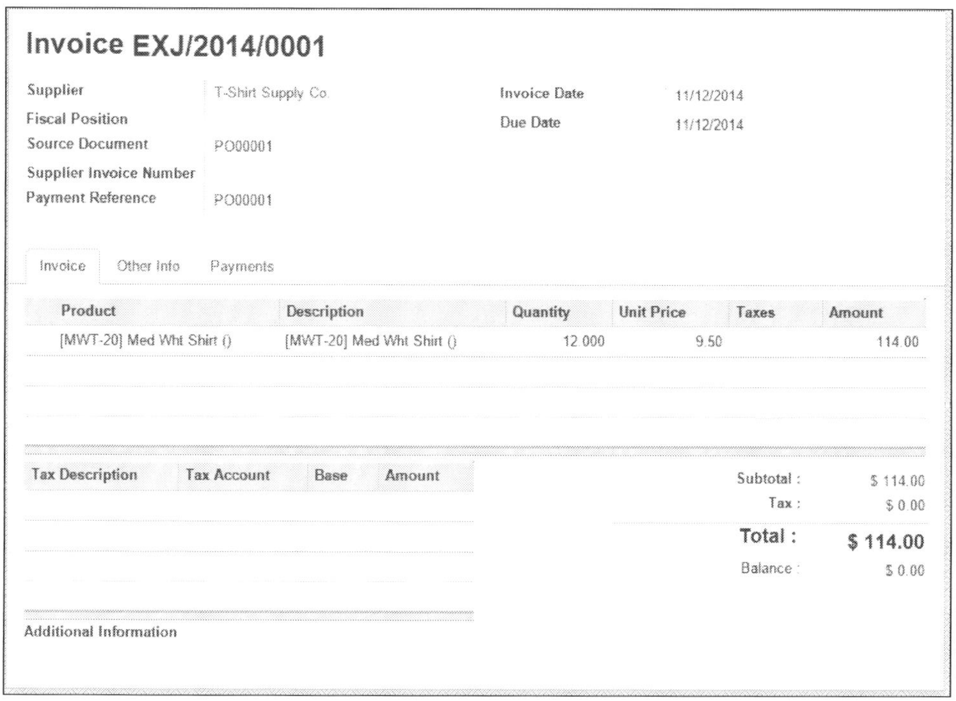

In the preceding screenshot, you can see the final paid invoice for our purchased products. At the bottom right of the form, it shows that we have a balance of zero.

Summary

In this chapter, we installed the purchasing application and set up a supplier to purchase products. Next, we successfully purchased products and received those products into the inventory. After our products were received into the inventory, we proceeded to pay the invoice to complete the payment cycle.

In the next chapter, we will take the raw materials we have just received into the inventory and use them to manufacture and deliver a finished product. We will create manufacturing orders to define the steps of the production process and allocate the required resources. Coordinating all of your resources, including machinery and manpower, can be a daunting and time-consuming task, but we are learning how Odoo makes this significantly more manageable.

5

Making Goods with Manufacturing Resource Planning

In this chapter, we will cover how you can use Odoo to manage the process of manufacturing products. Once you have received the required raw products into your inventory, you can begin manufacturing the end product. Part of the functionality of an ERP system is to assist you in scheduling these orders based on available resources. One of the resources is, of course, the raw product. Other resources could include available labor or the availability of a particular machine. Essentially, the goal is to schedule the manufacturing order at a time when all the resources are available and produce the product for an on-time delivery.

In this chapter, we will cover the following topics:

- Setting up the manufacturing process
- Defining our bill of materials
- Manufacturing our final product
- Analyzing the inventory report

Creating manufacturing orders

Manufacturing orders define the product you wish to build, the resources required, and when you wish to produce the product. In addition, they can contain information about work orders and routings that are related to that manufacturing order.

Producing the product

When it is time to actually produce the product, you then inform Odoo of each of the products produced and your manufacturing order changes to the Complete status. In a typical workflow, your raw materials are moved out of the inventory and your finished product is added into your inventory.

Delivering the order

After a product has been produced and has been put into the inventory, it can be packaged and delivered to the customer. Depending on the specific manufacturing environment, a product might not even sit in a physical inventory location at all and instead, it might be shipped almost immediately to the customer. Meanwhile, in another industry, you might have a product that is produced and then sits in a warehouse for months before delivery. Of course, it is always possible something gets produced and gets left in dead stock. In this case, you would never have a delivery order and instead use a process to determine how to manage that dead inventory.

Defining the workflow for your business

Much like configuring the CRM application, oftentimes the most complex part of setting up a purchasing and manufacturing system is not the ERP software itself. Instead, the real challenge is to understand the business requirements and how the current processes can best be implemented. If you have never set up a purchasing and manufacturing system before, it is highly recommended that you supplement your knowledge with additional source material on the subject. Refer to *Appendix, Locating Additional Odoo Resources*, for references to additional resources on ERP and manufacturing.

A real world example – producing a custom printed T-shirt

In Odoo, you manufacture products by creating manufacturing orders. For our example, we will be printing T-shirts that have a custom designed logo. The basic manufacturing process itself involves using a screen to apply ink to each of the T-shirts. For now, we don't need to know all the details of this process to begin using Odoo to help schedule and track the manufacturing of the product.

The basic steps in the process are simple:

1. Define a bill of materials that determines what items are needed to produce the final product.
2. Use a manufacturing order to print a design on the blank T-shirts.
3. Deliver the printed T-shirts to a customer.

Installing manufacturing resource planning

We must now install the **manufacturing resource planning** (**MRP**) application so that we can begin configuring our T-shirt production. By now, you should begin to understand the modular nature of Odoo. Install the MRP application just like you did with the other Odoo applications, go to **Settings** | **Apps**.

Clicking on the **Install** button installs the MRP application.

Creating your first manufacturing order

The flexibility of Odoo provides a variety of approaches you can take while setting up your system. Manufacturing can also become a complex topic and is one of the more challenging aspects of setting up any ERP system. For our first manufacturing order, we will ignore many advanced options.

> Keep it simple at first. There are many options and it will take time to understand them all. If you are new to manufacturing systems, it will take you longer to implement Odoo, and you should consider hiring professional consultants to assist you.

To create your first manufacturing order, go to the **Manufacturing** menu, choose **Manufacturing Orders**, and then click on **Create**.

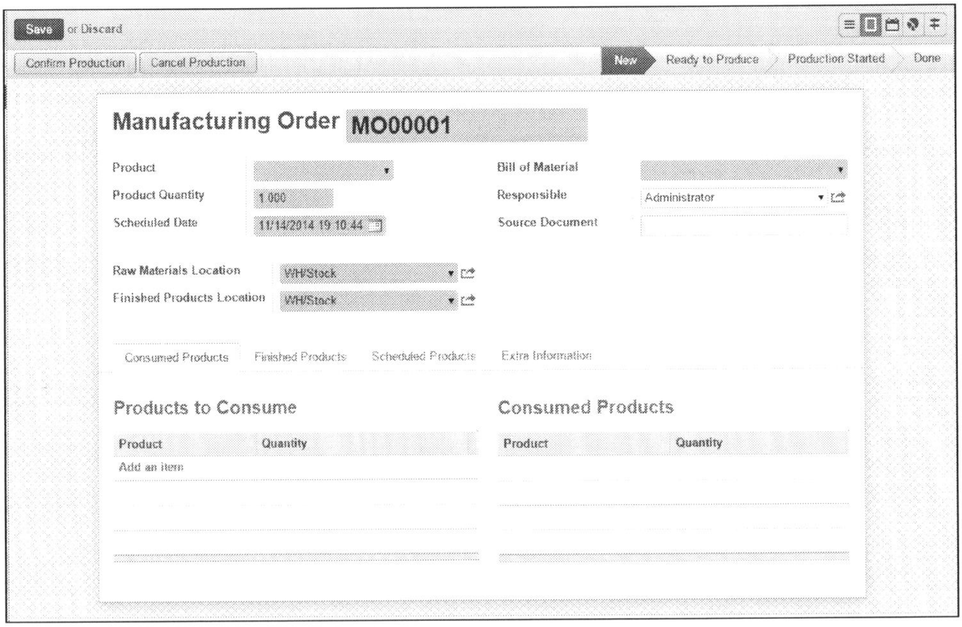

This is the manufacturing order as it appears just after you have hit **Create**. The `MO` prefix in the sequential order number that will be assigned stands for, you guessed it, **Manufacturing Order**. We will use this form to define our manufacturing order to print our custom designed T-shirts.

Take a minute to look through the various tabs and get an idea of the information that is collected for a manufacturing order. Don't worry if you don't understand all the options yet. We will begin with a simple product and look at some of the most important aspects of creating a manufacturing order. Later, we will explore some of the more complex manufacturing scenarios.

What product are we going to manufacture?

The only product we have entered into Odoo so far is the medium white T-shirt that is blank. Nothing is printed on the T-shirt when it is received from the supplier. Now, we want to create a manufacturing order that will produce a new product in which we print a design of the customer's choice on the T-shirt.

For our operations, we can still use the medium white T-shirt. But now instead of selling the blank T-shirt directly to our customer, it will be used as a raw material for our manufacturing order.

Let's first configure the final product that is to be created during the manufacturing process, that is, the complete T-shirt with the final design that will ship to the customer. For our example, it will be **Class of 2014 T-shirt**.

Odoo allows you the ability where it is appropriate to create a product on the fly. Let's create a product by clicking on the dropdown next to **Product** and choosing **Create and Edit...**.

Using the quick **Create and Edit...** option, you can add your finished products directly when creating a manufacturing order. In some workflows, where you might use a separate system for handling sales orders, this option can be a fast way to create the required finished products to push into the inventory.

Next, you will fill out the product form with the fields required for a finished product:

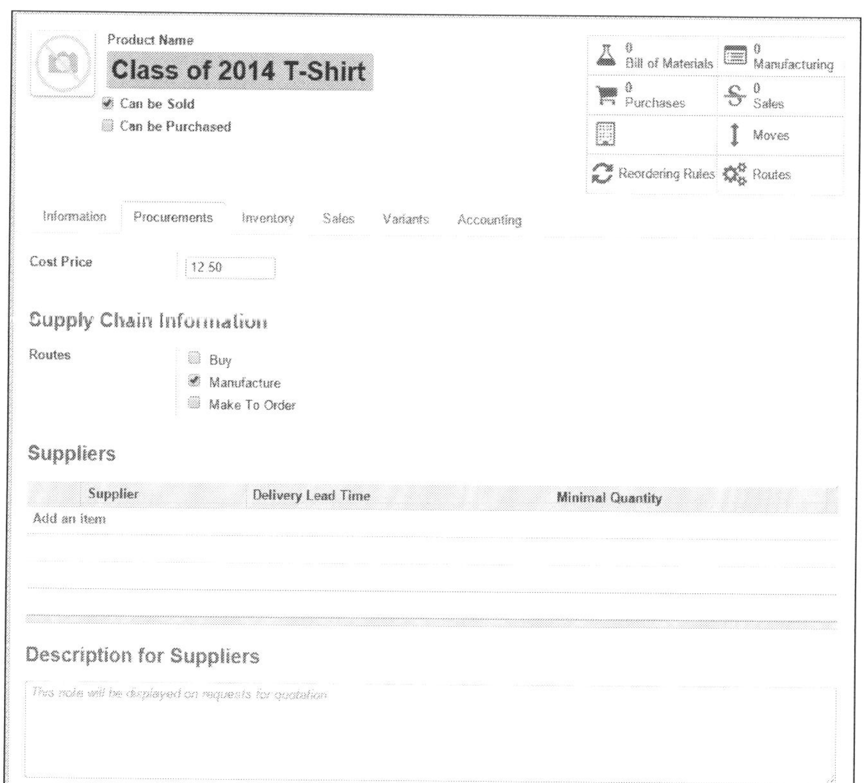

The product and procurement tabs should look familiar by now. In Odoo 8, we have routes that allow a lot of flexibility in defining complex workflows and supply management operations. Fortunately, the more common routes are already configured and we can check **Manufacture** to let Odoo manufacturing know that this product is part of the manufacturing workflow. Only products that have the supply method of **Manufacture** can be selected as a product on a manufacture order.

Notice at the top of the form that the **Can be Purchased** box is unchecked. This will keep this product from appearing in the product list on a purchase order. Since we cannot purchase this product directly from a supplier, we don't want it appearing in our product list when working within purchasing.

Building your bill of materials

A **bill of materials**, or **BOM** as it is commonly called, is essentially a list of products that are required to produce another product. You can think of it as the list of ingredients for a recipe. Odoo needs to know what materials are required for us to produce this **Class of 2014 T-shirt** product.

In complex products, a bill of materials can be nested. For example, it might take many products to make a subproduct and then several subproducts to make a final product.

> Don't let nested BOMs intimidate you. Once you understand how a simple BOM is processed, you will more easily see how you can group parts together. Think about grouping more complex BOMs by assembly and work centers. This makes it easier to see your inventory in real time as BOMs can be processed at each stage of your operations, properly using up materials and creating finished subassemblies.

For our first bill of materials example, we will be keeping the bill of materials simple. We are just going to require the white T-shirt. The rest of the operation, that is, printing the actual T-shirt, will be incorporated into the manufacturing order. In other words, if there are enough white T-shirts, this manufacturing order can be processed, and we can produce the final product. For now, the inks and screens will not be managed in the manufacturing process. This is an example of starting simple and adding more complexity as we build up the system.

In Odoo 8, a smart button at the top right of the form shows you a count of the bill of materials attached to this product.

Clicking on this button will bring up the bill of materials listing for that product.

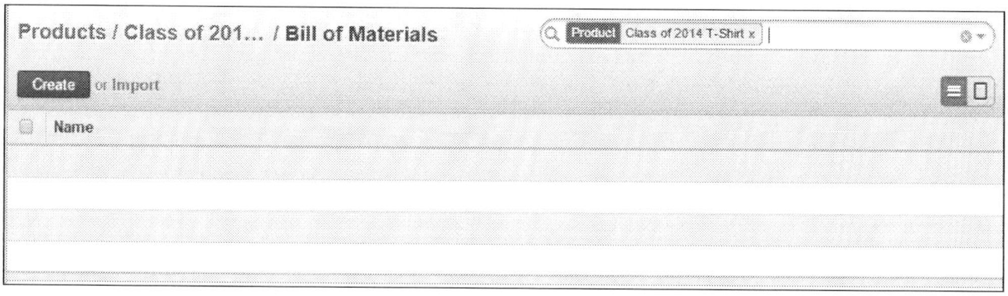

Naturally, this is a blank list, as we have not yet defined any bill of materials for this product. Notice that in the top-right corner is the product filter that is restricting this list view to only display the **Bill of Materials** that is for the **Class of 2014 T-shirt**.

Clicking on **Create** will now bring up a blank **Bill of Materials** form with the **Class of 2014 T-shirt** automatically prepopulated as the finished product to build.

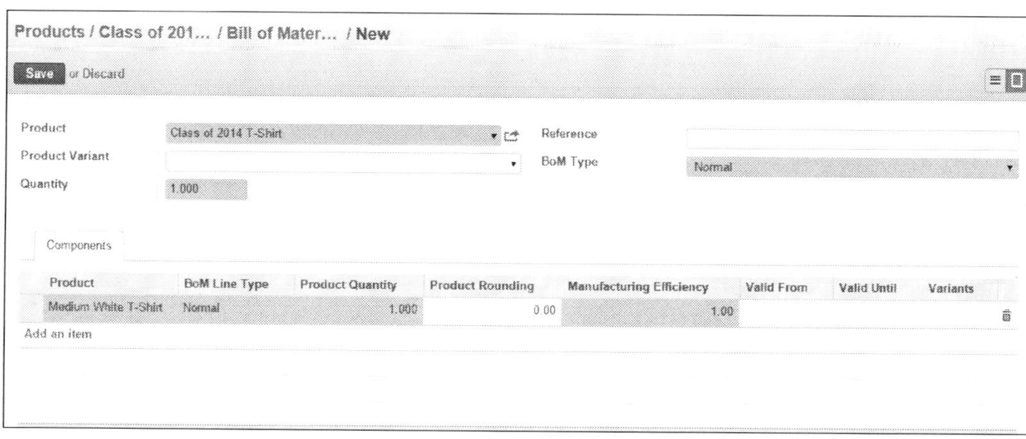

Many of the fields will be automatically filled out as Odoo knows we are creating a bill of materials for our **Class of 2014 T-Shirt** product. In this example, we have added **Medium White T-Shirt** to the bill of materials. Both **Product Quantity** and **Manufacturing Efficiency** are set to **1**. **Manufacturing Efficiency**, explained later in this chapter, is a percentage; therefore, an efficiency of one indicates 100 percent efficiency. When we manufacture one **Class of 2014 T-Shirt**, we will require one medium white T-shirt. Many times, if not most of the time, a bill of materials will contain multiple items. Regardless of the number of items in the bill of materials, the way it is processed is exactly the same.

It is possible that your manufacturing order or bill of materials screen might look slightly different than the ones you see here. One reason is that, depending on the applications that are installed and what options are selected, the forms might have some different content. Another common reason is that Odoo is currently getting frequent updates that can change the appearance of a given form.

Confirming production

Once you click on **Confirm Production**, you are ready to manufacture the product. Odoo will provide reasonable defaults that you can override as required. When production is confirmed, that does not mean that production has actually taken place. Confirming production has only informed the system that production is ready to proceed. You can tell we are ready to begin manufacturing because the **Produce** button is available.

Here is what our **Class of 2014 T-Shirt Manufacturing Order** looks like now:

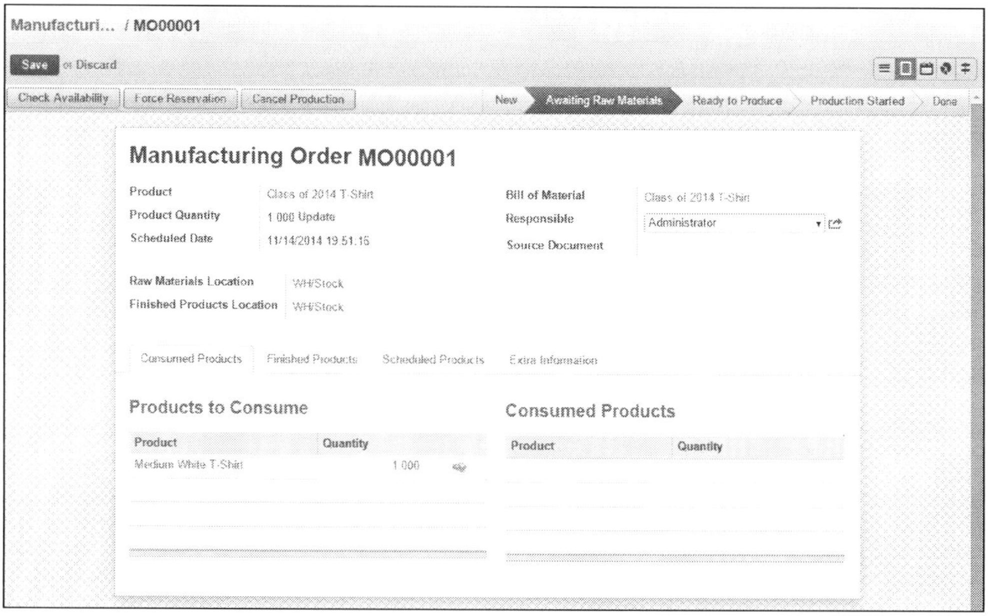

This is the manufacturing form showing the products waiting to be consumed to produce the order. In this case, it is our **Medium White T-Shirt**. You will also notice that this item is in red, and at the top of the form, you can see **Awaiting Raw Materials** selected as the current status. This informs us that we must check the availability of our raw goods before we can begin manufacturing this product.

Checking availability

Odoo manufacturing links into inventory automatically and will use available stock to complete the order. As we have already purchased Medium White T-Shirts in the previous chapter, clicking on the **Check Availability** button will remove the red highlight on **Medium White T-Shirt**, as well as move the state of the manufacturing order to **Ready to Produce**.

Be aware that at this stage, if you don't have the quantity available, Odoo will stay in the **Awaiting Raw Materials** stage until the product is acquired and put it into the inventory. Each time you click on **Check Availability**, Odoo will look into the inventory to see if we have the necessary products so we are ready to produce. Alternatively, you can click on **Force Reservation** to indicate to Odoo manufacturing that you in fact are ready to produce this product even if inventory within the system does not meet the necessary requirements. Note that doing this will give you negative inventory quantities in your warehouse.

After the raw product has been acquired and we are ready to produce our final product, the form will be updated and the state changed.

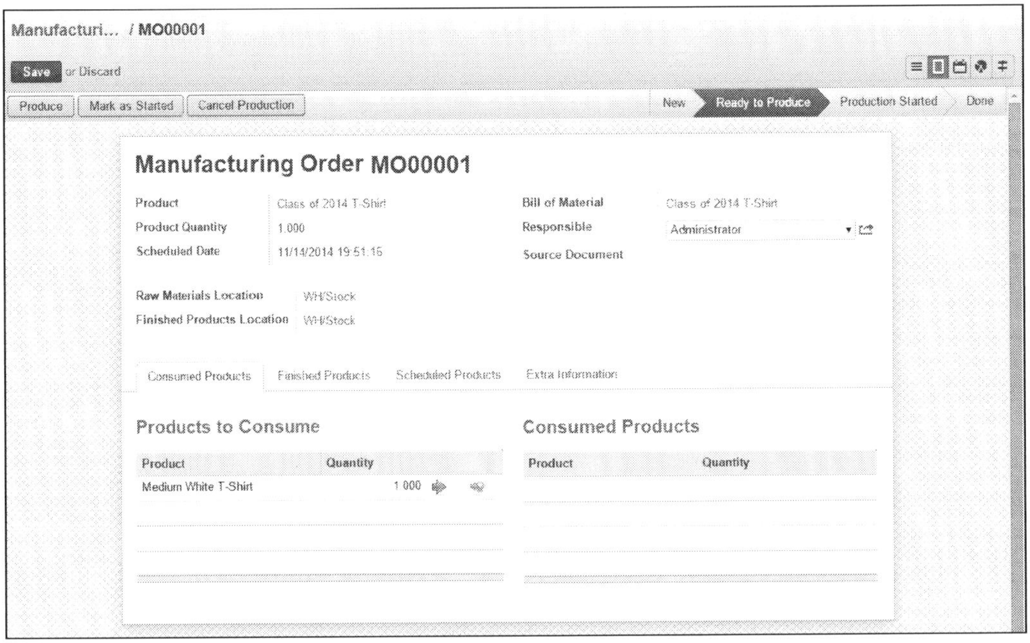

Here, we can see that we are in the **Ready to Produce** stage and that at the bottom we have a small green arrow next to our quantity in the **Products to Consume** section. This little green arrow is a shortcut to tell Odoo to go ahead and mark this product as consumed as part of the operation. With this mechanism, you can use the manufacturing order as a checklist so that a worker can go down and mark off each product as they use it for the manufacturing operation. Alternatively, you can click on the **Produce** button.

Producing the product

After you click on the **Produce** button, you will be prompted to confirm that the product has been produced:

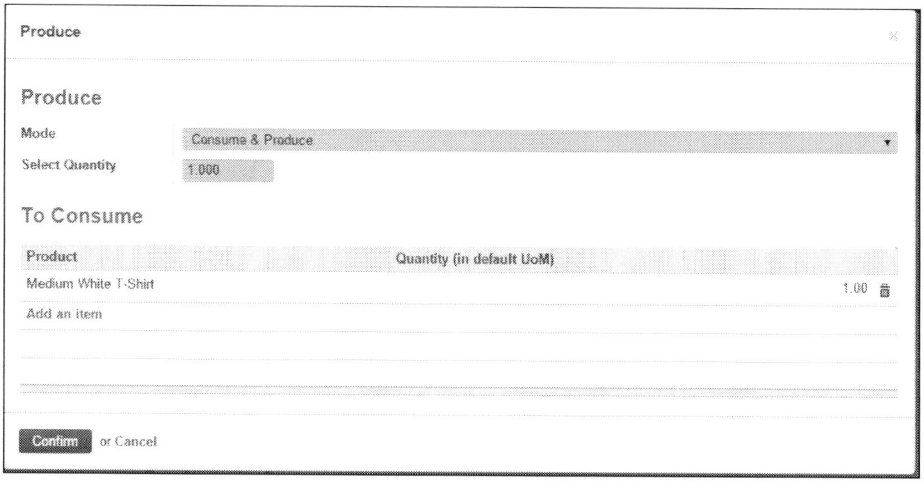

The mode option allows you to choose whether you want to consume the raw materials and produce the final product or simply consume the raw materials. This latter option might be used in long production cycles where you need to show the raw materials gone from inventory, but you want another step to actually produce the final product. For this example, we will **Consume & Produce** the final product.

Notice that you do have the option to add additional items on-the-fly or adjust the quantity that has been consumed as part of the operation.

Click on the **Confirm** button to produce the product.

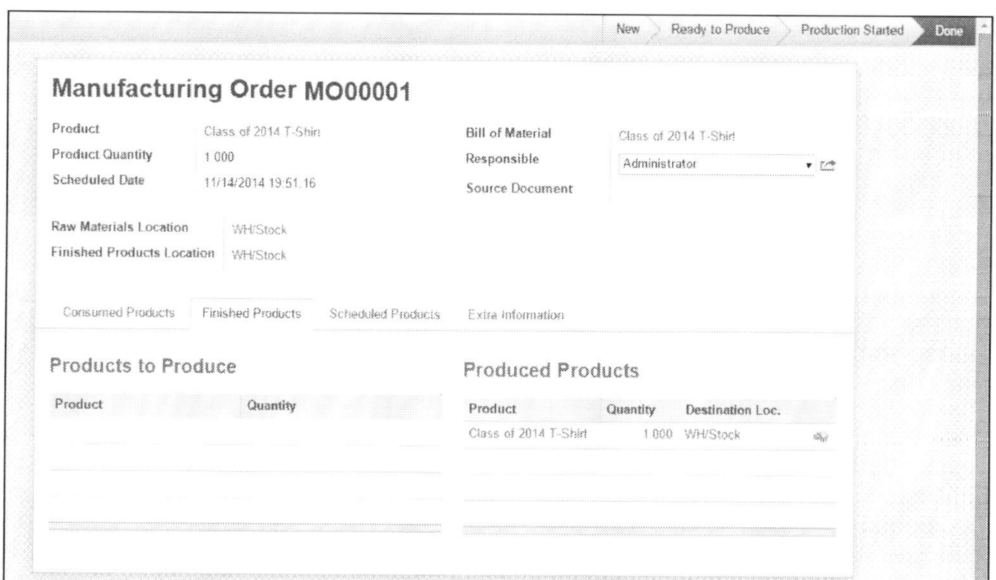

The product has then been produced and is now available in the inventory for sale. Notice that by navigating to **Manufacturing Order | Finished Products | Produced Products**, we can see the **Class of 2014 T-shirt** and the destination/location where it is in the warehouse.

Congratulations, you have just used Odoo to manufacture your first product!

Analyzing stock valuation

In our example, we have taken a raw material and increased its value by producing a finished product. One of the easiest ways to see the effect of our manufacturing order is to look at the stock valuation report, which can be found by navigating to **Reporting | Warehouse | Stock Valuation**.

When you select this option, Odoo provides you with a screen that gives you the option to see what the stock was valued at on a specific date. For now, we will just look at the current valuation.

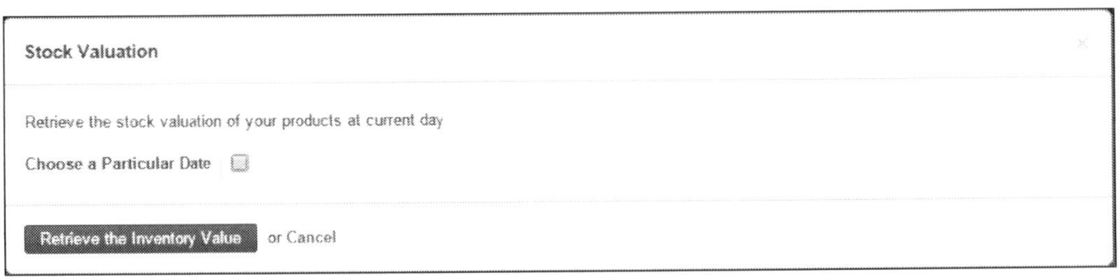

Click on **Retrieve the Inventory Value** to bring up the Stock Valuation view.

Here you will see that we now have one **Class of 2014 T-Shirt** and 11 medium white T-shirts. The inventory is accurately reflecting the purchases made by us, as well as the products consumed and produced by our manufacturing order.

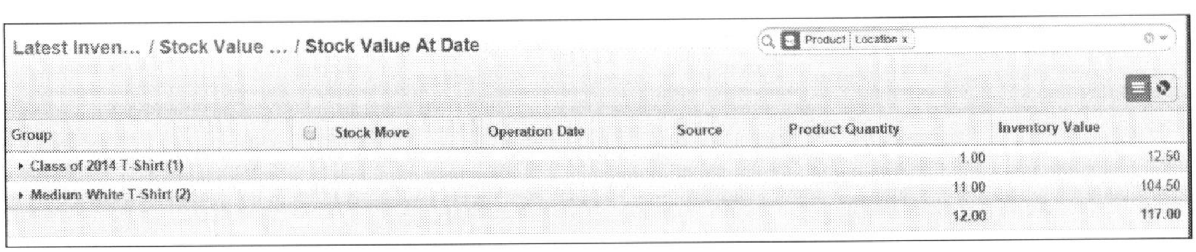

With this view, everything is collapsed and as a result, many of the columns are empty. For example in this view, you don't see anything under **Stock Move** or **Operation Date** because the data is rolled up. You can use the small triangles on the far left of the grid to drill down into the data and see more detail on how the stock value is derived. Here is the same data but expanded so you can see the detail:

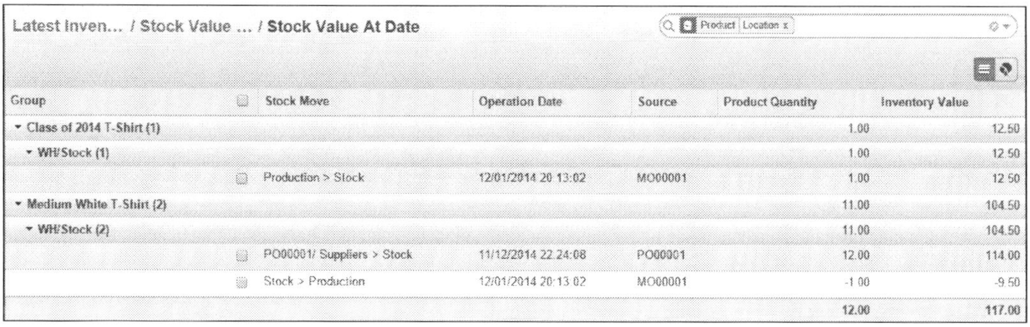
Latest Inven... / Stock Value ... / Stock Value At Date

Group	Stock Move	Operation Date	Source	Product Quantity	Inventory Value
▾ Class of 2014 T-Shirt (1)				1.00	12.50
▾ WH/Stock (1)				1.00	12.50
	Production > Stock	12/01/2014 20:13:02	MO00001	1.00	12.50
▾ Medium White T-Shirt (2)				11.00	104.50
▾ WH/Stock (2)				11.00	104.50
	PO00001/ Suppliers > Stock	11/12/2014 22:24:08	PO00001	12.00	114.00
	Stock > Production	12/01/2014 20:13:02	MO00001	-1.00	-9.50
				12.00	117.00

In a more detailed listing, you will see how you can get a great deal of information on the operations by looking at the stock move column. Here, we can see exactly where the product came from, where it went, and how it affects the product quantity for that location.

Managing routings and work orders

This first manufacturing order was very simple and our bill of materials only contained one product. In many companies, the manufacturing operations are more complex. For example, in some instances, depending on the attributes of the product, the manufacturing could involve different work centers or alternative steps to produce the final product. By default, Odoo's manufacturing application takes a more simplified approach. Going into the settings of the manufacturing application allows you to specify additional options.

Simply go into the **Settings** menu and select **Manufacturing** under the **Configuration** section on the left. Here, under **Planning**, you can check **Manage routings and work orders**. Once this option is checked, you will have the ability to manage more complex manufacturing processes inside Odoo.

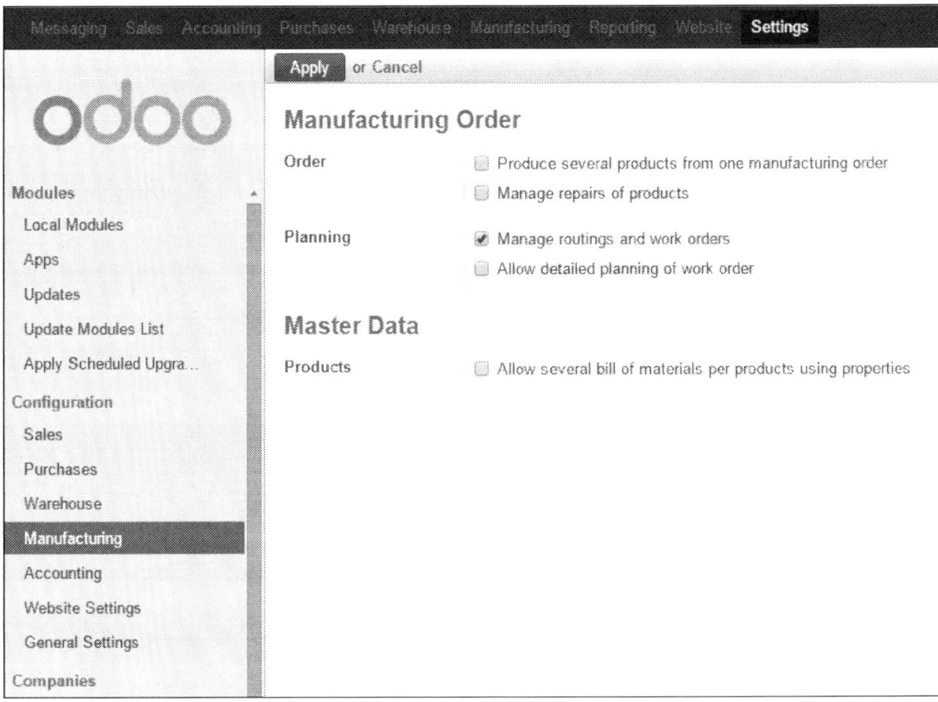

After you apply the changes, the menus will refresh, and new options will be added to the manufacturing application.

> Sometimes, when adding a new functionality to Odoo, such as applications or modifying settings, it can be helpful to do a *Shift* + Refresh on your browser to make sure Odoo is refreshed with the latest options.

Creating a work center

In our previous simplified manufacturing order, we specified the raw product required in a bill of materials and then turned that into a finished product. Now, we will expand this example to specify the human labor that goes into printing our Class of 2014 T-Shirt. In Odoo, we define the parameters in a work center.

For the purpose of our example, we will create a work center `Printing` that is responsible for taking the blank T-shirt and applying the design to create the final product. We begin by going to the manufacturing application and, under the configuration menu, choosing the **Work Center** option. Then, we click on **Create** to set up a new work center record:

In our example, we have named the work center `Printing`. In a full implementation, it would be common to have different work centers based around the work performed.

Defining a resource type

When setting up a work center, you are required to specify **Resource Type**. This setting can either be **Human** or **Material**. As you might expect, a human resource will primarily depend on human interaction in performing the work while a material resource would typically indicate a nearly automatic machine that, once configured, will perform the work unattended.

Setting capacity information

When defining a work center, it is possible to define **Capacity Information** that will allow you to estimate the cost and time required to produce your products. In our example, we are going to configure this work center so that we can estimate the time required to produce a T-shirt. Let's look at each of the capacity values.

Efficiency Factor

Efficiency Factor is a metric on how efficient this work center is at completing tasks. Often, the efficiency factor is most valuable in allowing you to tweak your work center's capacity without modifying many of the other variables. If, for example, you have an efficiency factor of 2.00 (or 200 percent) then the work center will complete twice as many tasks. For our example, we are leaving the efficiency factor as the default of 1.00 or 100 percent. Some consider it lazy work center design to modify efficiency values rather than more accurately setting other capacity settings.

Capacity per Cycle

The **Capacity per Cycle** option allows you to determine how many tasks the work center can do in parallel. For example, if you had a work center that could be configured with three workers and all three workers can complete a cycle at the same time, you could set the capacity per cycle to three. When a manufacturing order is then routed to the work center, the work center can complete three tasks at the same time. For our example, we will assume one worker and therefore, one capacity per cycle.

Time for 1 cycle (hour)

This option specifies how much time in hours it takes to complete one cycle. In our example, we are producing T-shirts. Therefore, this value indicates how long it takes to produce one T-shirt. In this example, we have specified that each T-shirt will take 2 minutes to produce by this work center.

Time before and after production

Many work center operations will have the time required for setup and tear down times outside of the time consumed by actually producing the product. This is certainly true for our example. It takes time for someone to prepare a printing press with ink before the first T-shirt can be printed. For our example, we have estimated 5 minutes of setup time. Likewise, when we are done producing the last product in our work order, it takes time to clean up and prepare for the next job. In this example, we have estimated 5 minutes of time at the end of production for clean-up operations.

Costing information

In the costing information section, you can also specify a product that is produced by a work center. In some manufacturing operations, a work center will always produce the exact same assembly or subassembly. For our example, we want our work center to be flexible, and it might print any number of finished products, so we are leaving the **Work Center Product** field blank.

Creating routing orders

After defining a work center, you need to define a way to specify under which conditions you should use the work center. This is accomplished by defining routings. For our example, we are going to keep it simple and use routing to send our manufacture order to the printing work center for the finished product to be produced. In a real world example, the job might use routings to go through many work center operations before the final product is produced.

To create a routing order, go to the Manufacturing application and choose **Routings** under the **Product** submenu. Click on **Create** to bring up the new routing form:

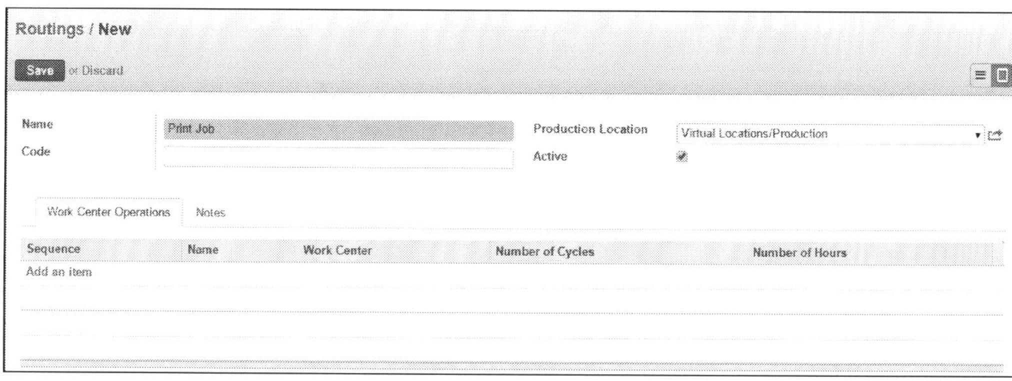

In our example, we have named the routing `Print Job` and specified the **Virtual Location/Production** location. This vertical location is used to provide a location in which the product is actually produced. Because the product is not actually stocked or physically counted during production, the location is considered a virtual location within Odoo.

Next, we will define our work center operation by clicking on **Add an Item** and bringing up the operation form.

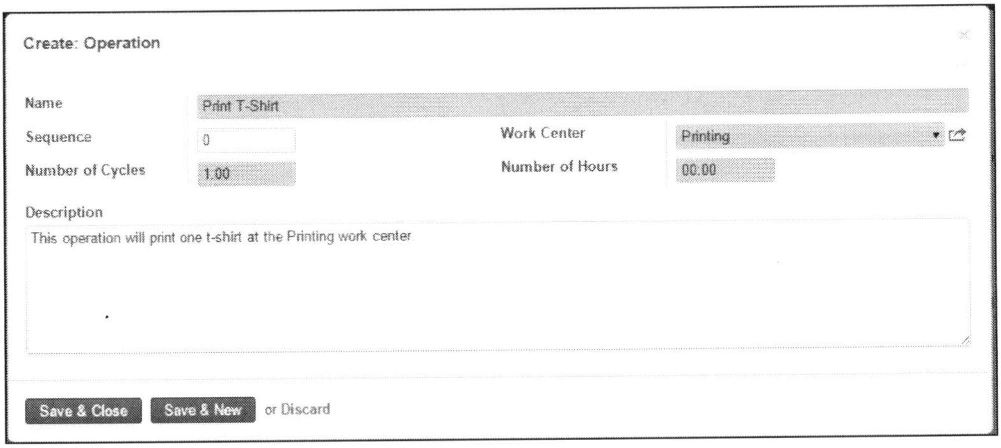

When defining our operation, we can name it whatever we wish, but in this case, I picked **Print T-Shirt**. This indicates this operation is more specific than the simple **Print Job** we are assigning to the routing order.

For complex routings, you can specify the sequence of the operations. For example, we could have a **Design** operation and a **Build Screen** operation before the **Print Job** operation. Then, we could specify a **Quality Assurance** operation and a **Packing** operation after the print job. You would handle all of these exactly the same way you set up the printing work center and created the required operations to produce the product. By starting simple and adding additional operations and complexity over time, you can often get up and running much more quickly than trying to track every little task right from the beginning.

Once you have set up your operation, your routing should resemble the following form:

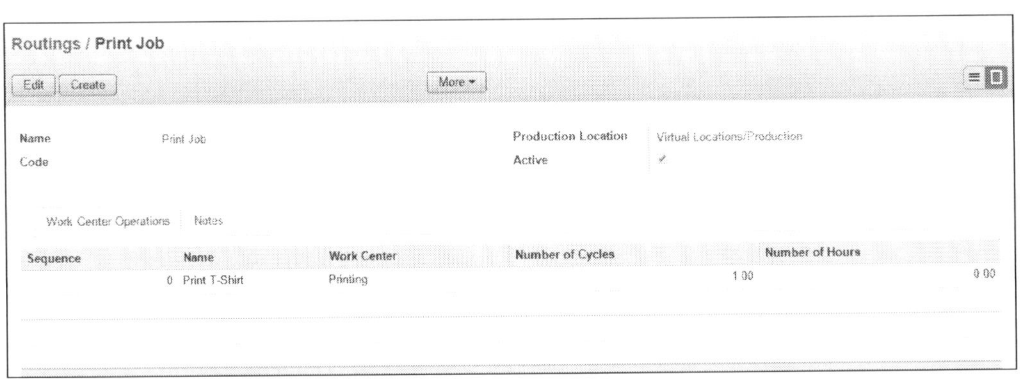

Here, we can see the finished order. One thing worth pointing out is that the number of hours specified in this routing is 0. Routings are very flexible and don't necessarily have to tie directly to a work center. In our example, we are letting the work center calculate the hours provided based on the quantity of the shirts we are producing. Alternatively, you can specify the number of hours directly in the routing.

Creating a manufacturing order with routing and a work center

Now that we have defined our work center and our routing operation, we can create a manufacturing order that will utilize our new production steps. In this example, we are going to produce 15 Class of 2014 T-Shirts.

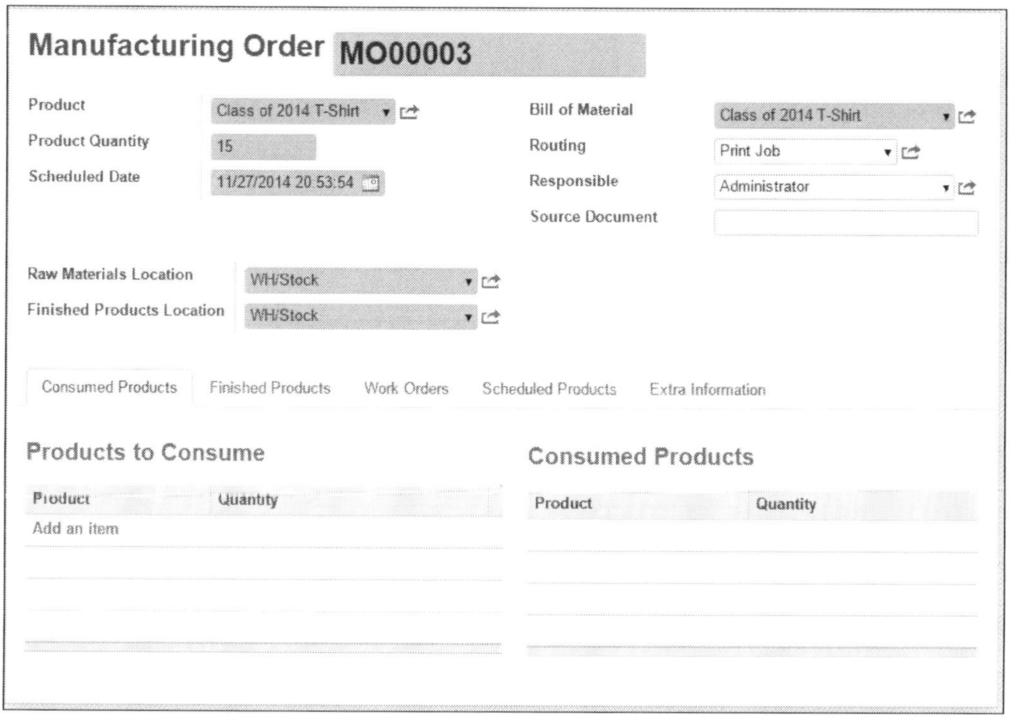

When we select the product, Odoo will now automatically assign the associated bill of the materials for the product. You will notice in the manufacturing order we have selected **Print Job** for the routing of this order. This is the key field that will send this job to the printing work center to be produced. Clicking on **Confirm Production** will load in the products that will need to be consumed, as well as the work orders that are required to produce the product.

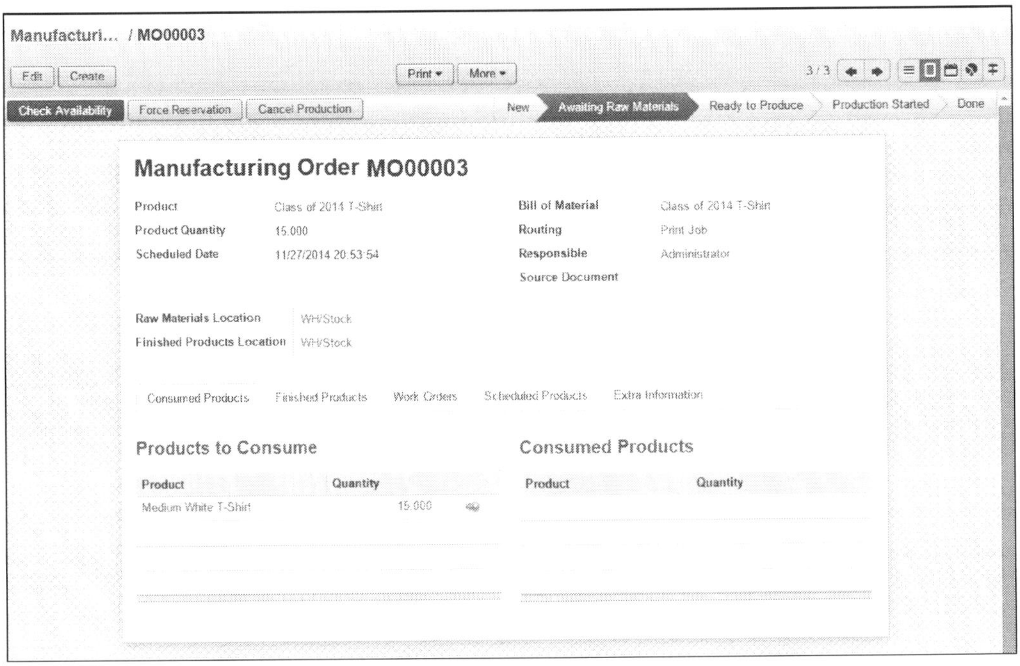

Once again, you will see that we are awaiting availability. The main difference is that now you will see the routing in the top-right corner is set to **Print Job**. This will route the manufacturing order to the Printing work center we created.

Now, when you click on **Check Availability**, unless you have purchased additional Medium White T-Shirts outside of the exercises in this book, you will not be able to continue on to production.

> Odoo does not give you a lot of feedback here. When you click on **Check Availability**, Odoo will simply leave the status at **Awaiting Raw Materials**. There is no warning message or another indicator displayed.

You can now either go in and use your skills from *Chapter 4, Purchasing with Odoo*, to create an order for additional medium white T-shirts, or you can alternatively click on the **Force Reservation** to tell Odoo you still wish to process this order despite the inventory showing a lack of available raw materials. For our purposes, we are going to assume that we have additional T-shirts available already and use this opportunity to try the **Force Reservation** option.

Click on **Force Reservation** to get the order ready for production.

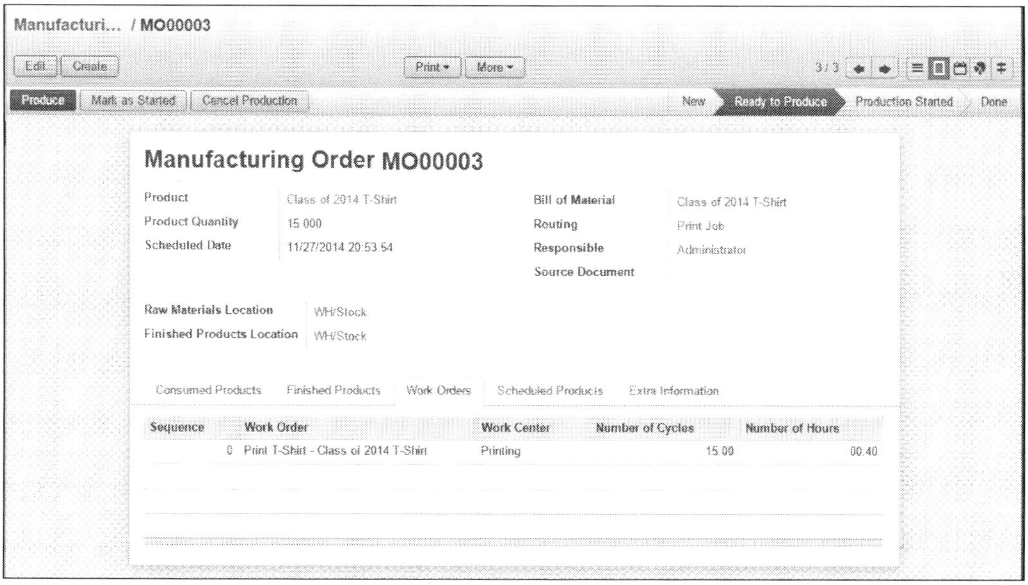

As you can see on the far right, it is estimated that it will take 40 minutes (00:40) to produce these 15 Class of 2014 T-Shirts.

How did we arrive at that number? It is a result of the capacity information we specified in the printing work center earlier in the chapter:

*Capacity Information: 5 minutes setup + (2 minutes * 15 shirts) + 5 minutes tear down time = 40 minutes.*

Producing the manufacturing order

Now you can click on **Produce** to send the manufacturing order to the work center and produce the 15 T-shirts. You will get a confirmation screen to confirm that you wish to create all 15:

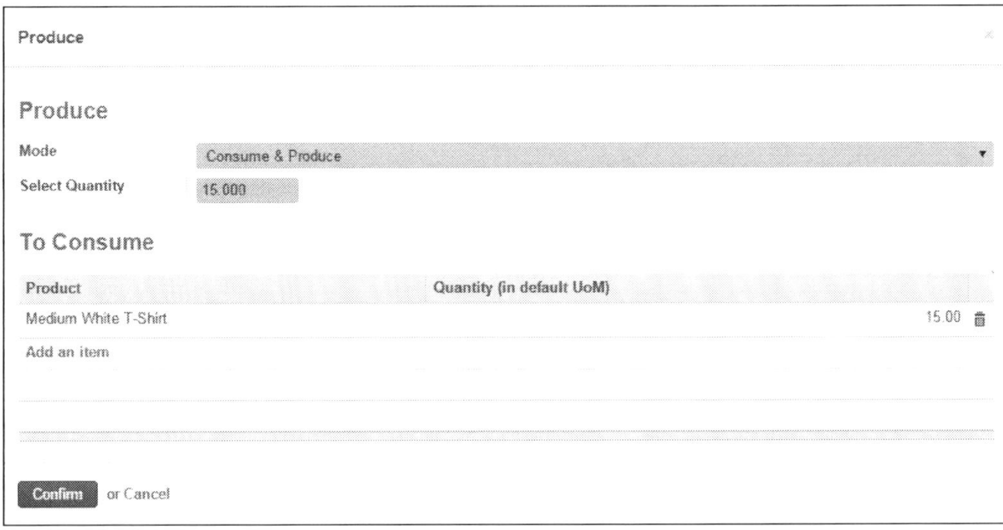

Just like before, you can tell Odoo that you are only consuming at this stage or you can confirm and produce. Clicking on **Confirm** processes the manufacturing order. After production, the state will go to **Done** and you will find the 15 T-shirts in your inventory ready for shipping.

Summary

In this chapter, we installed the MRP application to begin setting up our manufacturing process. A bill of materials was created to define what products would be consumed when our product was manufactured. Finally, we manufactured our final product and looked at the inventory analysis report to verify our results.

In the next chapter, we will take a closer look at accounting and other reporting options. Setting up your chart of accounts is an important step that we'll cover, as well as reviewing journal entries, creating invoices, and receiving payments. We will also be defining sales taxes and managing fiscal periods. Yes, there is a lot more to cover!

6
Configuring Accounting Finance

One of the nice things about Odoo is that you can get up and running fairly quickly without having to spend a lot of time setting up complicated accounting and finance options. Odoo does a pretty fair job of creating a basic chart of account structures as a point to get started and to get familiar with Odoo. When setting up a production system for your company. However, you will want to take time to properly define your accounting requirements.

In this chapter, you will learn how to configure accounting in Odoo. This includes:

- Installing the Accounting and Finance application
- Examining the chart of accounts
- Learning how the other applications create transactions in accounting
- Adding new custom accounts
- Configuring fiscal years and periods
- A quick overview of the available accounting reports
- Closing a period
- Creating journal entries

Defining the chart of accounts for your business

The backbone of an accounting system setup is the chart of accounts. Wikipedia defines a chart of accounts as follows:

> *"A chart of accounts (COA) is a created list of the accounts used by a business entity to define each class of items for which money or the equivalent is spent or received. It is used to organize the finances of the entity and to segregate expenditures, revenue, assets and liabilities in order to give interested parties a better understanding of the financial health of the entity."*

It is very likely that if you are setting up Odoo for an existing business, you will be asked to configure the chart of accounts in Odoo to match the account structure that the business is already using. Even if you are not tied to any existing chart of accounts, it is inevitable that you will need to have a firm understanding of how the accounting functionality in Odoo works if you are going to have a successful implementation.

If you are completely unfamiliar with accounting, then this chapter might prove somewhat challenging. It is important to get familiar with accounting basics if you want to succeed in implementing any ERP system.

Installing the Accounting and Finance application

Odoo configures a basic accounting structure when you install base applications such as Sales and Purchasing. To access all of the accounting configuration options, you must install the **Accounting and Finance** application. If this application is not already installed in your configuration, go to **settings** and click on **Apps** to pull up the available applications. Find **Accounting and Finance** and click on **Install** to install the application.

After you have installed the **Accounting and Finance** application, your menu structure at the top of Odoo will change. Before installing the application, you likely had an **Invoicing** menu that contained the necessary options for the Sales and Purchasing applications. Once the **Accounting and Finance** application is installed, the **Invoicing** menu will be replaced with an **Accounting** menu and will be populated with several more options.

Viewing the current chart of accounts

We will begin by learning how to view the current chart of accounts in Odoo:

1. Go to the **Accounting** menu and choose **Chart of Accounts** under the **Charts** submenu. You will be presented with a screen that lets you select the year and fiscal period for which you wish to review the Chart of Accounts:

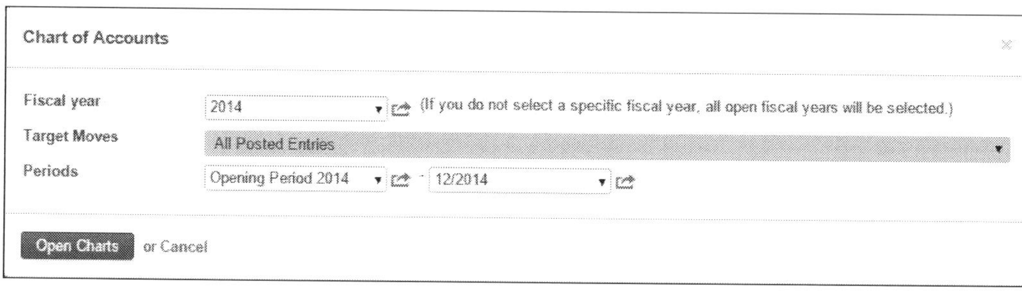

   Odoo will change, by default, the fiscal year to the current year, and the periods will also change, by default, to periods of the current month in the fiscal year.

2. Click on **Open Charts** to view the chart of accounts for the specified time frame:

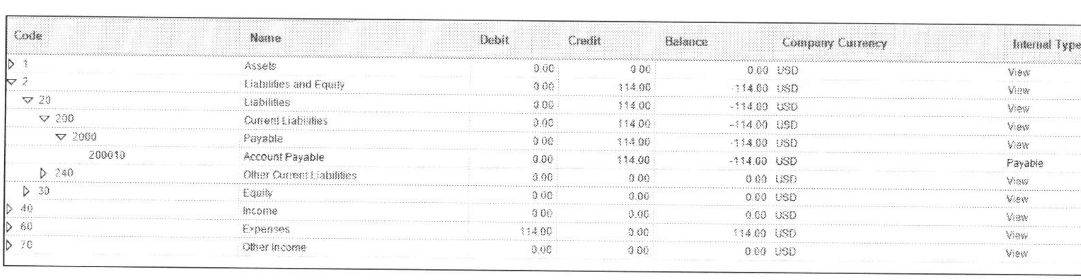

Code	Name	Debit	Credit	Balance	Company Currency	Internal Type
1	Assets	0.00	0.00	0.00	USD	View
2	Liabilities and Equity	0.00	114.00	-114.00	USD	View
20	Liabilities	0.00	114.00	-114.00	USD	View
200	Current Liabilities	0.00	114.00	-114.00	USD	View
2000	Payable	0.00	114.00	-114.00	USD	View
200010	Account Payable	0.00	114.00	-114.00	USD	Payable
240	Other Current Liabilities	0.00	0.00	0.00	USD	View
30	Equity	0.00	0.00	0.00	USD	View
40	Income	0.00	0.00	0.00	USD	View
60	Expenses	114.00	0.00	114.00	USD	View
70	Other Income	0.00	0.00	0.00	USD	View

In the previous screenshot, we see the currently configured chart of accounts in a hierarchical tree structure. The liabilities accounts have been opened up to demonstrate how Odoo nests accounts inside each other.

- 2 – **Liabilities**
- 20 – **Current Liabilities**
- 2000 – **Payable**
- 200010 – **Account Payable**

The ability to nest accounts inside one another allows reports to *roll up* totals, so that you can analyze the financial status of the company at any level. For example, you can look at the total of all liabilities or only look at the liabilities you currently have in accounts payable.

How were the transactions created in Account Payable?

Looking at the chart of accounts, we can see that we have transactions in the Account Payable liability account. Account Payable liability typically includes a total of the current invoices that you have open from your suppliers. When you purchase goods and you receive an invoice, Account Payable will increase by the amount of the invoice. When you pay the invoice, the Account Payable account will decrease by the amount you pay on the invoice.

To see the transactions that created the $114.00 in Account Payable, double-click on the 200010 account:

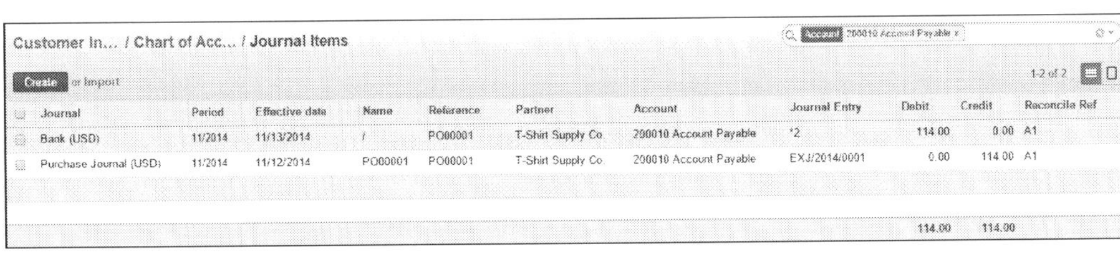

When we open the account, we see all the transactions that were involved. In the first column, we see the Journals from which the transaction came. **The Purchase Journal (USD)** and the **Bank (USD)** entries specify **PO00001** as the reference number for the transaction. This lets you tie back this payment to the original purchase order. Near the far right of the first line item, you will see the debit amount of **$114.00**. This was the entry wherein your bank account was debited the amount of the purchase, and removing the money from your account.

In the second line, the **Account Payable** account was *credited* $114.00 to reduce the liability that you owed for the product. With both these entries, you are accounting for the invoiced purchase order PO00001.

Viewing the other journal items

In the top-right corner in the Odoo search box, we can see that the view is limited to the **Account Payable** account. If we click on the small closed box on the account payable filter in the search view, we can see all the journal items.

Journal	Period	Effective date	Name	Reference	Partner	Account	Journal Entry	Debit	Credit	Reconcile Ref
Bank (USD)	11/2014	11/13/2014	/	PO00001	T-Shirt Supply Co.	200010 Account Payable	*2	114.00	0.00	A1
Bank (USD)	11/2014	11/13/2014	Check #123	PO00001	T-Shirt Supply Co	100002 Bank	*2	0.00	114.00	
Purchase Journal (USD)	11/2014	11/12/2014	PO00001	PO00001	T-Shirt Supply Co.	200010 Account Payable	EXJ/2014/0001	0.00	114.00	A1
Purchase Journal (USD)	11/2014	11/12/2014	[MWT-20] Med Wht Shirt ()	PO00001	T-Shirt Supply Co.	690000 Miscellaneous Expense	EXJ/2014/0001	114.00	0.00	
								228.00	228.00	

If you look carefully at the new list of journal items, you will see there are two additional transactions.

One of these transactions is a **$114.00** debit to the **690000 Miscellaneous Expense** account. When the purchase order was invoiced, Odoo credited $114.00 to Account Payable to reflect that the company owes $114.00 to the supplier in the company books. At the same time, Odoo created the $114.00 debit to the 690000 Miscellaneous Expense account. This is known as **double-entry accounting**. The result is that we can look at 690000 to see the total of our purchases.

When we paid the invoice, Odoo created the $114.00 debit to **Accounts Payable** to account for the fact that the company no longer has $114.00 in accounts payable liability. At the same time, Odoo credited the account **100002 Bank** for $114.00 to account for the money leaving that account.

If this is still a little confusing don't worry. We are now going to follow through a set of transactions from the Accounts Receivable side, so that you can better understand how Odoo handles accounting transactions.

Following transactions through the sales and accounts receivable process

In the previous example, we were looking at the chart of accounts and determining what transactions created the entries. Next, we will sell an item to a customer and see exactly how that transaction affects the accounting entries in the journal.

Let's begin by creating a new sales order.

Go to **Sales** and click on **Sales Order** to bring up the sales order listing. Click on **Create** to create a new sales order.

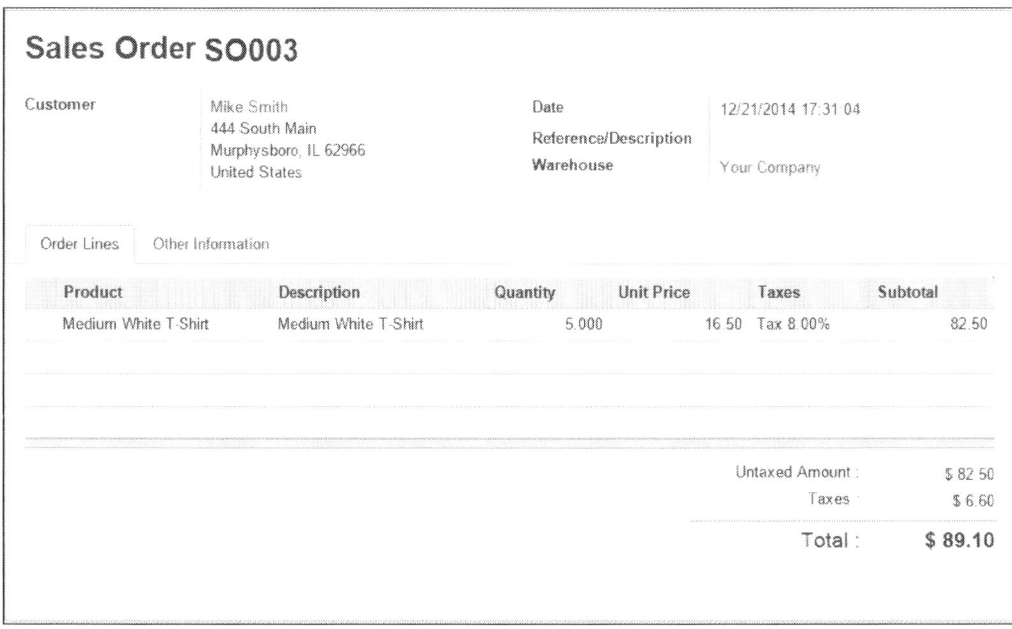

If you have followed along with our examples, then you will already have the customer and product entered to create the samples sales order. Otherwise, you will need to add a customer and a product if you wish to follow along on your computer. In this example, we have created a sales order for 5 medium white t-shirts. Make sure you **Confirm** your quotation to create the sales order.

> Odoo will automatically number the sales orders and other documents. In the preceding example, there have already been two sales order numbers used by the Odoo system. Therefore, depending on what you have already done with your current system, you might not have the same sales order number for your sample sales order.

At this point, if you were to go and look at the chart of accounts, you will not see any changes to the transactions. Why is this? The way Odoo is currently configured we must manually create an invoice. Only when we click on the **Create Invoice** button at the top of the screen will Odoo actually create accounting transactions.

Click on **Create Invoice** to generate a draft invoice for this sales order:

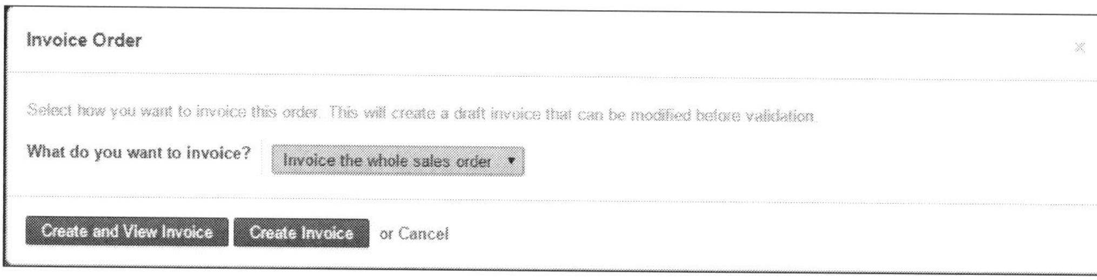

Click on **Create and View Invoice**:

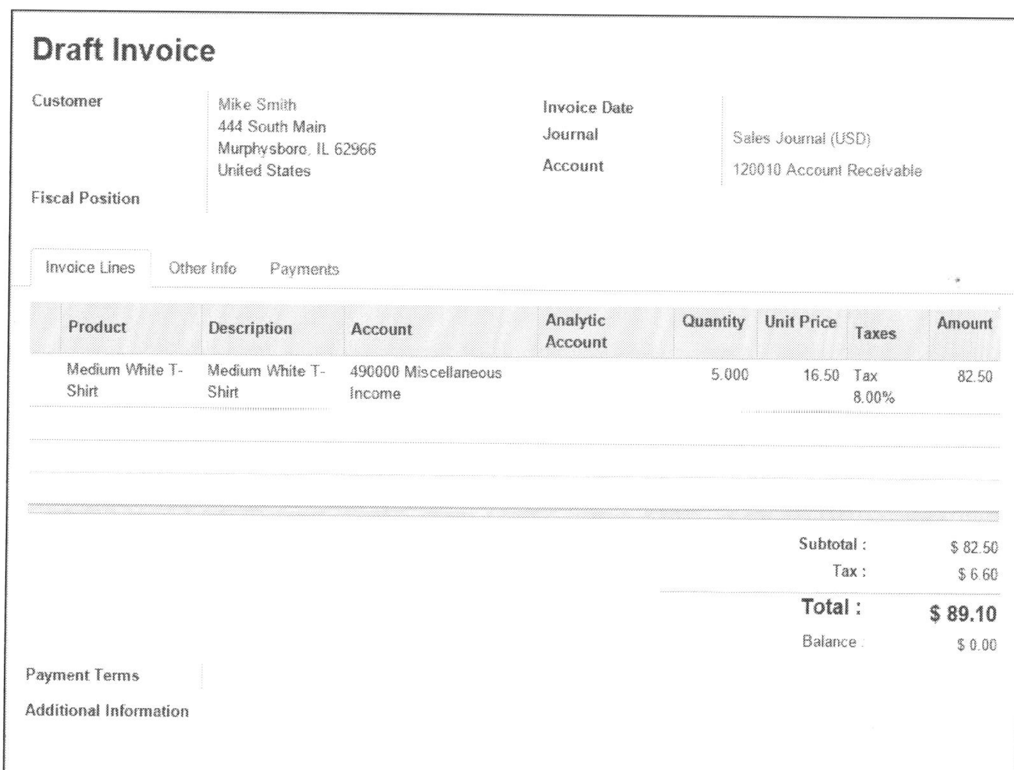

Because this is just a **Draft Invoice**, if you look at the chart of accounts, you will see no changes. However, if you look at the draft invoice, you can see the transactions that will be created once you validate the invoice. Notice that under **Account** in the header of the document, it reads **120010 Account Receivable**; this account will be debited to journal the amount the customer owes to the company once the invoice is generated.

In the line item of the sales order, you will see the **490000 Miscellaneous** account. This will be the account that will be credited for the sale of the medium white t-shirts that the customer has purchased.

Click on **Validate** to post the invoice and create the transactions.

Viewing the transactions created by validating the invoice

Now that we have validated our invoice, Odoo has automatically created the accounting transaction to increase our Accounts Receivable assets and the accounting transaction to record the sale.

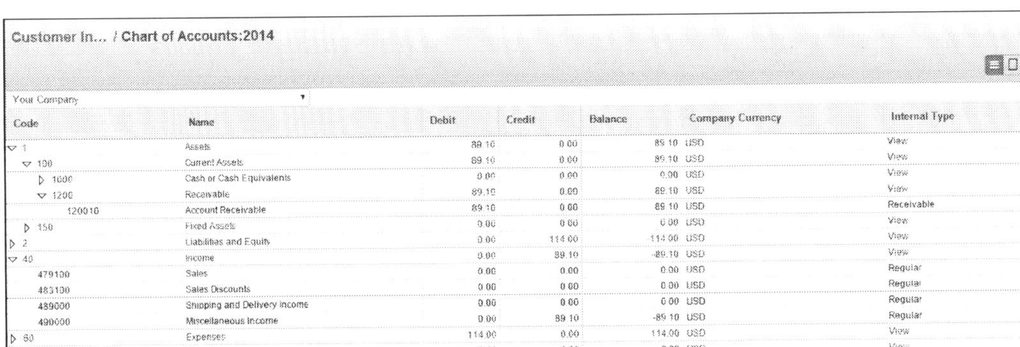

Customer In... / Chart of Accounts:2014

Your Company

Code	Name	Debit	Credit	Balance	Company Currency	Internal Type
1	Assets	89.10	0.00	89.10	USD	View
100	Current Assets	89.10	0.00	89.10	USD	View
1000	Cash or Cash Equivalents	0.00	0.00	0.00	USD	View
1200	Receivable	89.10	0.00	89.10	USD	View
120010	Account Receivable	89.10	0.00	89.10	USD	Receivable
150	Fixed Assets	0.00	0.00	0.00	USD	View
2	Liabilities and Equity	0.00	114.00	-114.00	USD	View
40	Income	0.00	89.10	-89.10	USD	View
479100	Sales	0.00	0.00	0.00	USD	Regular
483100	Sales Discounts	0.00	0.00	0.00	USD	Regular
489000	Shipping and Delivery Income	0.00	0.00	0.00	USD	Regular
490000	Miscellaneous Income	0.00	89.10	-89.10	USD	Regular
60	Expenses	114.00	0.00	114.00	USD	View
70	Other Income	0.00	0.00	0.00	USD	View

If you take a close look at the chart of accounts after posting the invoice, you will see that the **120010 Account Receivable** account has been debited by $89.10 to show the new current asset representing the customer invoice. The customer owes the company $89.10. As you create invoices and customers owe you money as a result, Accounts Receivable will continue to grow.

Next, notice the **490000 Miscellaneous Income** account has been credited with $89.10. This account will continue to be credited for the products you sell.

> For our example, we are using only one sales account to keep things simple. In most companies, you will have far more sales accounts to organize the various types of products sold.

Now, let's see what happens to these accounts when a customer pays their invoice.

Go to **Accounting** and choose **Customer Invoices**, then click on the invoice to bring up the form. Click on **Receive Payment** to bring up **Pay Invoice**:

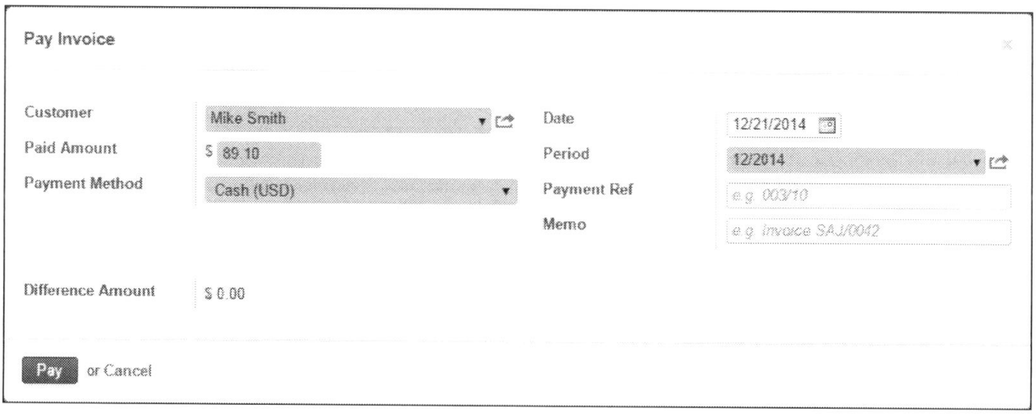

Odoo will automatically fill up the customer, paid amount, date, and period fields. For our example, we have chosen the **Cash (USD)** payment method. You have the option to provide both a payment reference and a memo to document that invoice payment.

Click on the **Pay** button to pay the invoice and create the appropriate accounting transactions.

The invoice is now paid and the journal entries have been automatically created. However, when it comes to money going in and out of the company, extra care is taken to make sure there is an opportunity to reconcile cash and bank transactions. For example, the Accounts Receivable clerk might receive a check from a customer and mark the invoice as paid. But how do we know for sure that the customer's check actually made it into the bank account?

For this reason, the journal item for the cash received to pay the invoice is created in an **Unposted** status. Let's view the journal entry:

Under the **Accounting** menu, choose **Journal Entries** to bring up the list of journal entries:

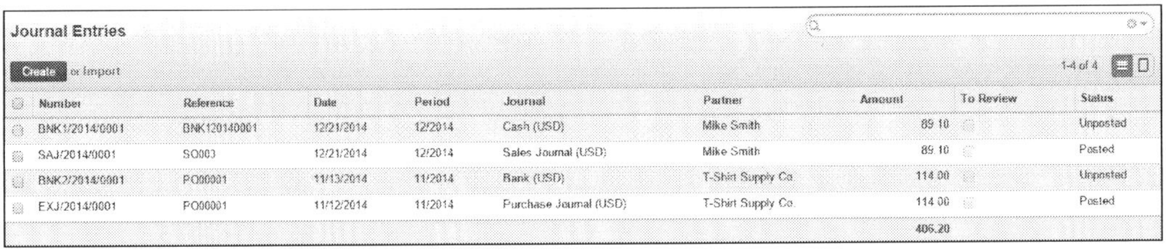

In the list, you will notice we have two unposted entries. One is the entry from the payment of the purchasing invoice of $114.00, which is to be taken from the bank account. The other entry is the cash customer payment of $89.10.

> In some systems, there is a dedicated step to handling daily bank deposits. With Odoo, you can implement a daily deposit workflow by leaving all deposits in a draft state and then at the end of the day, post the entries to the journal. By properly filtering unposted items, the total amount should equal the amount of your bank deposit.

Let's go ahead and post the cash entry for Mike Smith's invoice.

Click on the unposted cash payment for $89.10 to pull up the journal entry:

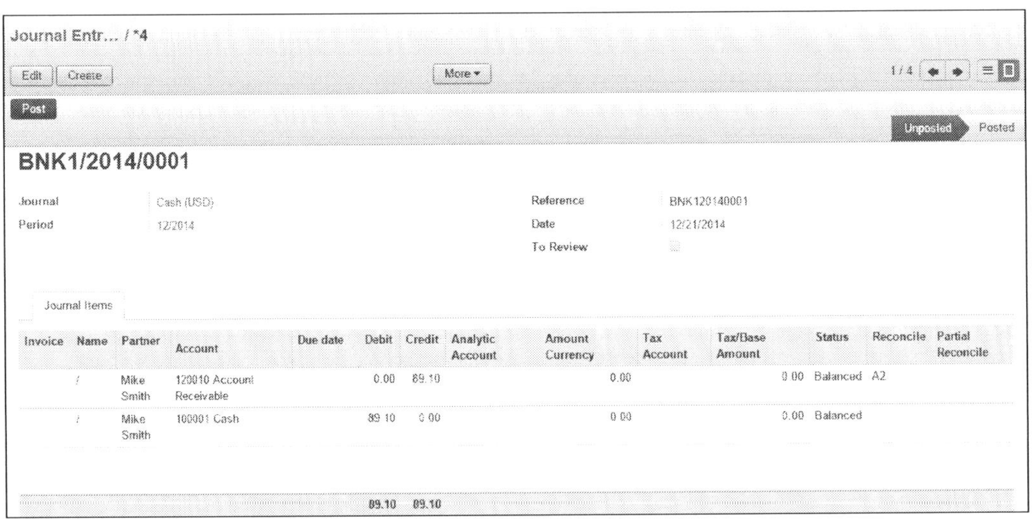

In this cash receipt, you will notice that we can see the details on exactly which accounts will be affected when we post the entry:

- **120010 Account Receivable** is credited with $89.10. This will reduce this asset account.
- **100001 Cash** is debited with $89.10. This will increase this asset account.

Essentially, this journal entry transfers the potential asset that the customer owes the company from accounts receivable into the cash account. The customer's account balance is reduced to reflect their payment.

Click on **Post** to post the entry.

Now that we have posted the entry, let's take another look at the chart of accounts to see how the Cash and Account Receivable accounts have been changed to reflect the transactions.

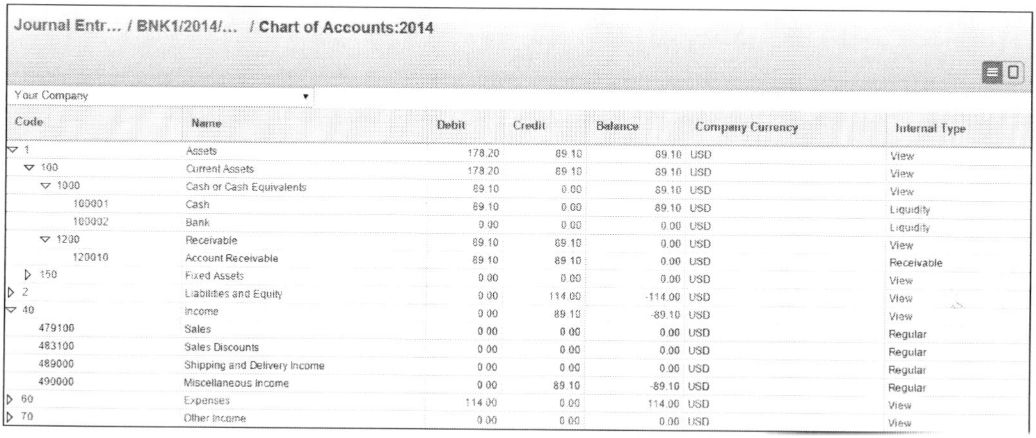

Journal Entr... / BNK1/2014/... / Chart of Accounts:2014

Your Company

Code	Name	Debit	Credit	Balance	Company Currency	Internal Type
1	Assets	178.20	89.10	89.10	USD	View
100	Current Assets	178.20	89.10	89.10	USD	View
1000	Cash or Cash Equivalents	89.10	0.00	89.10	USD	View
100001	Cash	89.10	0.00	89.10	USD	Liquidity
100002	Bank	0.00	0.00	0.00	USD	Liquidity
1200	Receivable	89.10	89.10	0.00	USD	View
120010	Account Receivable	89.10	89.10	0.00	USD	Receivable
150	Fixed Assets	0.00	0.00	0.00	USD	View
2	Liabilities and Equity	0.00	114.00	-114.00	USD	View
40	Income	0.00	89.10	-89.10	USD	View
479100	Sales	0.00	0.00	0.00	USD	Regular
483100	Sales Discounts	0.00	0.00	0.00	USD	Regular
489000	Shipping and Delivery Income	0.00	0.00	0.00	USD	Regular
490000	Miscellaneous Income	0.00	89.10	-89.10	USD	Regular
60	Expenses	114.00	0.00	114.00	USD	View
70	Other Income	0.00	0.00	0.00	USD	View

First, notice that now our Account Receivable (120010) balance is zero. We can see the debit of $89.10 that was created when we invoiced the customer. Then, we can see the $89.10 credit that was posted when we received the customer payment. Now, take a look at the Cash account (100001). It has a debit and a balance of $89.10. This is the cash that we have received from the customer.

Practice posting transactions and tracking the results

Remember that people spend many years and even get full degrees in financial accounting. It is important that you take time to learn how each process you implement will affect the accounts in Odoo. When implementing an ERP system for your company, take the time to get this right. It will save you a lot of pain in the long run.

Where are my taxes?

If you have been looking at the journal entries and following along, you might have noticed that the sales taxes are not reflected in the chart of accounts. By default, Odoo posts the entire transaction to the sales account. This was likely done in order to make Odoo a little easier to implement for people that are new to accounting. You don't have to trouble yourself with setting up special tax accounts. Fortunately, Odoo provides a very easy way to see your sales tax liability.

The chart of taxes appears right under the menu item for chart of accounts:

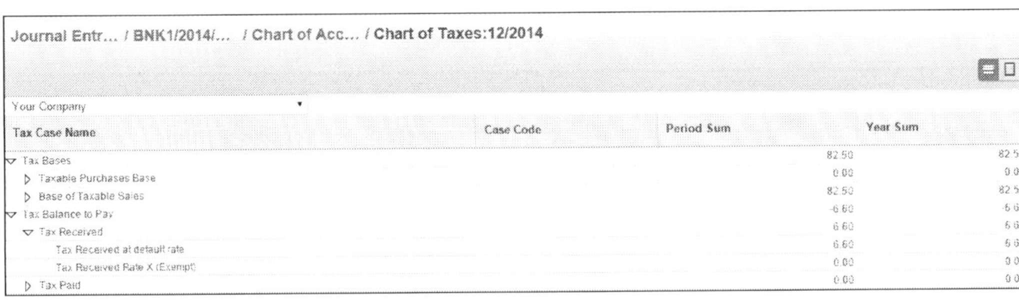

Here, in this tax report, you can see the **Tax Received** totaling to $6.60 from Mike Smith's t-shirt order. This setup will work for some companies but many companies are going to want to have their sales tax payable represented in their chart of accounts.

Specifying the account for your sales tax

As we have discussed, by default, Odoo does not configure sales tax to post to a specific general ledger account. To configure Odoo in order to create the appropriate journal entry in Sales Tax Payable, open up the tax entry form.

Under the **Accounting** menu, choose **Taxes** under the configuration section at the bottom of the menu. Then, click on the **Tax Type** that you would like to configure. In our example, we have opened up the 8.0 percent sales tax rate:

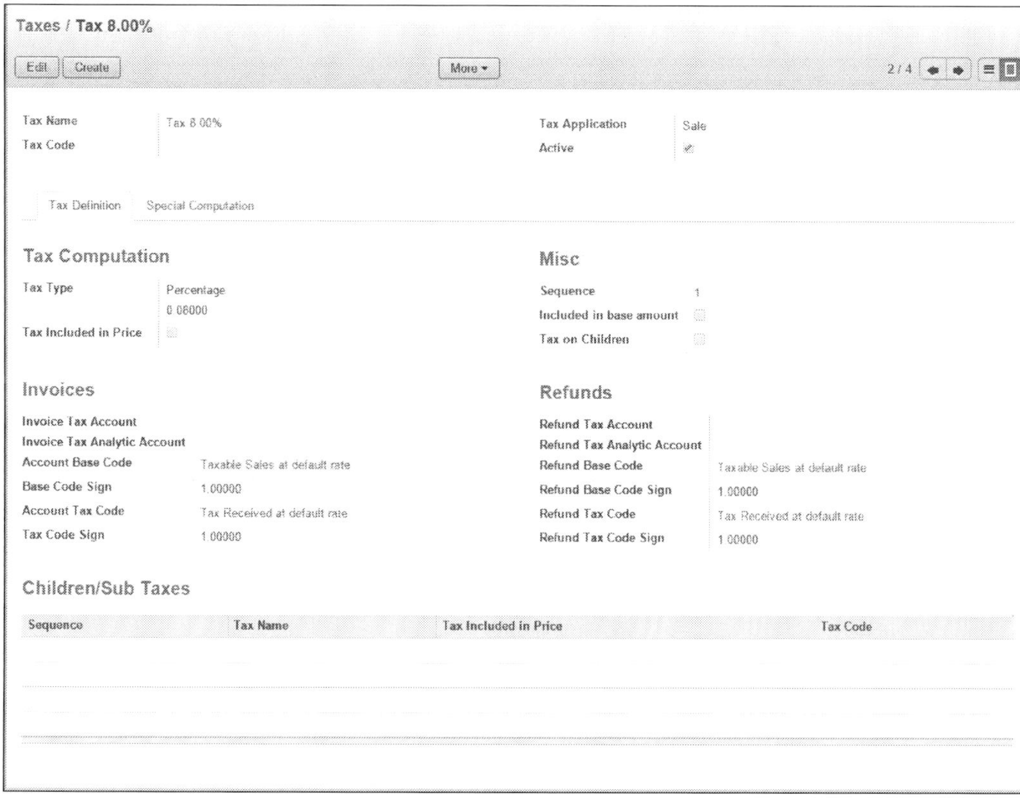

First off, notice that **Invoice Tax Account** is blank. By default, the taxes just go against expenses as you saw in the previous example and you use a separate report to look at your tax liability. For some operations, this makes things easier but for many businesses, you will want to setup dedicated tax accounts.

As you can see by looking at this form, there are a lot of configuration options for taxes. Fortunately, we only have to concern ourselves with a few options to configure Odoo to post to a specific account. Instead of leaving **Invoice Tax Account** blank, we will send our taxes to an alternate account.

Click on **Edit** to edit the sales tax record.

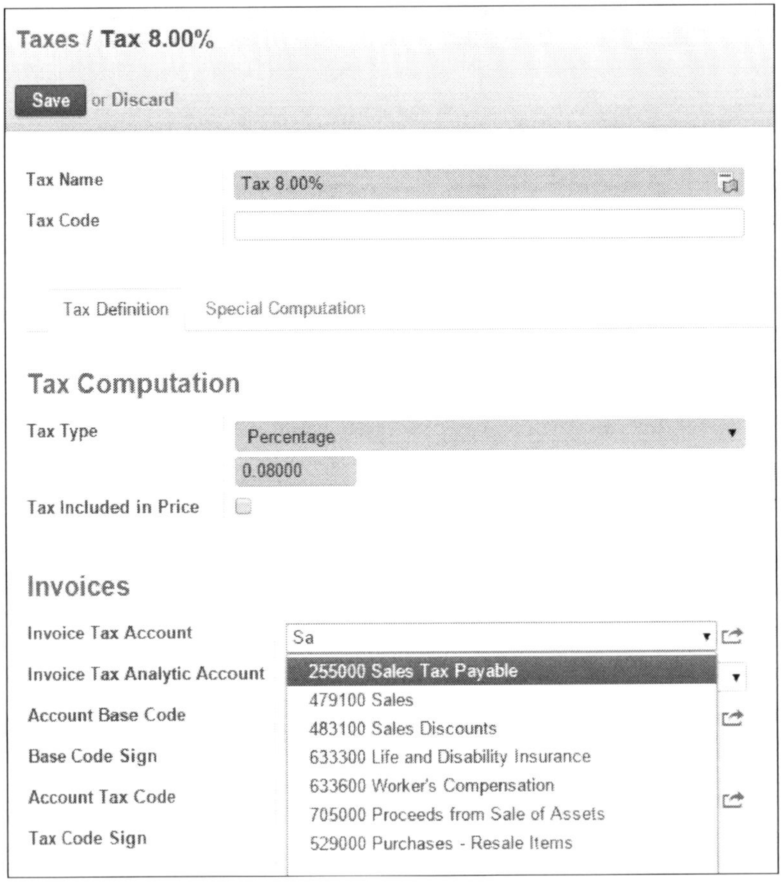

After clicking on edit, we choose to expense the 8.0 percent tax to the **255000 Sales Tax Payable** account when an invoice is posted. This account typically comes with the standard Odoo chart of accounts. With this configuration, Odoo will now credit the taxes to this account.

As an example, we created another invoice for Mike Smith that resulted in $5.28 in taxes:

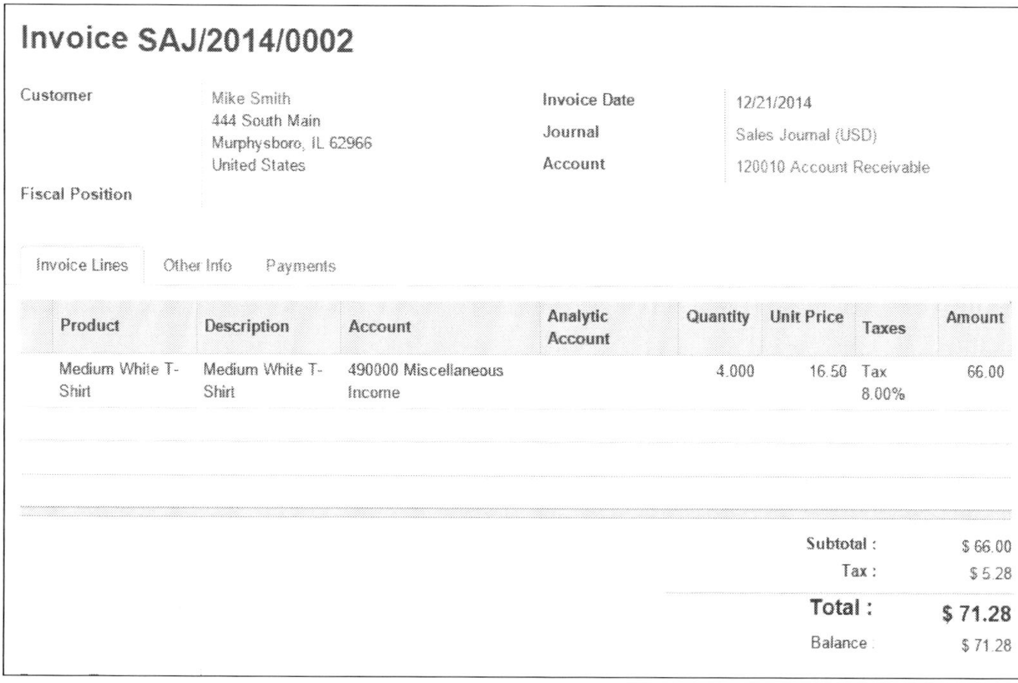

We can now see this tax represented in the chart of accounts in the Sales Tax Payable account:

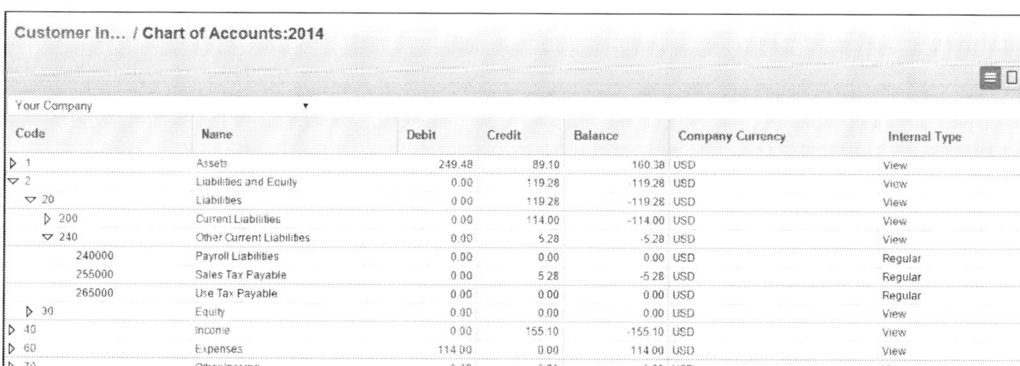
Customer In... / Chart of Accounts:2014

Your Company

Code	Name	Debit	Credit	Balance	Company Currency	Internal Type
1	Assets	249.48	89.10	160.38	USD	View
2	Liabilities and Equity	0.00	119.28	-119.28	USD	View
20	Liabilities	0.00	119.28	-119.28	USD	View
200	Current Liabilities	0.00	114.00	-114.00	USD	View
240	Other Current Liabilities	0.00	5.28	-5.28	USD	View
240000	Payroll Liabilities	0.00	0.00	0.00	USD	Regular
255000	Sales Tax Payable	0.00	5.28	-5.28	USD	Regular
265000	Use Tax Payable	0.00	0.00	0.00	USD	Regular
30	Equity	0.00	0.00	0.00	USD	View
40	Income	0.00	155.10	-155.10	USD	View
60	Expenses	114.00	0.00	114.00	USD	View
70	Other Income	0.00	0.00	0.00	USD	View

Setting up your own accounts

Up to this point, we have used the standard United States chart of accounts template provided by Odoo. Most companies, however, will need to modify this chart of accounts or even set up an entirely different chart of accounts to match the needs of their business. As an example, we are going to add an additional sales account specifically for t-shirts so that we can better organize our sales into types of products.

To setup a new account, go to the accounting menu and then down to the configuration section and choose **Accounts**. Odoo will present you with a listing of all your current accounts in Odoo. Click on **Create** to add a new account:

Notice in our screen that we have specified the account code as `479110`. Why did we choose this as the account code? Odoo had already provided `479100` for the general sales account. Therefore, `479110` was an appropriate account code to choose for our T-shirt sales. For the name of the account, we simply choose **T-shirt Sales**.

In addition to specifying the account code and name, we must set the account parent. Even though this is not a required field, you need to be careful and select the appropriate parent for the account. In this case, the parent account is **40 Income**. This will group the T-shirt sales with the income of other products the company sells.

The other important setting is **Account Type**. Odoo needs to know the type of account you are setting up. So for example, if you were setting up an account that was to track the costs of products that you purchase often to produce your products, you would specify an **Expense** account type.

> Take time planning your chart of accounts in Odoo. Even if your company has already been using an existing chart of accounts, it is always a good idea to evaluate the current chart of accounts and make any improvements, given the current state of the business.

Specifying a new account for your product category

With Odoo, you can manage accounts at the product category level. Therefore, all products under a given category can utilize the same account settings. Let's create a new product category, `T-shirts`, for our medium white t-shirt and assign that category to the `479100 T-Shirt` sales account that we created. We can later add all T-shirt products under this category.

Go to the **Sales** menu, and in the **Configuration** section, choose **Product Categories** under the **Products** submenu. This lists the current product categories:

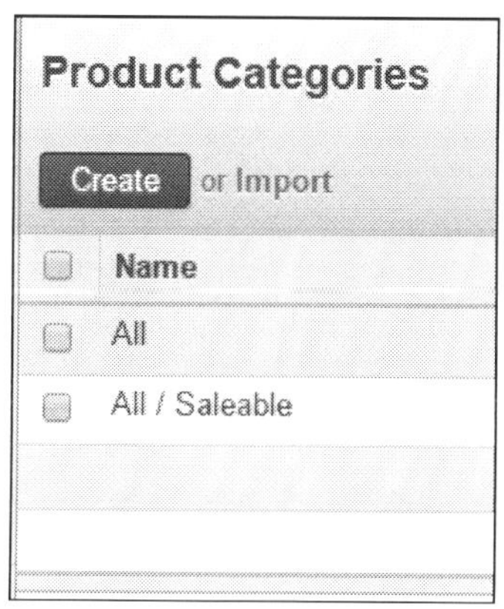

At this point, you will see that we only have two categories. Click on **Create** to create a new category for our T-shirt products:

We have named our new category `T-shirts`. All t-shirt products can now be grouped under this category. Also notice that we have set a parent category **All / Saleable**. This allows you to view the t-shirt products, along with all the other products, when you choose the parent category.

Most important from the accounting standpoint is that we have assigned the **Income Account** property, **479110 T-shirt Sales**, that we have set up in the chart of accounts. When an invoice is posted that has a line item attributed to this product category, the amount for that line item will be posted to **479110 T-Shirt Sales**. For the expense account, we have specified the built in **529000 Purchases - Resale Items**. This will change our expenses that are related to products in this category to that account.

> **Exercise**
>
> Now try going into the product record for the medium white t-shirt and set the product category to `T-shirts`. Create a sales order, turn it into an invoice, and validate it. View the chart of accounts and you will see the income against your t-shirt in the specified income account.
>
> Remember that it is important to practice using Odoo until you are comfortable setting up accounts and clearly understand where the transactions are posted. A little bit of time and effort put in during the configuration will save you a lot of time later.

Configuring your fiscal year and periods

Companies are typically required to report financial information on a monthly, quarterly, and yearly basis. While configuring Odoo, you must specify the fiscal periods that your company uses for reporting. By default, Odoo configures your installation with an opening period for adjustments, then a period for each month in the year starting in January.

While many companies have a December 31st closing date for their year, there are quite a few companies that have fiscal years that begin and end on other dates. There are many reasons why a company might have an alternative fiscal year structure. In Odoo, we can view and edit the accounting periods by going into the configuration section of the accounting menu and choosing periods:

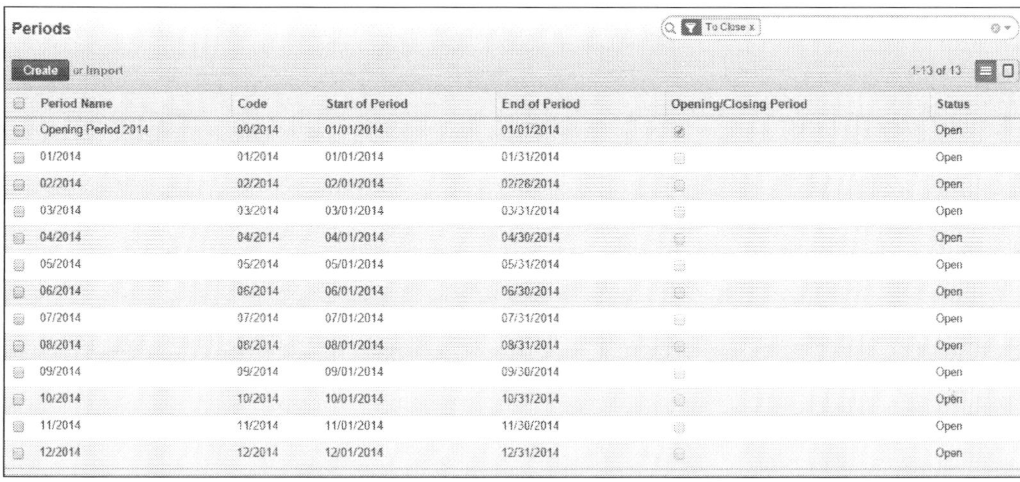

Period Name	Code	Start of Period	End of Period	Opening/Closing Period	Status
Opening Period 2014	00/2014	01/01/2014	01/01/2014	✓	Open
01/2014	01/2014	01/01/2014	01/31/2014		Open
02/2014	02/2014	02/01/2014	02/28/2014		Open
03/2014	03/2014	03/01/2014	03/31/2014		Open
04/2014	04/2014	04/01/2014	04/30/2014		Open
05/2014	05/2014	05/01/2014	05/31/2014		Open
06/2014	06/2014	06/01/2014	06/30/2014		Open
07/2014	07/2014	07/01/2014	07/31/2014		Open
08/2014	08/2014	08/01/2014	08/31/2014		Open
09/2014	09/2014	09/01/2014	09/30/2014		Open
10/2014	10/2014	10/01/2014	10/31/2014		Open
11/2014	11/2014	11/01/2014	11/30/2014		Open
12/2014	12/2014	12/01/2014	12/31/2014		Open

As you can see, each period is defined with starting and closing dates. In this view, you can modify the periods to meet the needs of your business. On the far right of the listing, you will notice a status column. This tells you whether the period is open or closed.

Examining the available Legal Reports in Odoo

Like nearly all accounting and finance systems, Odoo provides the standard reports you would expect including:

- General Ledger
- Trial Balance
- Balance Sheet

- Profit and Loss
- Financial Report

These reports are a bit buried near the middle of the **Accounting** menu under the **Reporting | Accounting Reports | Legal Reports**:

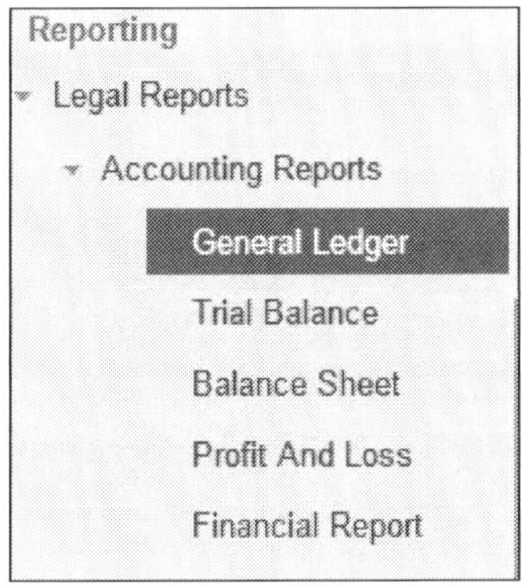

Each report you select will bring up an appropriate wizard that lets you specify the criteria for a given report. After you have made your selections and generated the report, you will be prompted to download the PDF file that contains the results. While going through each of these reports with all the screenshots is beyond the scope of this book, you are encouraged to spend some time examining each report, and make sure you understand how it fits within the reporting requirements of your business.

> As you add more and more data to your system, some of the accounting reports will take additional time to process. As part of the testing, before you go into production, you should take the time to make sure all of your accounting reports run at acceptable levels of performance using data that will simulate real-world conditions.

Closing a period

When you have completed all the transactions for a given period, it is a good idea to close that period to prevent any additional new postings. This is important because you do not want your future transactions to accidently post to a previous period of time because of a user error. To close a period, simply click on the period you wish to close and click on the **Close Period** button in the form. You will be presented with a form to confirm that you wish to close the period.

Once you have closed a period, it is possible to reopen the period if you must post a transaction to that period. Simply click on the period again and click on the **Re-open Period** button.

Creating journal entries

While Odoo will create many journal entries automatically when you perform various operations in the system, it is inevitable that, at some point, you (or your accountant) will wish to create a manual journal entry. A manual journal entry allows you to adjust account balances in a way that can easily be tracked and audited.

For our example, we are going to create a journal entry that will account for a small investment by one of the company owners. When someone puts money as an investment into a company, they are not buying anything and they are not selling anything. While there are other potential methods, a simple journal entry is a straightforward way to accurately record the transaction.

To enter a journal entry, go to the accounting menu and select **Journal Entries** in the **Journal Entries** section and click on the **Create** button:

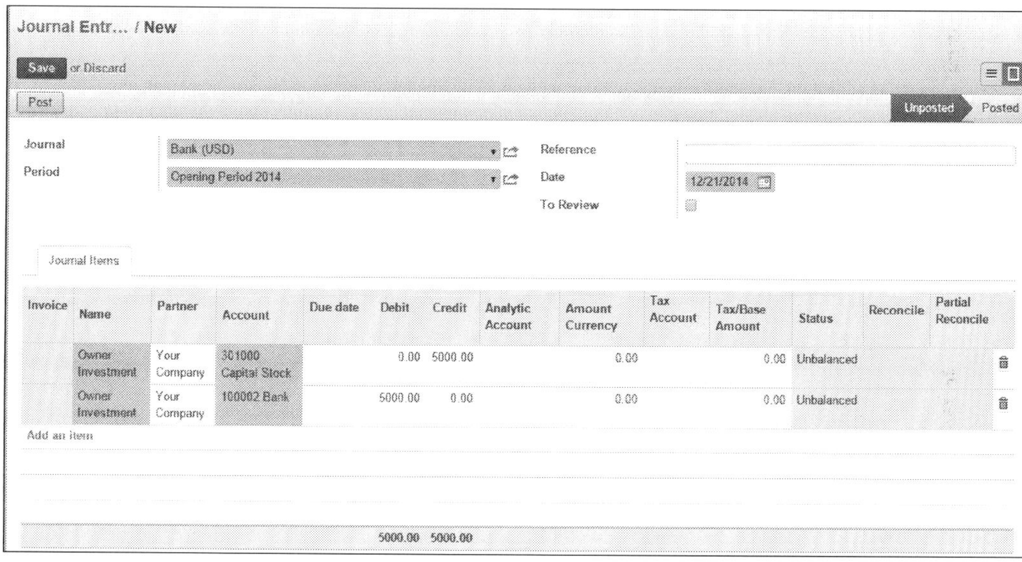

First, when you create a new journal entry, you will need to pick which journal and period to post to. For this situation, we used an example of how to post to the bank journal in the opening period to represent the owner's investment into the company.

> There is also an **Opening Entries** journal that you can also use to help you better organize opening entries for your company.

We are considering the $5000 investment as a cash investment by the owner, so we have posted this into the bank journal. Next, you can select the period you wish to post the journal entry to.

Whenever you create a journal entry, you will add at least two line items. Furthermore, the line items must balance out. In our example, we are putting $5,000 in funds from the owner into the company bank account.

Typically, any investment the owner puts into the company must also be recognized as a liability for the company. Why? The money does not really belong to the company. Instead, the $5,000, in this case, is considered the owner's equity. The owner is entitled to get that money back, and therefore it is booked as a liability. You can verify this by opening up the chart of accounts and looking at the list of main accounts. **Liabilities and Equity** are grouped together and are then divided out as you drill down into the account hierarchy.

Odoo sets up a **Capital Stock** account that allows us to post the $5,000 we have put into the bank as capital stock for the owner. Once you save your journal entry, it is in the form of a draft. To post the journal entry and have it appear in your chart of accounts you must click on the **Post** button.

After we have posted, we can look at our balances in the chart of accounts. You will notice that our assets now include the $5,000 investment, and the **Capital Stock** account in the **Liabilities and Equity** section of the chart of accounts represents the liability the company now has to the owner who invested:

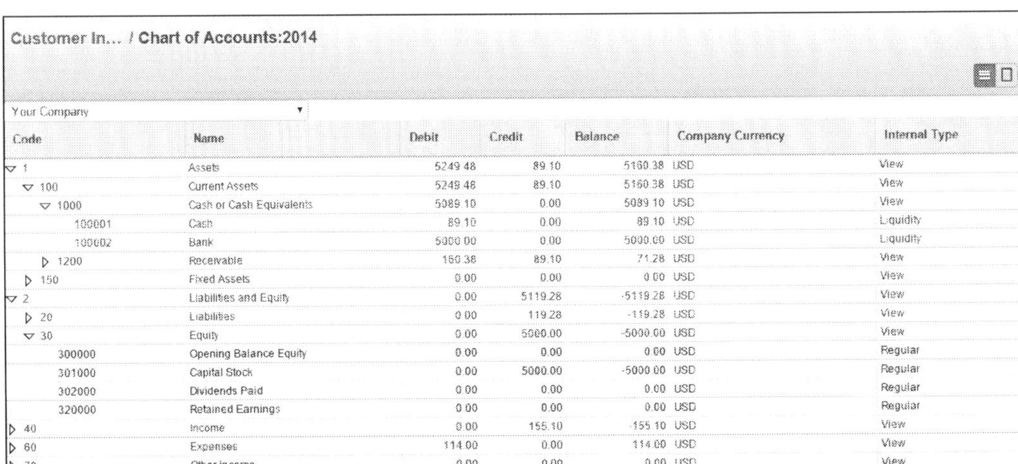

Customer In... / Chart of Accounts:2014

Your Company

Code	Name	Debit	Credit	Balance	Company Currency	Internal Type
1	Assets	5249.48	89.10	5160.38	USD	View
100	Current Assets	5249.48	89.10	5160.38	USD	View
1000	Cash or Cash Equivalents	5089.10	0.00	5089.10	USD	View
100001	Cash	89.10	0.00	89.10	USD	Liquidity
100002	Bank	5000.00	0.00	5000.00	USD	Liquidity
1200	Receivable	160.38	89.10	71.28	USD	View
150	Fixed Assets	0.00	0.00	0.00	USD	View
2	Liabilities and Equity	0.00	5119.28	-5119.28	USD	View
20	Liabilities	0.00	119.28	-119.28	USD	View
30	Equity	0.00	5000.00	-5000.00	USD	View
300000	Opening Balance Equity	0.00	0.00	0.00	USD	Regular
301000	Capital Stock	0.00	5000.00	-5000.00	USD	Regular
302000	Dividends Paid	0.00	0.00	0.00	USD	Regular
320000	Retained Earnings	0.00	0.00	0.00	USD	Regular
40	Income	0.00	155.10	-155.10	USD	View
60	Expenses	114.00	0.00	114.00	USD	View
70	Other income	0.00	0.00	0.00	USD	View

Summary

In this chapter, we examined how Odoo generates transactions and how you can use the Chart of Accounts to look at how those transactions originated. We examined both the Accounts Payable and Accounts Receivable accounts and how an invoice is posted. There are certainly more advanced Odoo topics such as bank reconciliation and recurring entries, which are beyond the scope of this book. Refer *Appendix, Locating Additional Odoo Resources*, to locate additional resources for more advanced Odoo subjects.

In the next chapter, we will discover how to back up and restore databases, as well as how to manage user access and group permissions.

7

Administering an Odoo Installation

With Odoo, within just a few minutes, you can have several applications installed and begin working with the system right away. In the previous chapters, we have already covered a great deal of functionality without spending a lot of time on configuration, access rules, languages, or other administrative topics.

Now we will take a closer look at important topics to consider when administering an Odoo installation. The topics we will cover in this chapter include the following:

- Basic administration of an Odoo installation
- Backing up and restoring Odoo databases
- Creating users and assigning access rights
- Internationalization, including currencies and language translation
- How to manage document sequences
- Multicompany configurations

Basic considerations for an Odoo administration

Like most IT installations, successful Odoo installations require proper planning and maintenance. Care must be taken in documenting important configuration details, and you must always have a business continuity plan in place that focuses on getting your Odoo installation back up and running within an acceptable period of time.

Having an implementation strategy

While you are learning Odoo and prototyping how you may use it for your business, you may not care much about a clear implementation strategy; however, once you have made the decision to use Odoo for your business, it is important to plan this strategy. While you may not have time to write out a 150-page detailed strategy, it is important to take the time to document your minimal plan before you begin setting up servers and installing Odoo.

The breadth of the project management and administration of an ERP system is beyond the scope of this book; however, there are several basic implementation considerations to keep in mind.

The development, staging, and production servers

One of the first considerations you will need to make when contemplating an Odoo installation is how you will configure servers for various Odoo instances that may be required during planning, deployment, and final production operations. For example, you don't want to be making modifications to Odoo's functionality in your live production system. Instead, you should always make changes and modifications in a development instance of Odoo where you can test your changes outside of the live database.

In addition to a development server and production server, it is often desirable to have an Odoo installation that users (and in some cases, business partners) can use to train and learn the operations of the system. Sometimes this installation is known as the staging server. This server will typically have all the tested changes and functionality of the live system but will be loaded with test data and configurations that are useful for training.

Each installation will have its own requirements and constraints. What is important is that you make these decisions early on in your Odoo configurations so that you can properly administer the installations all the way, from development to production.

Clear documentation of all Odoo configurations

Once you have decided what Odoo servers you require and how those installations should be configured, it is important that you create a clearly defined method to document all the details that go along with the setup. This can be as simple as a text or Microsoft Word document that is in a known place and is kept up to date. It can be as complex as using a full-blown project manager. Using cloud organization tools such as Dropbox, Evernote, and Google Documents provides you with several options on how you can document your Odoo installations.

It will be up to your own business policies to determine exactly where you store this information and how much detail you keep. One bit of advice is that it is almost always better to err on the side of having too much detail rather than too little. You will naturally need to be aware of how you secure user names and passwords and have a clear policy on how that information is securely stored.

Focusing on business continuity

Any business information system is only as good as its ability to recover from something going wrong. Despite having more reliable hardware and software, data can still get corrupted. Even the most dedicated employee can accidentally post bad data. The best security can be defeated. While everyone is trying their best, there are certainly still bugs lurking in Odoo's applications as you are reading this. No amount of planning can prevent a problem from occurring. This is why one of the most important tasks in administering an Odoo installation is making sure that you always have a clear recovery strategy.

Here are a few important tips to keep in mind:

- Regularly test your backups for recoverability. Backing up your data regularly does not mean that it is quickly recoverable. All too often, businesses may go months or even years without testing if the data they are backing up is recoverable.
- Have a strong archive of backups. Perform daily backups along with weekly and monthly snapshots. Oftentimes, data can be bad, deleted, or corrupted long before anyone knows anything has gone wrong. Someone might accidentally delete a set of old entries, and it may not be until a few months later that a manager writing a report finds critical holes in the data.
- Have contingency system options. Even if you plan on hosting locally, consider having a cloud server configured where you can run your Odoo installation in a pinch. Too often, you can have the backups ready to go, but if you are waiting on hardware to be fixed or a part to be delivered, you are going to extend your downtime. If you plan to use your development server as a backup production system, make sure you have the proper tested procedures in place. Don't make blindly optimistic assumptions about your system contingencies. Test them at least once or twice a year.
- Make sure you know how long it takes to fully recover your Odoo installation and what data would need to be re-entered into the system. If you back up nightly, and it takes you four hours to get your installation back up and running, make sure your internal business processes are clear on exactly what steps are required.

- Know exactly how much downtime costs your business and plan accordingly. Companies such as eBay and Amazon are in crisis if they are down for even a few minutes. More than an hour of downtime for them would make international news. While you may not have their uptime requirements, it is important that you understand exactly what risk your business does face if your Odoo installation goes down for two minutes, two hours, or even two days.

Backing up your Odoo database

It is critical in a production environment that, at minimum, you back up both your working Odoo application directories and the associated Postgres databases. Ideally, you will have server snapshots and a clear, tested business continuity plan in place. Still, it is valuable to know that Odoo provides a built-in database backup tool. I use it frequently in a variety of Odoo installations.

Before going ahead, it should be noted that this function will not be applicable to all Odoo installations. If you are running in a hosted Odoo environment where you have been provided a login and password to your database, then you will be provided with a specific backup procedure. Make sure you fully understand how it works and have a way to test and ensure that it functions as expected.

The easiest way to get to the backup database function is to navigate directly to the database manager. By adding `/web/database/manager` to the end of your Odoo URL, you will be taken directly to the Odoo database manager. The **Create a New Database** form will appear:

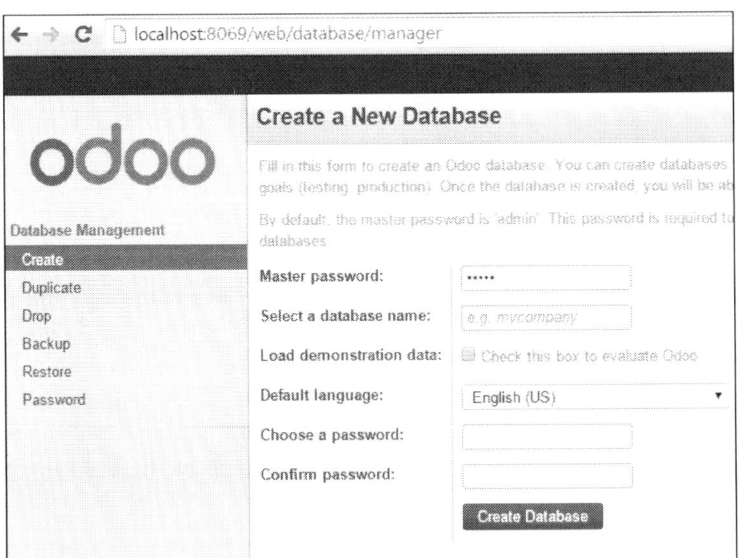

In the left menu under **Database Management**, you will see the **Backup** option. You may click this to bring up the Odoo Backup Database utility.

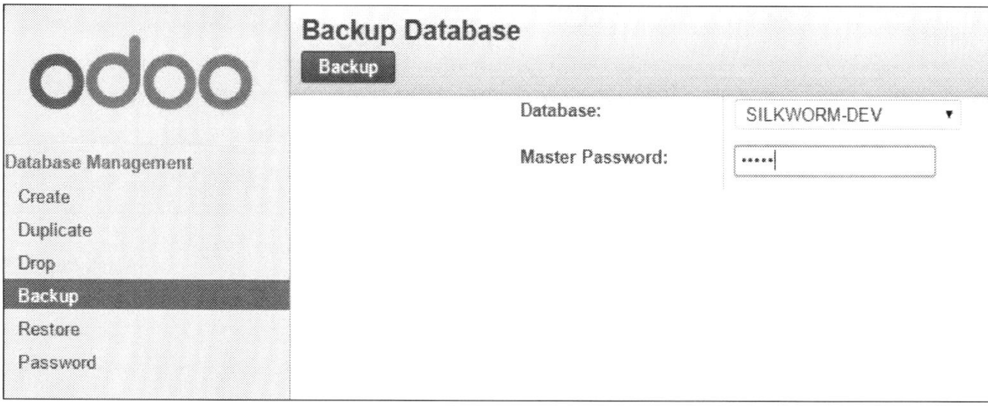

> Sometimes if you are having trouble with an Odoo installation, such as internal server errors and other system-related issues, you can navigate directly to the database manager to back up your database and perform operations that may help you recover from the problem.

You can use the pop-up list to select the database you wish to back up. Then, provide the **Master Password**. By default, this master password is admin. If the password is wrong, you will receive an **Access Denied** error.

Once you have selected the database and provided a valid master password, click the **Backup** button to begin backing up the database. The database will then download through your browser just like any other file you download from the Internet. If your database is extremely large, there is a chance that the file may not be easily downloaded.

Restoring an Odoo database

The ability to back up a database does little good unless you have the ability to restore the database and get it up and running again. Click the **Restore** button in the **Database Management** menu to bring up the **Restore Database** form:

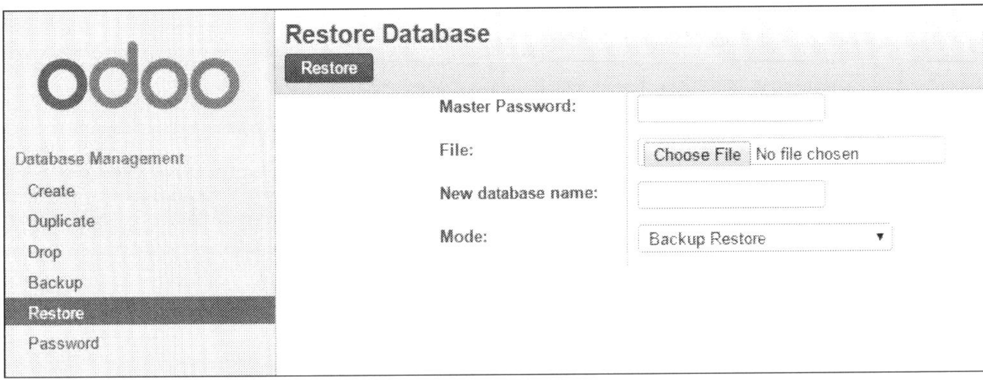

Here, specify the master password and choose the file you wish to restore. Once you have the file selected, you will need to specify a new database name within which the database will be restored.

You also get the option to choose either **Backup Restore** or **Copy of an existing database** as the **Mode** for restoration.

Administering users in Odoo

In any ERP system, it is important to understand completely how users and user access rights are managed. When Odoo is first installed, an admin account is created automatically. This is a superuser account, and it is the only one like it. In some systems, any account can be given full administration privileges. Odoo, however, gives permissions to the administration account that no other user in the system has.

> Specifically, all access rights are bypassed when using the administrator account. Much like the root account in Linux or Ubuntu, you always need to protect your administration account by using a strong password and keeping it secret.

Selecting a user to administer

Let's begin looking at how to select a user in Odoo and how they are tied to partner records within the rest of the Odoo applications.

To access the list of users, click on **Settings** in the main menu and then select **Users** under the **Users** section in the left-hand side menu:

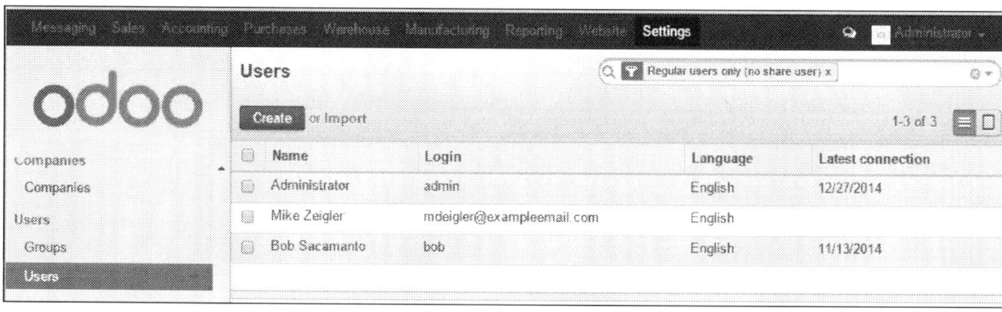

Click on **Mike Ziegler** to bring up the user and look at the additional options that are available:

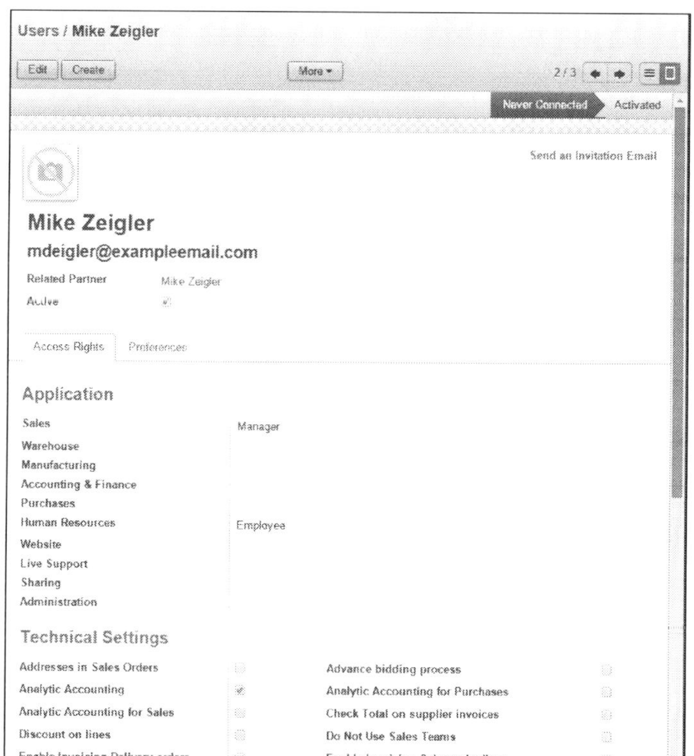

When you pull up a user in your own Odoo installation, it is unlikely that the contents of the preceding screenshot will look exactly like yours. Depending on the types of applications installed, the available application and technical settings will change. Also, it is common to see different versions of this window depending on the Odoo build you are running.

Understanding related partners

In Odoo, every company, customer, vendor, and user has a related partner record. In the user window, you can see the specified related partner for that user along with a hyperlink to bring up the partner record.

Go ahead and click the related partner link **Mike Zeigler** to bring up the partner record:

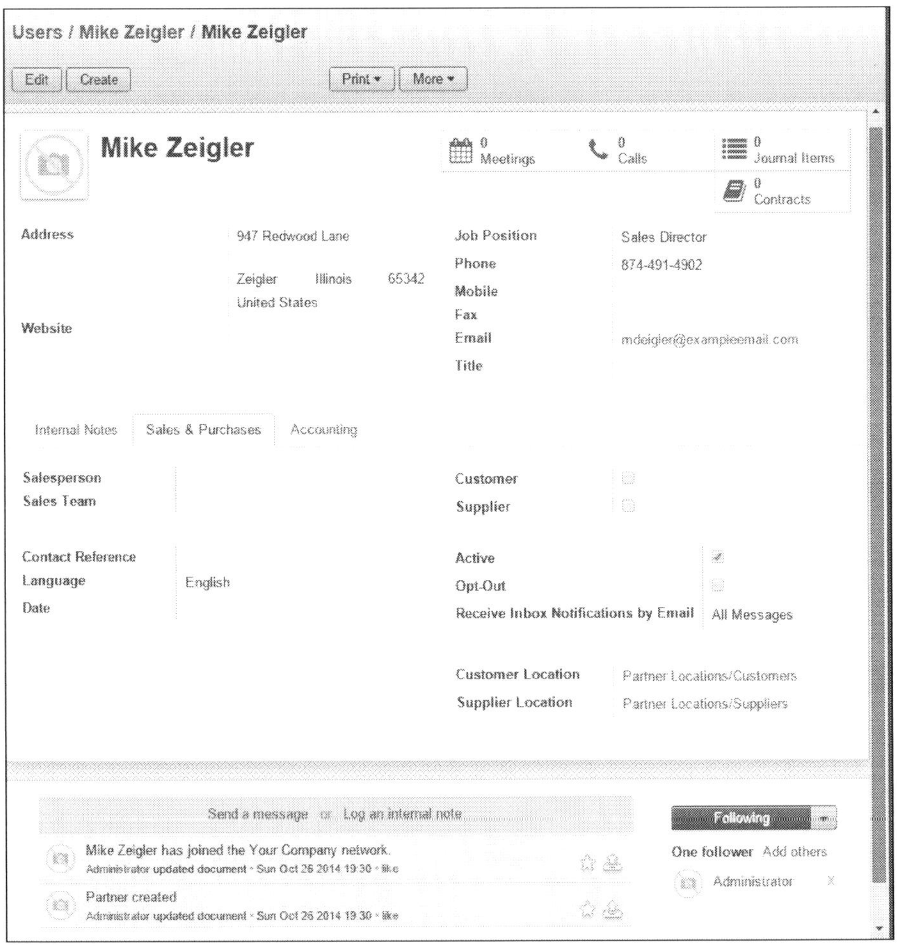

Here, we have selected the **Sales & Purchases** tab in the form so you can see that the **Customer** and **Supplier** checkboxes are not selected. If we wished, we could make Mike Zeigler a customer and/or a supplier in addition to being a user by selecting the appropriate checkbox. In many systems, there are separate files for vendors, customers, and employees. Odoo, however, considers every person a partner. In this case, this is the partner record for Mike Zeigler. We have filled in a little bit of address information.

When managing users, just remember that if you can't find what you are looking for inside the user record, it may be inside the associated partner record.

Managing user preferences

Using the breadcrumbs at the top of the form, we can navigate back to the user record and take a look at the preferences page:

In this section, we can specify important localization options that can dramatically change the user experience. We can specify one of the many dozen languages that Odoo supports, as well as the timezone and default sales team of the user.

Under the **Menus Customization** section, we can specify **Home Action** for our user. This is the action we want to occur when a user logs in to Odoo or when they navigate to the home page of the installation. Odoo provides friendly names for the various operations in the system.

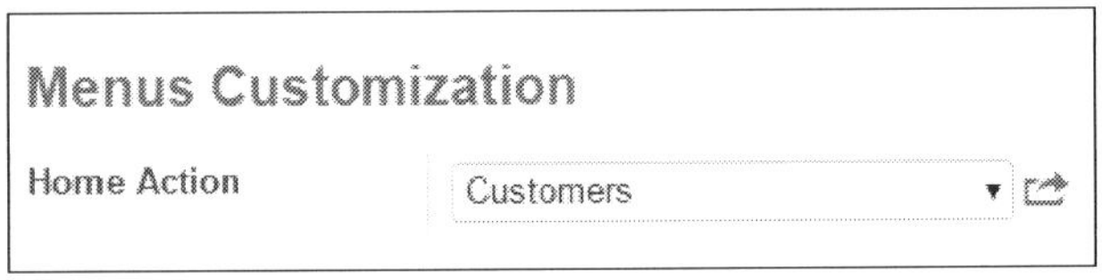

In the preceding example, we have set **Home Action** to **Customers**. The next time Mike logs in to Odoo, he will automatically be taken to the Customers listing in Odoo.

Finally, the **Preferences** section lets you manage your **Messaging and Social** options for the user.

Currently, there are only two options to receive inbox notifications by e-mail. Either he will never receive notifications or he will receive all the messages. You also can ask Odoo to display suggested groups for the user to join. Odoo makes this determination based on other users in the system, what sales teams they have joined, and other factors.

Finally, you can use the **Signature** rich text area at the bottom to specify a signature footer for the emails sent by this user.

> If desired, the user can change their own signature at any time by choosing **Preferences** from the menu in the upper right-hand corner of the screen.

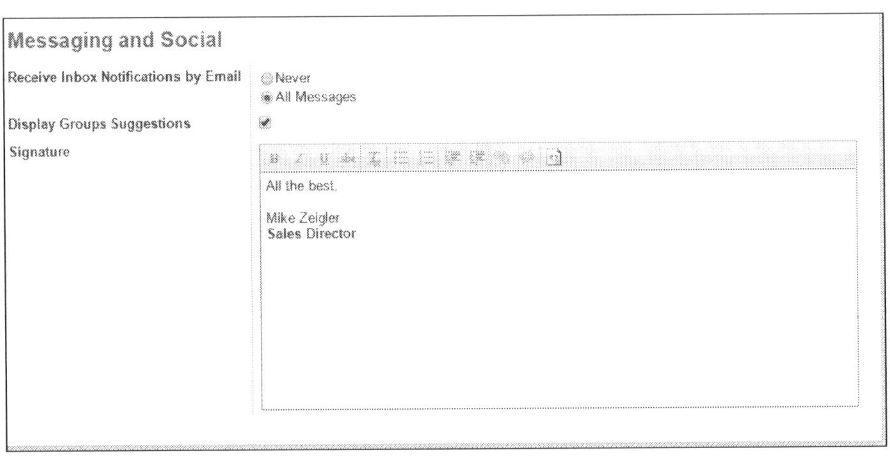

> Remember that if you are an administrator making these changes for another user, changing these settings will require that user to log out of the system so that their session is updated with the changes.
>
> If you are setting up multiple users, don't forget that you can use the **Duplicate** option under the **More** menu at the top of the form to make a copy of a user. This can be handy if an employee has left and has been replaced by another. You can deactivate the old employee profile and duplicate it for the new employee.

Understanding groups in Odoo

In Odoo, you give users permissions by assigning them to groups. Once a user is assigned to a group, they have all the permissions and options that are associated with that group. Users can belong, and often do belong, to more than one group. To see the list of groups that are currently available in your Odoo installation, go to the **Settings** menu at the top and then choose **Groups** under the **Users** section on the left.

As you will see, Odoo has several groups. Fortunately, once you understand how groups work, you will easily be able to determine exactly what options are available to a user when you put them in a specific group.

For our example, let's examine the **Sales / Manager** group. You can find this group by scrolling down the list of groups or use the search to narrow the list until you can find the group you are looking for.

As with other lists, clicking on the **Sales / Manager** group in the list of groups brings up the form:

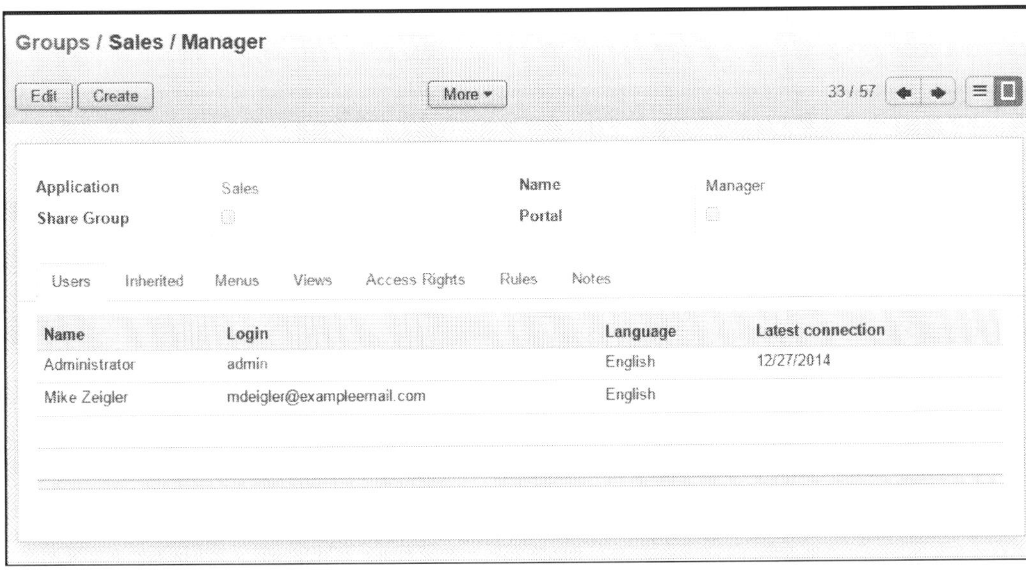

At the very top of the form on the left, you can see that a group is always associated with a given application. In this case, the group is associated with the **Sales** application. On the right is the name: **Manager**. Odoo automatically adds the / in between the application and the name when displaying the full name in the list.

As you can see, the first page lists users that are assigned to the group. Naturally, you can add and remove users from this group as required. You will also notice there are seven pages on this form that you will be using to configure exactly what permissions this group will offer to member users.

Understanding group inheritance in Odoo

Managing access permissions in any ERP system is always a challenge. Odoo makes managing user permissions easier by allowing you to inherit permissions from multiple groups and then define a new group that automatically includes all the permissions from those groups. With proper planning, you can create groups that provide your users with the permissions they require.

Let's take a look at the groups inherited by the **Sales / Manager** group.

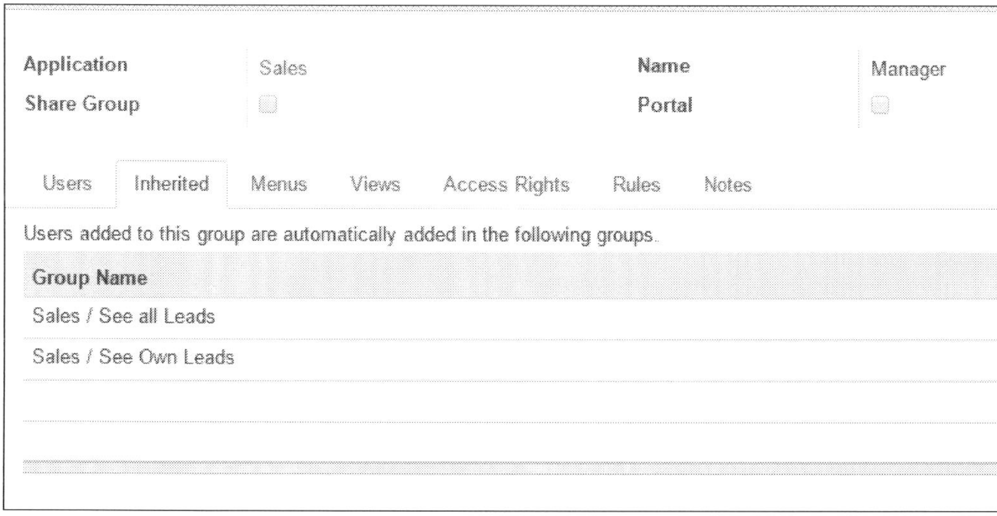

The **Sales / Manager** group has both the **See All Leads** and the **See Own Leads** groups included in the **Inherited** list. Just like the instructions say, users added to the **Sales / Manager** group will automatically be added into the **See All Leads** and **See Own Leads** groups.

With this in mind, manager groups such as this will most often include all the other groups that have more restrictions in the system. In this case, looking at the **See Own Leads** group will let you see the most restrictive group permissions for the Sales group.

Defining menus for your group

Groups provide you with a direct way to determine which menus users in that group have access to. In the case of the **Sales / Manager** group, we have additional menu options listed. Members of the **See all Leads** or the **See Own Leads** groups will not see these menus unless they are also members of **Sales / Manager**.

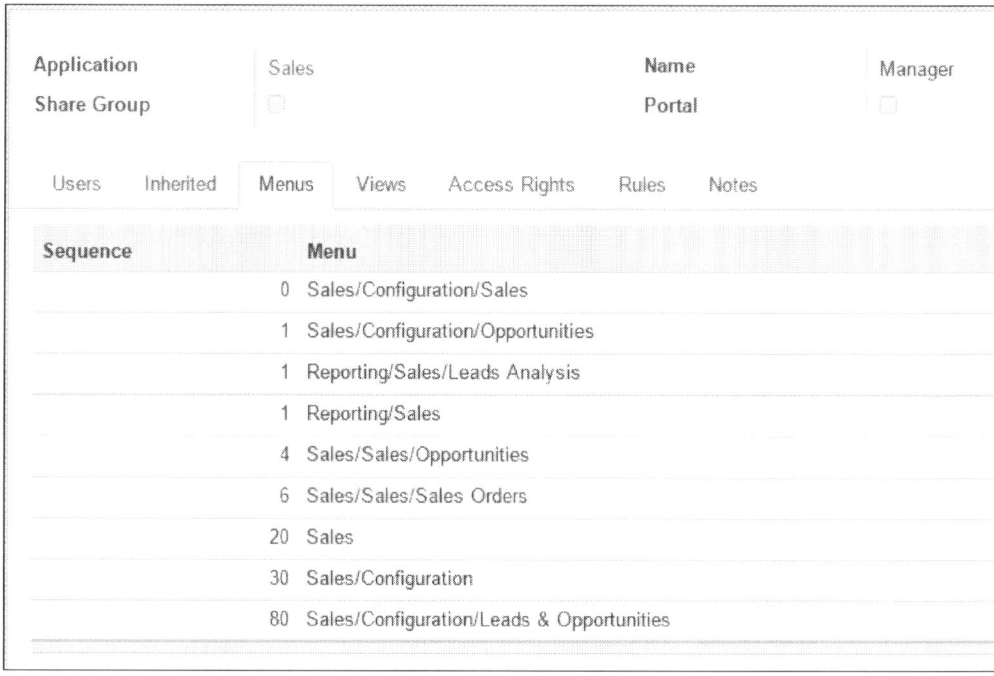

If, for example, you wanted to allow users in the **See All Leads** group to view the **Leads Analysis** report, you could remove the menu from the list in this manager group and add the menu to the **See All Leads** group. Because the manager group inherits from the **See All Leads** group, they will still be able to see the menu in addition to users that are only in the **See All Leads** group.

Now with the new website applications, Views can be used to limit what information is displayed on a web form. In the following example, we can see how the public group has rights to the view that allows them to log in to the website.

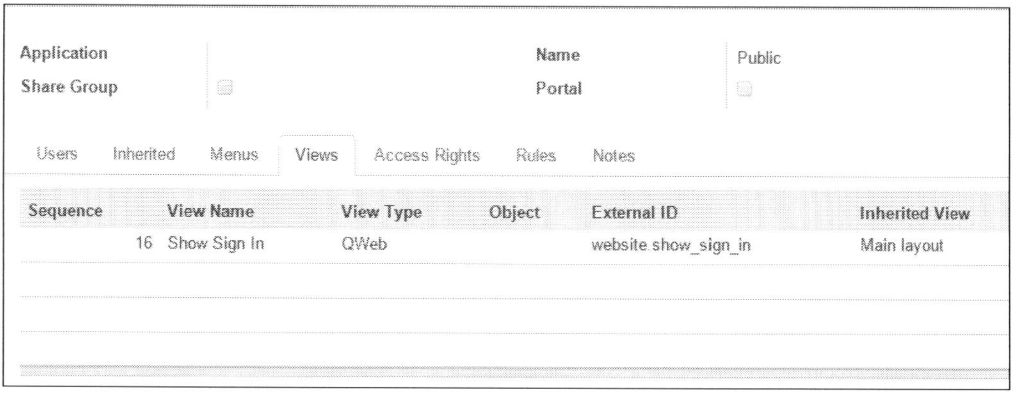

Also, notice that views can inherit from other views. In this case, the **Show Sign In** view is inheriting from the **Main layout** view.

You can expect that there will be more administration of Views and their groups in future versions of Odoo as more website tools are developed.

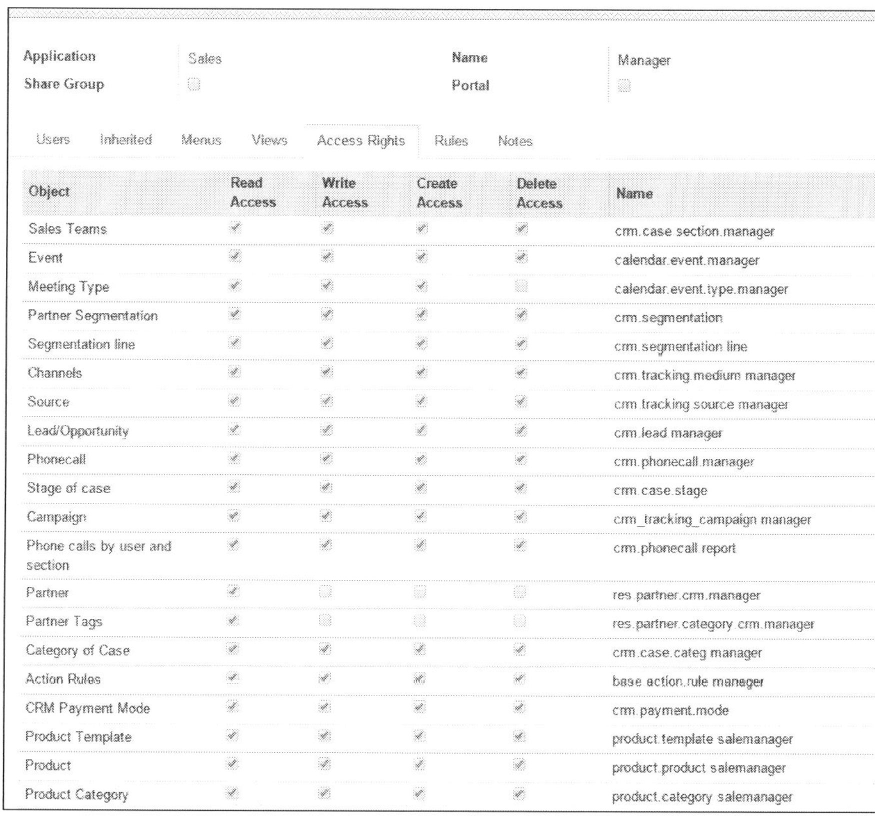

Access Rights is where you define exactly what models the group has access to. In Odoo, the term model represents a business entity object and its related operations. You can determine for each object if the group should have any combination of Read, Write, Create, or Delete access. For example, in the preceding listing, we can see the Sales / Manager group has the ability to read, write, and create meeting types, but they cannot delete meeting types.

Now, let's take a quick look at the access rights of the **See Your Own Leads** group.

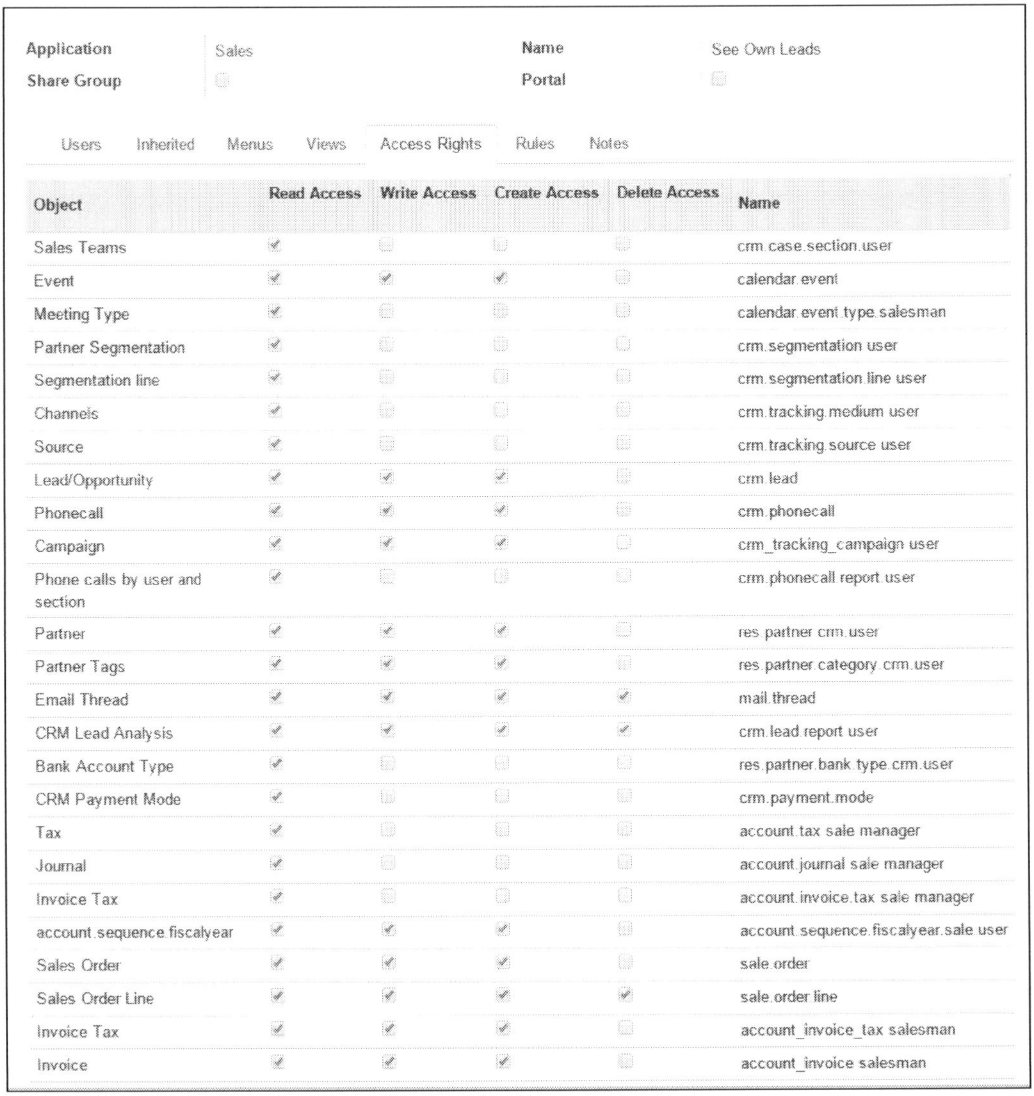

The manager group we looked at previously had a lot of permissions to create and write records; but the **See Own Leads** group only has read access for many objects, such as Meeting Type, Channels, Tax, Journal, and so on. This group can see the information, and it can be selected on forms and reports, but they do not have permission to modify records in those objects.

Understanding record rules in Odoo

Sometimes in a system, you want users to have access to a particular model but not to all the records in that model. For example, you may want users to have access to phone calls within the system. But, for some groups, you only want the user to have access to the records of their own phone calls, not the phone calls of everyone in the system. When you need to control user access based on the contents of records within a model, you can define **Rules**.

For this example, we are looking at the rules for the **See Own Leads** group. Because this is a highly restricted group, there are many rules that limit users in this group to only see the records that are personally associated with them.

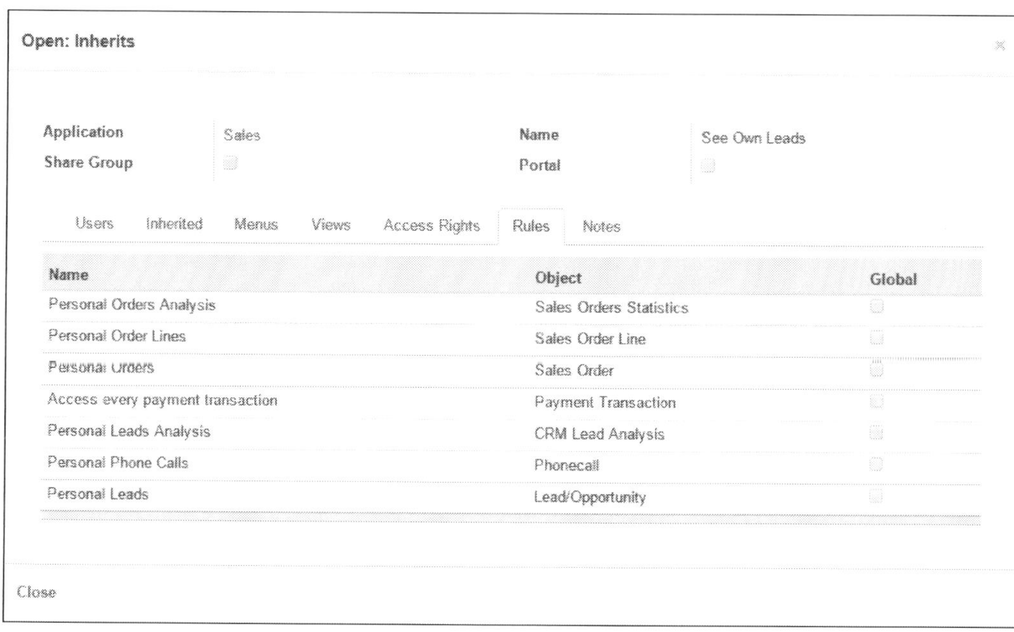

Typically, manager groups will have few or no rules because they do not have restrictions on what records they can access. Groups such as **See Own Leads** have quite a few rules so that the users can't see records that do not belong to them. Let's take a quick look at the **Personal Orders** rule to see how we can construct a rule that limits what records a user can access.

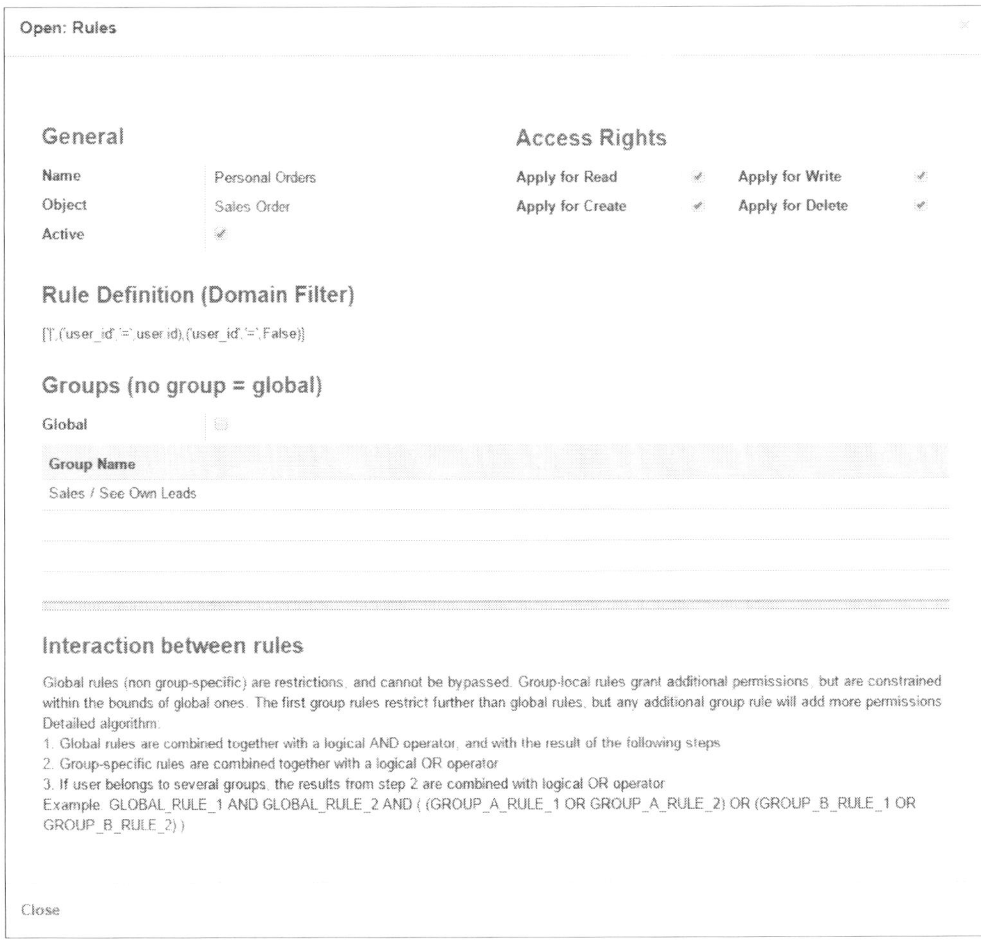

Odoo provides a pretty good description at the bottom of the form on how rules interact. If no groups are specified in the list, this means this rule will apply to everyone—all groups. As you can see on the right, you can specify the access rights for this rule. So you could have a rule in which a user can access (read) certain records, but they cannot create, write, or delete records.

The most important part of the rule is the **Rule Definition** or **Domain Filter**. This filter is applied to each record to determine whether that record should be available. While the syntax may look cryptic, you can see that the system is checking whether the user ID is equal to the current user ID. This filter will be true if you are specifically looking at your own records or records that have not been assigned to any specific user.

> When making your own rules, copy and paste the rules from a similar rule to make it easier to get the syntax right. Also, be careful about changing rules in a live system. It is possible that an error in your syntax could make it impossible to access certain parts of the system.

Internationalization in Odoo

Even with a conventional English installation of Odoo, it is possible to configure it to work with a variety of languages, time zones, and currencies without downloading any additional add-ons. Odoo has robust features for configuring a global ERP system that can meet the demands of today's multicultural business environment.

As with most Odoo features, you only need to configure the international features you require for your business. For example, you may do business entirely in US dollars but would like to offer Odoo in Spanish for some of your workstations, users, or portal customers. On the other hand, if you are purchasing from a supplier in an alternative currency, you may choose to create a special price list that allows you to do business in that currency.

Configuring language translation

Like many of the other options in Odoo we have discussed, business requirements should drive how you configure your system. For our real-world example, it has become increasingly desirable to offer a native Spanish Odoo interface for some employees. Let's see how we can configure Odoo to provide other language alternatives.

Fortunately, Odoo makes this very easy. Under the **Settings** menu, simply choose **Load a Translation** under the **Translations** section on the left.

You will find quite a few languages to choose from in the list. At the time of writing this book, there are more than 80 languages to choose from.

> Many of these languages are community supported and translation will certainly vary. Furthermore, ERP systems can often be confusing even for users that speak the language fluently. Take the time to train users so they understand all their processes well.

You should use **Overwrite Existing Terms** if you have made custom modifications to a language translation and now wish to overwrite them. You also can tell Odoo to perform a translation on the websites as well.

After the language is loaded, you will get a confirmation message and instructions on the next step you need to take to begin using the installed language:

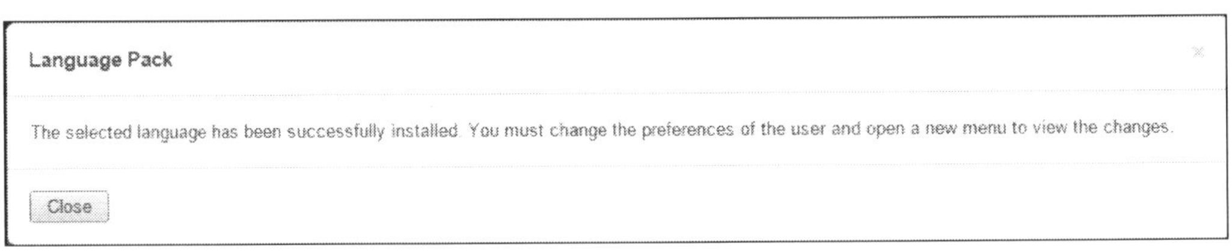

Now that we have installed the new language, we can assign that language to our users and even our customers and suppliers. As seen in the following screenshot, we have set Mike Zeigler's language choice to Spanish. Odoo also allows you to specify the timezone either by the GMT offset or by common regions. In this case, we have chosen Cancun as the timezone.

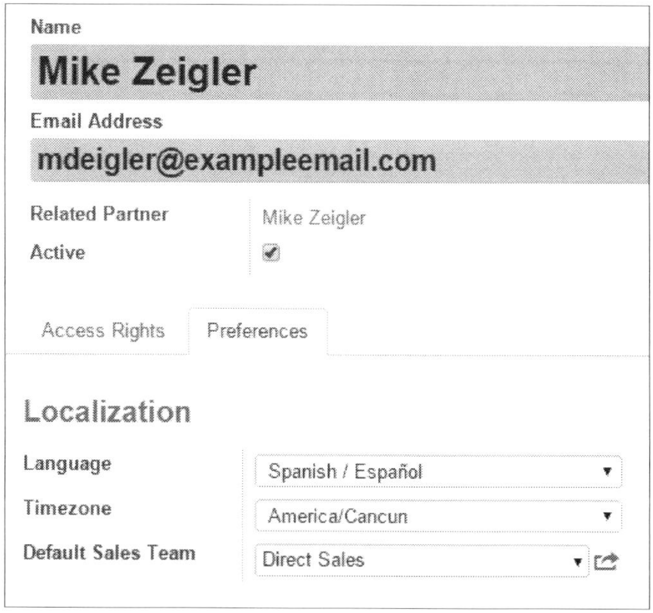

After the changes are saved and the user has logged back in, we will see that their interface has changed over to Spanish.

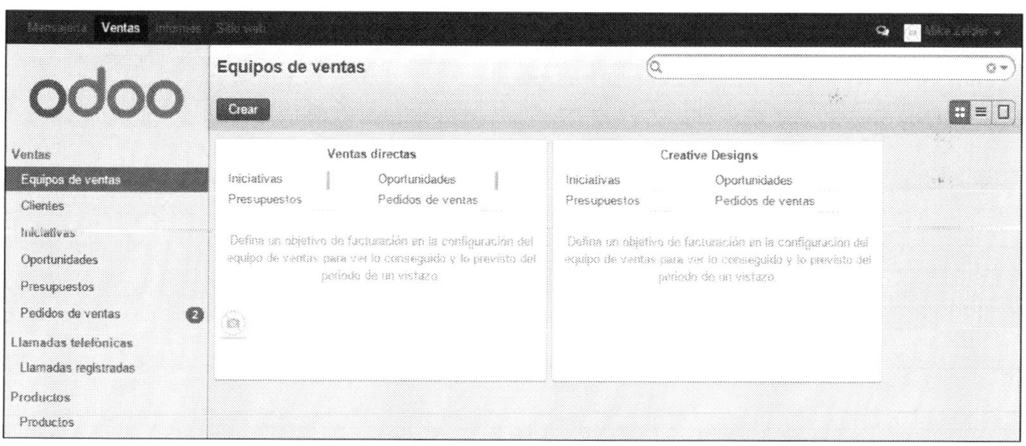

Using translation features to customize Odoo for your business

Even if you do not plan to use Odoo's translation features for alternative languages, they can be useful to change forms to better fit a given business requirement.

To see the translated terms for a given language, navigate to **Settings**, and under **Application Terms**, choose **Translated Terms**.

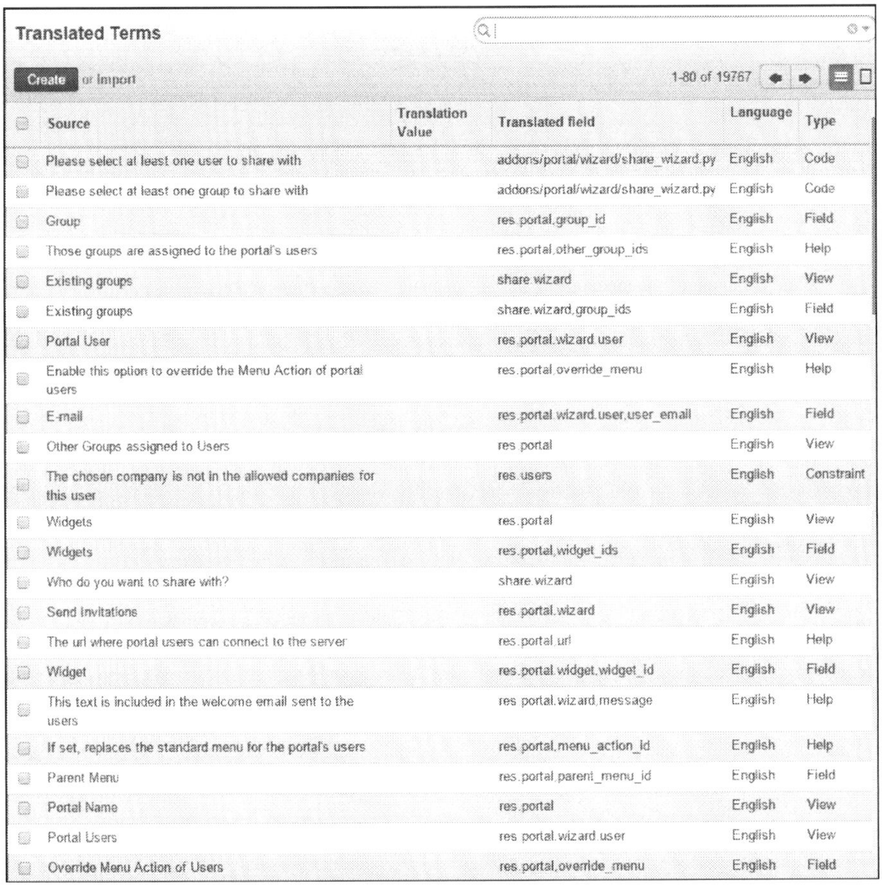

Source	Translation Value	Translated field	Language	Type
Please select at least one user to share with		addons/portal/wizard/share_wizard.py	English	Code
Please select at least one group to share with		addons/portal/wizard/share_wizard.py	English	Code
Group		res.portal,group_id	English	Field
Those groups are assigned to the portal's users		res.portal,other_group_ids	English	Help
Existing groups		share.wizard	English	View
Existing groups		share.wizard,group_ids	English	Field
Portal User		res.portal.wizard.user	English	View
Enable this option to override the Menu Action of portal users		res.portal,override_menu	English	Help
E-mail		res.portal.wizard.user,user_email	English	Field
Other Groups assigned to Users		res.portal	English	View
The chosen company is not in the allowed companies for this user		res.users	English	Constraint
Widgets		res.portal	English	View
Widgets		res.portal,widget_ids	English	Field
Who do you want to share with?		share.wizard	English	View
Send Invitations		res.portal.wizard	English	View
The url where portal users can connect to the server		res.portal,url	English	Help
Widget		res.portal.widget,widget_id	English	Field
This text is included in the welcome email sent to the users		res.portal.wizard,message	English	Help
If set, replaces the standard menu for the portal's users		res.portal,menu_action_id	English	Help
Parent Menu		res.portal,parent_menu_id	English	Field
Portal Name		res.portal	English	View
Portal Users		res.portal.wizard.user	English	View
Override Menu Action of Users		res.portal,override_menu	English	Field

Notice that in the second-last column the first page has all English translations and that the record count is 19,767. Nearly every message, menu, and label in Odoo is driven off the translations in this table. That is how Odoo can easily adapt and support dozens of languages; but we can also use these translations to change terms to make them more business-friendly for our requirements. For instance, you could change Fiscal Position in Sales to Tax Status or change Meetings in the Calendar module to Activities. Neither will affect how the system works; these are just labels.

International currencies

As you saw, it was quite easy and straightforward to configure Odoo for multiple languages. Currencies, however, will require more planning and testing during system configuration. Unlike languages, multiple currencies have the ability to directly modify the amount of money you are receiving or paying out. If the system has misconfigured currency settings, you are almost guaranteed to have inaccurate transactions within your system at some point. Make sure you thoroughly test all scenarios when working with multiple currencies in Odoo or any other ERP system.

To set up multiple currencies in Odoo, navigate to the **Settings** menu and select **Accounting** under the **Configuration** settings:

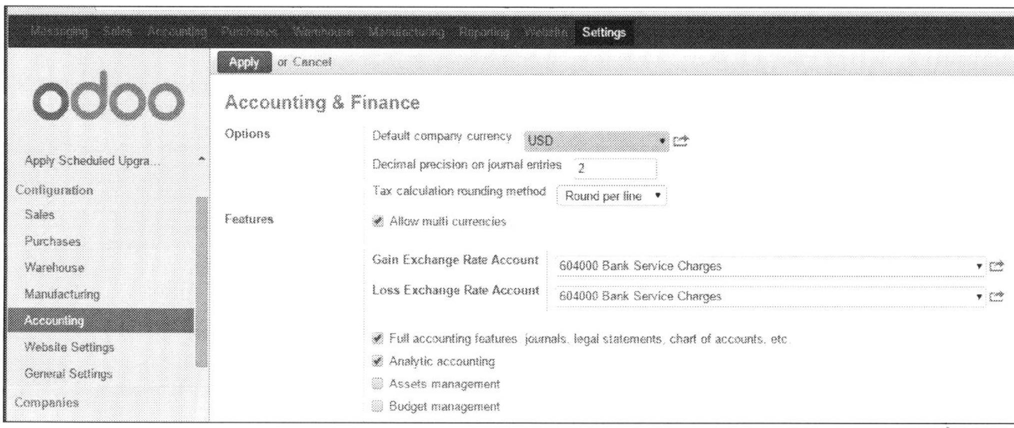

Under **Features**, the first option is **Allow multi currencies**. Check this and you will get the option to select the accounts to which the differences between exchange rates will be posted. When setting up a full production system, you will want to assign appropriate accounts as discussed in *Chapter 6, Configuring Accounting Finance*. However, you can post to Bank Service Charges as an appropriate typed income/expense account for the purpose of this example.

Once you click on **Apply**, Odoo will work for a few seconds and then return you to the same screen. You will not notice the changes in multicurrency until you look at how some of your documents now appear in Odoo.

> As with configuring other Odoo options, it is a good idea to use *Shift + refresh* in your browser to force Odoo to present any new menus or settings resulting from your changes.

Purchasing in a different currency

After you select multicurrency, the purchasing system immediately allows you to begin purchasing products in alternative currencies. Create a new purchase order and observe the new currency selection available at the top of the form.

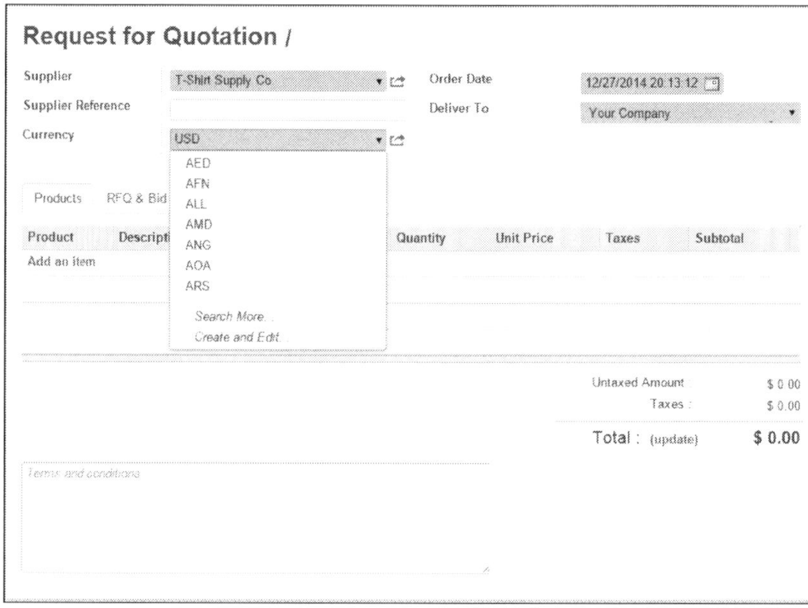

At the time of writing this book, there are 160 currencies in the list. Once you choose a currency, you will see the symbol change at the bottom of the purchase order to show that you are now purchasing in the new currency.

If you continue, however, and try to add a product to your purchase order, you will quickly find out that unit cost does not auto-populate from the cost you have specified in the product file. As you are now using multiple currencies, either you need to provide detailed pricing information, or you must enter the amount on each purchase order you create.

Managing supplier price lists

Now that we know we are going to have suppliers from whom we need to purchase in a different currency, let's see how we can set up a price list for this alternative currency so that when we order products, we do not have to re-enter our costs.

We must first turn on multiple supplier price lists. Select **Settings** and then **Purchases** under the **Configuration** section. There, check the **Manage pricelist per supplier** option and click on **Apply**.

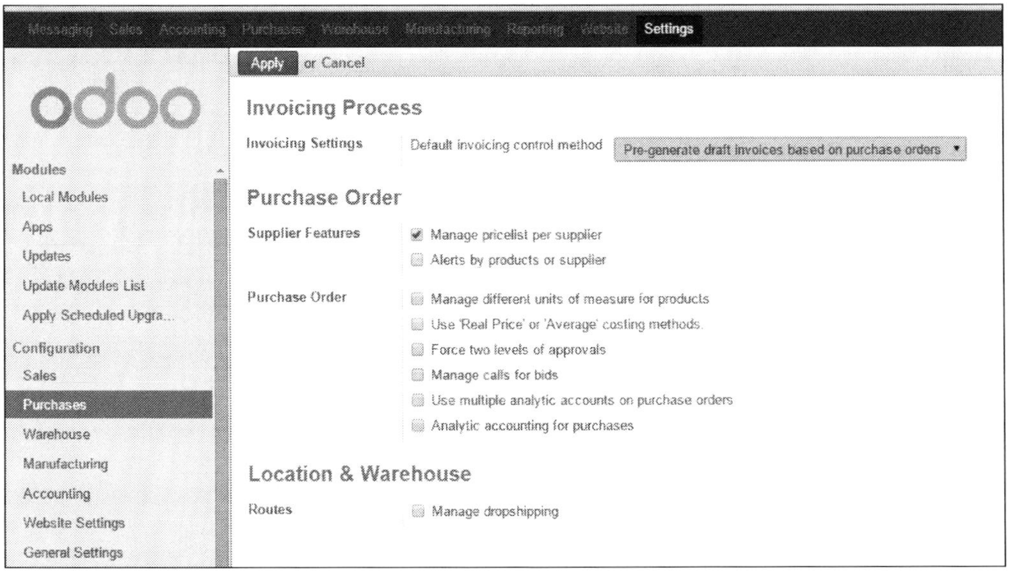

After we have turned on the option to manage pricelists per supplier, in the **Purchase** menu, we can expand the **Pricelists** section under **Configuration** and choose **Pricelists** to see the one default pricelist that is already installed.

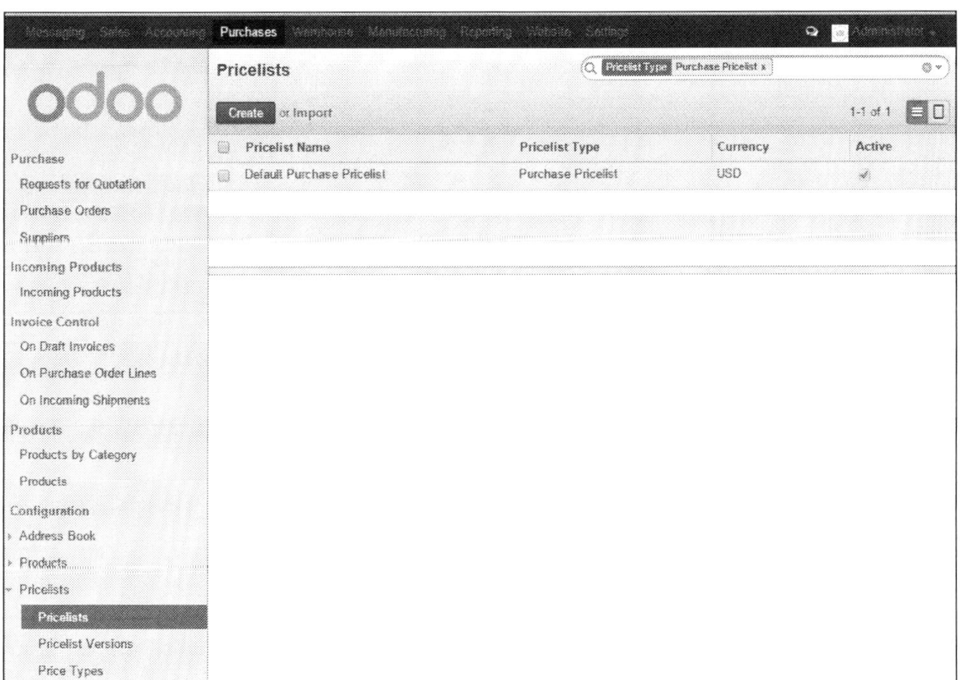

Before making any changes to your existing configuration or adding a new pricelist to your own system, I highly recommend you look at how the existing pricelist is configured. Fortunately, adding a price list for the EUR currency is easy. Create a **Default Purchase Pricelist** and simply give it the EUR currency. The rule is a minimum quantity of zero. This way the pricelist will apply to any product.

Here is the pricelist record configured to handle the EUR currency:

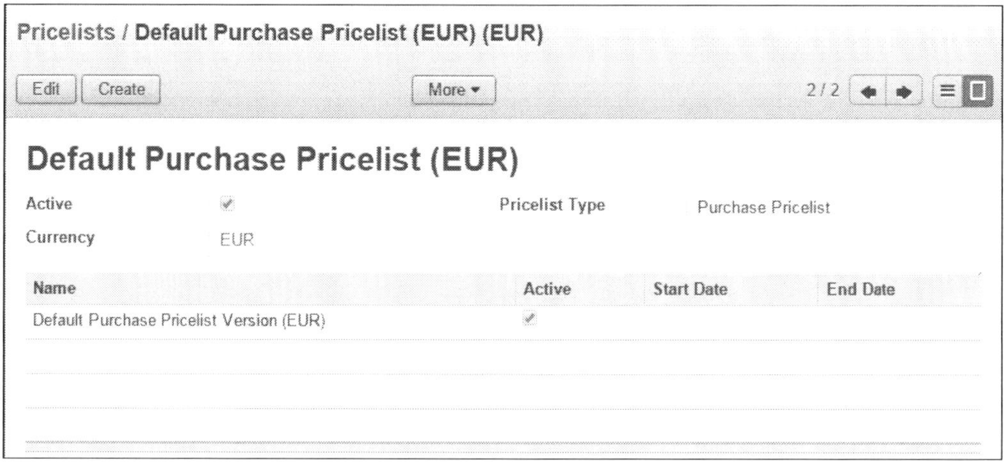

Now we can assign this pricelist and use it to price products in EUR within our purchasing system.

Managing sequences in Odoo

When you are setting up a system for your business, there is a very good chance that the default naming of documents and the number sequences that Odoo defines may not be ideal. A simple example is that you most likely do not want your invoices starting at number 00001 when you may already have produced thousands of invoices. You would want the numbers to start where the old system left off.

Additionally, sequences in Odoo don't just manage the numbering of your documents. They also manage how the document name looks inside Odoo. To see the current sequences defined by Odoo, navigate to the **Settings** menu and choose **Sequences** under **Sequences & Identifiers**.

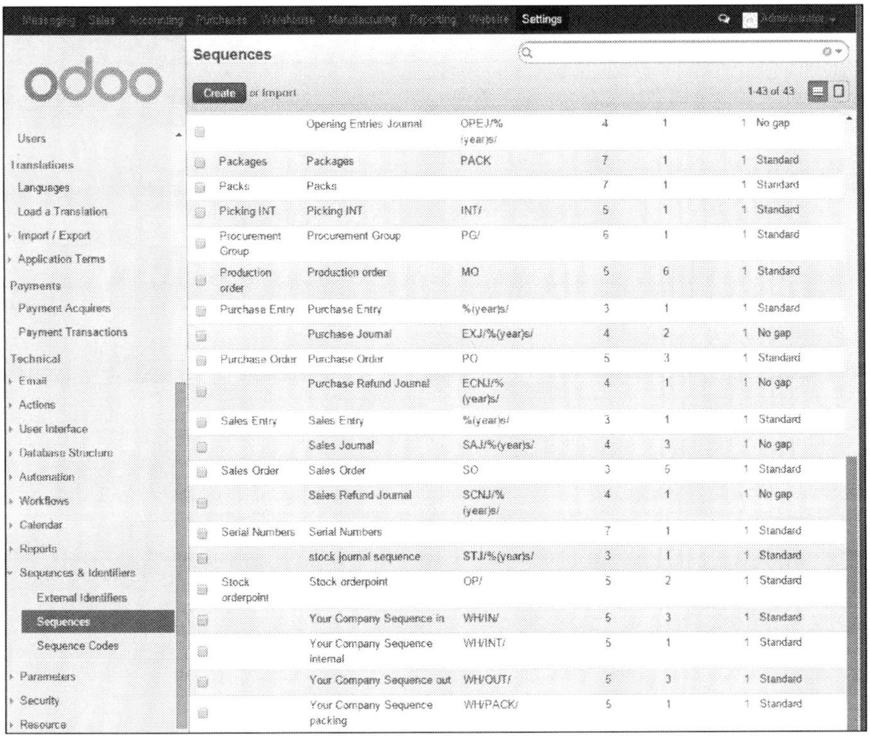

Here, we have scrolled down so you can see the sales order sequence. Click on it to bring up its details.

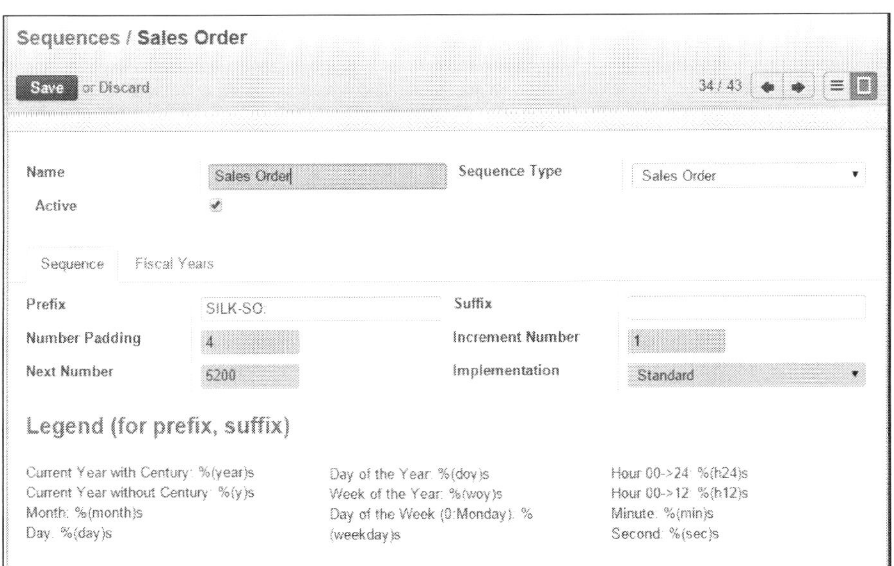

The prefix SO is generic and could potentially match a document identifier from another company.

For this example, we have changed the **Prefix** of the sales orders in our Odoo installation so that they will begin with `SILK-SO`. It is common in a business situation that you may wish to prefix your documents with a notation that identifies that document specifically to your company. Also, notice we have bumped up the **Next Number** to 5200.

After you save the changes to the sequence, any new documents will now use the new sequence definition.

Multiple companies in Odoo

Odoo has the ability to manage multiple companies within the same database. This feature allows you to consolidate some of your system administration and manage operations that are more complex. Multiple-company configuration is an advanced topic. You should be very comfortable with working with single-company configurations before you begin looking into multiple-company configurations. Also, Odoo's warehouse management and analytic accounting abilities are often a more preferable way to manage operations than by configuring multiple companies.

A good general rule is that if they are not separate legal entities, then most likely they should not be set up as multiple companies in Odoo. However, every business requirement is different, and the ability to use multiple companies in Odoo may allow you to easily implement a solution that otherwise may have been rather difficult with just a single company.

To set up Odoo to begin using multiple companies, navigate to the **Settings** menu and under **Configuration**, choose **General Settings**:

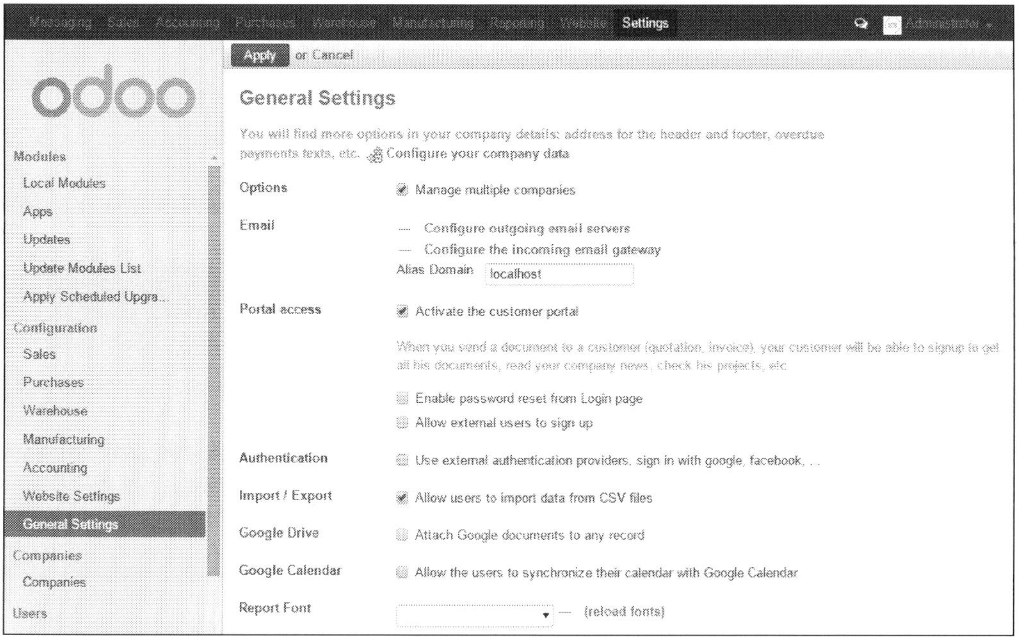

After you have checked **Manage multiple companies** and clicked on **Apply**, Odoo will work for a few seconds to configure the installation for multiple companies. Note that this operation can take more than a few seconds on some systems.

First off, by default, Odoo does not turn on multicompany operations for a user even though you have configured multicompany operations through the general settings. Even the administrator user must go in and check the option to **Manage multiple companies**.

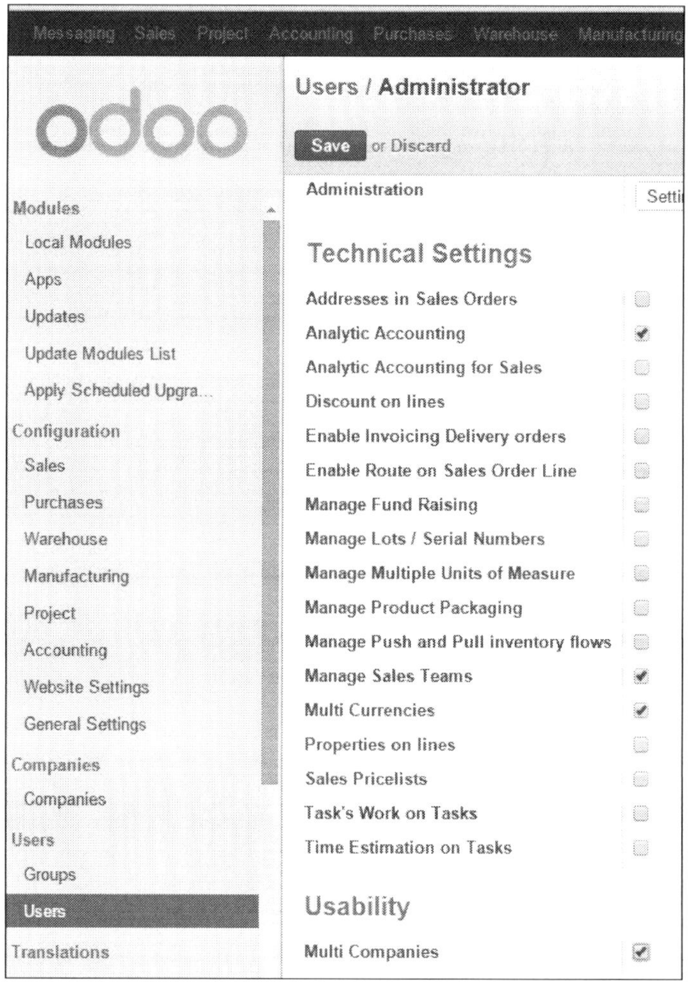

As with other operations that may make major changes to your Odoo installation, use *Shift* + Refresh to tell your browser to reload Odoo completely.

Setting up a second company in Odoo

Now we can create a second company. With Odoo, you can have multiple companies that are all independent of each other, or you can have child companies to which you can link charts of accounts and other operations to roll up into the parent company. For example, we have created a new company named `Euro Shirts` and have set `Silkworm, Inc.` as the parent company.

For our example, we choose **France** and using the Euro as the default currency.

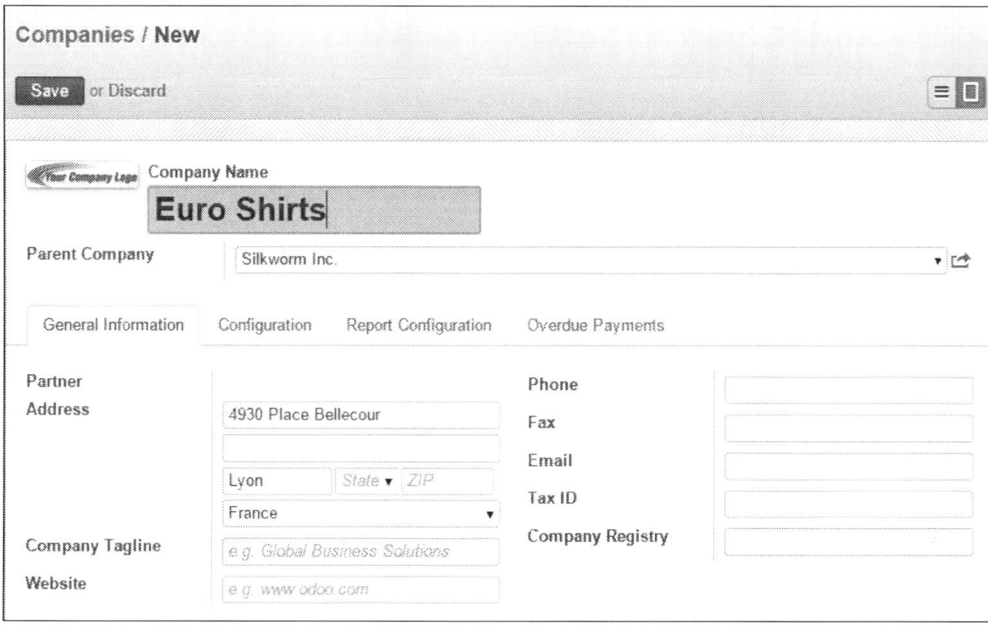

Now that we have defined a second company, we will go into our **Accounting** settings and see how we can define our chart of accounts.

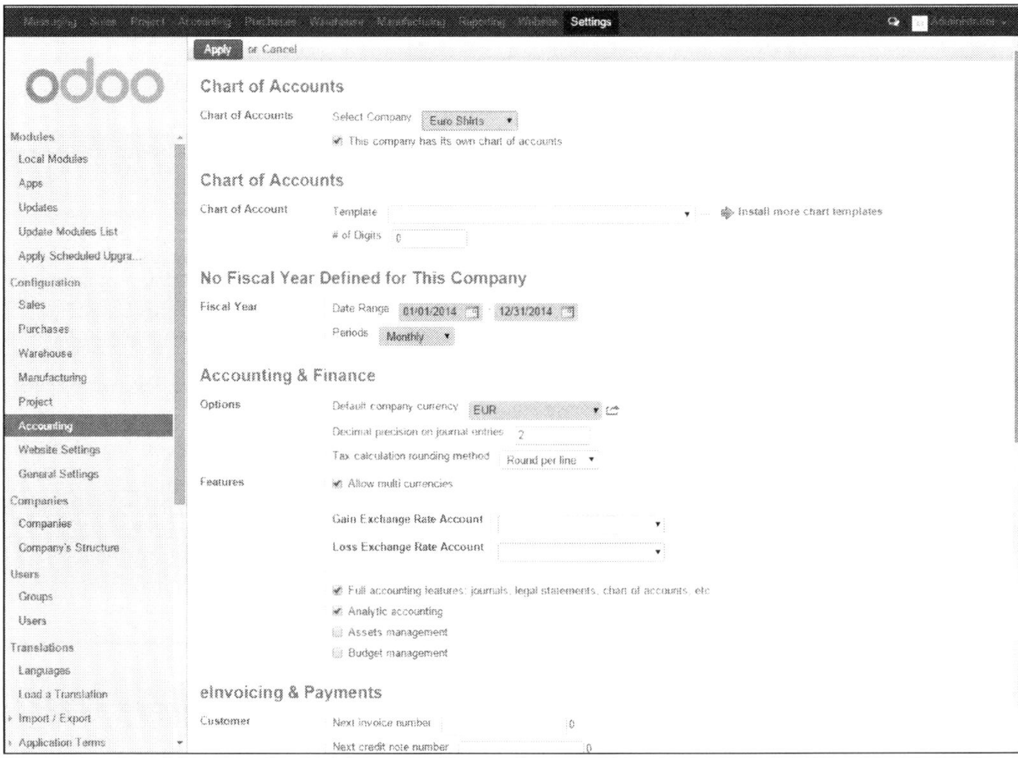

Notice that we now have the opportunity to set up a chart of accounts specifically for our new company along with its fiscal years. Also, take note that at the very top of the form we have specified that **This company has its own chart of accounts**.

Implementing a multicompany solution

As was previously stated, setting up a multicompany system is complex. While the system will work much the same as it did previously, it is important that you understand how a multicompany system affects every operation within the system. Customers, users, suppliers, and the chart of accounts all tie into multiple company operations. This chapter gives you the basics to get started with configuring a multicompany setup, but the final configurations will take a great deal of planning and fine-tuning to have a truly successful installation.

Summary

In this chapter, we examined some of the things you should consider when administering an Odoo installation, such as planning your server configuration and establishing good practices to ensure business continuity in the case of failure. We discovered how to back up and restore databases, as well as how to manage user access and group permissions.

Later in the chapter, we looked at internationalization and configured Odoo to handle multiple languages and international currency. We learned how to change Odoo sequences so your documents can have the formats and numbering that work for your business requirements. Finally, we took a brief look at setting up a multiple company configuration in Odoo.

In the next chapter, we will take a look at Human Resource applications and how you can configure Odoo to make it easier to recruit, interview, hire, and manage employees.

8

Implementing the Human Resources Application

Over the past few decades, companies have had increasing demands placed upon them to keep track of employee-related information. Odoo has a variety of applications that can help your company organize this information regarding your employees. Some of these applications, such as timesheets and attendance records, can become critical processes to help a company control costs. In this chapter, we will look at how you can integrate the Human Resources application.

Specifically, this chapter will cover the following:

- Installation of the Employee Directory
- How to create employees, setup job titles, and enter employee-related information.
- Learn how to create employee timesheets to track time
- Use analytic accounting to track time related to tasks
- Learn about Odoo's recruitment features

A modular approach to Human Resources

Like the rest of Odoo, the Human Resources application allows you to implement the functionality you need today, and then later, add additional modules. This approach makes it much easier to start using Odoo right away, to solve specific company needs. The best way to be successful with implementing a system is to plan ahead and implement in stages. Once you are successful at putting one application in place, then you can move on to putting additional applications in place.

Installing the Employee Directory

When you install the base Odoo applications, you get the ability to manage system users, but you will notice that there are no menu options for entering and managing employees. To begin working with the Human Resources application, you will need to install the base Employee Directory application.

Go to the **Settings** menu and install the **Employee Directory** application using the same process as the previous Odoo applications.

After you have installed the **Employee Directory** application, you will see a new menu at the top, **Human Resources**. Clicking on the menu will take you to the list of employees. The default view for employees in Odoo 8 is the Kanban view:

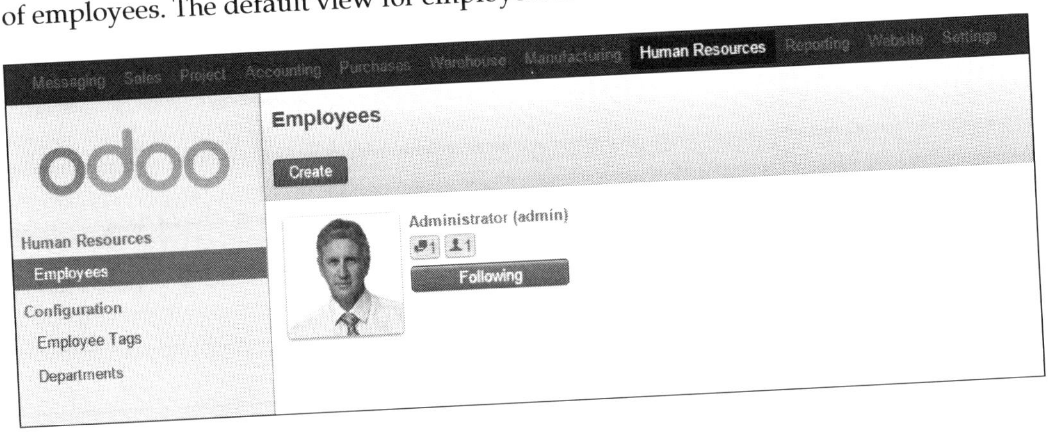

The Administrator account comes with an image already loaded for the user. So the gentleman you see in the preceding screenshot is likely the same in your Odoo 8 installation.

> If you have added users besides the Administrator account, they will be considered employees and included in the list. All users are employees, but not all employees are users.

Creating a new employee

Clicking on the **Create** button will bring up the form for you to begin entering a new employee into Odoo:

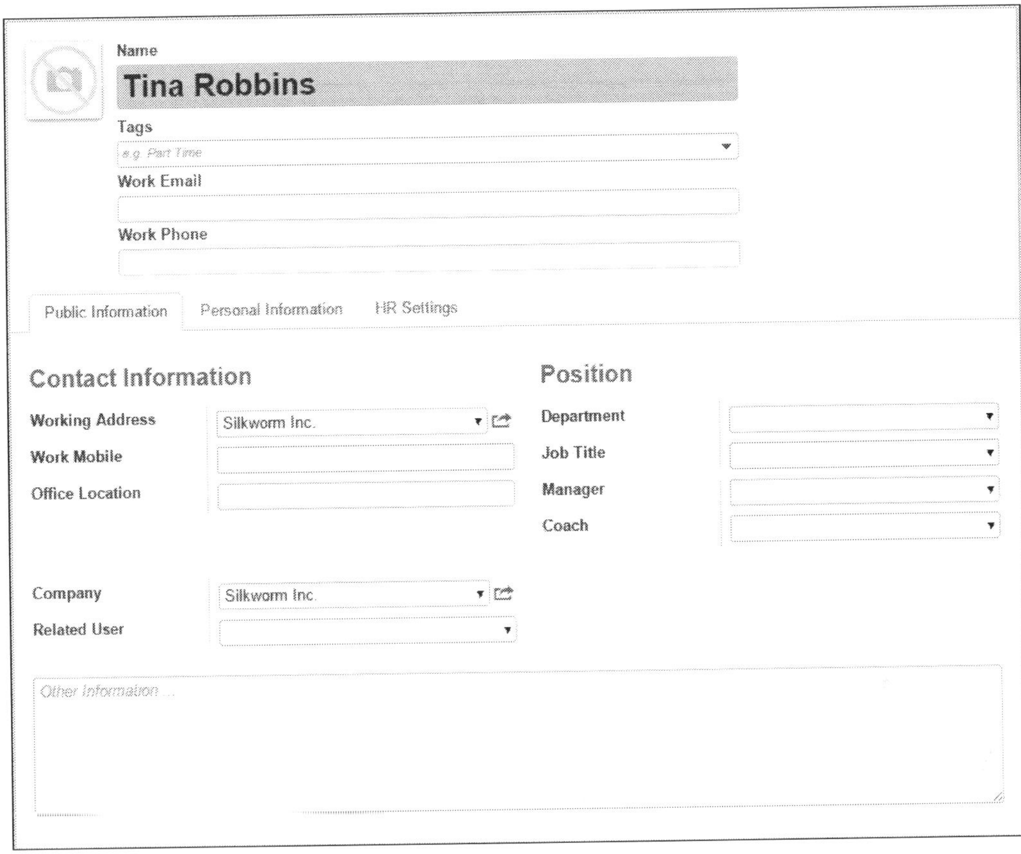

The only required field in the employee form is **Name**. All the other fields are optional. Odoo will default the working address to the company address. While most fields are self-explanatory, we will go over several of the more important fields to take into consideration.

Related User

In the **Contact information** section, the **Related User** field will allow you to associate the employee with an existing user account in Odoo. Simply select the user from the pop-up list and choose which user you want associated with the employee. It is also possible to add users on the fly by choosing **Create...** from the **Related User** dropdown.

Department

The employee's department is a common way for a company to organize employees. In our example, we are going to create a production department.

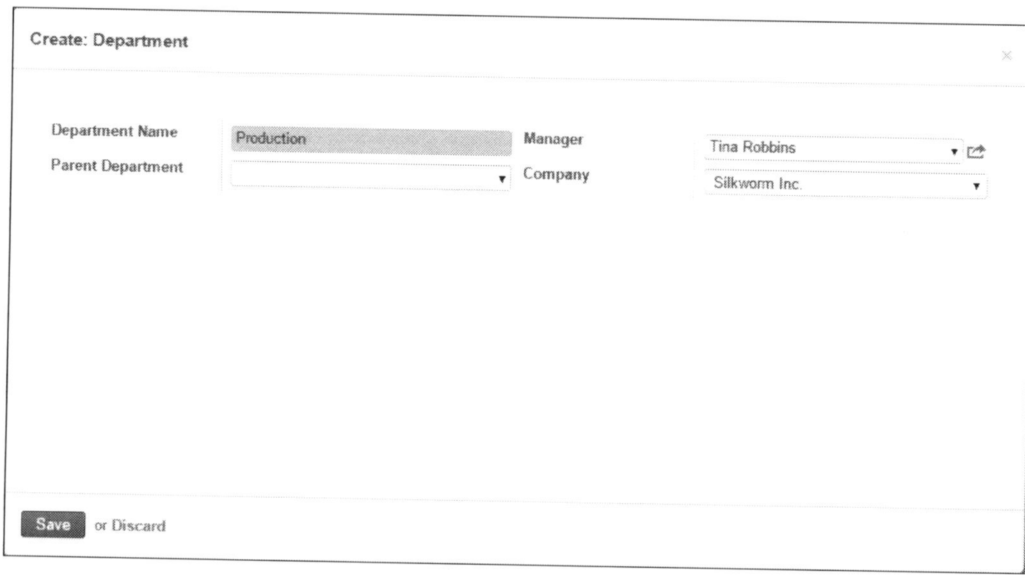

In this screen, we have set the **Department Name** field to `Production` and set the **Manager** field of this department to **Tina Robbins**. Also, you will notice that the **Parent Department** field allows you to create a hierarchical structure of departments of your company. Typically, you will wish to look at the organization chart of a company and take some time in preparing the company department structure.

Job Title

The **Job Title** field allows you to manage job titles for employees inside of Odoo.

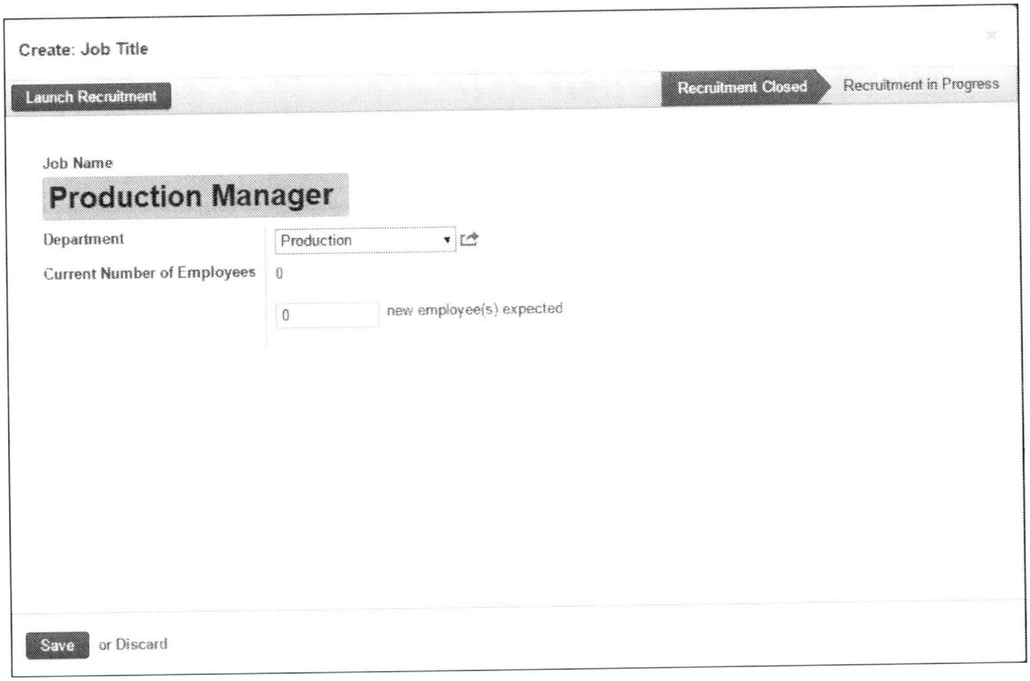

Here in the preceding screenshot, we created a job title of **Production Manager** for **Tina Robbins**. As you can see from this form, the job titles are tied to departments. This means that to properly configure Odoo, you would need to create job titles across departments. Therefore, you do not necessarily want to simply name a job `manager`. This would make it difficult, when looking at the list of job titles, to know which department that manager is associated with.

You will notice that there is a count of the current number of employees as well as a place to enter the new employees that are to be expected. At the top, there is a **Launch Recruitment** button, which we will cover later in the chapter.

Manager and Coach

The **Manager** and **Coach** fields on the employee's screen can be used to specify any other employees that are already in Odoo. The manager is often called the supervisor in some companies and might be involved in approving the employee's timesheets, leave requests, performance appraisals, and so on. The **Coach** field is just an optional field that you could use to specify any other relationship the employee has that is valuable to the position.

An employee's personal information

The **Personal Information** tab on the employee's screen contains an individual's private details that are pertinent to the human resources department, such as home address, date of birth, and citizenship status.

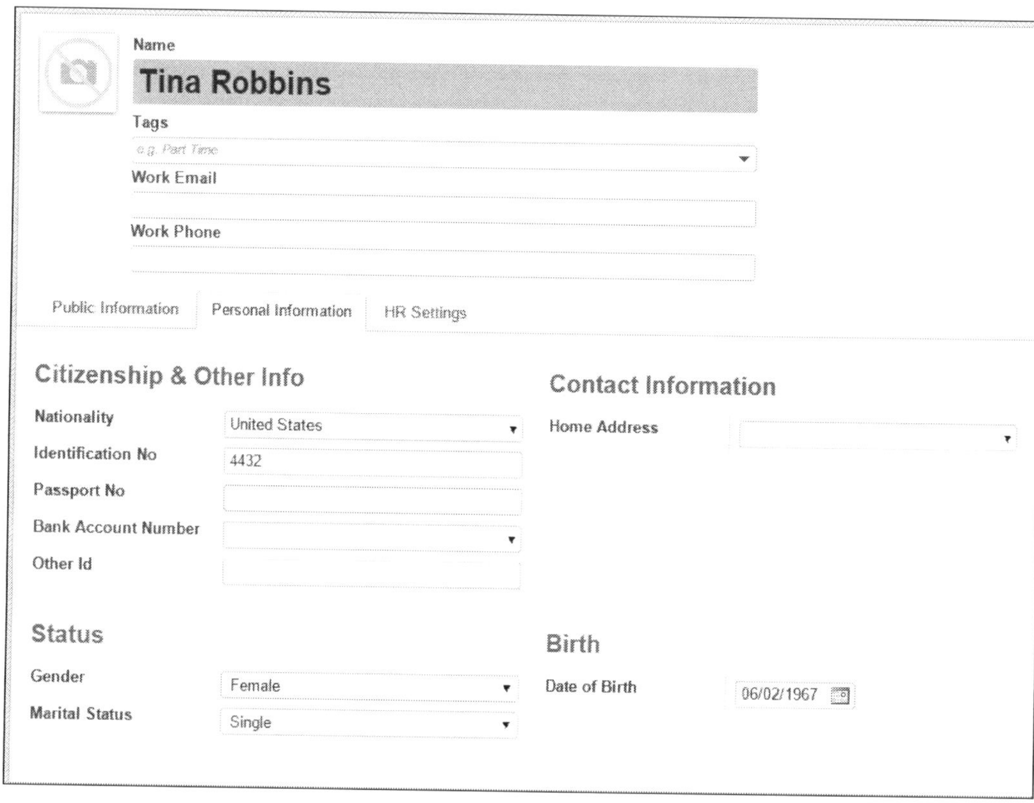

The nationality field allows you to select from the complete list of countries that comes preloaded in Odoo. Typically, the **Identification No** field would be used for an employee badge. Odoo includes a **Passport No** field on the form, which might be required in some cases where a company is required to report citizenship information to the government. The **Other Id** field can be used to collect any other information that might be a part of the human resource record of the employee.

If you decide to enter a home address for the employee, you will be taken to another screen. Near the bottom of the form, you have the ability to specify gender, marital status, and date of birth for the employee.

Under **HR Settings**, the only field on the form after installing the **Employee Directory** field, is a field to determine whether the employee is active. If you wish to make an employee inactive, simply uncheck the **Active** checkbox.

Timesheets

Odoo allows you to install a Human Resource application that will allow you to track employee time and attendance. Timesheets are the most useful feature when you have jobs that require you to account for employees' work hours and assign these hours to projects or customers. To use this feature, install the **Timesheets** application.

Once you have installed the timesheets application, the **Human Resources** menu will be expanded to include a new section called **Time Tracking**. It is in this section that you'll manage and validate timesheets.

Looking at your current timesheet

We can begin by clicking on **My Current Timesheet** to bring up your timesheet for the current week. If you are logged in as Administrator, you can choose to view any timesheet. In this case, we are viewing the timesheet for **Tina Robbins** and have clicked on the **Add a Line** button to create a new line on the timesheet.

> In Odoo, you will need to set up an account to track time and attendance before you can begin entering hours into your timesheet.

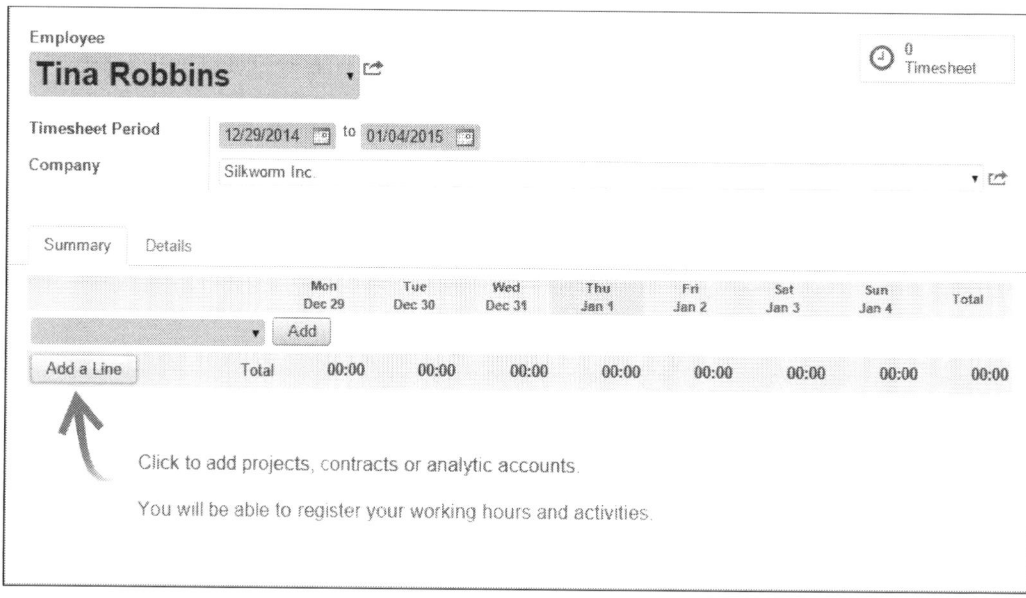

An introduction to analytic accounting

When you begin tracking time, it is important for you to consider how you want to report that time spent by employees and whether you would like to tie it to a specific customer. This is where analytic accounting features in Odoo are extremely valuable. In *Chapter 6, Configuring Accounting Finance*, you learned how to set up a basic chart of accounts. Analytic Accounting allows you to track finances into alternate accounts to analyze costs and revenue by project, by time period, or by other user-defined analytic operations.

For our real-world example, we are going to set up an analytic account to track our **Art Production** time. When you click on **Add a Line**, you will be prompted to select an account.

> An analytical account allows you to track costs and other financial information separately or from a different perspective than your standard accounts. For the most part, it is managers and directors who are going to be interested in analytical accounts as opposed to the financial department who will be focused primarily on general accounts.

After a little bit of configuration in setting up the account, Odoo can take care of the rest once we enter the hours into the timesheets.

Adding a new analytic account to Odoo

To add an account, we use Odoo's ability to add a record on the fly by typing `Art Production` and then selecting **Create and Edit...** from the small drop-down menu:

Odoo will then display the form that allows you to specify details for the `Art Production` account:

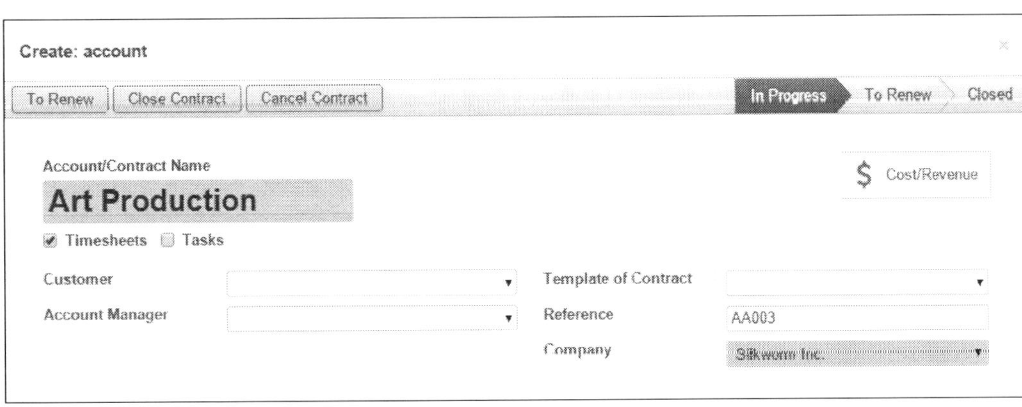

In the previous screenshot, we set the account name to `Art Production`.

With analytic accounts, you have the ability to tie the accounts to specific customers or account managers. This allows you to perform specific job costing and be very precise about how you track your sales and costs related to tasks within your company. For example, you might have an internal project to renovate the break room. Rather than modifying your chart of accounts to track that one-time project, you can set up an analytic account and use it to track those related expenses. As you can pick the account on any timesheet, you can easily manage how the time is reported.

If you want to track projects by contracts or projects there is a **Contact Information** section at the bottom of the form to associate with the time allocated to the account:

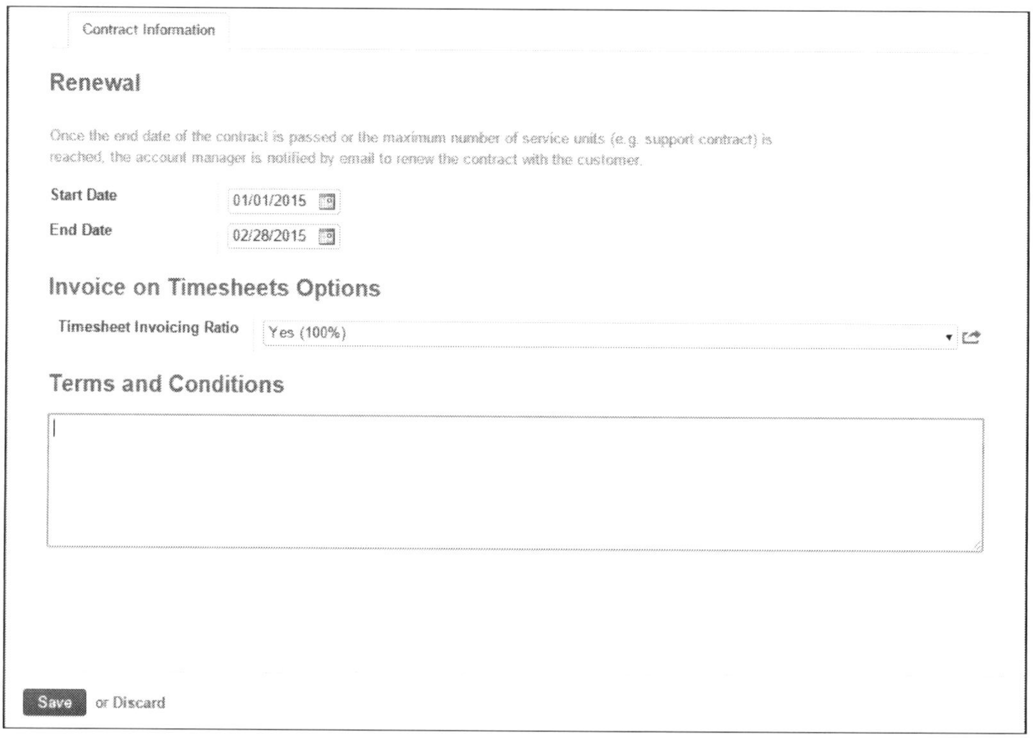

Odoo has the capability to specify a start and end date for contracts and automatically notify the account manager when it is time to contact the customer to renew. **Timesheet Invoicing Ratio** lets you specify how much of the invoice is paid up front and how much is paid out during the remaining period of the contract. Use the text area under **Terms and Conditions** to specify any details on the contract requirements.

Configuring the employee to enter timesheets

There is one more step you need to take before you can begin entering timesheets for an employee. When we installed the Timesheets application, additional options were added to the **Human Resources** section of the employee form. An entire new section called **Timesheets** was added with the ability to select a product to associate with the employee's time, as well as an analytic journal that organizes the timesheets.

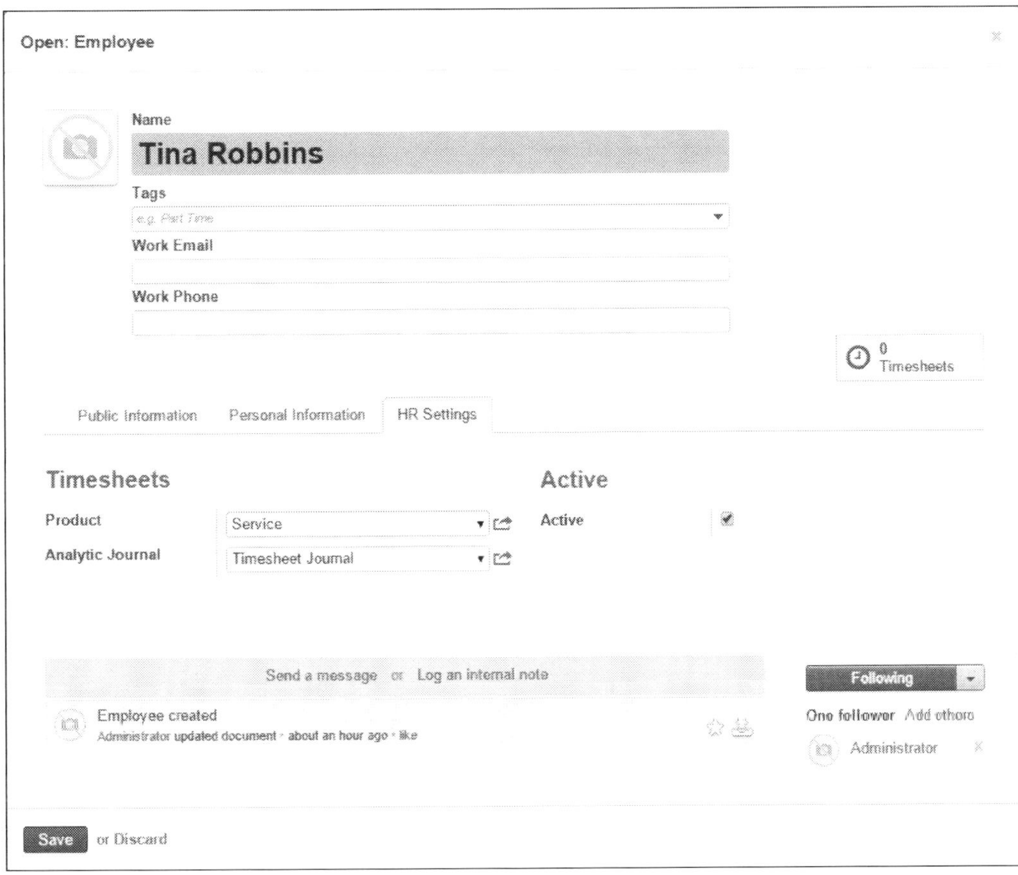

> If you do not specify the analytic journal for the employee, you will not be able to create a timesheet and submit it to a manager for approval.

Tracking employee hours with the timesheet

After you have set up the account, you can enter the number of hours into the timesheet. For more complex timesheet requirements, you can create additional accounts and then add as many lines as you need to properly account for all the hours worked.

Here is the timesheet after the week has been filled out for **Tina Robbins**:

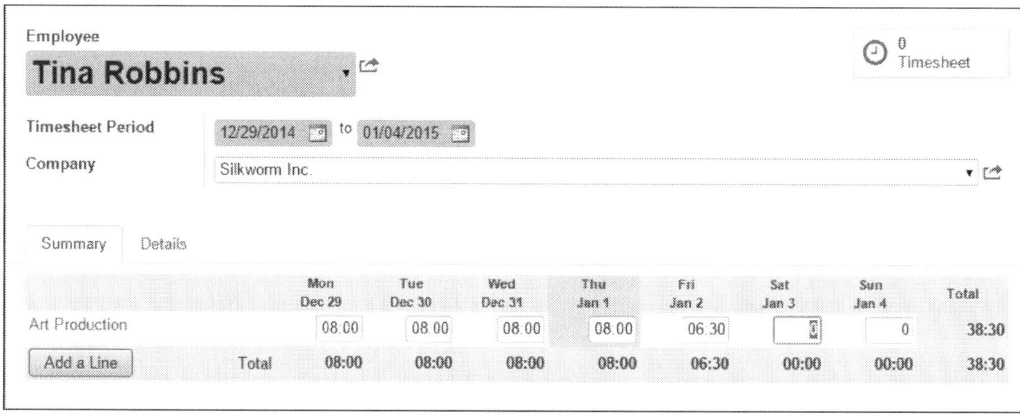

You can enter additional details on the work performed by clicking on the **Details** tab:

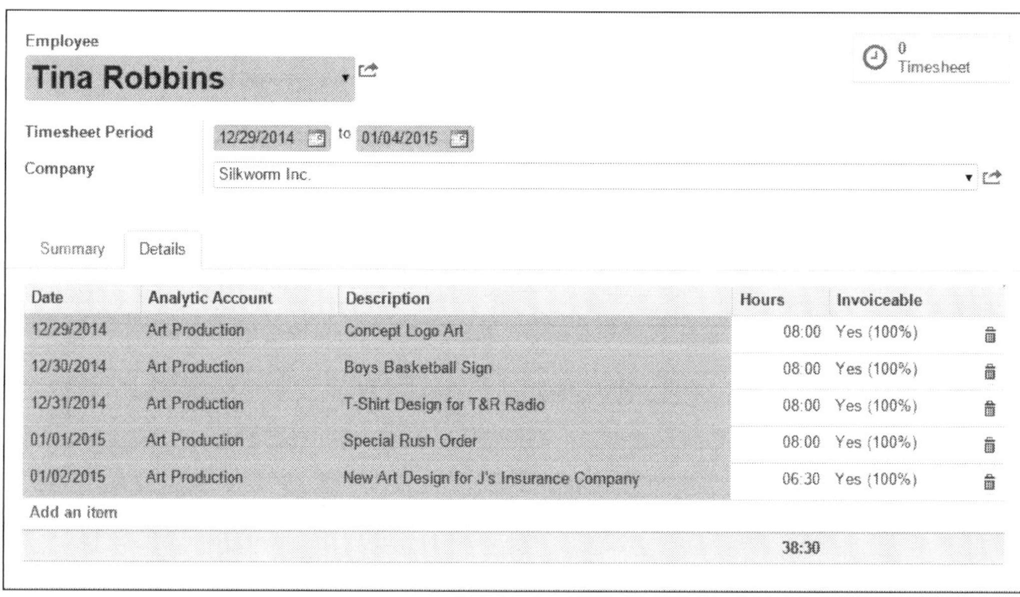

In addition to specifying a description or changing the analytic account the time needs to be attributed to; you can also determine what percentage of the time on the timesheet can be invoiced. This will allow you to manage invoices in which the time performed by the employee, is part of a contract.

After the number of hours is entered, the timesheet can be submitted to the manager by clicking on the **Submit to Manager** button in the top-left corner.

Validating timesheets

Once a timesheet has been submitted to a manager, the timesheet will appear under the **Timesheets to Validate** section for that manager when they login to Odoo:

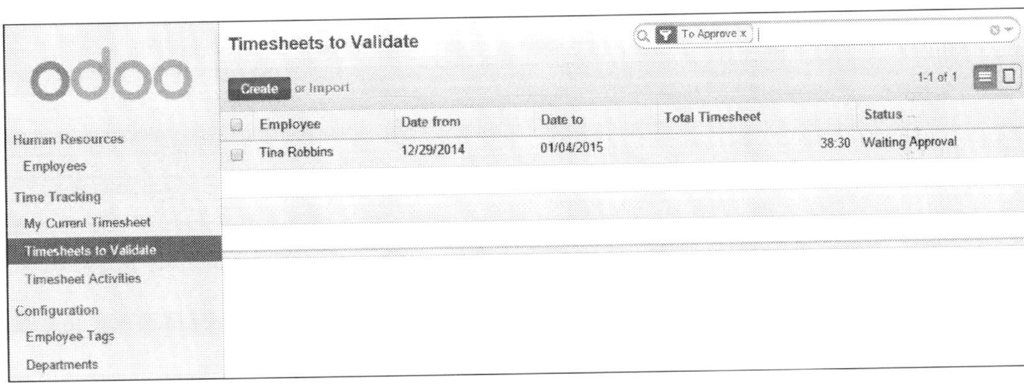

To validate a timesheet, simply click on the timesheet you wish to validate, and click on the **Approve** button. If you wish to decline a timesheet, click on the **Refuse** button instead.

Leave Management

In addition to managing and approving daily timesheets, it is also possible to install an Odoo Human Resources application that will manage holidays, leaves, and other information related to employee time off. We install **Leave Management** in the same way as the other Odoo applications.

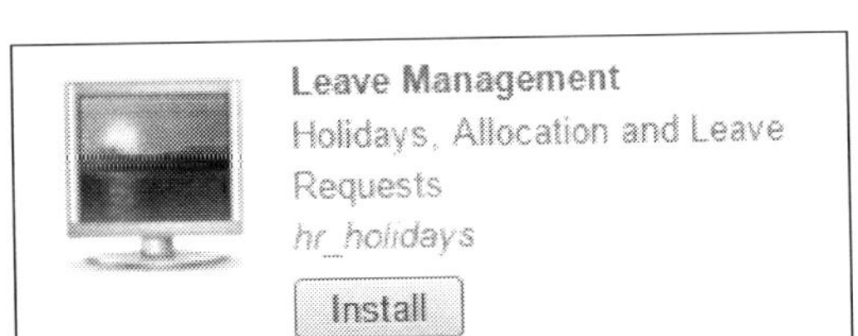

After you have installed the **Leave Management** application, you will have a new section added under the **Human Resource** menu; the **Leaves** section. The primary purpose of this Leave Management application is to provide an easy mechanism for employees to request leave and for their managers to approve or deny the request.

Creating a leave request

When you click on the **Leave Requests** menu option, you are taken to a calendar that will show your current leave requests. Naturally, if there were no prior leave requests made, or there are none for the current month, then the calendar is empty.

Click on a day in the calendar to tell Odoo to schedule a leave request beginning on that day.

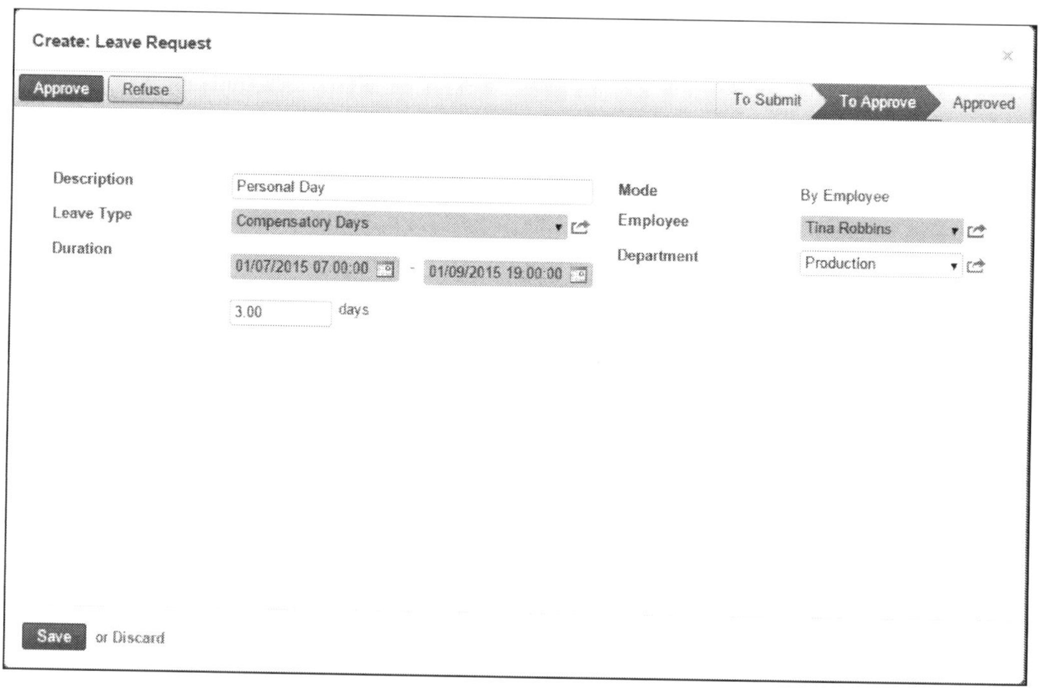

In this example, we requested personal time off for a period of three days. Personal days differ from observed or national holidays because they are not taken by everyone in the company, though they are often scheduled around a holiday to maximize consecutive days off.

Leave Type

For our example, we have chosen the **Compensatory Days** leave type. This implies that the employee is taking this leave with pay. Alternative leave types can be managed for reporting purposes.

Duration

When you change the **Duration** field using the date range fields, Odoo will automatically recalculate the **days** field.

Mode

The **Mode** field deserves special explanation and dramatically changes the way in which this leave request is submitted. For our example, we are submitting the leave request for a single employee. By using the **By Employee** tag mode, you can submit leave requests that match all employees who share the same employee tag. This can be useful if you need to schedule leaves for entire sets of employees.

Employee

This field lets you set the employee for whom the leave is requested.

Department

This field lets you set the department for which the leave is requested.

Submitting for approval

When requesting leave, clicking on the **Save** button is all that is required to save the information and send it on to the assigned manager of the employee for approval.

Approving leave requests

Clicking on the **Leave Requests to Approve** option in the **Leaves** section of the **Human Resources** menu pulls up the list of leave requests for approval. In our example, we can see the leave request we have submitted for Tina Robbins:

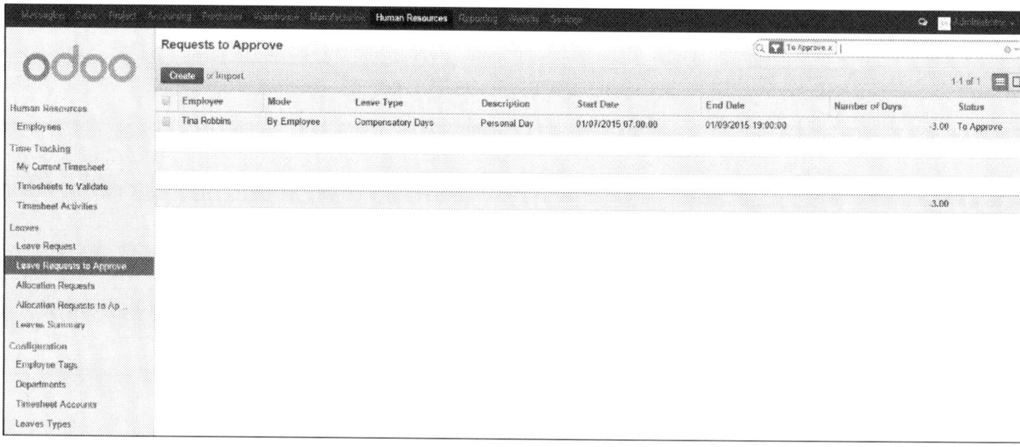

Much like the timesheet approval, you can simply click on a request and then choose **Approve** to approve the request, or **Refuse** to deny the request.

Leaves Summary

To see all the leaves that have been approved, click on the **Leaves Summary** option under the **Leaves** section:

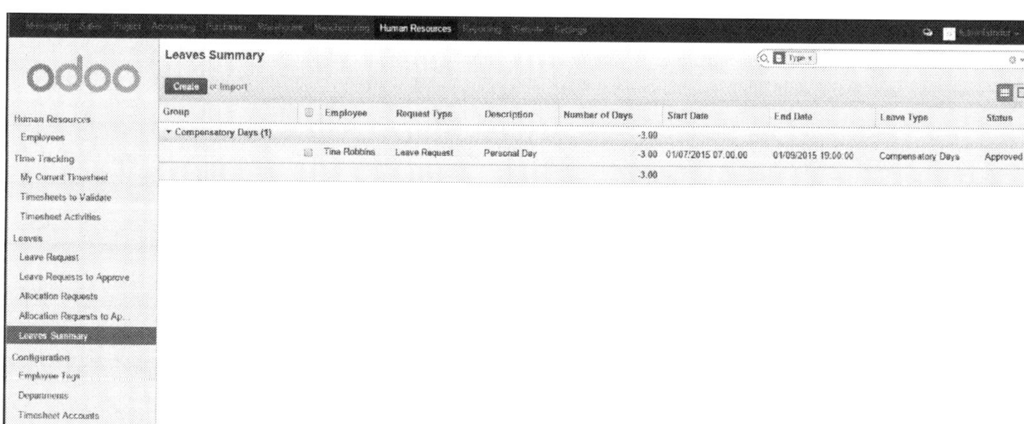

By default, this report groups by the leave type. Using the grouping and filtering options of Odoo, you can configure the leaves summary to display information on the leaves that you require.

Recruitment Process

Many Human Resource departments can spend a great deal of time managing the recruitment process. Odoo provides an application that can help organize the information and make it easier to keep a track of the communication required when hiring new employees.

Install the **Recruitment Process** application, as you have installed the other Odoo applications:

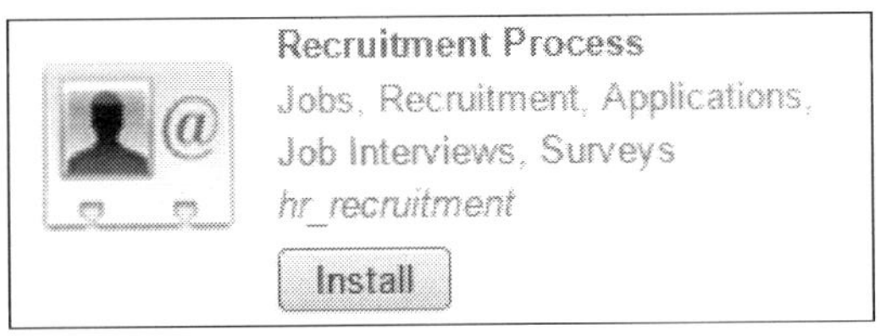

After the Recruitment Process application has been installed, Odoo will add an additional section to the **Human Resources** section, as well as new options under the **Configuration** menus at the bottom.

Defining the recruitment stages

The Odoo Recruitment Process application organizes the recruiting process in stages. This is in much the same way that an opportunity in the CRM application is organized in stages. The goal, of course, is to find new employee leads and then convert them into company employees. To look at the stages that Odoo sets up by default, go down to the **Configuration** section under **Human Resources** and choose **Stages**.

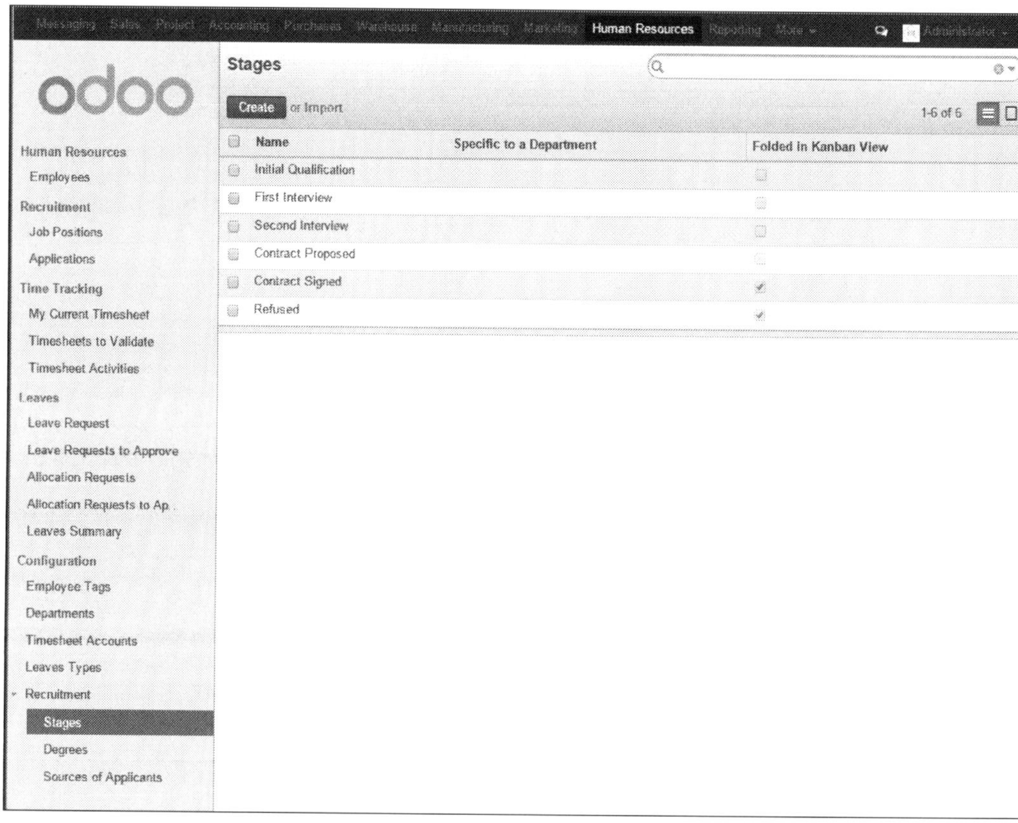

Stages can be created, edited, and deleted just like other records in Odoo. Odoo also allows you to specify that some stages are specific to a given department. Let's implement this in a practical example. In our company, we are going to say that the second interview is only required for the Sales department.

Let's start by adding a new department named `Sales` and restricting the **Second Interview** stage to the **Sales** department.

Here are the resulting stages after the previous changes:

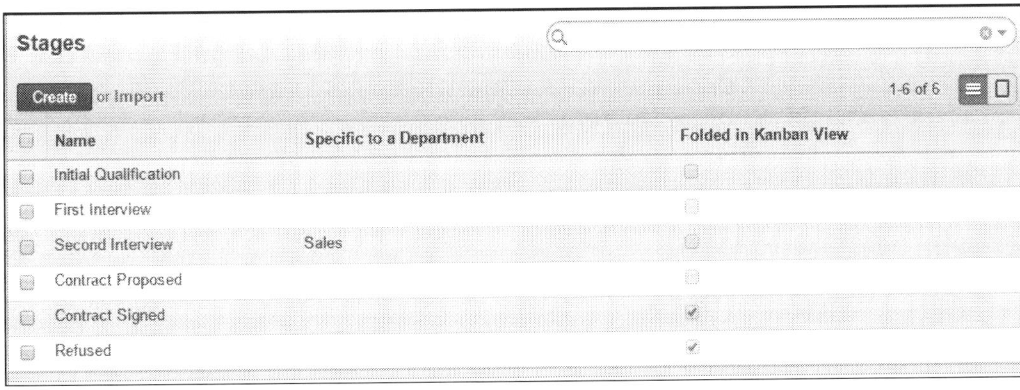

Recruiting for a new job

Tina Robbins has been very busy in her position as Production Manager. It has been decided that there is a need to hire a Production Assistant to assist her in her duties. With the new recruitment application installed, we can now create a new job position and start the recruiting process.

Click on **Job Positions** under the **Human Resources** configuration section, and click on the **Create** button:

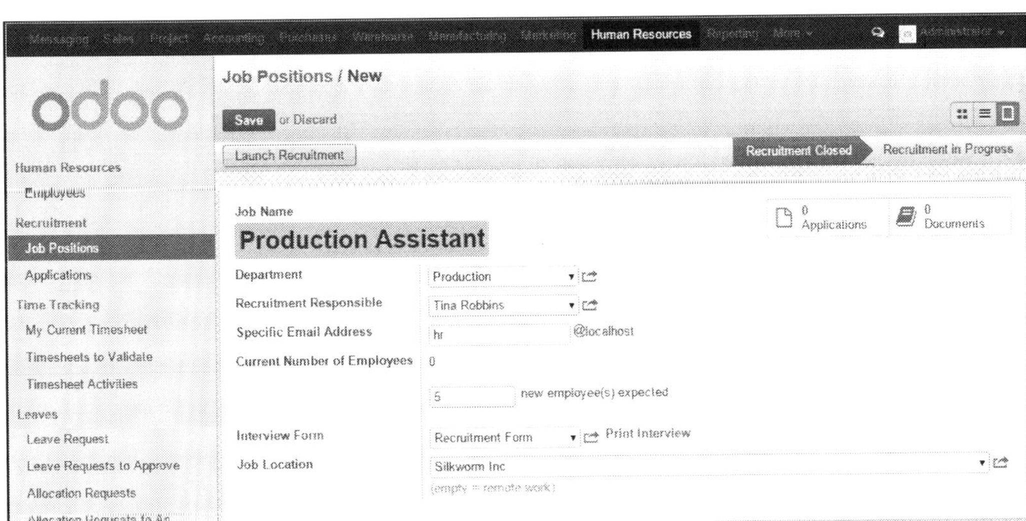

Here, we have filled in the details for our **Production Assistant** that has been assigned the position, to the **Production** department.

We can now click on **Launch Recruitment** to begin recruiting for this position. This essentially flags the recruiting process as active and makes it easier to determine which positions you are currently hiring for.

When we go back and look at the **Job Positions** section in Odoo, we will find that the Kanban view now displays details about the job position that we created, along with a progress dial that shows our headway toward hiring a total of five employees.

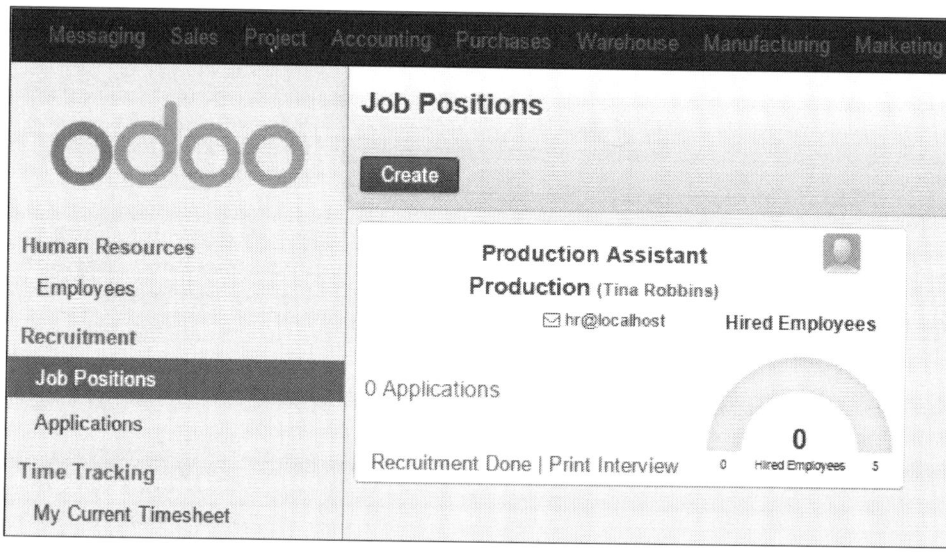

The Print Interview hyperlink

The **Print Interview** hyperlink on the Kanban view allows you to select a PDF job survey file to download. By default, the survey contains generic questions that you would typically ask an employee at a job interview.

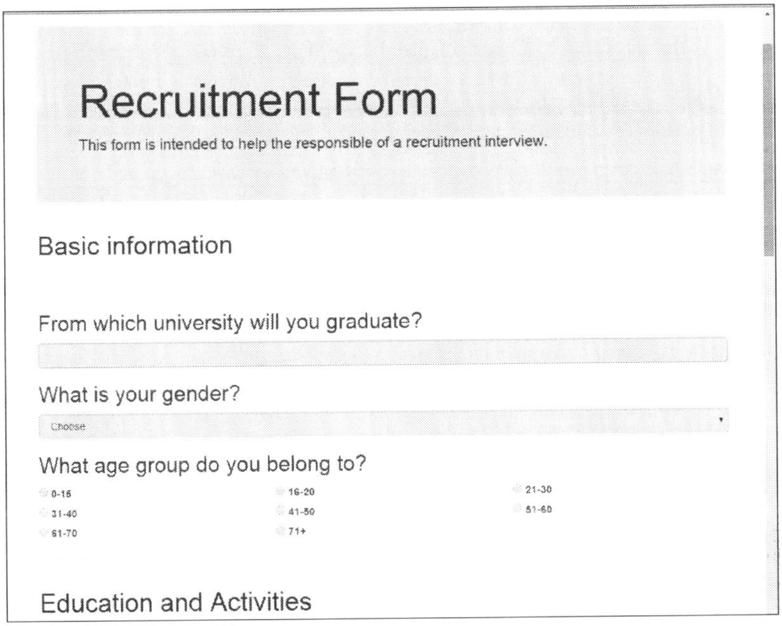

This survey could then be printed and e-mailed or presented to a prospective employee to fill out before an interview. The survey application provides a fairly robust form that you can use to design your own surveys.

You can edit the recruitment form by opening up the job application for the production assistant and clicking on the icon on the right, next to **Recruitment Form**.

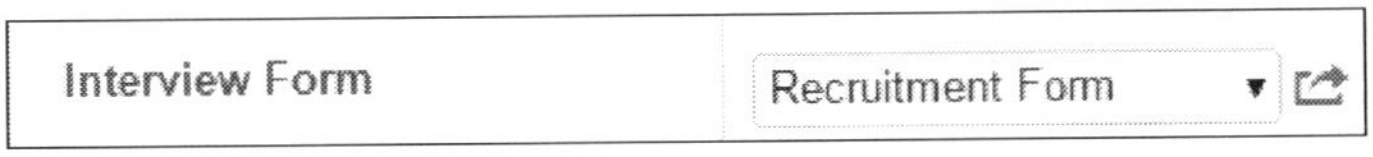

After you click on the icon, the survey editor comes up. This allows you to change the interview form to what you want.

> At the time of this writing, the terminology used in the Recruitment Form, Interview Form, and Job Survey is a bit confusing. Despite labeling them differently in the system, they are all referring to the same survey document in Odoo.

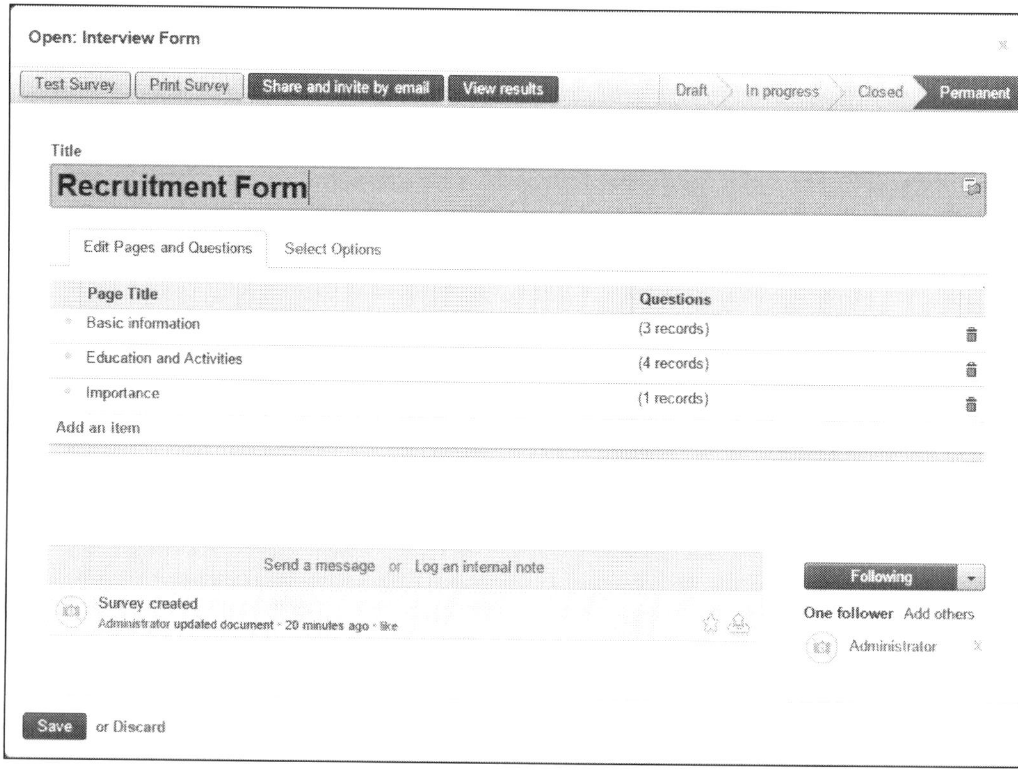

Surveys can be organized around the job function and can be valuable for prescreening employees before a formal interview.

Creating an employment application

When a potential employee sends in an application, resume, or another trigger that allows you to document their interest in working for your company, you create a recruitment application.

Under the **Recruitment** | **Applications** section, click on **Create** to create a new application:

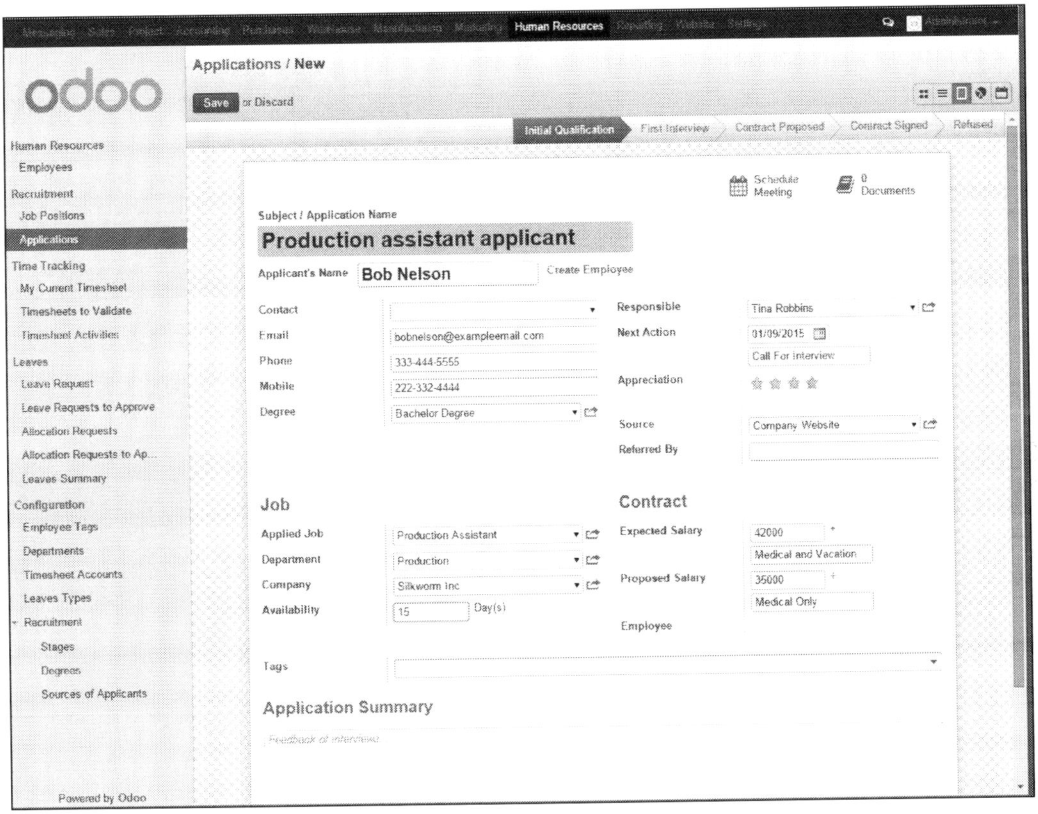

This form has a lot of fields to be potentially filled out. By default, the only required field for the application is the subject. The rest of the information can be collected throughout the recruiting and interviewing processes.

Most of these fields are self-explanatory. Notice that at the top right, you can see the progress of this employee through the various stages.

Hiring employees

Let's go ahead and hire this Bob Nelson guy. Thankfully, the Odoo Recruitment application will create the employee for us by simply clicking on the **Create Employee** hyperlink next to the applicant's name.

Looking at the employees list, we can now see that **Bob Nelson** is an employee in the **Production** department with the title **Production Assistant**:

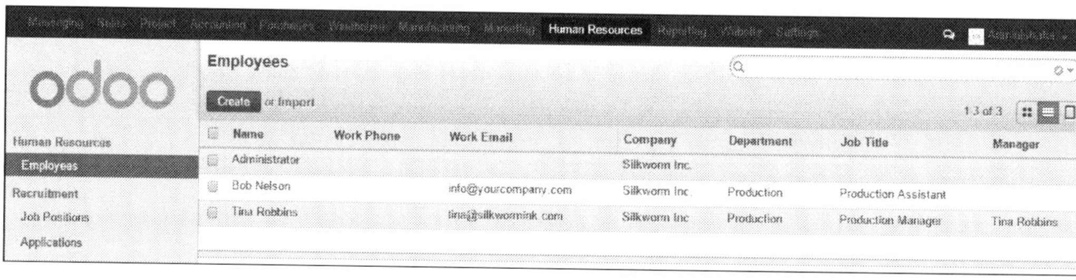

Summary

In this chapter, we examined the various Human Resource applications available in Odoo. We installed the base Employee Directory followed by applications that managed time and attendance, as well as leave requests. Finally, we installed an application that allowed us to manage the recruiting processes of new employees. We walked through completing an employment application, and finally, turning the potential applicant into an employee.

In the next chapter, we will look at the Project Management application in Odoo and how it can be used to improve service quality for customers. Project Management allows you to organize from the most simple projects, to complex projects involving multiple tasks. Furthermore, you can even track the time related to projects, and display project information in a variety of graphical formats to make it easier to track your deadlines.

9
Understanding Project Management

In this chapter, we will explore a very flexible application that allows you to manage projects and link them into other applications in Odoo. The Project Management application allows your company to manage project stages, assign teams, and even track time and job costs related to projects. Analytical accounting features give you even greater control of how project costs can be linked to your company's general ledger.

This chapter covers the following topics:

- Discovering the various uses for Project Management
- Linking projects with customer accounts
- Assigning teams to projects
- Creating custom project stages
- Adding, assigning, and organizing tasks
- Tying into analytical accounting and employee timesheets

The basics of Project Management

Depending on your industry and the types of projects you may encounter, the **Project Management** application can be set up to manage independent projects, or instead, it can be configured to manage projects related to customers or sales orders. With additional modules, it is possible to link the **Project Management** application into virtually any aspect of Odoo. For example, you could simply use the **Project Management** application to track the various stages and tasks involved in a company event. Who is going to be responsible for finding the location? When will you need to send out invitations? Who is going to set the agenda? When is an employee going to go and pick up the sound system? In this instance, the **Project Management** application is simply being used to track a single project that is not associated with the customer.

In other instances, you might want to use the **Project Management** application to track projects that are organized around your customer records. A common example would be a construction firm. After assigning the project to a customer, you can track various stages of the project's life cycle. Employees can be assigned tasks, and using the Odoo messaging system you can share project details with your customers. It is in this configuration that the Odoo **Project Management** application can add real value to an Odoo installation and provide better integration with your accounting system with less effort than a stand-alone project management tool.

Installing the Project Management application

To access the project managing features, you will need to install the Project Management application.

Go to the **Settings** menu and install the **Project Management** application using the same process as the previous Odoo applications.

The real-world project example

Like in other chapters, we will use a real-world example to demonstrate the functionality of Odoo's **Project Management** application. In the silkscreen industry, it can be common to have extremely large projects that can span across many types of apparel and print designs. For this example, we are going to create a project to manage creating an entire line of sports jerseys for an organization called *Lil League*.

When defining our project, it is important to look at the scope of our project and why it will be valuable to use the project manager to organize the various tasks involved. With our Lil League organization, we are dealing with multiple teams with varied logo designs, the number of players, the sizes of the apparel required, and the printing of different players' numbers and names. There are often multiple deadlines to manage and a number of people that might need to approve various phases of the project as they are completed. Using the **Project Management** application, we can better track this information and tie it into sales orders and other Odoo functions.

Creating our first project

After the **Project Management** application has been successfully installed, we can go to the Project application and create a new project.

The basic steps we will perform are as follows:

1. Create a new project record
2. Name the project
3. Assign the project to a specific customer
4. Assign team members to the project

To begin with, under the **Project** application, select **Projects** in the menu on the left, and then click on the **Create** button:

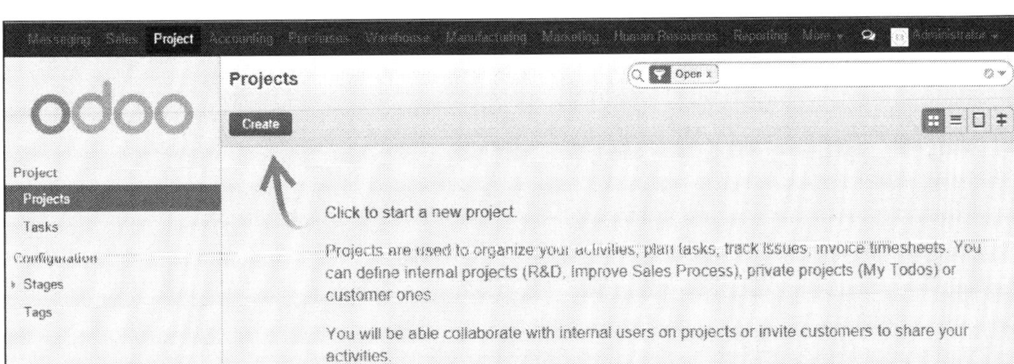

After you click on **Create**, the project editor will allow you to enter various details about your new project. For our example, we will start out defining the name of the project, `Sunny Hill Lil League`, and assign the project to a customer that we created, `Sunny Hill Sports`. Assigning a customer is optional, but in this example, we are identifying the customer as the primary league contact.

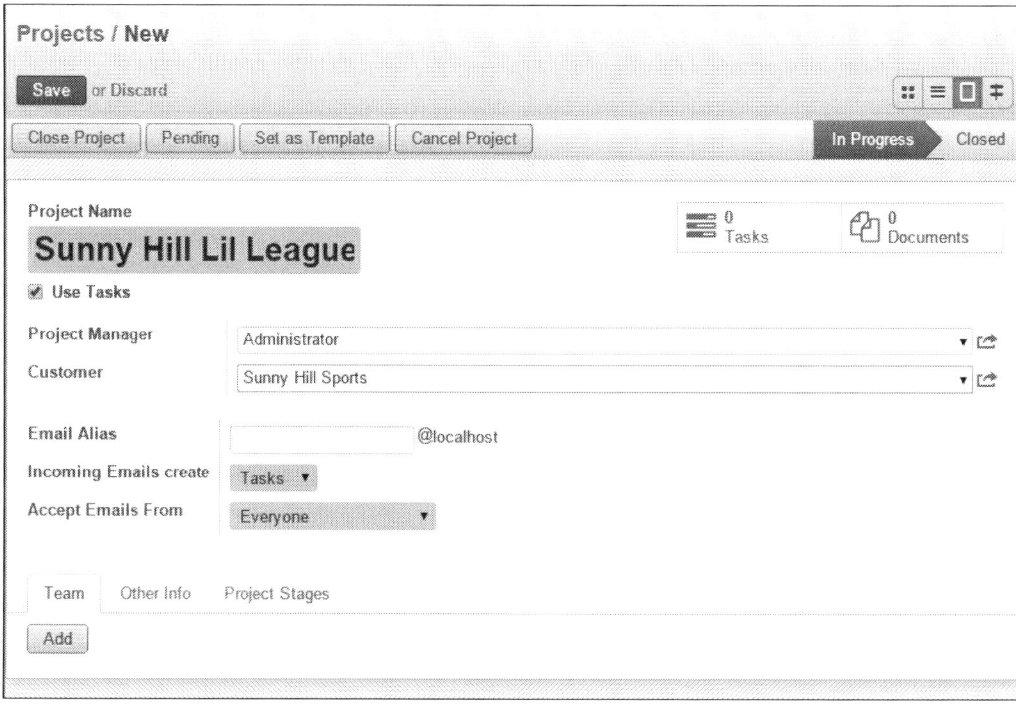

You will notice that the project is set to **In Progress** in the top-right corner. You will also notice that you can assign someone as **Project Manager** as well, though this is not required.

If the **Use Tasks** checkbox is checked, then you will see the **Project Stages** tab in the form. Different projects can naturally have different project stages that they go through on their way toward completion. For our example, we will leave the **Use Tasks** checkbox checked. A little later, we will go through how to define the various stages for our project.

Assigning project teams

In the first tab that is labeled **Team**, you can add team members to the project. Click on the **Add** button, and you will be provided with a list of the available team members in your company. To filter the list or to locate a particular employee by name, simply type it into the box in the upper-right corner.

Using the checkboxes to the left of a person's name, you can add multiple project members to the project team at the same time. To mark everyone who is included in the list, use the checkbox at the very top in the header row.

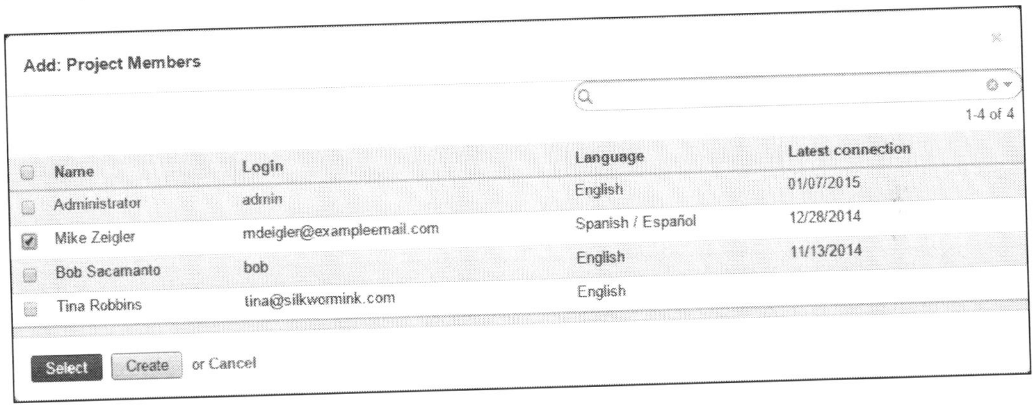

After you have selected all of the **Project Members** options you want to add, click on the **Select** button to add them to the project team. Next to each member on the project team in the project edit screen you will see a small **x**. Clicking on this **x** will remove that team member from the project.

Setting other project information

In the second **Other Info** tab, we can record additional information related to the project. We can adjust privacy settings for the project, provide a start date and an end date for the project, currency, as well as determine sequence settings. Finally, you can specify a parent for the project so that you can nest projects inside of other projects to provide more flexibility in managing extremely complex projects.

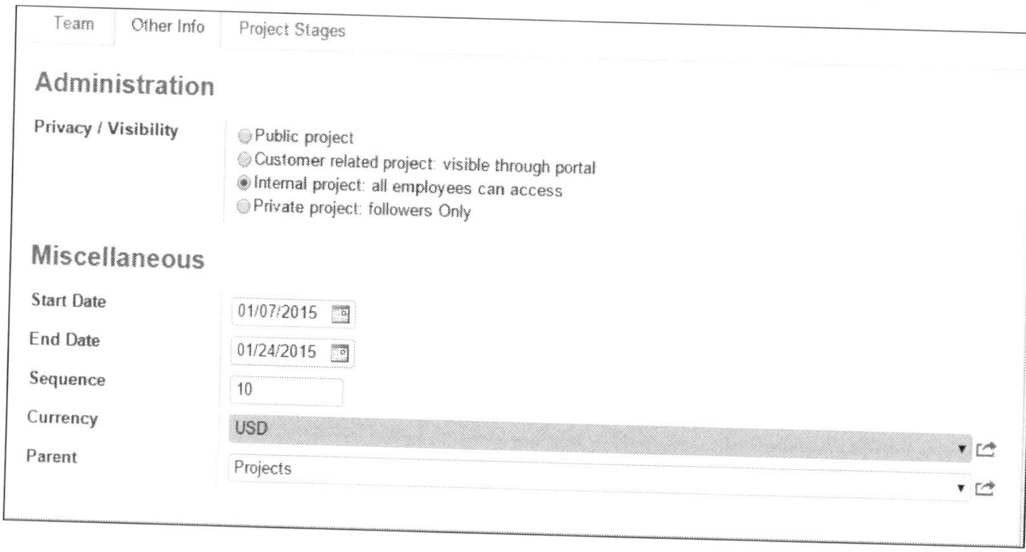

Under the **Administration** heading, we see that we can define **Privacy / Visibility** settings for our project. Now with Odoo 8, you have the ability to define the visibility four separate ways:

- **Public project**: This option allows you to make a project completely public so that someone can access it without having any login in Odoo.
- **Customer related project: visible through portal**: This option will allow the customer assigned to the project to access the project. To facilitate this, Odoo will send a link to the customer so they can login to the portal and see the project.
- **Internal project: all employees can access**: This option is the default setting. It restricts project access to internal employees. This option, however, allows all employees in the company access to the project.
- **Private project: followers Only**: This option is the most restrictive project. With this setting, only the followers specifically assigned to the project are allowed access.

As we can rearrange projects into any order we want within the Kanban view, Odoo provides a **Sequence** number to determine the exact order of the projects. If you have multicurrency turned on, you will also have the opportunity to provide the currency related to the project. This will be used when calculating budgets and other expenses related to the project.

The **Parent** field provides the capability to nest multiple projects inside another project. If, for example, we wanted to treat each Lil League team as a separate project, we can group them under this project using the **Parent** field in this form. In this way, an entire smaller project can itself become a mere step (or **Task**) along the way to completing the larger, more complex **Parent** project. We can examine all projects in Odoo as they are ultimately contained in the **Projects** collection.

Understanding project stages

In the third tab, we can define the stages for the project. This tab will only be available if the **Tasks** checkbox in the upper-left corner is checked.

The **Project Management** application has a set of default project stages that will be automatically populated when you create a new project. You can then add, edit, and delete **Project Stages** as required, to meet the needs of each specific project.

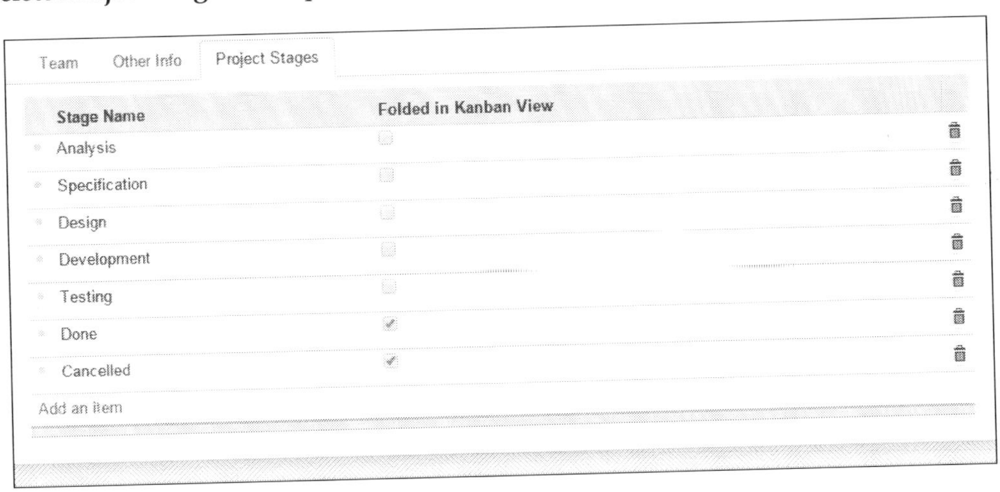

In the **Project Stages** tab, you have both the **Stage Name** option and the option to fold that status in the Kanban view.

> In Odoo 8, the stages inside the Project Management and the CRM applications were simplified by removing a field named `related status`, which corresponded to the stage name.

Defining project stages for a specific project

For the purpose of our example, there are several changes we would like to make to our **Project Stages**. While **Specification** and **Design** are very appropriate stages for our real-world example project of printing team jerseys, the stages of **Development** and **Testing** could be much better defined. Instead of **Development**, the stage could better be described perhaps as **Manufacturing**. Instead of **Testing**, the stage could better be described as **Quality Assurance**.

While the stages we might want to change will depend on the project, for the silkscreen printing industry, we can anticipate that we will most often wish to use these new definitions for nearly *every* project. Let's redefine them once, so that the new stage descriptions can be used in all future projects.

To edit **Project Stage**, simply click on the row you want to change. In this case, we will begin by changing the name of the **Development** stage.

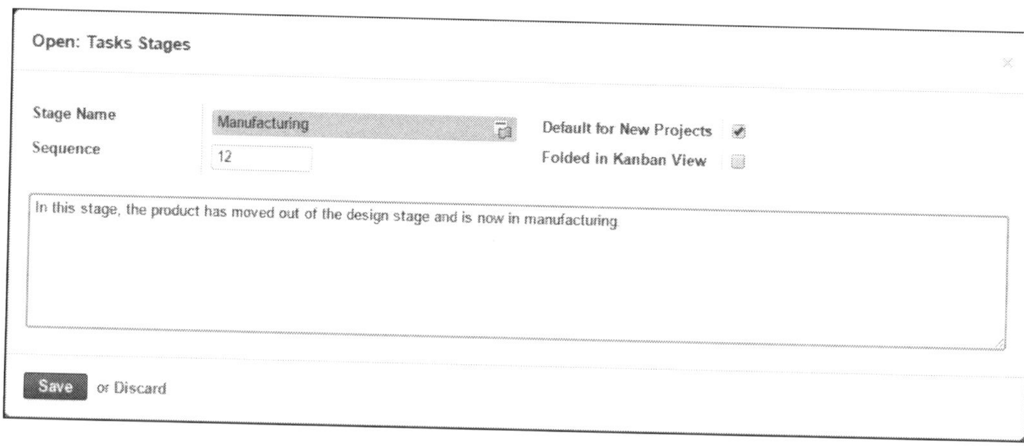

In this example, we have simply changed the stage name from **Development** to **Manufacturing**, which better describes the stage for our project. We have also kept the **Default for New Projects** checkbox marked because we can anticipate that most of the projects for this company will involve manufacturing. If needed, the **Sequence** option could be changed here to reorder the stages of the project.

The **Folded by Default** checkbox tells Odoo how to handle stages that have no tasks assigned to them in the project view. If the **Folded in Kanban View** checkbox is checked, then the Kanban view will make this stage invisible when there are no tasks. If the checkbox is not marked, Odoo will show the stage in the Kanban view even if there are no tasks currently assigned to this stage. We will keep this checkbox unmarked.

The following screenshot has the new stage list after it has been modified with stage names more appropriate to the Lil League project for our example:

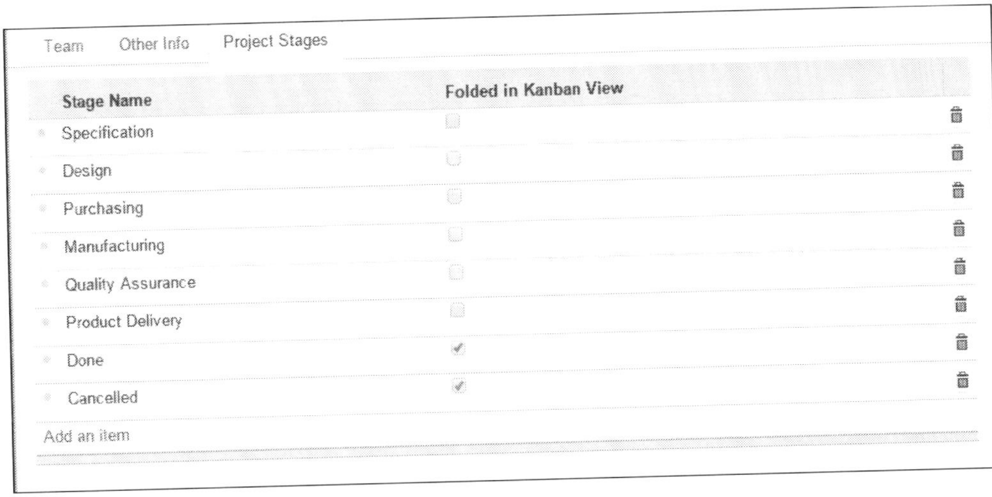

In addition to changing **Development** to **Manufacturing** and **Testing** to **Quality Assurance**, we have also added stages for **Purchasing** and **Product Delivery**. Finally, we have removed **Analysis** from the list of stages.

> The little bullet to the left of the **Stage Name** option will allow you to drag and drop stages to reorder them in the list; this is much quicker than editing the **Sequence** field of each stage. Clicking on the little trash can icon on the far right of the row will remove a stage from the list.

With these stages in place, we can now assign tasks that will help us manage the project through the various stages.

Now with our project stages defined, we can begin defining tasks for our project.

Defining project tasks

The main unit for tracking the various activities involved with a project is a project task. We will create a new task by navigating to the **Task** menu in the **Project** application and clicking on the **Create** button. Here, we'll define the various aspects of the task:

- the name of the task (this is required)
- The stage to which the task belongs (also required)
- The project to which the task is assigned

- The deadline date of the task
- The responsible party assigned to the task
- Any tags you would like to associate with this task
- A description of the task

For our example, we have filled out the task as seen in the following screenshot:

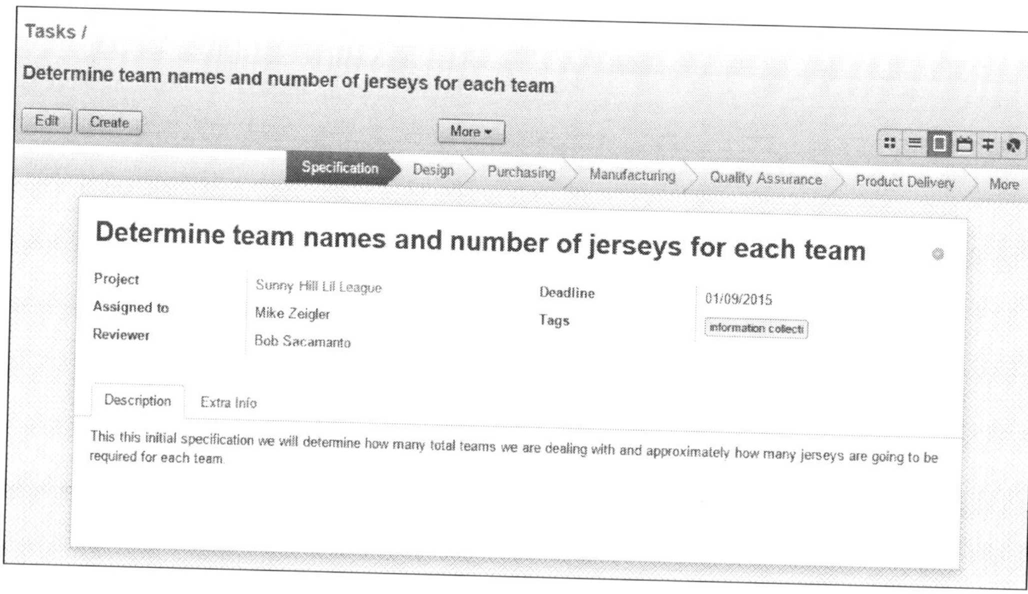

At the top of the form, you will see all of the project stages and the current stage highlighted in blue. In this example, **Specification** is the currently selected stage. When in the edit mode, you can click on these stages to directly assign the task to a given stage. This can be changed as the project progresses, so you are not locked into keeping a task assigned to the same stage throughout the project.

One of the important aspects of good project management is assigning responsible parties for each and every task. The **Assigned to** field allows you to specify who is ultimately responsible for the completion of the task. Odoo also allows you to optionally specify someone's name in the **Reviewer** field to check that the task has been completed and has met the necessary requirements.

The **Tags** field can be valuable to better track and organize tasks. In our example, we have defined an **information collection** tag. This tag can then be assigned to any task that is related to collecting data regarding the project.

Defining additional task information

The **Project Management** application also allows you to define additional information for project tasks. This information includes:

- **Priority** of the task
- **Sequence**
- **Customer**
- **Starting Date** and **Ending Date** in **Gantt View**

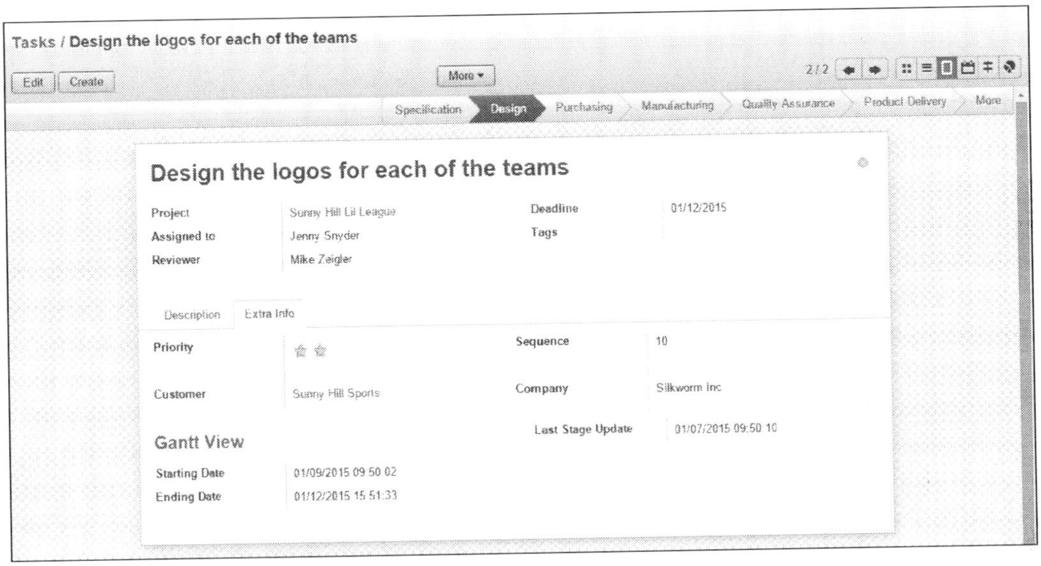

In our example, we have used the same customer throughout the entire project. For complex projects, you might have several customers that are part of various tasks in the project.

Creating additional tasks

For our real-world example, we are going to define several tasks at various stages. These tasks include:

- Approval of the logo designs
- Collection of the names and numbers of the players on each team
- Identification of suppliers for the product
- Estimation of costs and pricing for the raw product

- Placement of purchase orders for the raw product
- Creation of a printed prototype jersey for customer approval
- Scheduling of the print jobs
- Printing of the jerseys
- Inspection of each jersey for defects
- Packaging and shipment of the jerseys

After entering our tasks and assigning them to the various stages, we can look at tasks, more easily, in the Kanban view. In this view, you can drag and drop tasks to move them to different stages and reorder the sequence of tasks.

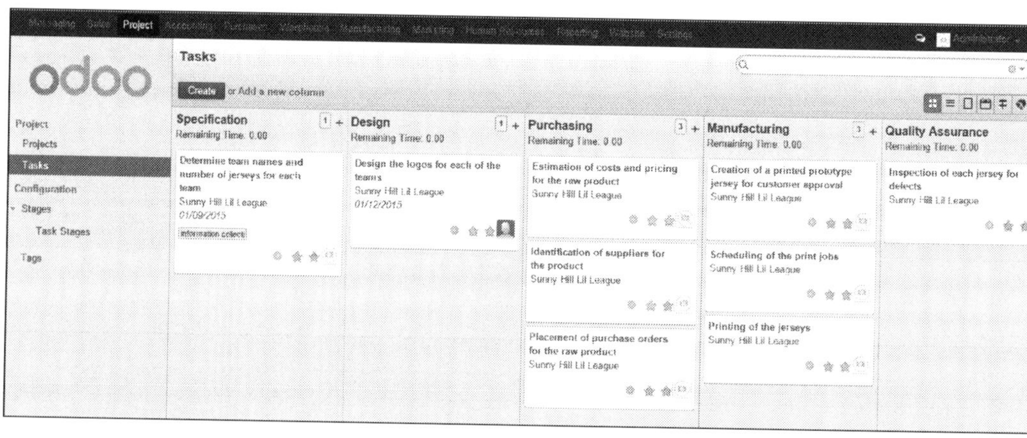

Each task is represented as a card and provides the name of the task, the project, and the due date for the task. Tags such as **information collection**, are also displayed on the card.

If you hover over the little icon shaped like a head, you will see the name of the person who is assigned to the task and who is, therefore, responsible for it.

> The small arrow in the upper-right corner of each Kanban card will bring up a popup menu that will allow you to specify the color of the card to visually organize your tasks, as well as an option to edit or delete the task.

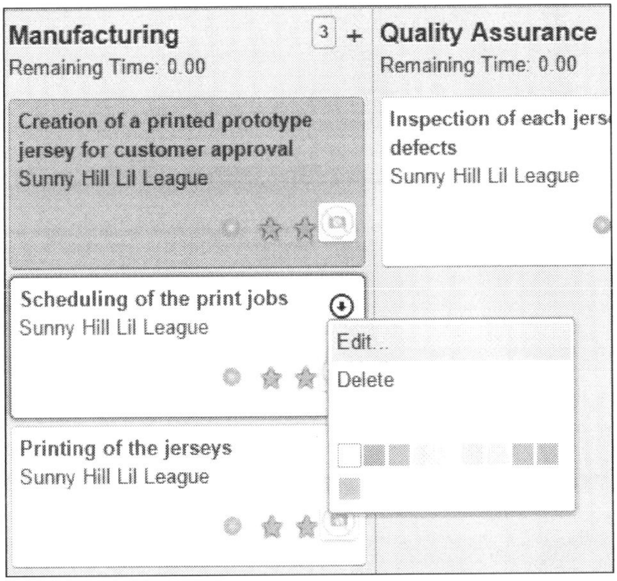

The preceding screenshot shows you how to change the color of the Kanban card by clicking on an available color from the palette.

You might also want to see the tasks in both a list view and a Gantt chart view. The icon for the Gantt chart view looks like this: ╪.

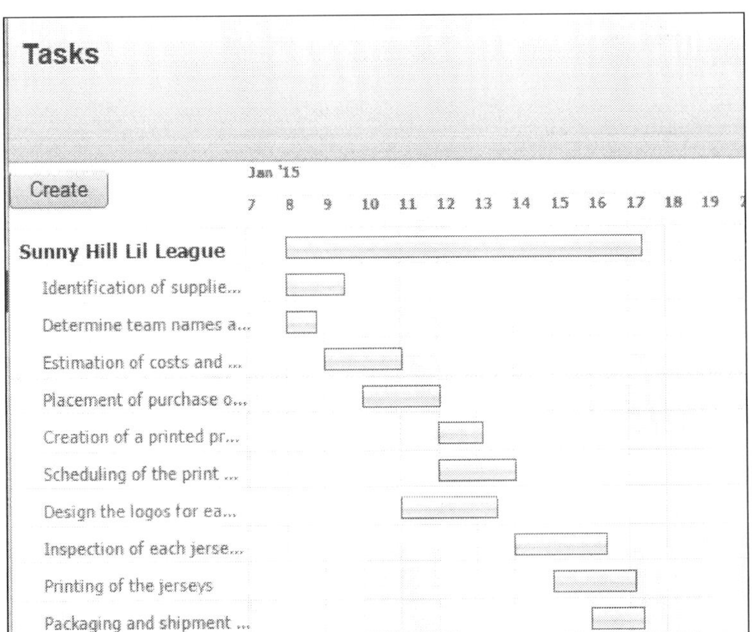

The tasks are shown in a Gantt chart view format in the preceding screenshot.

Using this view, you can adjust the time of a given task by clicking on and dragging the edges of the task bar. You can also click at the center of a bar and drag a task left or right to reposition it in the Gantt chart view. You cannot, however, drag tasks up or down to reorder them.

If you move your mouse over a task and hover there, you will see a small pop-up box providing you with additional information about the task. This is demonstrated in the following screenshot:

> Don't waste your time trying to double-click or right-click on a task on the Gantt view. Unfortunately, Odoo does not provide a direct way to edit tasks from the Gantt view.

In addition to the Gantt view of the tasks, you can also pull up the tasks in the calendar view mode. While in the calendar view, on the right you can see the color legend showing each person that is assigned to the tasks.

Fortunately, unlike the Gantt view, in the calendar view, you can double-click on a task to bring it up for editing. You can also use the standard drag and drop features of the calendar to set a new due date for the task.

Completing project tasks

As you complete project tasks, you can bring them up and click on the **Done** button. At this point, the task falls out of the currently assigned stage and is moved to the **Done** stage. One easy way to see which tasks have been completed is to look at the tasks in the list view. In this view, you will see a green progress bar as well as **Done** written in the **Stage** column for every task that has been marked as complete:

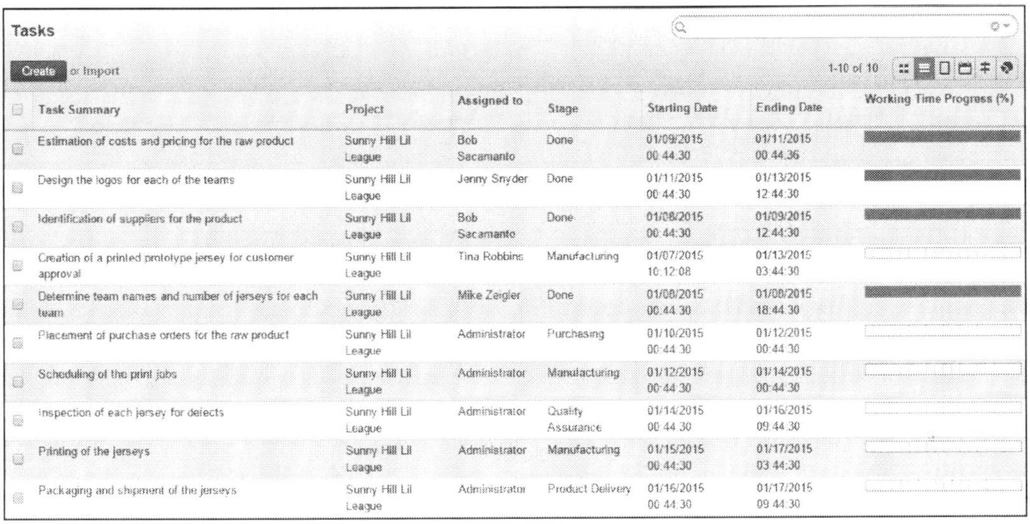

As you can see in the screenshot, we have marked off four of the tasks as complete or **Done**.

> If, for some reason, you accidently mark a task as done or you find out later that there is additional work needed for a task, you can edit the task and click on the **Reactivate** button. The task will then return to its previous stage and will no longer be considered done.

Calculating project costs and time

To calculate project costs and time, you can install the Human Resources application, **Timesheets**. This application lets you create timesheets for your employees that let you specify the number of hours worked per day. If you have been following along, you should already have this application installed from *Chapter 8, Implementing the Human Resources Application*.

To complete the integration so that you can use timesheets with the project manager, you must also install the module **Bill Time on Tasks** so that you can associate each task with the hours the employee worked on that task.

Once **Bill Time on Tasks** is installed you will see that if you bring up a project in Odoo, a new **Timesheets** button is available.

If you click on the **Timesheets** button, you will get a list view in which you can create new timesheet entries. In this example, we have attributed one hour of art design to the project.

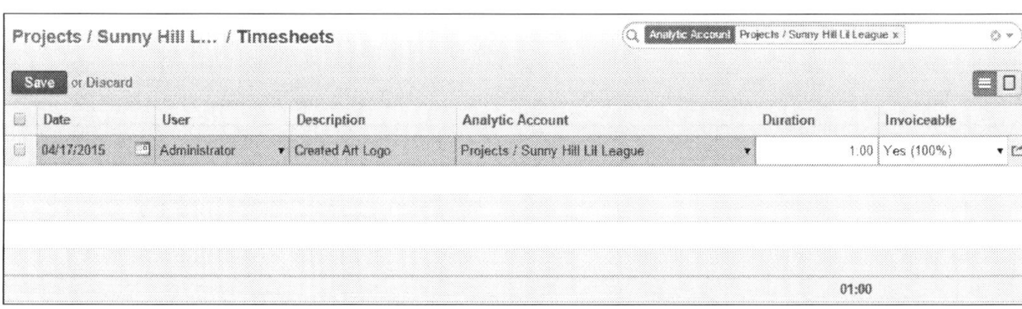

You can see that we have specified the project and the duration, and we have indicated that this is billable time that can be invoiced. If you want, you can double-check under **Invoiced Tasks** to see the entry and the amount that will be invoiced once the timesheet has been processed. You can learn more about using timesheets and analytical accounting in *Chapter 8, Implementing the Human Resources Application*.

Summary

In this chapter, we examined the **Project Management** application. We created an example of a real-world project involving our Lil League organization. After setting up our project and assigning team members, we defined the various stages that would be involved in completing the project. With the stages defined, we were able to go through and assign various tasks to the stages along with their dates of completion. Finally, we looked at the various ways in which you can view the tasks and how you can complete them.

In the next chapter, we will explore how you can create advanced searches and custom dashboards in Odoo. As a company uses its system from day to day, the amount of data collected can grow quite rapidly. Being able to locate pertinent records in a speedy fashion is vital for optimum business operation. We'll discover how to utilize all of the handy searching, filtering, and dashboard presentation tools that are at our disposal within Odoo.

10

Creating Advanced Searches and Dashboards

In this chapter, we will cover advanced searching, custom filters, and dashboards. We begin by looking at how Odoo searches the various datasets within the system. Next, we explore more advanced search options and discuss how you can save these filters so they can be easily accessed when you need them. Finally, we discuss the Odoo dashboard capabilities and how we can improve usability for users.

The topics covered in this chapter include the following:

- Identifying users' search requirements
- Understanding default filters versus custom filters
- Grouping items in a list
- Setting and saving advanced search conditions
- Creating dashboard content and layouts

Determining the search requirements for your business

One of the tasks that can often be frustrating and time consuming for users is trying to find the information they need. When datasets are small and simple, there is not much of an issue. As the number of records in the system grows, it can become increasingly difficult to find information.

When implementing an ERP system, you will want to take the time to work with users and get familiar with the data they use each day. If you are working with a purchasing system that only produces an average of 10 purchase orders a day, you will have far less concern over advanced searching in that application. However, if you have 20 purchasing agents cutting 450 purchase orders a day, it will be critical that the users have a firm grasp on the search functionality of the system. Trying to locate a particular order can be like trying to find a needle in a haystack.

> Take the time to sit with users and watch them use the system. Often, users will need to lookup the same types of data repeatedly in their daily interaction with the system. These are the activities that you will want to set up custom filters for and perhaps even include them on the user's dashboard.

Fortunately, Odoo offers a robust searching mechanism as well as the ability to create dashboards to display information that the user might need to look at frequently.

For the purposes of this chapter, we will create a new database with the demonstration data so you can better see the searches in action.

Creating a database with demonstration data

Often, it can be valuable to test certain features in Odoo without having to enter a lot of data. When you create a database, Odoo offers a way to optionally populate it with demonstration data. Since this chapter is focused specifically on searching and displaying data, we will load up a database with the sample data provided by Odoo.

Accessing the database manager

While it is possible to access the database manager by clicking on links in the login screen, there are times when that link is not available. One reason can be because the website application has been installed. In this case, the manage databases link is hidden from the home page.

> Sometimes, if your Odoo server is throwing internal server errors or you are having other problems with your database, you can resolve the issue and at least make backups of your data, by going directly to the database manager.

To access the database manager directly in the default installation of Odoo, you can use `http://localhost:8069/web/database/manager`.

Naturally, you will need to change the server address and port to match your Odoo installation.

When creating our database, we check **Load demonstration data** so that our database is prepopulated making it easier to present example search techniques.

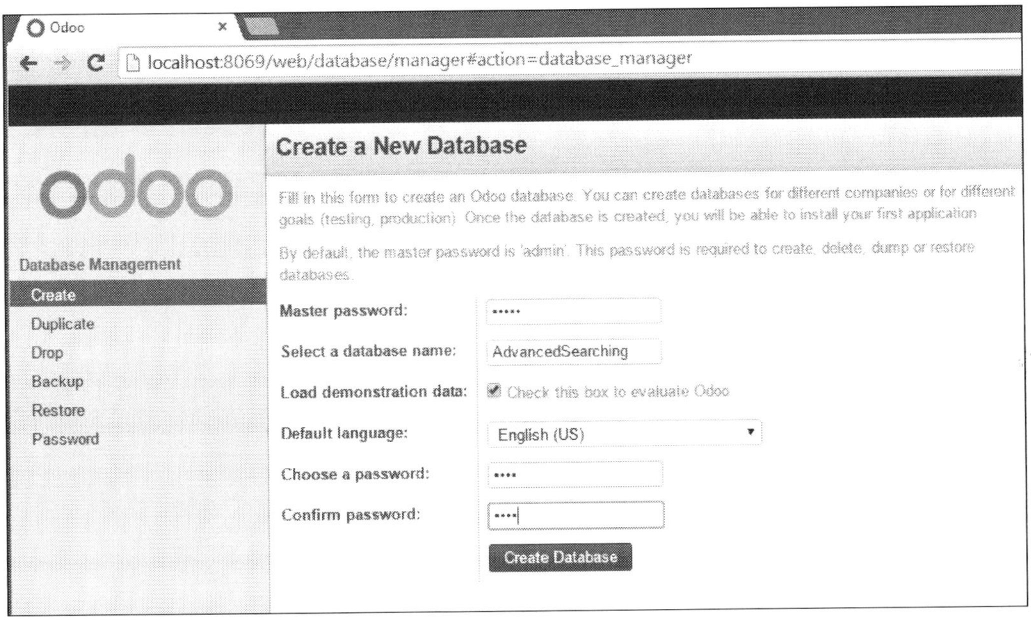

After you click on **Create Database**, Odoo will set up the new database. So that we have an application to work with, we will install the **CRM** application.

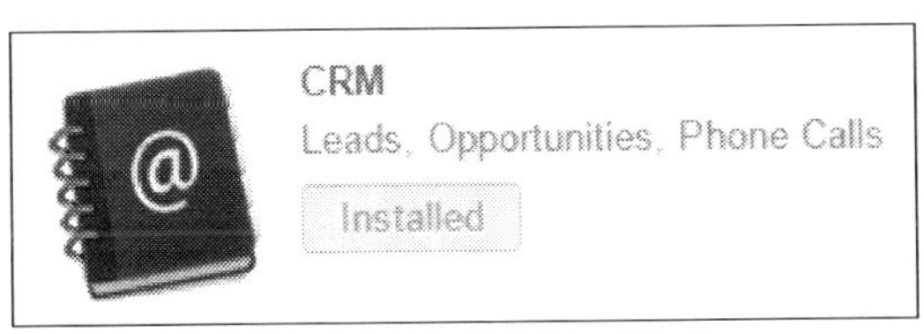

Searching in Odoo

Odoo provides a standardized search box at the top right in all of the list and Kanban views. Depending on the menu item, some forms come with predefined filters already set for the list.

If you navigate to **Sales** and select **Customer**, you can see the search box in the upper-right corner with the **Customers** filter preassigned.

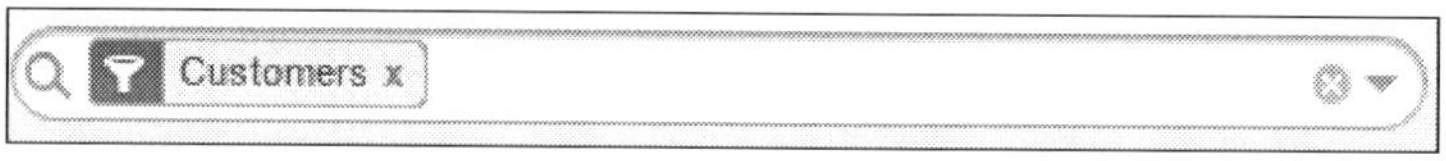

Some lists open with a predefined filter that will limit the primary dataset. In the preceding screenshot, you can see that the list view **Customers** has a customer filter applied, by default, when you open the form. Odoo stores customers, vendors, and employees in the same central database table. The **Customer** filter prevents the other types of data, such as vendors or employees from being displayed in the list.

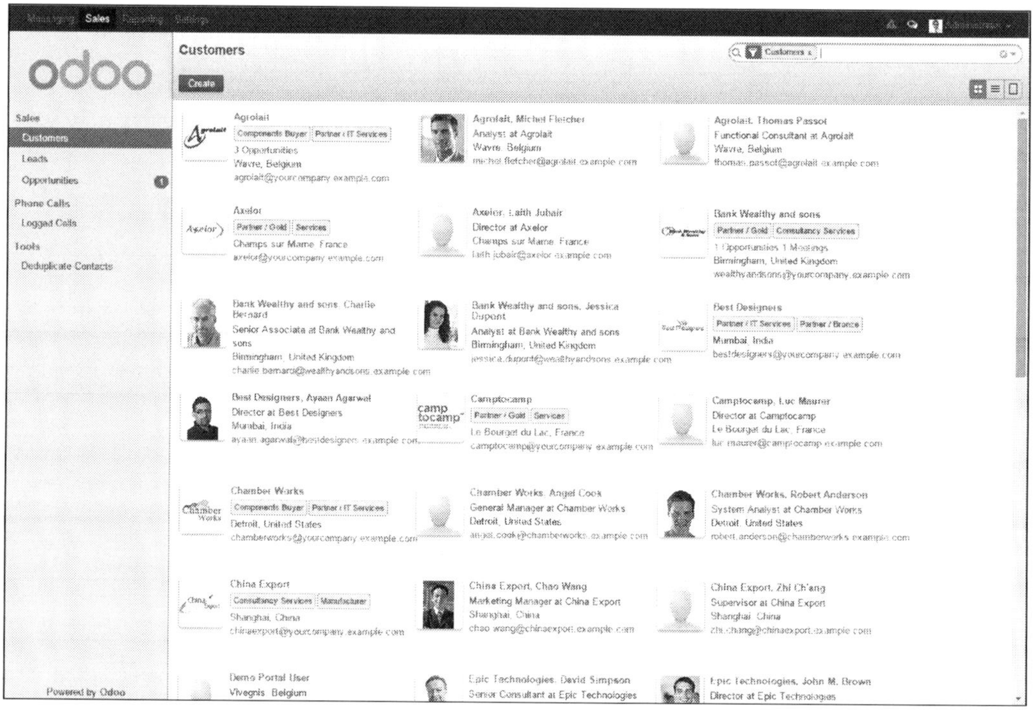

In this instance, if you clear the **Customers** filter by clicking on the small close box in the tag, you will have a list with not just customers. Instead, Odoo will return partners, users, suppliers, and contacts as well. The **Customers** filter is applied by default in this view.

> Sometimes, users can get confused if they accidently remove the filter. If you are not getting the results you expect, always double-check the filter in the top right and if necessary, navigate from the view and back again to refresh the default filter.

Basic searches are handled easily in Odoo. Just go into the search box, begin typing, and press the *Enter* key. Odoo will then look at the primary search fields for the type of data you are searching for, and show you the results in the list or Kanban view.

In the following screenshot, you can see a simple search:

In this example, Odoo has returned all the customers that have Bank in their name.

Now, we can see that there are two filters applied. The default filter **Customers** that was already there when we opened the customer list and the **Name** filter that will limit those customers to just the names that include Bank.

> The small space between the two filter tags means that both conditions are required for a record to be included in the results list (A and B).
>
> When two filter tags are butted up against one another without a space between them, it denotes that records might meet either condition (A or B).

Odoo will remember your search criteria as you move between list, Kanban, and form views. Once you go to another menu item, the search criteria will reset to the default search when you return.

The small magnifying glass in the far left of the search box will allow you to repeat your search again. This would be most useful in an environment in which transactions are coming in quickly and you want to refresh your results with the latest data.

The preceding screenshot shows the search again magnifying glass, which is to the left of the **Customers** filter.

As you type in the search box before hitting the *Enter* key, Odoo will display the available filters in a small drop-down list, directly under the search box. In the previous versions of Odoo, with each letter you type, the results list will narrow down. In Odoo 8, the search has been redesigned to display all the available filters including **My Partners**, **Persons**, **Customers**, **Suppliers**, and **Available for mass mailing**.

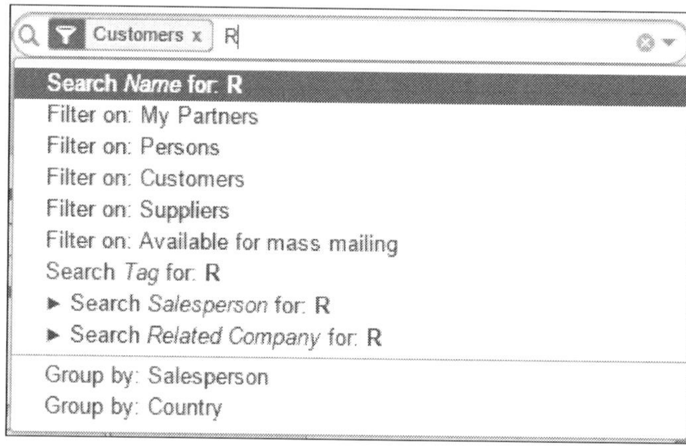

Type the letter R into the search box. You will notice how **R** is now in bold where it will be applied to the filter. Also, notice that to the left of **Search Salesperson** is a small triangle; clicking on this triangle will show an example of the results in the list:

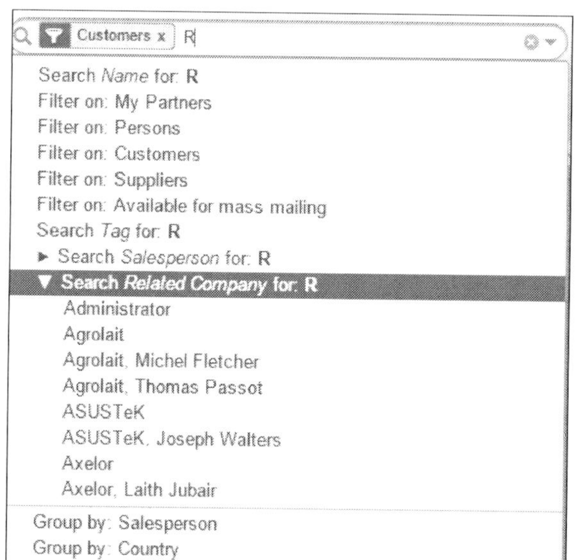

Using filters in list views

Odoo provides default filters for all of the list views. Applying a filter will limit the records that Odoo is displaying. You can apply one or more filters depending on your needs. The available filters and by what fields you can group, will vary depending on the data you are viewing.

For example, the **Products** view will have a completely different set of filters and group options compared to the **Customers** view.

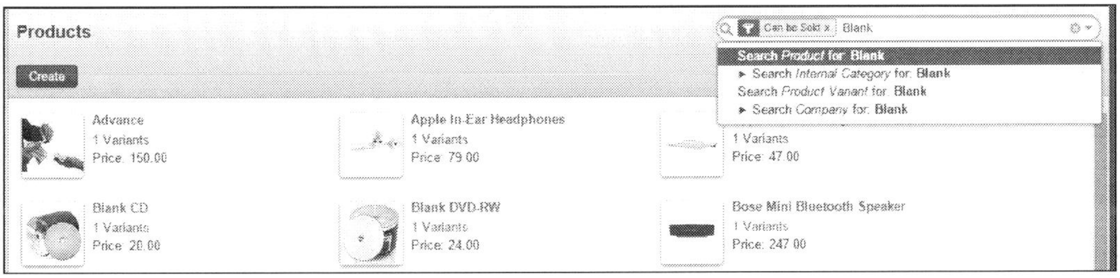

While each search box will have different default filters and group by options, the functionality is the same. In Odoo 8, you access all the search features by clicking on the small triangle on the far right of the search box.

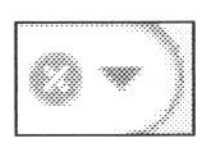

When you click on this, Odoo will expand the search area to show all the search features. Let's return to the **Customer** list and click on the small triangle to bring up the advanced search options:

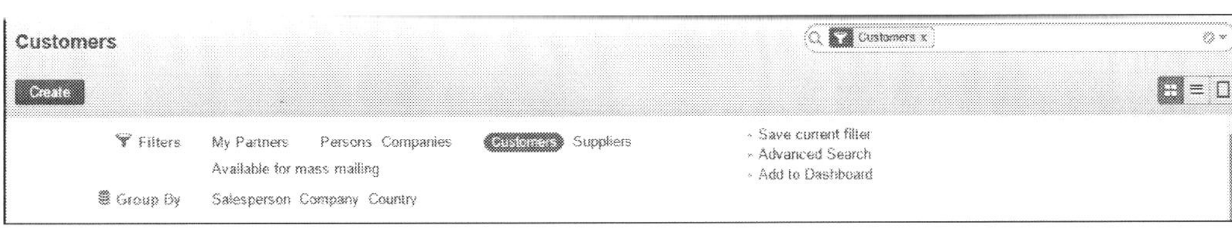

There is an area at the top that contains the default **Filters** and **Group By...** options. The second section on the right of the search area is the **Save current filter** option, where all of the user-defined filters will be stored for later use. Next, there is the **Advanced Search** option and finally an **Add to Dashboard** option to append the current search criteria to a dashboard.

In the example dropdown in the preceding screenshot, you can see that we have highlighted the filters that have been applied, **Persons** and **Customers**. The tags for the filters are also displayed inside the search box. With these two filters applied, Odoo will show the contacts or persons who are also customers. Clicking on a filter applies the filter immediately and refreshes the result list.

Naturally, the list of available filters will change depending on which set of records you are viewing. Clicking on a filter that is already highlighted will remove that filter from the search.

Grouping information

In addition to filtering your results, you can also group data in most Kanban and list views using the **Group By** option. When you group data in a Kanban view, you will get a column for each category. You can then use the horizontal scrollbar at the bottom of your window to look through the items. This will be ineffective for items in which there are a very large number of groups.

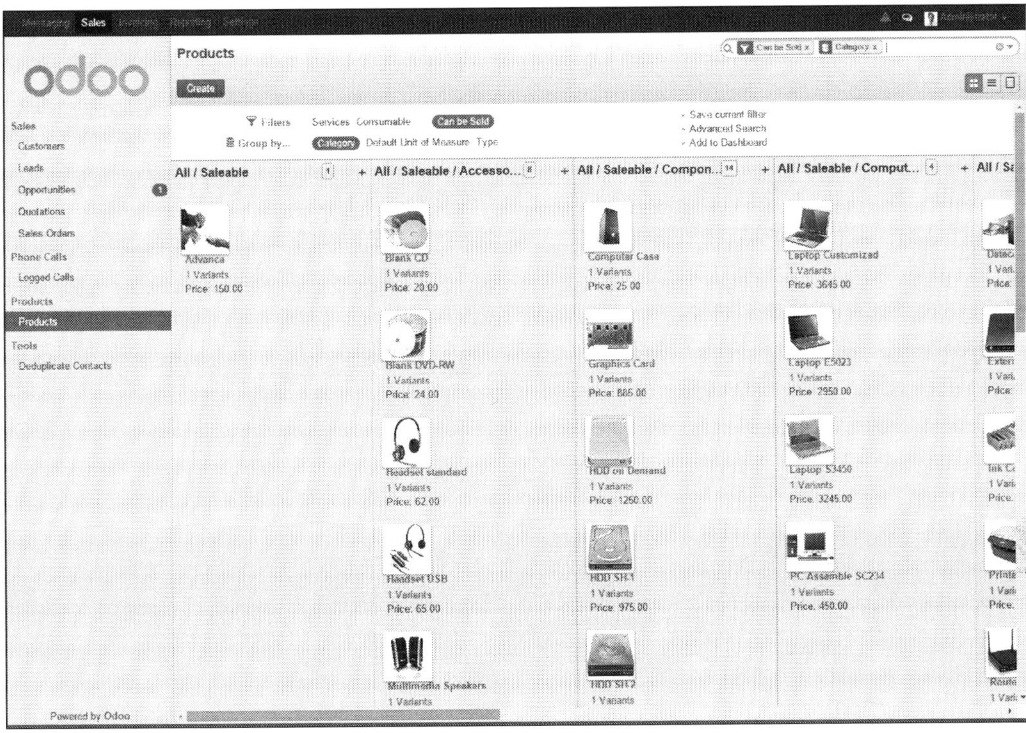

The preceding screenshot shows **Products** in the Kanban view, to demonstrate how a user will need to scroll not only up and down but also left and right to get a view all of the items.

> You need to be somewhat careful when grouping in a Kanban view. If you group on a field that has many results, you will have to scroll a long way to the right to even turn off the filter. In this case, it is usually faster just to click over to another menu and come back to restore the default search settings.

Grouped data is often more easily represented in a list view.

When you group data in a list, a little triangle appears to the left of each group header. Clicking on this triangle will display the rows grouped under that header.

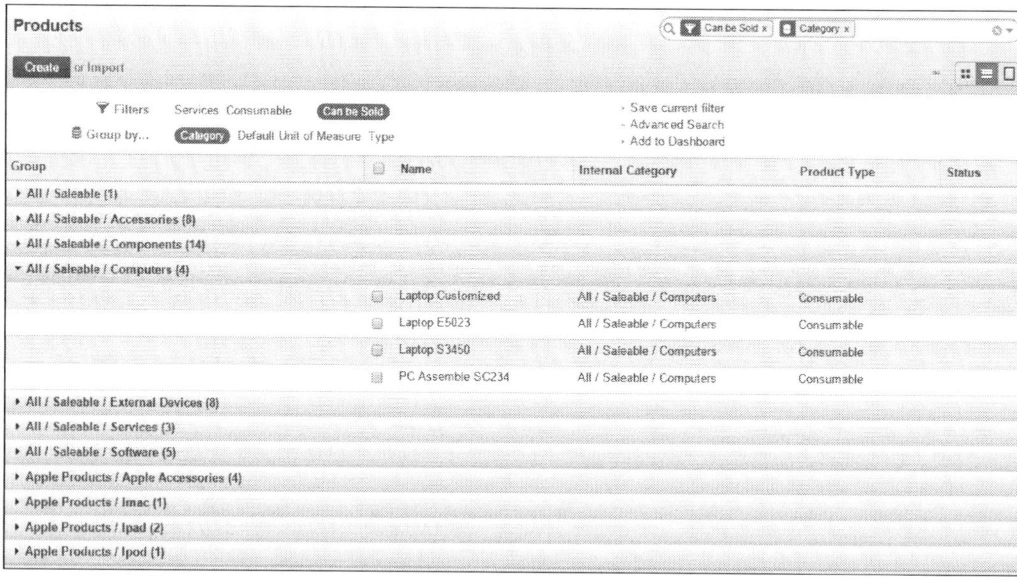

Filters and groups can be combined together to produce a list of results. To clear all search conditions and groupings at once, click on the circled **x** on the far right of the search box.

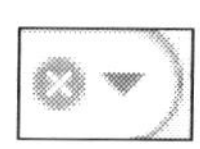

As shown in the previous screenshot, we have filtered by products that can be sold, by selecting the **Can be Sold** option in the **Filters** section; we also grouped our data by category, by selecting **Category** in the **Group by...** section. Next, we expanded the **Computers** category by clicking on the small triangle to the left. You can then see the list of products that are included under the **Computers** category. As with filters, clicking on **Category** again will remove the grouping. You can also nest groups inside of other groups simply by selecting additional items under **Group by...**.

> Grouping can be a great way to look at data. Unfortunately, with extremely large datasets, grouping lists can be very slow because far more records must be processed if you are filtering and browsing data.

Performing an advanced search

While the default filters might help us find most of the data records we seek, it is inevitable that there will come a time when we will need a more customized search. To create an advanced search, click on the down arrow on the right of the search box and then click on **Advanced Search** to expand the available options. Here, you will get a drop-down list of fields that can be used to set our search criteria.

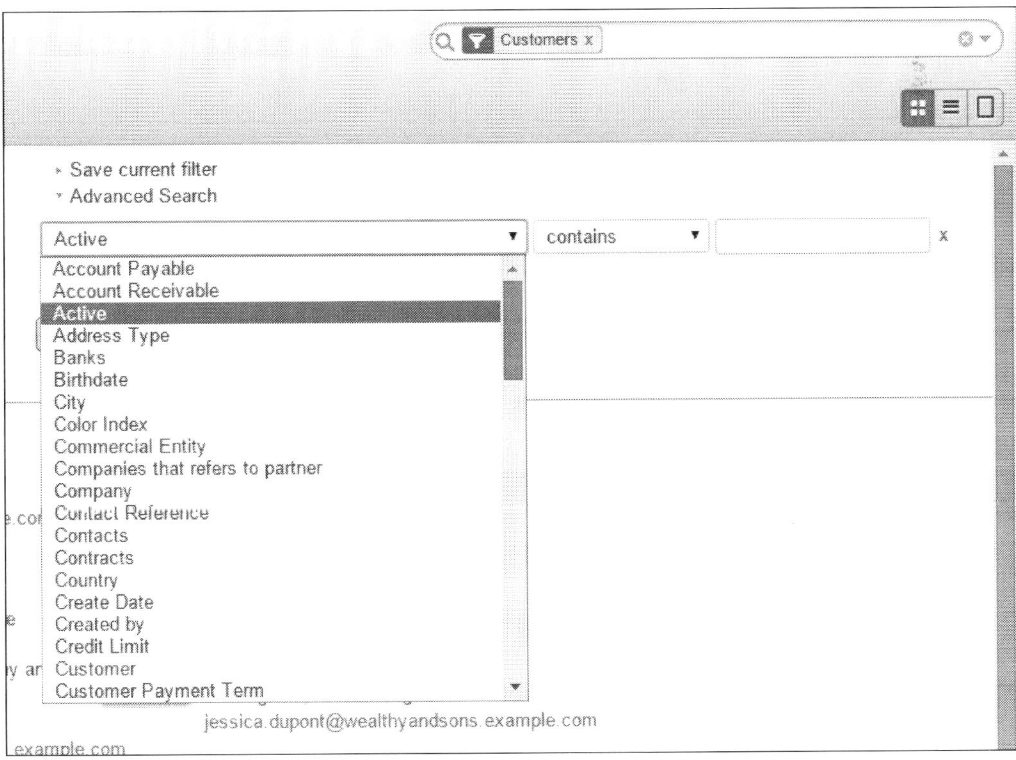

Choosing a field from the list will allow you to select from the available search operators as well as specify the data for which you wish to search. Click on **Add a condition** to enter further criteria. Clicking on the small **x** to the right of a search condition will delete that condition from your **Advanced Search**.

> In Odoo, you will often find it a best practice to make records inactive when they are no longer required. For example, if you discontinue a product, you will often find yourself unable to delete that product because there are transactions tied to it. Therefore, you will want to make that product record inactive. By default, Odoo will hide inactive records. If you need to retrieve inactive records, use **Advanced Search** to create a condition where the **Active** field `is false` and then apply it to this filter.

You can continue to add additional criteria to your **Advanced Search**. When you have specified all the criteria you want to use in your search, click on the **Apply** button to apply the custom filter.

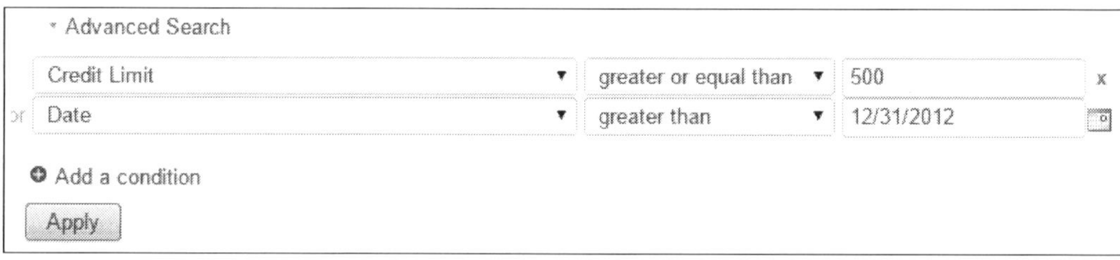

In the **Advanced Search** option, we have specified two conditions: **Credit limit** must be greater or equal than 500 or the date that the customer was acquired must be greater than **12/31/2012**. Many users can get confused and believe that this filter would imply that both **Credit Limit** and **Date** must meet our criteria, but it is not so. Notice, the faint little **or** to the left of the second condition.

Specifying multiple advanced searches

As you can see in our previous example, Odoo will always use an **or** operation between each of the conditions you add to the search. But what if we want a search where the credit limit is greater than `500` and the date the customer was acquired is greater than **12/31/2012**? To accomplish this, you must first apply the advanced search with only the credit limit condition defined. That will limit the results to only records of customers that have **Credit Limit greater than** `500`. Then, you can go back and add a second advanced search that only contains the **Date greater than 12/31/2012** condition.

Just remember that if you want both conditions to be true, then they must be applied separately. If you want either of the conditions to be true, then add them together in one search.

In the previous screenshot, we created a search that will return customers that have a credit limit greater than or equal to 500; or a customer acquisition date greater than 12/31/2012, and each of those customers must also have a total receivables less than 1000.

Saving your advanced searches

While advanced searches are quite powerful, they can often take a bit of time to configure and get the results just like you want them. Fortunately, Odoo allows you to save your searches so that you will not have to build them from scratch each time. To save a custom search, click on the little triangle next to **Save current filter**, provide a name for the search, and then click on **Save**.

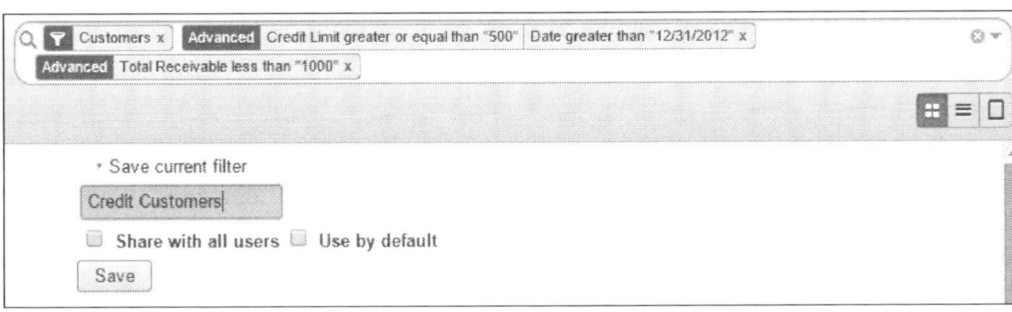

Once you click on **Save**, the filter is added to your list of **Custom Filters** and can be applied just like the default Odoo filters. In addition, you can also have the option to save the custom filter for all users, and even set a custom filter as the default filter to be applied when you bring up the list.

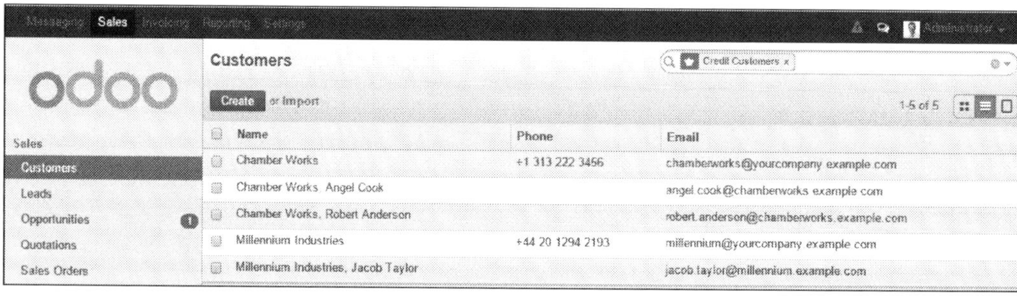

In the preceding screenshot, we applied the custom filter, **Credit Customers**, which we just saved. As you can see, the criteria at the top no longer shows all the detail in the advanced search and instead, uses the name you provided when you saved the custom filter.

> There is no easy way for an end user to see what the criteria of their search is, after they have named and saved their search for later use. Like in our example, **Credit Customers** is all we will see when returning to the search later. Until Odoo provides an easier method, users should be encouraged to document their searches.

The ability to save advanced searches into your own custom filters and make them available for other users, allows you to better customize Odoo for your business requirements.

Adding information to your custom dashboard

Dashboards allow you to take information that you need to look at frequently and put it together in one place. Odoo has a very flexible dashboard system. Each user has a personal dashboard named `My Dashboard` provided with the default Odoo setup.

To add a new result set to your dashboard, simply click on the little triangle next to **Add to Dashboard**. By default Odoo, will prompt you to add the search list to your own personal dashboard. However, if you wish, you can add the results to any dashboard by selecting the name of that dashboard in the list and clicking on the **Add** button.

In this example, the current **Credit Customers** filter we created in the previous step will be added to **My Dashboard**, which can be found as the first option under the **Reporting** menu.

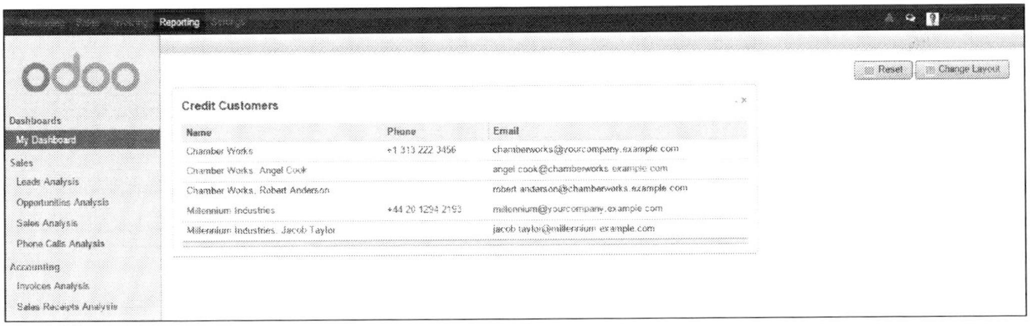

Odoo provides a variety of layouts so you can customize the appearance of the dashboard according to your preference. For example, you might want to have two columns of lists summarizing your sales or, if there are view columns, you might choose to have a column of three lists.

Clicking on the **Change Layout** button will bring up a small pop-up window to allow you to select an alternate layout.

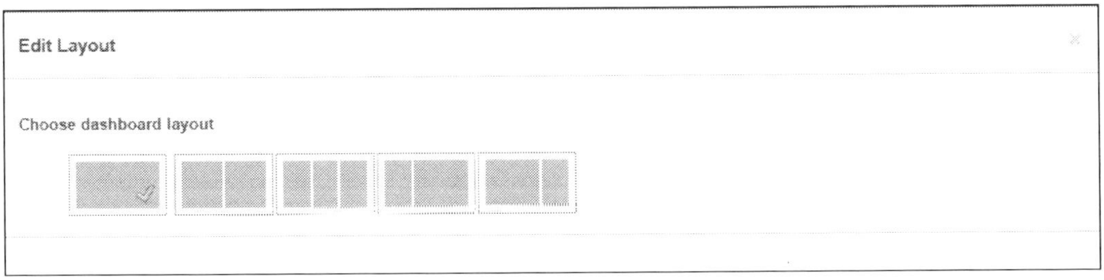

In the top-right corner of each item added to the dashboard, you can click on the little underscore icon to collapse the report area down to just its title. To arrange items on your dashboard, simply click and drag the item to drop it in the desired location. Finally, you can remove an item from the dashboard by clicking on the close box in the upper-right corner of the item.

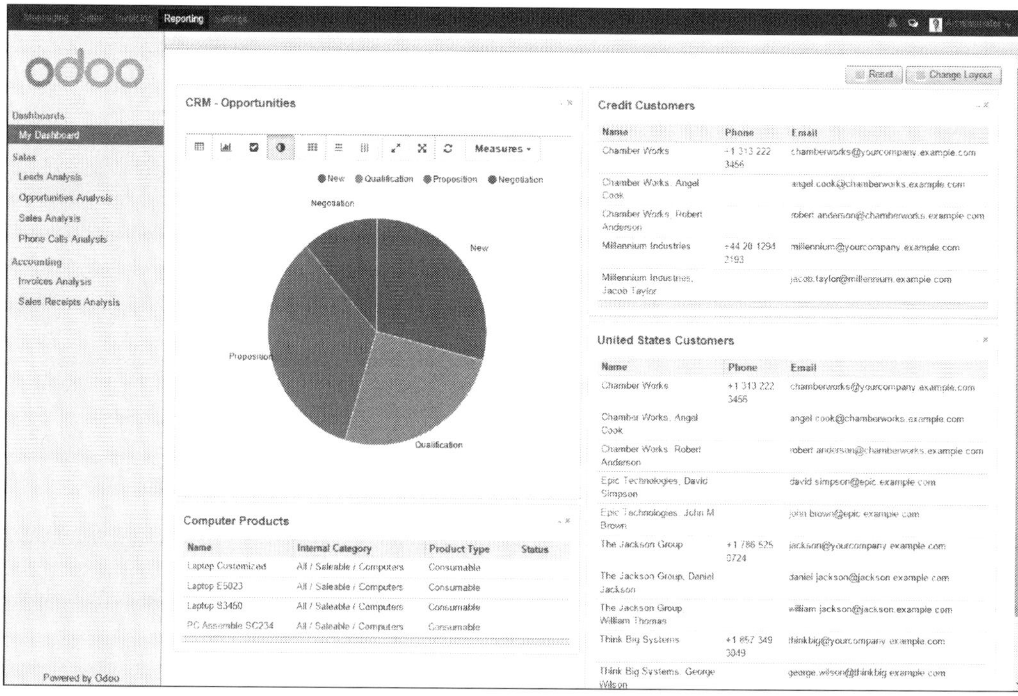

In this example, we have added a few more items to the dashboard and arranged them into two columns. Adding a graph is just as easy as adding a list view to the dashboard. In this example, we went under **Opportunities**, changed the view to graph, and then added it to our dashboard. For graphs, there is a toolbar above the graph that allows you to change properties that determine how the graph is displayed.

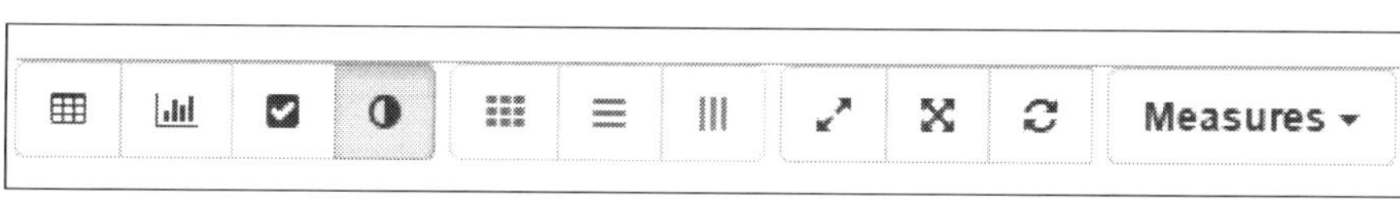

The first group of four icons on the left determine the main format for how the data is displayed. This can be either data in a table, bar graph, line chart, or pie chart. In this example, we have selected the pie chart. The next three buttons are heat maps that are only active if you are using data in a table form.

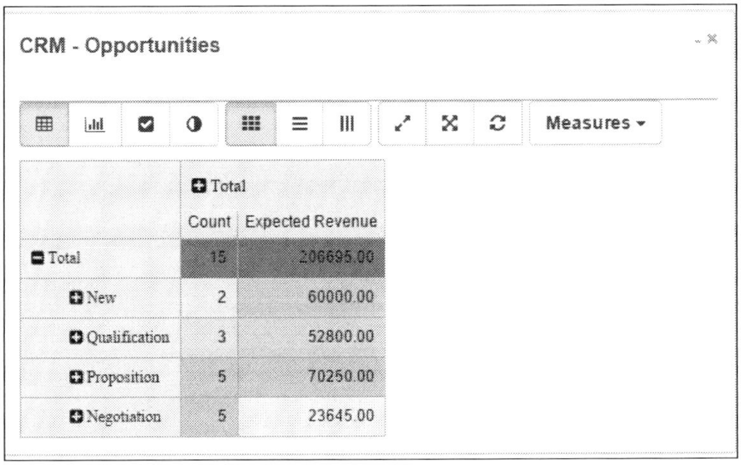

As you can see, the heat map will darken the larger numbers and lighten the smaller numbers.

The third group of icons allows you to swap the axis of the data, expand all the rows and columns, or refresh the data to update it if there have been any changes since the data was displayed.

The **Measures** drop-down menu allows you to pick which data items you want to plot in your table or graph:

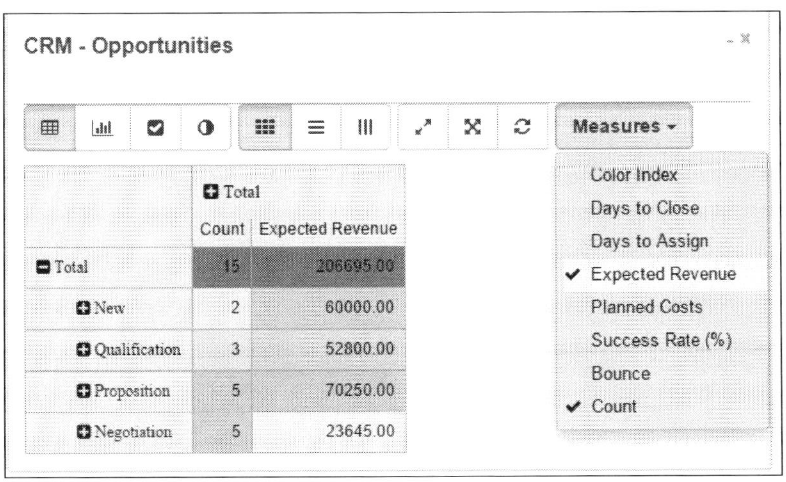

Summary

In this chapter, we examined Odoo's advanced searches and dashboards. Advanced searching allows you to search on a variety of fields as well as save your searches so you can easily pull them up later. Using these features, you can more easily find the data you are looking for, and place the data that you need frequently into your own personal dashboard.

In the next chapter, we will explore Odoo's powerful new website builder that integrates with Odoo business applications and e-commerce solutions.

11

Building a Website with Odoo

In this chapter, we will look at, perhaps, the most important new business application added to Odoo in version 8, the Odoo Website Builder application.

In this chapter, we will cover the following topics:

- Introducing **Content Management Systems** (**CMS**) and how they make it possible to manage websites
- Modifying pages with Odoo's Website Builder
- Inserting and customizing blocks
- Learning to use important Odoo website blocks
- Editing the menu of your website and organizing pages
- Selecting themes for your website
- Promoting your website

What is CMS?

The Website Builder application available for Odoo 8 can be considered, what is commonly known as, a Content Management System or CMS. A CMS provides a collection of tools that allow you to structure, organize, and manipulate your website without having to interact directly with the inner workings of your website. A key feature of a CMS is the ability for nonprogrammers and those with little technical expertise to create and edit content on the website once the initial structure of the site has been designed.

Odoo is entering into a very crowded market that has a great variety of both open source and paid CMS products, from which you can choose to build your website. Here are a few of the most popular website CMS, all of which at this point have considerably more configuration options and greater levels of adoption.

WordPress

WordPress is arguably the most popular CMS that companies choose to deploy for their website. More than a decade of maturity and a massive install base means that there are plenty of themes, add-ons, and professionals that can support a WordPress website. In addition, WordPress is open source, based on PHP, and continues to be developed aggressively and in more recent versions, it is targeting improved social networking features.

Joomla

Also, enjoying great popularity in the crowded CMS market, written in PHP and open source, is Joomla. This CMS, while perhaps not as often deployed as WordPress, has thousands of available plug-ins and can be found under some very prominent sites on the Internet. A few of the more high profile sites that use Joomla for their CMS include Harvard University and the Guggenheim Museum.

Drupal

No list of popular CMS solutions would be complete without Drupal. Like the other two, this CMS is also PHP-based and open source. For the most part, Drupal has more advanced capabilities and would be considered for sites more complex than perhaps you would use to build in WordPress. While there are fewer available themes for Drupal than for Joomla or WordPress, that has not kept Drupal from being the CMS for very popular websites including Popular Science and Sony Music.

Evoq or DotNetNuke

This content manager, previously known as **DNN** or **DotNetNuke**, has recently been through its own rebranding effort, much like OpenERP became Odoo. So according to their own news release, DotNetNuke is no more, and is now to be known as **Evoq**. While not nearly as popular as the other three listed, Evoq has the distinction of being a Windows Server based solution that uses Microsoft's .NET platform. Some big names using Evoq for their CMS include Hilton and Samsung.

These are just a few of many CMS options; others include Typo3, Frontpage, PublishMe.se, and Plone, all of which are very popular throughout Europe. The type of CMS you need depends heavily on your requirements for your website. Do you need to edit content frequently? Would you like to have a shopping cart that integrates with your accounting system? Does your website need to be mobile-friendly? These are all questions to consider when choosing a CMS.

Why use Odoo Website Builder for your CMS?

With so many CMS solutions available that have far better support and mature features, a very valid question is: *Why would I use Odoo's Website Builder for my CMS?* Not only is this a good question to ask, it is vital when building a website for your company that you pick the tools that work best for your given situation and requirements. So let's quickly look at some of the pros and cons to get a quick look at what are the strengths and weaknesses of using Odoo as the CMS to build your website.

The potential advantages to using Odoo as a CMS

While Odoo is still new and does not offer the proven track record and the number of successful websites as the CMS products, which were previously mentioned, there are still some very compelling reasons to consider Odoo as your CMS:

- One-click setup, if you already have Odoo installed.
- Very easy-to-use features, such as fast page editing and simple controls.
- Great support for mobile devices.
- Powerful built-in language translation support.
- Seamless integration with Odoo to leverage many of the applications already available. This includes CRM and Marketing applications but is especially true for the e-commerce application that will be covered in the next chapter.
- A growing number of professional themes that will make the Odoo Website Builder an attractive option in the years to come for those who are already using Odoo.
- Good built-in promotional tools.

The current limitations of using Odoo as a CMS

Despite a growing list of positive reasons to consider Odoo as your CMS, there are also some reasons why its current version might not be the CMS for every solution:

- Very limited support among hosting companies, website designers, and consultants. If your Odoo website breaks, you are reliant on Odoo experts to fix your website.

- Limited CMS functionality for version control of your web pages.
- Difficulty configuring custom URLs and utilizing subdomains.
- Complex (and sometimes confusing) security of web pages and assignment of access permissions.
- There are a very limited set of themes available that work directly with Odoo and the professional themes that are available are expensive.
- Immaturity of the CMS itself might cause volatility in the years ahead as new features are added making it a challenge to move your website between databases of various Odoo versions.
- Lack of an easy way to move websites or webpages between Odoo databases, which can add to integration, testing, and deployment challenges.
- Possible vulnerabilities if the publicly-accessed web portal's connections to customer, employee, and accounting data are not amply tested for security holes.

Deciding what is best for your company

Currently, Silkworm, the company we are using for our real business example, does not use Odoo for their CMS. That said, we expect this could change in the years ahead and the previously mentioned positive benefits of using Odoo for your website might be enough to make it a good choice.

Backing up the website you make in your Odoo database

If you do use Odoo's Website Builder for your website, backup your database often. All of the web pages you create are stored inside your database. So you must back it up to make sure you have a copy of your website. Additionally, you'll want to make sure you keep your Odoo application files backed up as well, because static themes, images, and CSS files that are located there must be available to properly display your website.

Installing the Odoo Website Builder

One of the greatest reasons to consider Odoo's Website Builder is that you can try it out in a matter of seconds. Just install the Website Builder like you would any other Odoo application. Go to **Settings**, choose **Local Modules**, and search for **Website Builder**:

Once you click on **Install**, Odoo will install the required modules and automatically redirect you to the home page of your new website. Also, you should be presented with a Website Builder tutorial that will walk you through some of the basics of building your website.

Here, we can see the initial web page presented by Odoo:

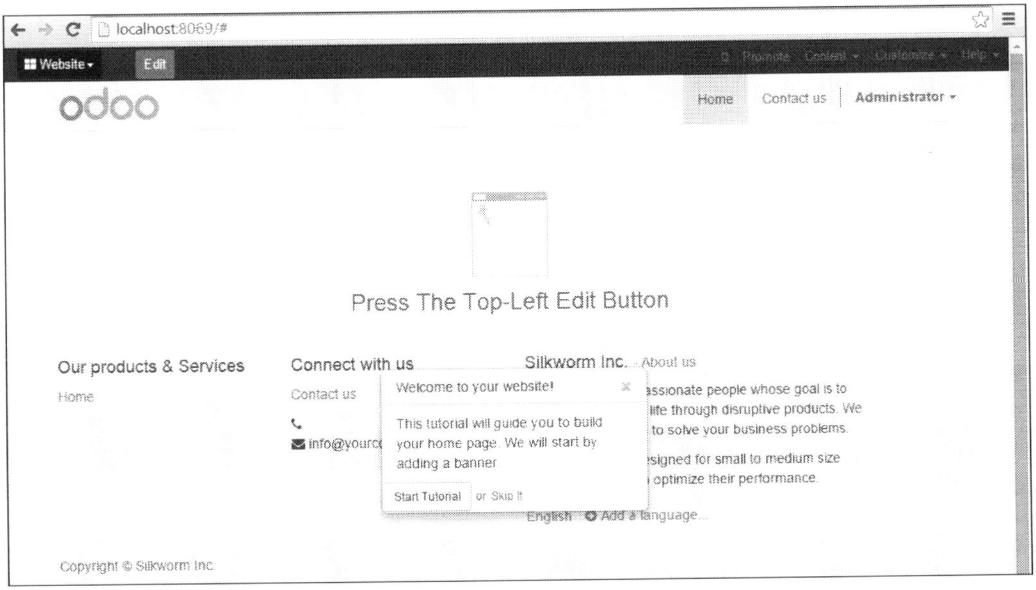

In the middle of the screen, the tutorial presents the **Welcome to your website!** message and a brief introduction of what the tutorial will cover. We will go ahead and use this tutorial to highlight the basic features of the Odoo Website Builder application:

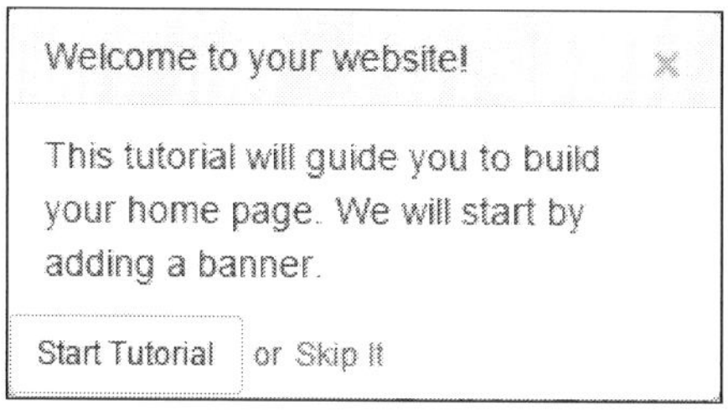

Clicking on the **Start Tutorial** button will direct your attention to the **Edit** page button at the top-left corner of the screen. This button is available on every page while you are on your Odoo website. Clicking on this **Edit** button will toggle your page into the edit mode so you can make changes to your website.

Click on the **Edit** button to begin editing your home page.

After clicking on the **Edit** button, your page should refresh to display the toolbars and options available to edit your web page.

Here, we will see that the tutorial will prompt you to insert blocks into your page. This is the action you will take anytime you want to add additional content to your web page.

> Building blocks can house text, images, or a combination of these in various formats, such as an image with text above, beside, or below it, or large, bold heading text with smaller paragraph text below it. Also, note that the instructions that walk you through each step are just for the tutorial that is run the first time. Once you have completed the tutorial (or have closed it intentionally), it will no longer give you interactive directions.

Click on **Insert Blocks** to add new content to your web page:

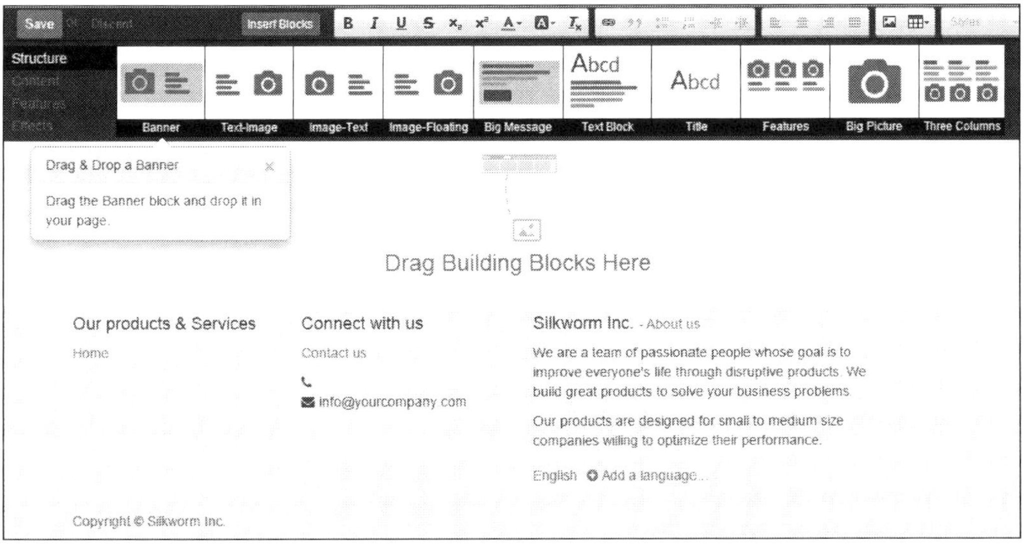

Once you click on **Insert Blocks**, the page refreshes to display a list of blocks available under the **Structure** category on the far left. The tutorial then prompts you to drag and drop a banner block from the toolbar on to your web page. The **Drag Building Blocks Here** prompt in the middle of the page shows you exactly where you must drop your first block on the page.

Click on and hold your left mouse button over the banner block and drag it out onto your web page. The web page will immediately update to show you the banner along with a snippet of text with a button to the left.

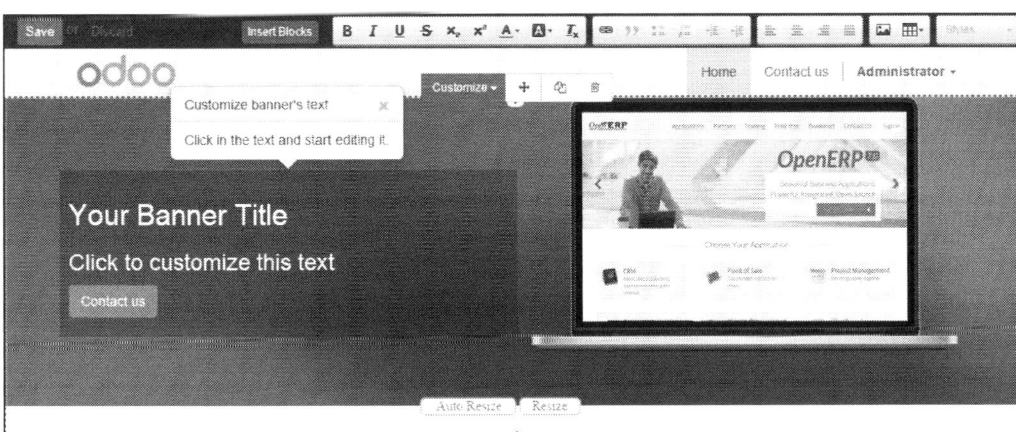

Odoo's simple tutorial continues prompting you to now change the title of your text to whatever you choose. All of the editing is performed right in the page itself. Just use your mouse to select the text like you would in any simple text editing program. Also notice that at the top, you have the ability to modify text to make it bold, underlined, italic, or other properties such as color.

After a few changes, the Odoo Website Builder tutorial will come back, once again calling attention to a very important function which is selecting the parent container of any object you are editing.

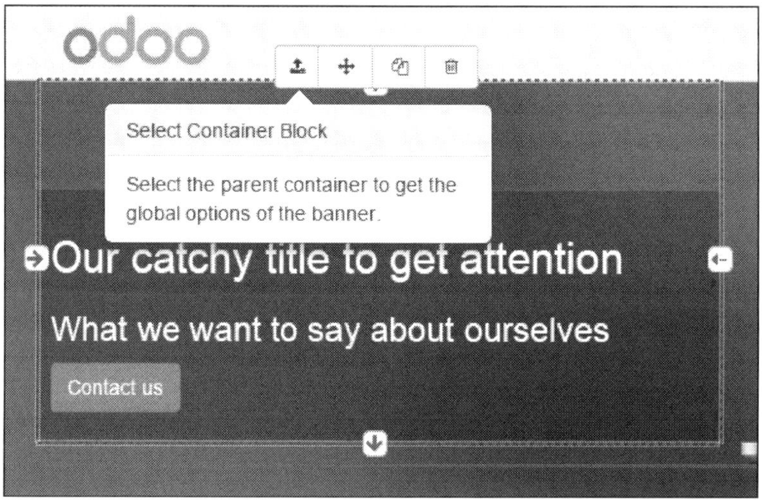

As you can see in the preceding screenshot, the icon on the far left is what you use to select the parent container from within any object you are editing. When you click on this icon, the focus changes to the parent of that object and you get access to all the options within that container.

> In most instances, you will have parent containers that contain other objects. It is unusual that you would have containers nested within containers. Container Blocks hold content objects, such as text headings, text paragraphs, or images. Therefore, you can't drop a container block inside of a content object.

Modifying the settings of a block

Once you have a block selected, you will get a context-sensitive **Customize** menu that will give you options to modify how the block displays its contents. In this example, we have the ability to change background images as well as change the picture itself.

One nice feature is that as you navigate the menu, it will show you what the current option is that you have selected. So in the following screenshot, we can see that the background of the image for this specific object is **Color Splash**:

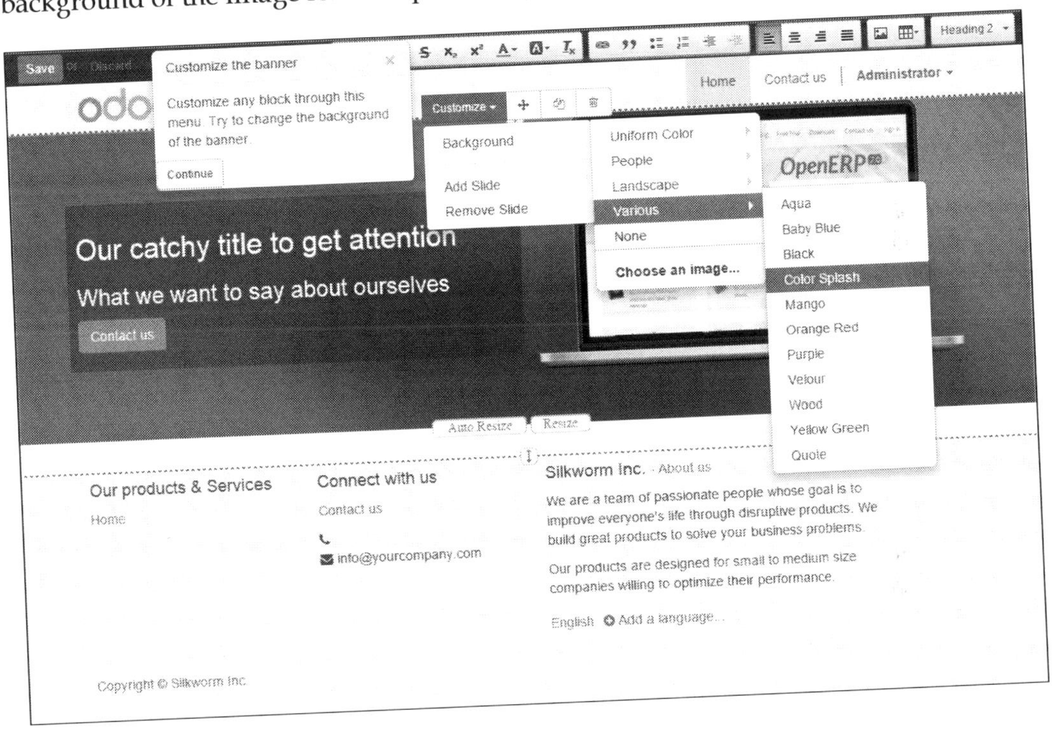

You might also notice that in this menu is the option to **Add Slide** and **Remove Slide**. You will use these options to create other banner text objects, which the user could then navigate and go through the pages on your website. Experiment with adding and removing slides to see if it creates the look and feel you want for your website.

Adding additional blocks to your web page

Odoo's tutorial prompts you to add another block to your page; specifically the **Features** block. This block provides you with a three-column features list that provides a simple foundation to describe three options for a given product or service.

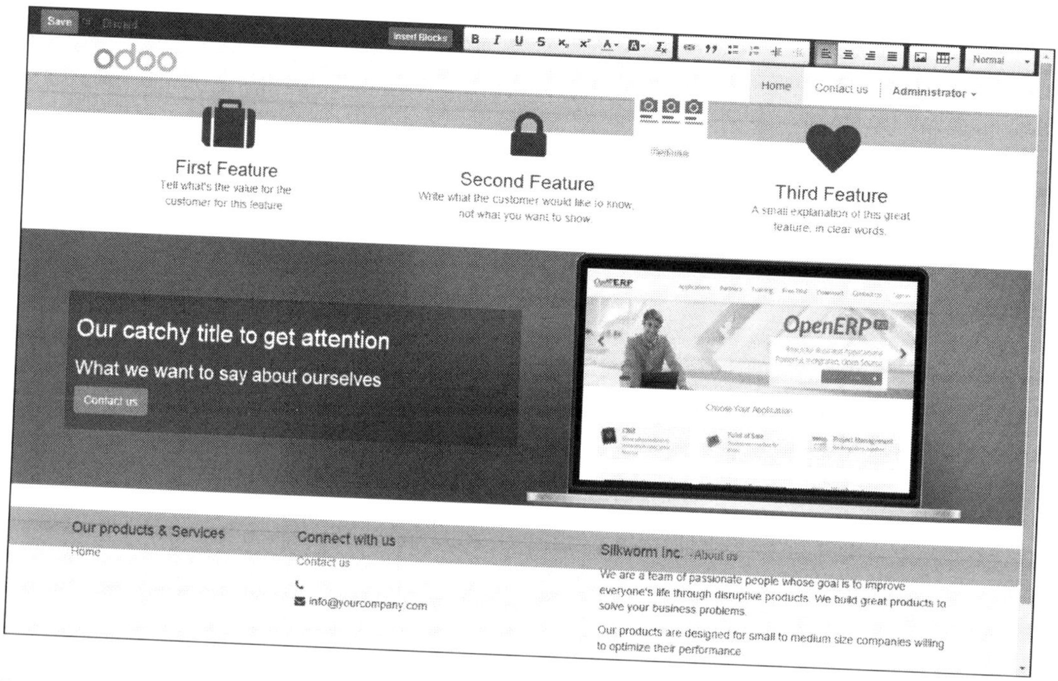

In the preceding screenshot, I have intentionally shown you the purple place holders that indicate where you can drag and drop your blocks. You will notice that in this example, there are two specific places that you can place the **Features** block. One slot is above our banner, the other is at the bottom where the purple bar sits on top of the **Our products & Services** heading. You can only drop the **Features** block in these two places where the purple indicators are showing. For example, you could not drop the features block under **Our catchy title to get attention**.

Saving your web page

After making these changes, the Odoo tutorial will prompt you to save your changes using the **Save** button on the top-left corner of the page:

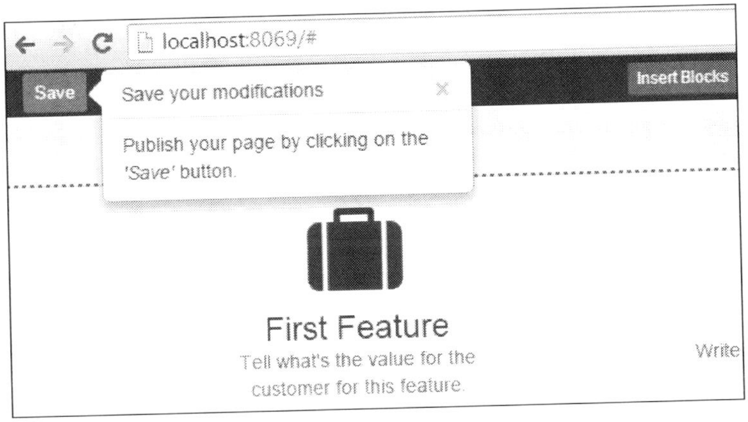

After you click on the **Save** button, the page will refresh and we can see our web page as it will appear to the visitors that come to our site:

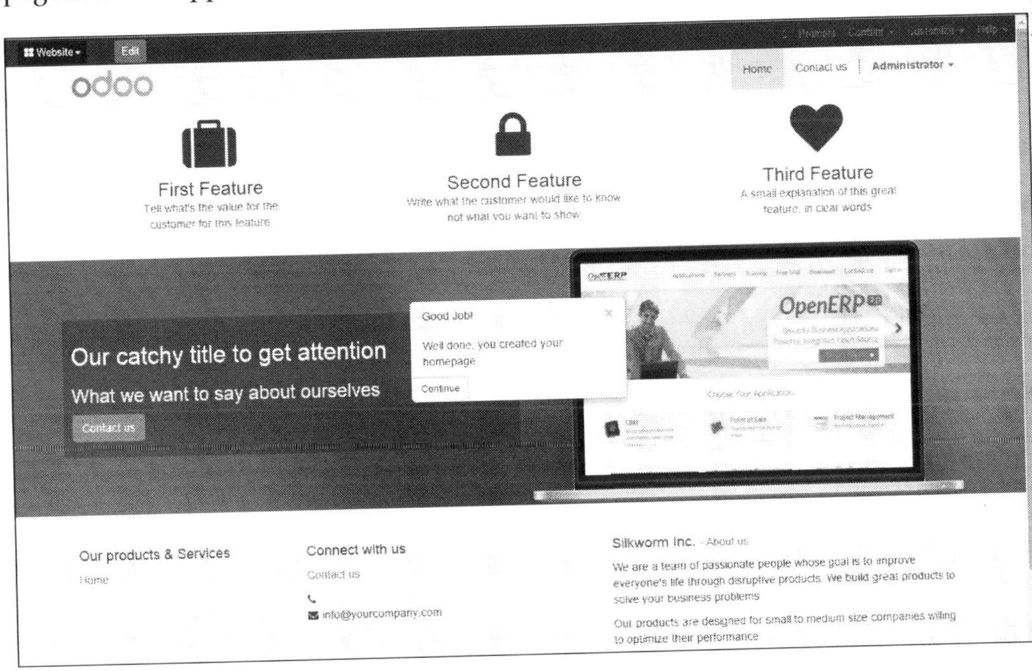

Odoo's tutorial will give you a little congratulations message for successfully saving your website and completing this part of the tutorial. You've now learned how to edit web pages, add new content blocks to these pages, and save those changes. As you can see, it is pretty easy to create web pages in Odoo using the Website Builder. Still, expect to spend a bit of time learning how the various objects can be combined and edited to get the results you desire.

Now, that we have a simple web page setup, you can go on with the tutorial by clicking on the **Continue** button.

Previewing your website on a mobile device

Certainly one of the compelling reasons to consider Odoo's Website Builder for your CMS is that it was built from the beginning to support mobile devices. This feature is so central to the Website Builder application that if you have been following along, the tutorial will now prompt you to see how your webpage will appear on a mobile device.

Click on the **Mobile Preview** button to see how your web page will look on a typical mobile device:

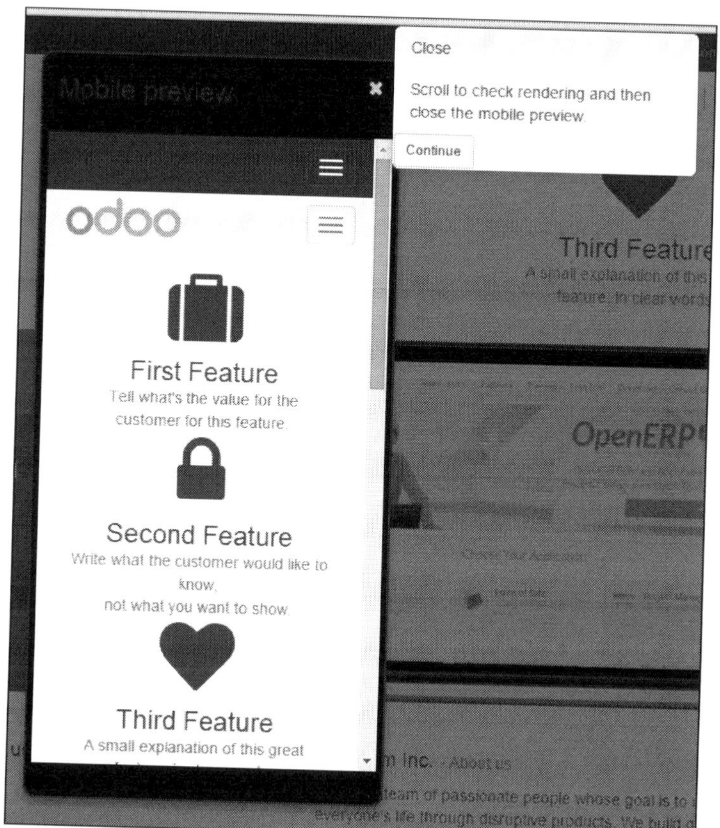

While you should still double-check all of your web pages on real mobile devices before you deploy your website, this feature is very valuable for getting an idea of what your pages will look like on mobile devices.

Adding new pages and menus to your website

Now, it is time to take a look at how we add new pages and menus to our website. Typically, it is a good idea to lay out your ideas ahead of time by deciding what pages you need and how your menu structure for your website should look. I personally believe that it is better to start out simple and add additional complexity as you go. Still, there are some pages you might already know you must have on your website so you might as well go ahead and add them.

Odoo's tutorial prompts you to use the **Content** menu to add menus and pages:

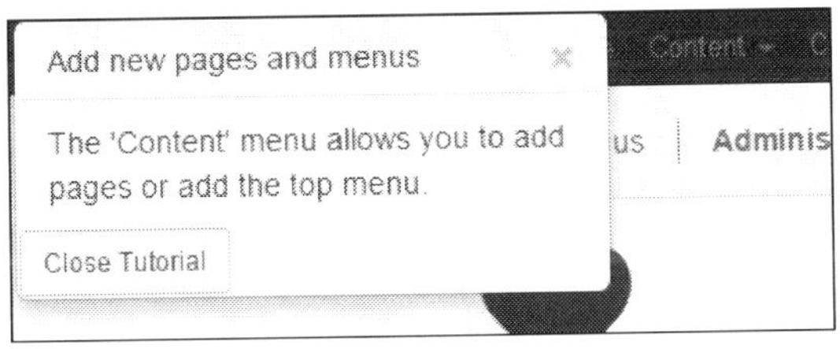

At this point, it is the end of the tutorial provided by Odoo. Still, this brings attention to the **Content** menu we will use to add a new page to our website and continue exploring some more advanced aspects of Odoo's Website Builder.

Adding a new page

Under the **Content** menu, choose **New Page** to bring up a simple form to add a new web page to our website:

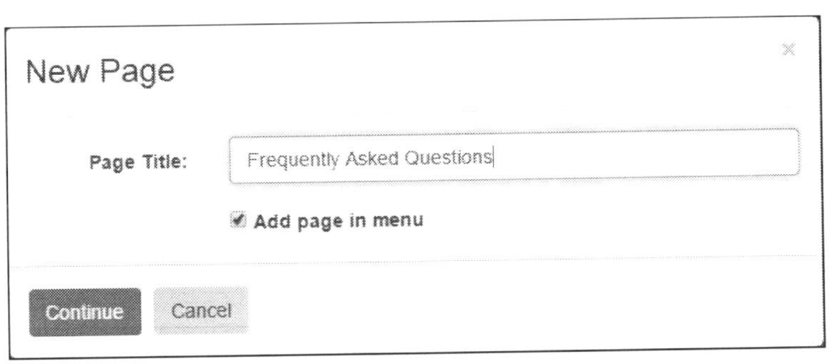

In this example, we have named our page **Frequently Asked Questions**, a page that is common on many websites. We have also left the checkbox, **Add page in menu** checked so that our page will be added to our menu automatically when the page is created.

Simply, click on the **Continue** button and the web page is added and ready to be edited just like we edited the previous web page.

Creating your Frequently Asked Questions web page

In the following example, we have edited the page and inserted a **Frequently Asked Questions (FAQ)** block into the page and added some of Silkworm's frequently asked questions content.

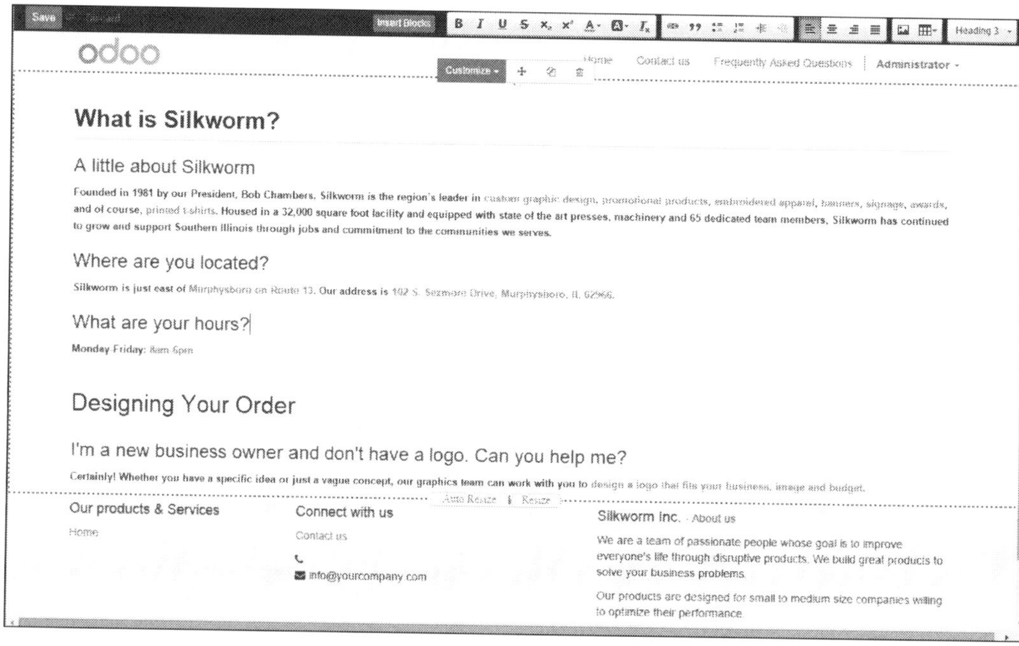

You get to the **FAQ** block by selecting **Features** on the far right once you have clicked on the **Insert Blocks** button:

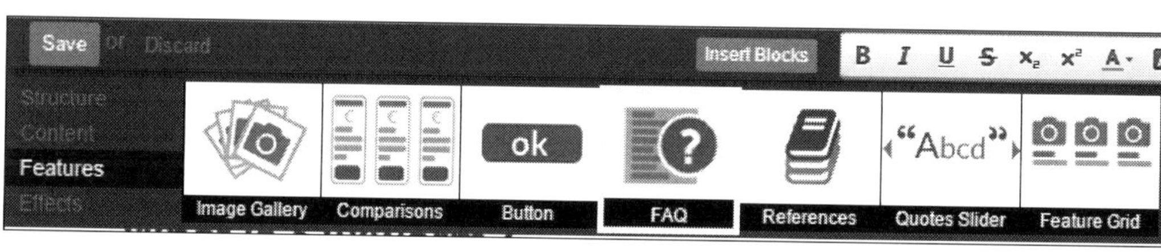

In the preceding screenshot, we have highlighted the **FAQ** block that we used to create our Frequently Asked Questions web page. Experiment with the different blocks to learn what they do so you can put them to use when designing your own web pages.

> When editing a block, click on any content object to access the Customize menu. This allows you to change whether a text block spans the width of the page or not, and whether it has a background color or background image. For blocks containing images, Customize allows you to select an existing picture or video from a library or upload a new one. Transform will allow you to rearrange, resize, and rotate these images.

Managing menus on your website

Under the **Content** menu, you can choose **Edit Menu** to organize the menu structure for your website;

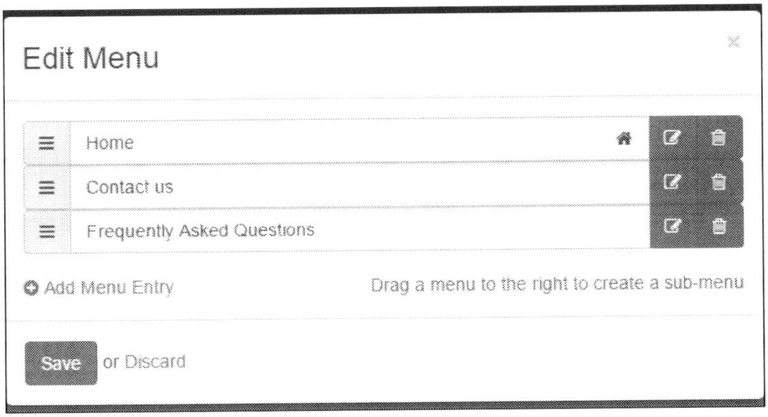

Using this simple **Edit Menu** form you can reorganize your menus by using the sliders on the far left to click and drag them into the order you desire. Any menu you drag to the top will automatically become the home page of the website and get the little icon of the house on the far right to designate the page.

Dragging a menu to the right will nest menus within other menus. A nested submenu will appear in a list slightly indented. Using these basic methods, you can create a hierarchy of menus to contain your pages in any structure you choose.

> Currently, you can only nest menu items one level deep. You cannot have submenus within submenus.

Adding a new menu to your website

Click on the **Add Menu Entry** link to bring up a form that allows you to add a new menu item to your website.

Here in this example, we have added a new menu named `Silkworm Design Tool` and specified an external link to directly connect the design tool that Silkworm currently uses, for people who wish to design orders on another website.

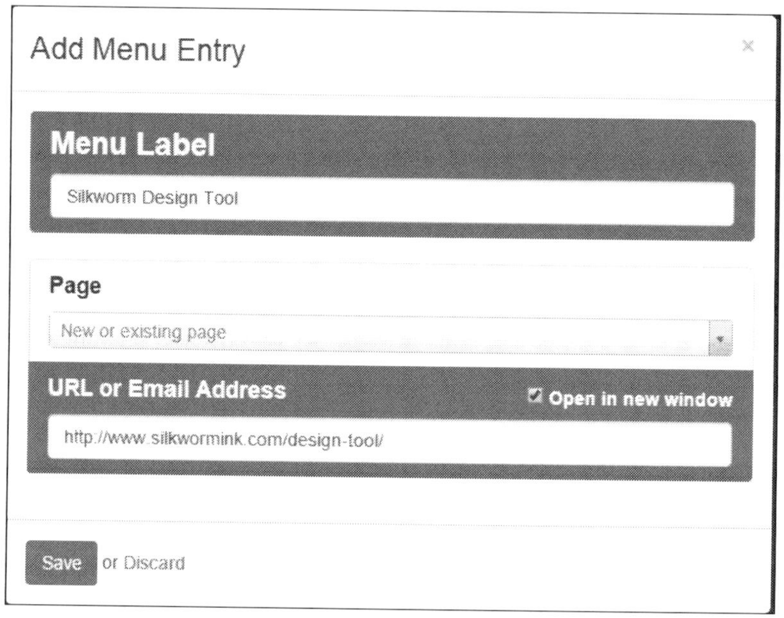

The form allows you flexibility in assigning a menu to an existing page, creating a new page, or specifying a URL or e-mail address to link to the menu. You also have the option to specify that the menu should open the page in a new window.

Changing themes in Odoo

One of the features that is attractive in most CMS solutions is the ability to change the theme of your website without having to modify your content. Odoo's Website Builder provides the ability to modify your theme by selecting the **Change Theme** option under the **Customize** menu.

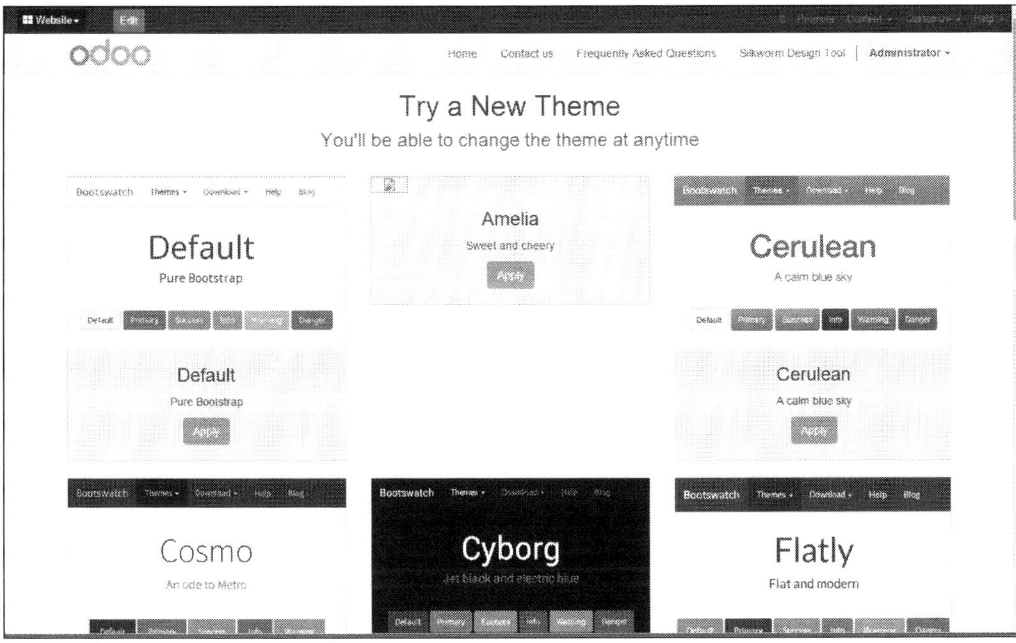

With this build of Odoo 8, you have the option to select from a variety of free Bootstrap themes. Simply click on **Apply** and your website will then be updated with the new theme.

> Bootstrap is a very popular, easy-to-use framework to create mobile-friendly websites using HTML5 and CSS languages. Bootstrap themes are templates that provide CSS stylesheets necessary to easily achieve the look you want for your website. To learn more about Bootstrap, visit `http://getbootstrap.com/`.

In the following screenshot, we can see how our Frequently Asked Questions page looks after we have applied the Cyborg theme:

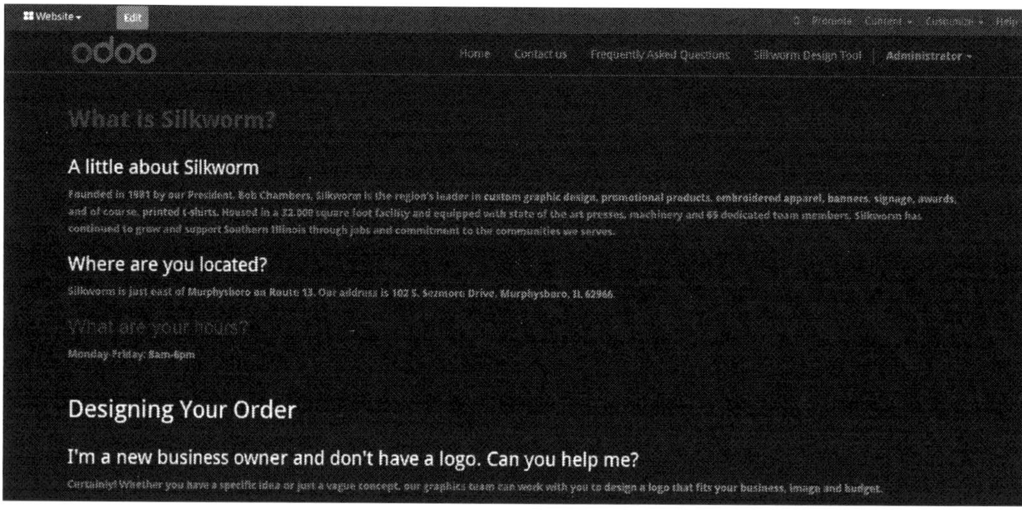

As you can see, simply by changing the theme of your website, you can create a dramatically different look.

Promoting your website

One of the other nice features of Odoo's Website Builder is the built-in promotion toolset for your website. Not only is it helpful to use the promotion option for each of your web pages, it is vital. If you don't specify the title, keywords, and descriptions for your page, Odoo will provide default information to search engines, such as Google. This is never a good idea because your website will be difficult to differentiate from all the other websites whose webmasters neglected this step. Make sure to take the time to at least provide a proper title and description for each of your web pages.

To promote your web page, navigate to the web page you wish to promote and click on **Promote** in the Website Builder menu. Odoo will then bring up the promote form:

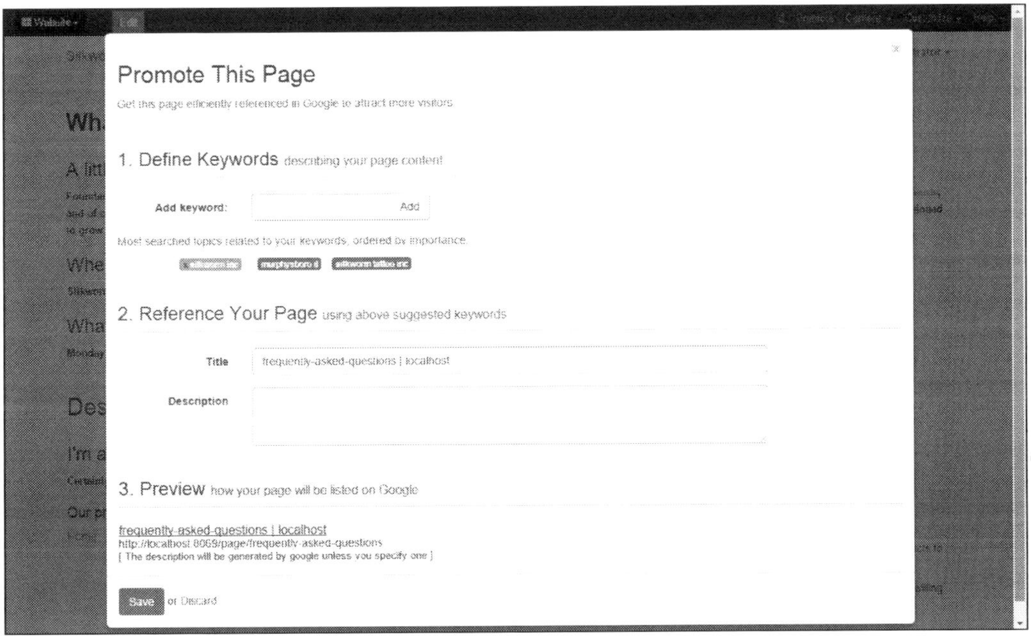

For this example, we have intentionally left the fields as they were when the form was brought up so you can see why it is so critical that you specify the title and description for each of your pages. Notice how Odoo has named our page and that the preview at the bottom is nothing like what we would want to have listed on Google.

Specifying keywords for your website

Search engine optimization (SEO) is a huge topic that can fill an entire book all on its own. One of the major aspects of good SEO is to know what keywords are the most popular for the page you wish to promote. Odoo provides a handy little tool so that as you specify keywords, Odoo will let you know associated keywords that are also popular within Google.

In the following screenshot, we enter the keyword `t-shirt`, and we can see the associated keywords that might be good to include within the content of our web page to get better results in search engines:

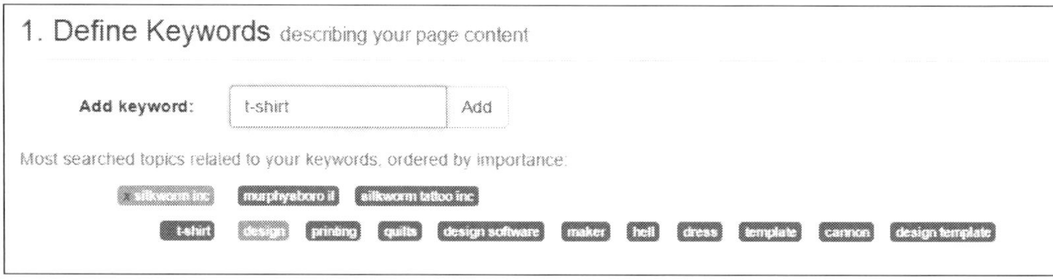

In the results, next to **t-shirt** you will see these suggestions: **design**, **printing**, **quilts**, **design software**, and so on. Notice how design is shaded in blue; this is because Odoo is indicating that this keyword is located within our web page. If, for example, we added the word **printing** within our FAQ page, we would then see the keyword colored blue accordingly.

Creating a title and description for your website

Take the time to make a description that includes high-quality keywords and accurately describes the content of your web page. There are many fine books available to help you better promote your website and provide advice on how you can get the best results in search engines.

In the following example, I have added a few keywords to the title as an example of how Odoo will color the keywords you have selected. The purpose is to try and have as many keywords as possible in your title and description so that you can get better results for your page. In this case, design and printing are important keywords that I have included in the title based on the feedback from Odoo's keyword research.

> Note that this is only for an example, and it is far more important to have accurate descriptions than to simply make a title based on popular keywords.

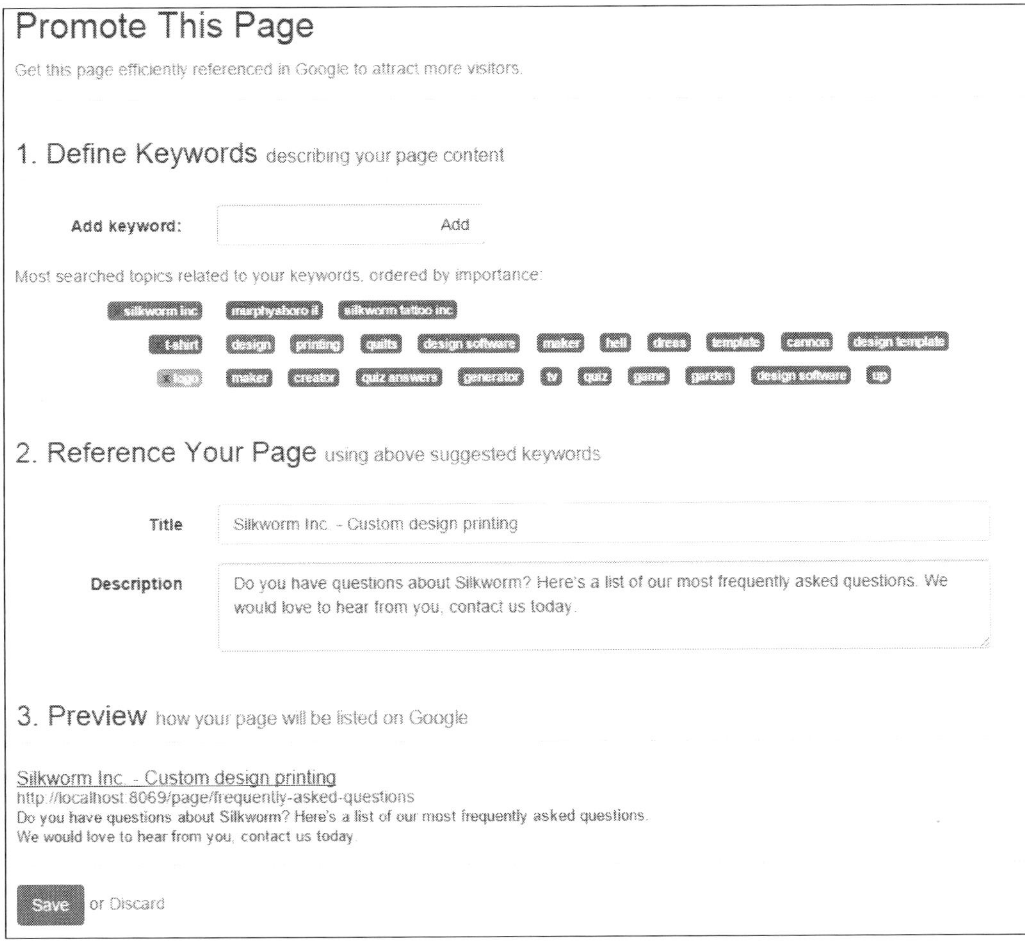

Now, that we have an accurate title and detailed description, the preview of our Google listing is much more attractive and functional.

Summary

In this chapter, we took a look at Odoo's exciting new Website Builder. We touched upon Content Management Systems (CMS) and some of the other more popular options. We then demonstrated how to install the Website Builder and followed along with Odoo's simple but effective interactive tutorial to learn the basics.

You then learned how to add new pages to websites, configure, and edit menus for the website and how to insert additional blocks and content into our pages. Finally, we finished up by learning how to change themes to give our website a new look and promote our web pages for good search results and a proper description within Google.

In the next chapter, we will look at how to use our new website to host an e-commerce shopping cart that integrates directly with our products in Odoo.

12

Implementing E-Commerce with Odoo

In the previous chapter, we took a look at the new Website Builder application and how it can be used as to easily create a website. Now that we know the basics of getting the website up and running, this chapter will show you how you can extend a simple website to become a full e-commerce site that can take and manage orders. Even better, this functionality ties directly into sales management, which you learned about in *Chapter 3, Exploring Customer Relationship Management in Odoo*.

The topics covered in this chapter are as follows:

- An overview of e-commerce and how it is implemented in Odoo
- How to install e-commerce and view the default web store
- Configuring and modifying your online store
- How to use product variants such as color and size to provide customized options for the products you sell
- Advanced product options such as alternative products, accessories, and categorizing your product
- How to set up a payment processor

Odoo and e-commerce

As I'm sure you are already well aware, **e-commerce** is a term that describes offering your products and services to customers electronically; typically on an Internet website. Over the years, e-commerce has made its way into more and more markets. There are increasing options to make payments on websites and now many mobile applications include the ability to make micro-transactions. E-commerce now covers a very wide field of options.

Popular e-commerce platforms

Like Odoo's late entry into the Website Builder/CMS market, Odoo is also introducing e-commerce functionality into a very mature market with several options. While there are hundreds, if not thousands, of viable e-commerce platforms out there, here are a few of the most popular.

Magento

A list of popular e-commerce applications would not be complete without Magento. Magento is open source, very popular, and was often the choice to integrate with Odoo. Even with Odoo's new e-commerce option, Magento will continue to be a selection for some Odoo customers who need more advanced functionality than what Odoo can currently offer.

Volusion

Volusion is also a very popular e-commerce platform that takes an entirely different approach. Instead of an open source solution, Volusion is a hosted solution in which you configure your website and cart using their tools. They offer many different pricing models, as well as a free 14-day trial. While not for all companies, Volusion can be a fast solution for companies to get up and running without any concern for the installation of software.

Shopify

While Shopify is very popular and is a hosting solution like Volusion, Shopify also directly markets Point of Sale solutions as well. This means that it could be a good solution for companies that want to have an online presence but also have retail operations in which Shopify would be an appropriate Point of Sale solution. Also, like Volusion, Shopify offers a variety of pricing options and a 14-day free trial.

Yahoo Small Business

Also a hosted solution, Yahoo Small Business offers a straightforward online shopping cart and what you would expect in a basic e-commerce solution. Yahoo has some advantages compared to the other services; they offer easy advertising integration, local marketing options, and robust e-mail handling.

Odoo as an e-commerce platform

In Odoo, e-commerce is implemented within the Website Builder. This means that the Website Builder is a dependency to use Odoo e-commerce, and Odoo will install the Website Builder if it is not already installed in the database. Also, in addition to adding a great deal of functionality to the Website builder, e-commerce also adds a lot of additional options to products in Odoo so they can have variants, appear in multiple categories, create associations with alternative products, and other options as well.

While other e-commerce platforms might have more features, there are some significant advantages to using Odoo e-commerce. Especially, if you are already using or are planning to use Odoo as your primary accounting / ERP system. Products you enter into Odoo automatically integrate with your e-commerce website. The orders you get automatically come into Odoo.

Best of all, Odoo e-commerce is extremely easy to set up.

Installing Odoo e-commerce

You install Odoo e-commerce like other Odoo applications.

After clicking on **Install**, Odoo will refresh the browser and you will be taken to the store page that Odoo has added to the website menu. As before, Odoo has a tutorial that takes you through the basics of the Odoo website. Here, we can see the basic Odoo shop setup that has been displayed using data that we entered throughout the book so far:

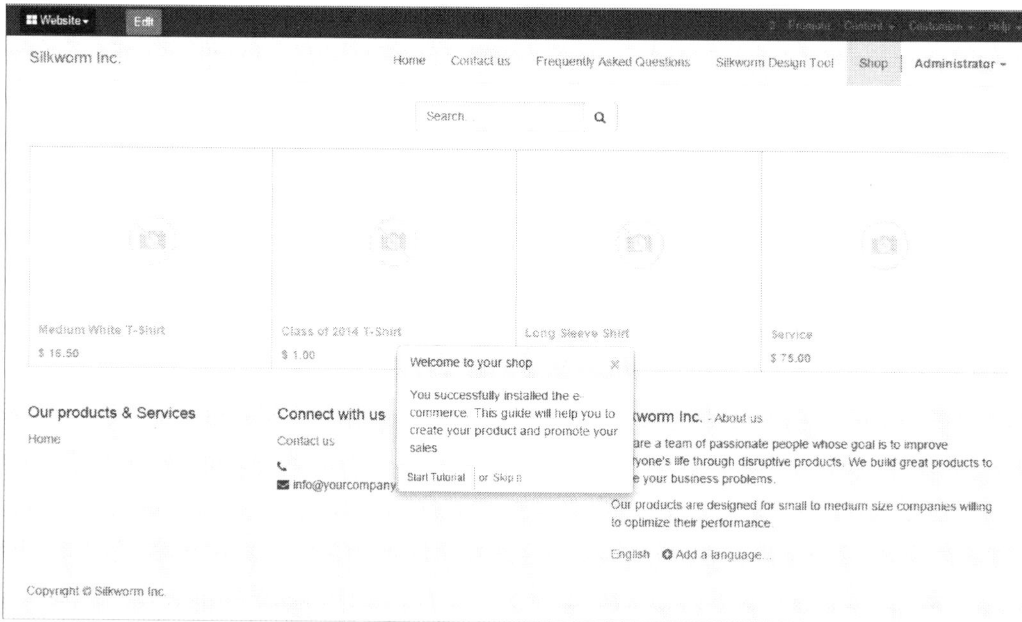

You may have noticed that there is a place holder to show you where the pictures for your product will be displayed once you add a picture for the product. We will see how to do that later in the chapter.

It certainly is an easy setup and the fact that all your products come in and everything is tied into the base Odoo applications is much less complex than alternate solutions such as synching Odoo to an external e-commerce system such as Magento.

The basics of Odoo e-commerce

You will notice a few things right away. There is a search box at the very top of the page that will allow you to search for products on the store. It is also worth mentioning that the footer is shared between all pages on the website.

Click on **Start Tutorial** and Odoo will prompt you with a handy feature that allows you to enter products directly from the website. In other words, you don't have to go into the **Sales** menu in Odoo and click on products and add the product there. You can do it right from this shop page.

Choose **New Product** from the **Shop** menu and Odoo will prompt you to enter the name of the product:

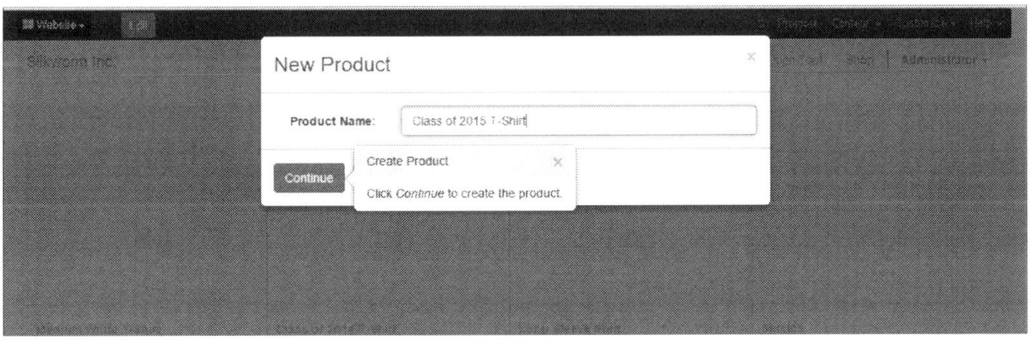

In this case, we have filled in the name of a new product that we want to add to our store and we are now prompted to click on the **Continue** button to add the product.

Odoo then refreshes the web browser to show the new product page your users will see when they navigate to the product. Here, you can edit and add content to the product page, just like you learned in the previous chapter on the Odoo Website Builder.

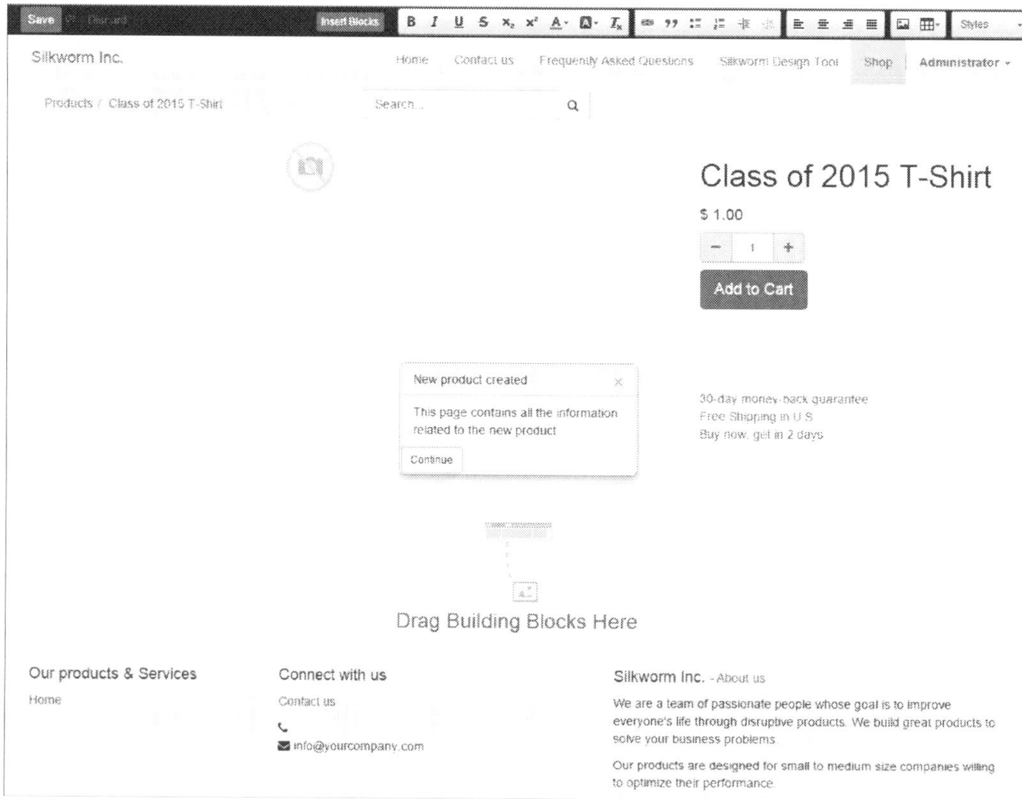

While the page is not much to look at yet, you can see the basics. The price is right under the name of the product, under that a place to change your quantity, and then the button that will add that product to a shopping cart. Under the basic products, you can see the prompt to **Drag Building Blocks Here** that gives you all the same tools you had when you were working with a standard web page.

Setting the product price from the e-commerce page

Another nice feature of Odoo e-commerce is that you don't have to go all the way back to the product list inside the standard Odoo business applications. You can change the price right on the website.

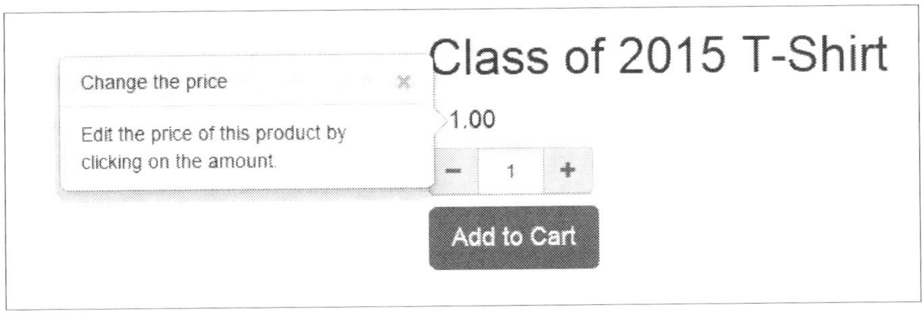

While it might seem like a small thing, the ability to change the price on the web page can help with workflow, and you will not have to switch back and forth between the two different views.

Adding a picture to your product

If you are going to have an e-commerce site, you are going to have a picture for your product. Now, the Odoo tutorial prompts you to add a picture for the product:

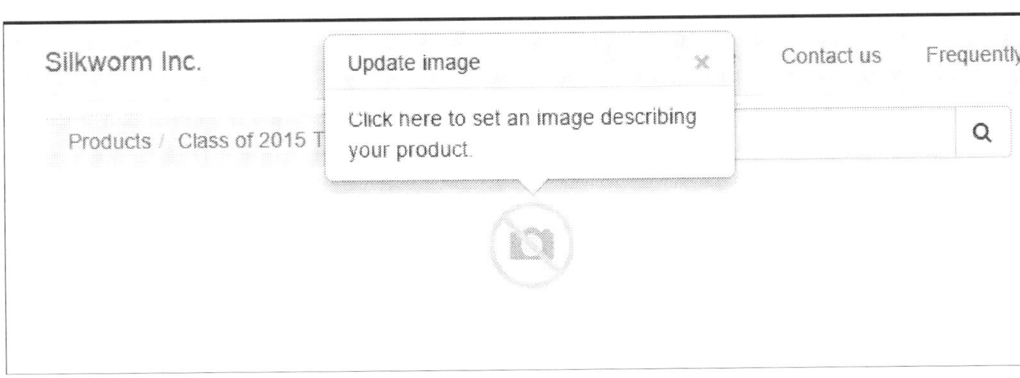

Then, you will be presented with Odoo's picture selection wizard, which allows you to choose pictures from a gallery, your own computer, or even through a URL:

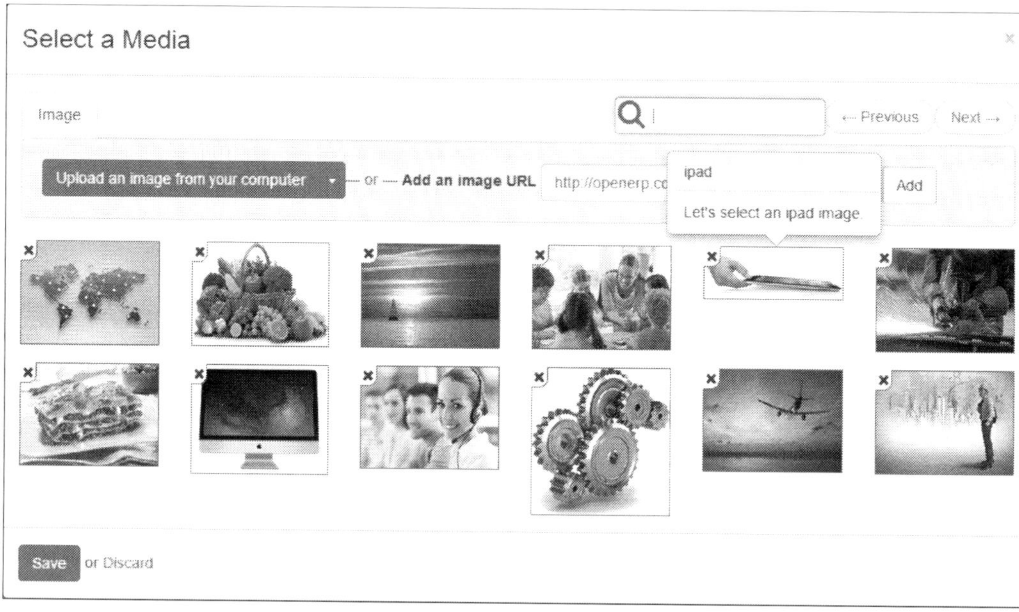

The tutorial provided by Odoo prompts us to pick an iPad image. However, notice that the **Upload an image from your computer** button and **Add an image URL** near the top. You will most likely use these more frequently than the built-in gallery pictures that Odoo provides.

We will go ahead with the tutorial and select the iPad image, and then, click on **Save**. Odoo will then refresh the page to show an iPad image added to our product page.

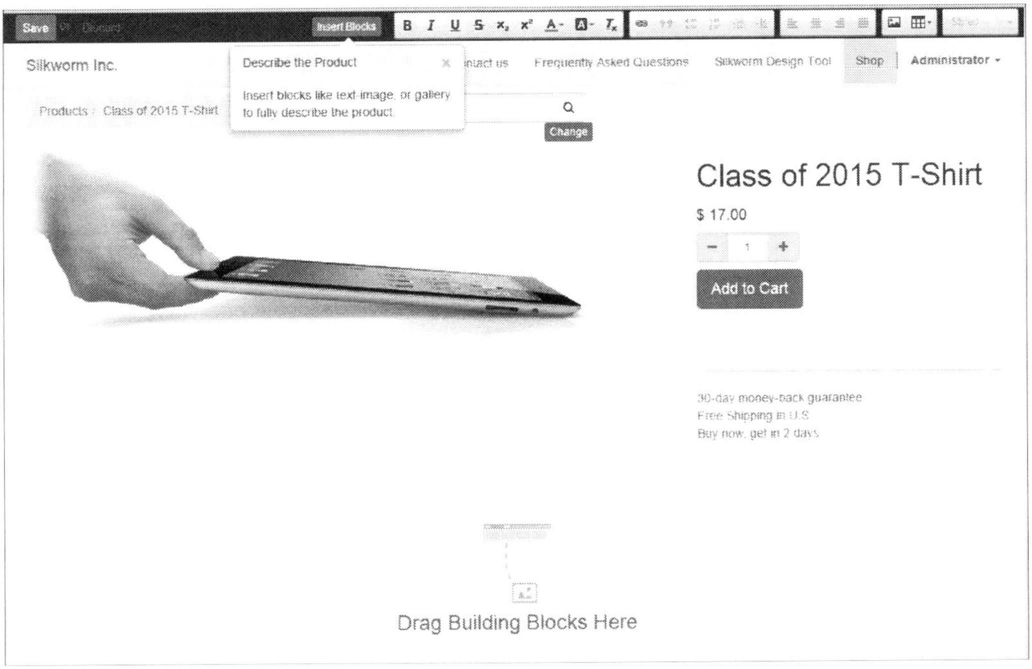

We now see our new iPad image and the tutorial prompts us to insert blocks to add to our product page. This is what you will use to describe your product.

Describing the product

Now, by following the tutorial, you can click on **Insert Blocks** and drag the **Big Picture** block onto the page. Take some time to learn what blocks are available and use them to make a product page that meets the needs of your customers. You can review *Chapter 11, Building a Website with Odoo*, on the Website Builder to learn more about inserting blocks into web pages.

After you have finished inserting blocks and editing pages, click on the **Save** button to commit your changes.

Publishing your product

By default, both new and existing products that were already in Odoo are not published to the website. You can see them when logged in as an administrator or another user with the appropriate permissions. But until you publish the product, they will not be seen by anonymous website users.

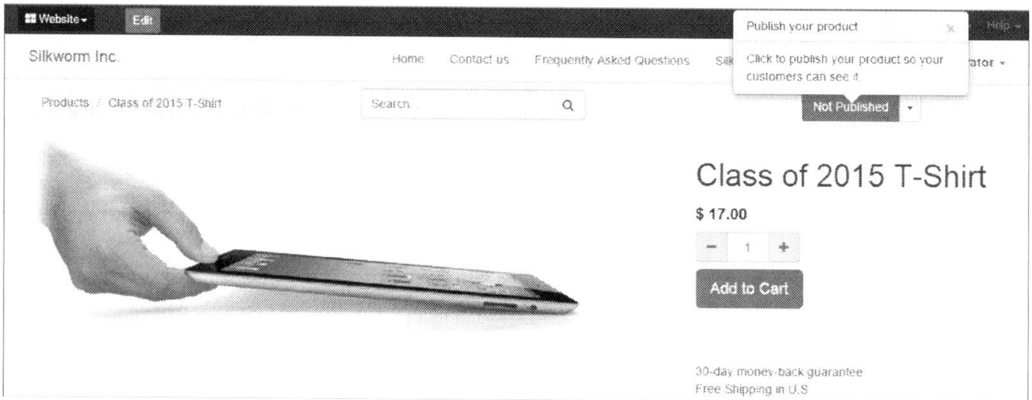

When you click on the red **Not Published** button, the button will change to green and will now display **Published**:

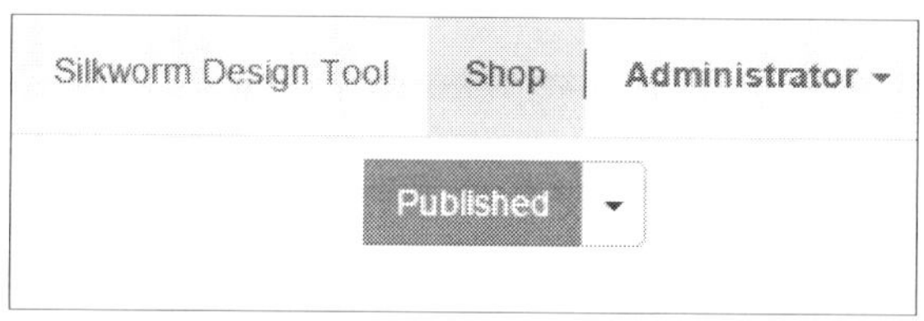

Your product is now published and is visible to anyone who can access the website store. By clicking on the button again, you can set the product back to the **Not Published** state. At this point, the interactive tutorial that Odoo uses to introduce you to the e-commerce application is completed.

Additional configuration options for your Odoo shop

When you first install Odoo e-commerce, it gives you a default layout to get you started. However, there are several options available that you can use to change how your shop looks and the information it displays. Now, let's take a look at a few of these.

You will want to choose **Shop** from the main menu so that you can see your changes. Clicking on the **Customize** menu on the right will give you a list of several options that you can check or uncheck to change the appearance of your online store.

> The **Customize** menu is available on every page but the options that are available in the menu change depending on what page you are on.

Let's check the **Add to Cart** option to add a small image to each product that will allow visitors to easily add the product to the shopping cart.

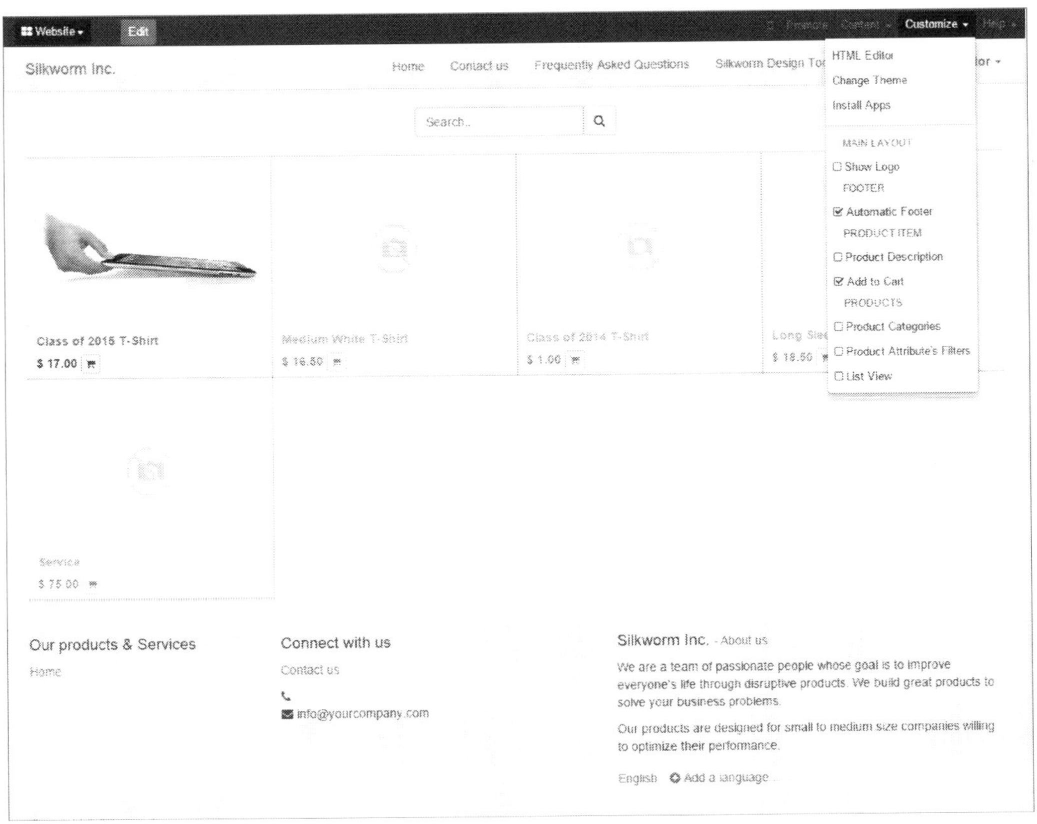

In the preceding screenshot, you can see the available list of options, and now can see that the little shopping cart icon is to the right of the price on each product. Experiment with the other options available inside the **Customize** windows to get the appearance you want.

Modifying the order of the products in the store

There are also other store options available to you if you edit the shop page. One of them is the ability to reorder the products. Click on **Edit** at the top of the page and then hover over products to see the **Options** menu.

We will choose under **Promote** and then **Push to top** to send **Medium White T-Shirt** to the top of the page:

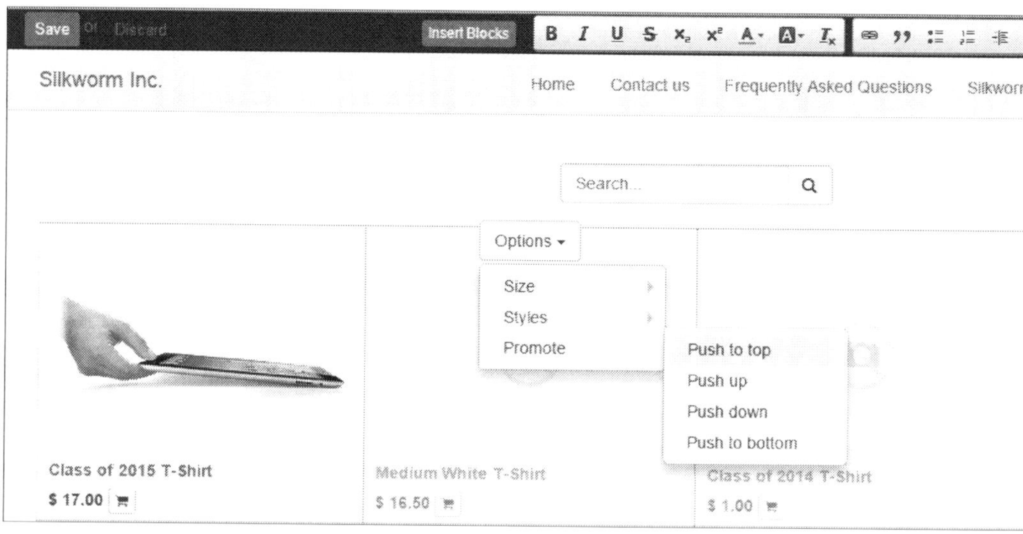

As you can see in the menu, it is possible to promote a product to the top quickly but it could be time consuming to move around a lot of products.

> On the product page, you can quickly adjust the order of the products by setting sequence numbers directly. Simply open the product form, and you can specify the sequence number under the sales tab.

Take a few minutes to explore the other options in the menu. The size options allow you to change the size of the product that shows up in the grid, giving you the opportunity to make more interesting shop layouts. The **Styles** options give you the option of adding a sale ribbon to the product, as we can see in the following screenshot:

Setting up product variants

Another nice feature that comes with the e-commerce application is the ability to create product variants. This is a particularly important feature for the business case we have been using throughout the book. Product variants allow you to offer different options for the same product. For example, a t-shirt and most other apparel products will often come in various sizes and colors. A computer company might offer a product with different memory options.

To create product variants, we need to navigate to the product we wish to create the variants for. Let's create variants for **Class of 2014 T-shirt**.

After you are out of the edit mode in the Website Builder, choose **Sales** from the website's menu in the top-left corner of your screen. Then, choose products and bring up **Class of 2014 T-Shirt**.

Choose the **Variants** page and you will see the grid where we will be adding in the variants.

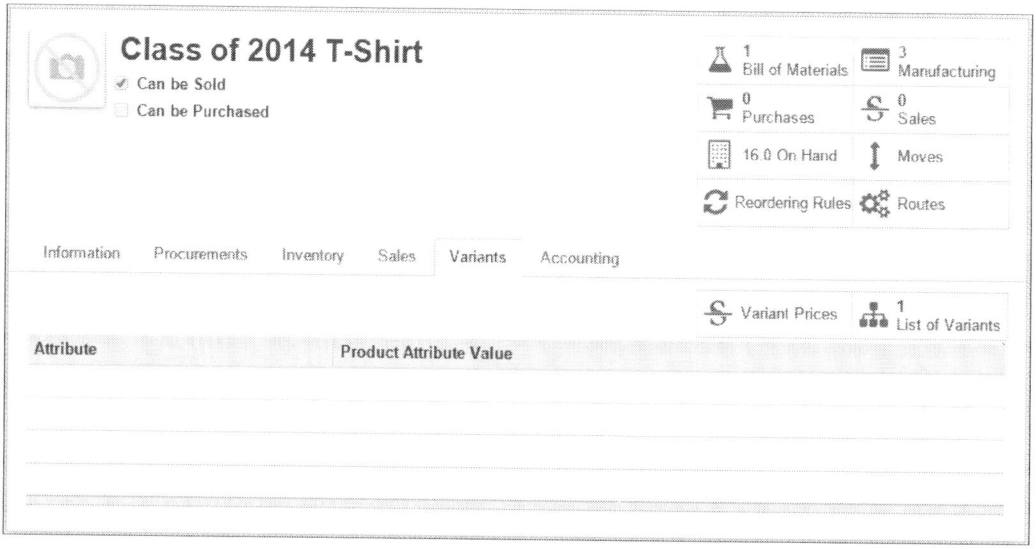

Notice that on the right, there is a separate button to bring up **List of Variants** and it has **1** in the button. You always have one variant that is the base variant for the product.

Now that we are where we need to be click on the **Edit** button at the top of your page and let's add some variants to our product.

To add variants, simply edit the product, choose the **Variants** tab, and click on **Add an Item**. In the **Attribute** column, you provide the label you want to use for your attributes. We will create attributes for both **Color** and **Size**. In the **Product Attribute Value** column, you add in each of the available values. Here, we will list out the available sizes and colors for our product:

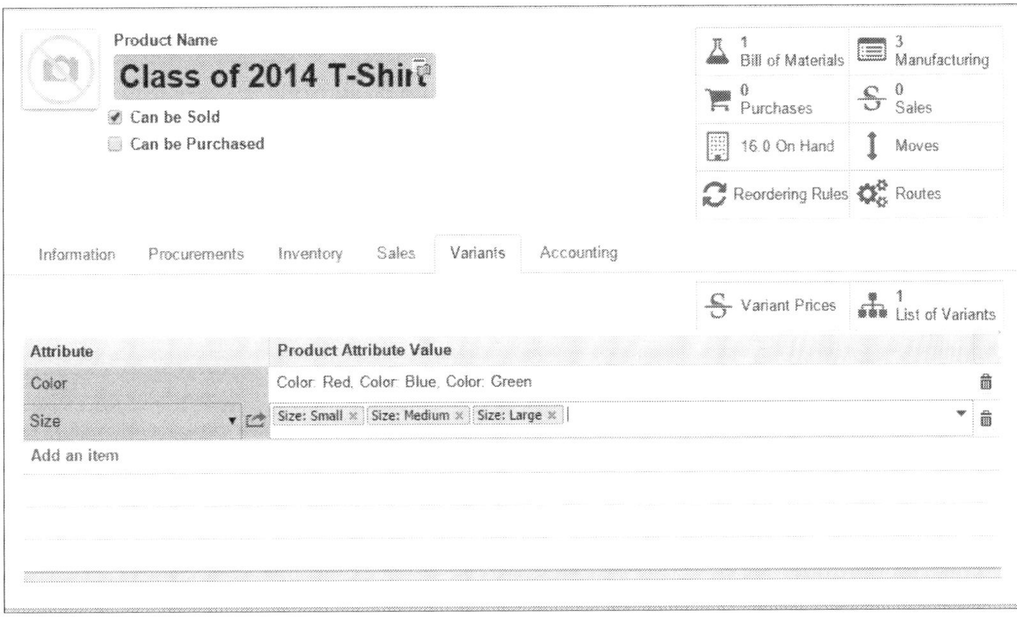

As you can see in the preceding screenshot, we have created two attribute categories. One for **Color** and one for **Size**. For the color attribute, we have specified red, blue, and green. For the size attribute, we have specified small, medium, and large.

Save the product and then go back to the website shop and see the options now as they appear on the product page.

Advanced e-commerce product options

In addition to the basic options we have covered so far, Odoo also offers several advanced options on the product's page that gives you more control over how it appears on the store. These options include specifying multiple categories, alternative products, and accessories as well as direct control over the sequence of the item on the store.

Once again, you will need to go to the product page:

In the preceding screenshot, we can see that we have specified quite a few advanced options. Instead of our product just showing up in one category, it will now show up in the **T-shirts**, **School**, or **2014** categories. This gives you more flexibility in designing your e-commerce store.

> To see your categories on your website, you will need to go under **Customize** while on the store page and check the product categories option.

Alternative products

Often times, when customers purchase one product, it is likely that there will be alternative products that might also be appropriate. It might be that it is another brand of product, or perhaps a deluxe version of the model they are currently viewing. For our example, we choose the 2015 as a potential alternate.

Now, when the user comes to the product page, they will see the alternative product displayed at the bottom.

Accessory products

These are products that are likely to accompany or compliment the purchase of the product on the page. For our business example, we will choose a sports logo that would perhaps be a pin or even an extra print location on the shirt. A more standard e-commerce example would be if you purchase a tablet computer, then you would be prompted to purchase a case, a stylus, or perhaps a warranty.

The accessory products are presented when you add a product to the cart.

Looking at the shopping cart

While we have primarily been focusing on configuration, people are coming to your store to (hopefully) buy merchandise or services. Let's see how the shopping cart looks for them by adding the **Class of 2014 T-shirt** product to a shopping cart:

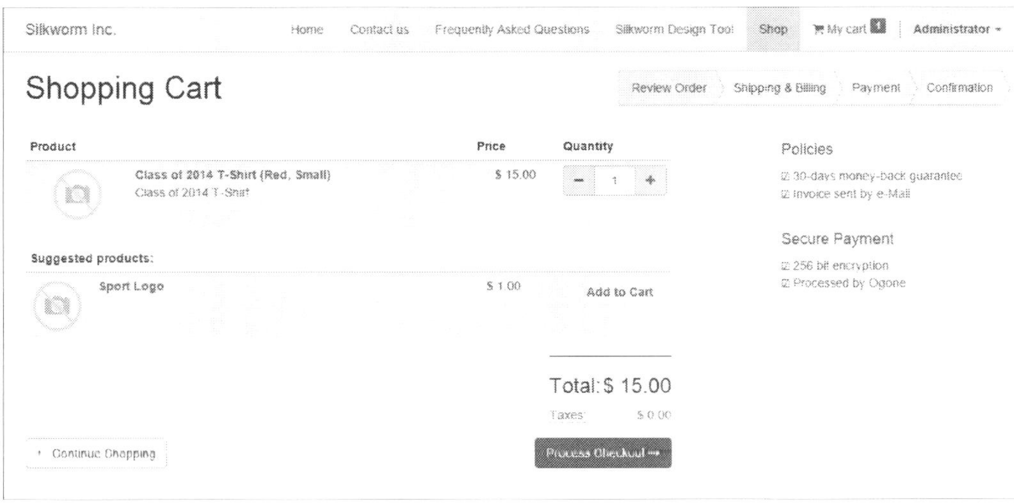

You will notice that the **Sports Logo** product has been added as a suggested product to our shopping cart, along with a link to add it to the cart. Odoo's shopping cart works as most e-commerce shopping carts do. After you adjust your quantity here and are finished shopping, you can click on **Process Checkout**, which will take you to the form that collects your shipping and billing information. A progress bar at the top right of the form keeps the user informed of the steps in the process.

Seeing the draft sales order in Odoo

As soon as an item is added to the shopping cart, the order will appear as a draft within Odoo in real time. Just go into sales and look at the list of quotations, and you will see your e-commerce order:

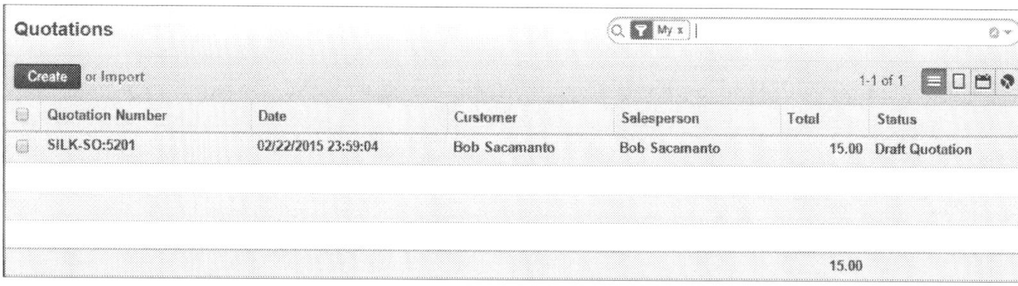

If the user abandons the order without checking out, it simply remains in the draft mode and you can delete it later. This can actually be good in order to see how many of your users might have added something to a cart but didn't make it all the way to checkout.

> Even if the user doesn't check out, this information can be valuable to see what customers are looking for.

Checking out

Like every other shopping cart application, after you have decided what you want, you must provide your billing address and shipping address. Odoo, by default, assumes that the shipping address will be the same as the billing address.

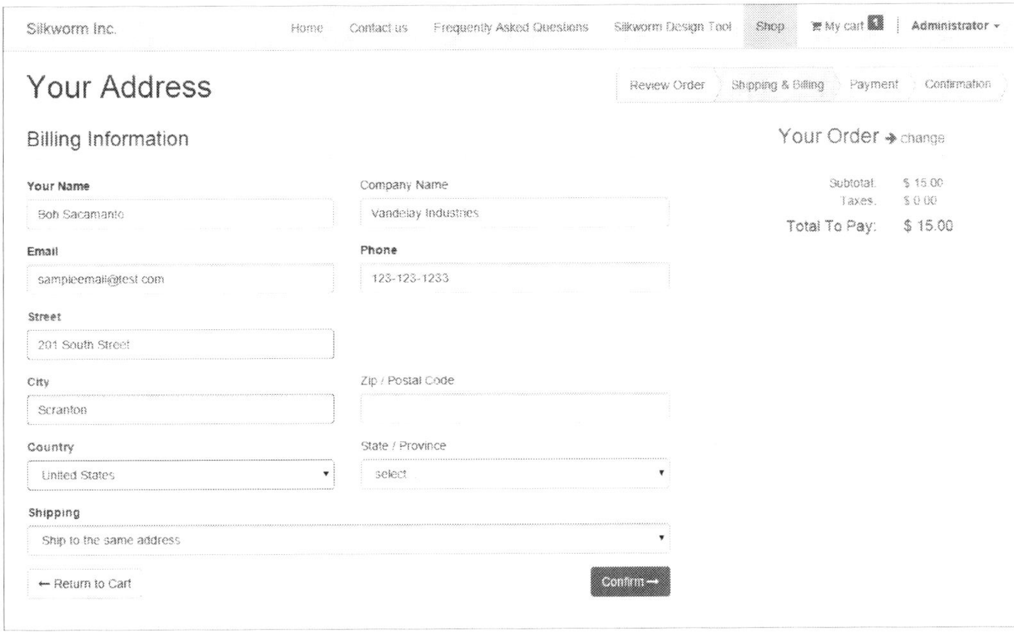

Here, we have filled in the form and intentionally confirmed it so that you could see the required fields that had not been filled out: **Street**, **City**, and **Country**. It is important to notice that, by default, Odoo does not require the zip code or state to confirm the order. In our chapter on customization, we will look at how we can make these fields required, if we want.

After clicking on **Confirm**, you are prompted to select a method of payment:

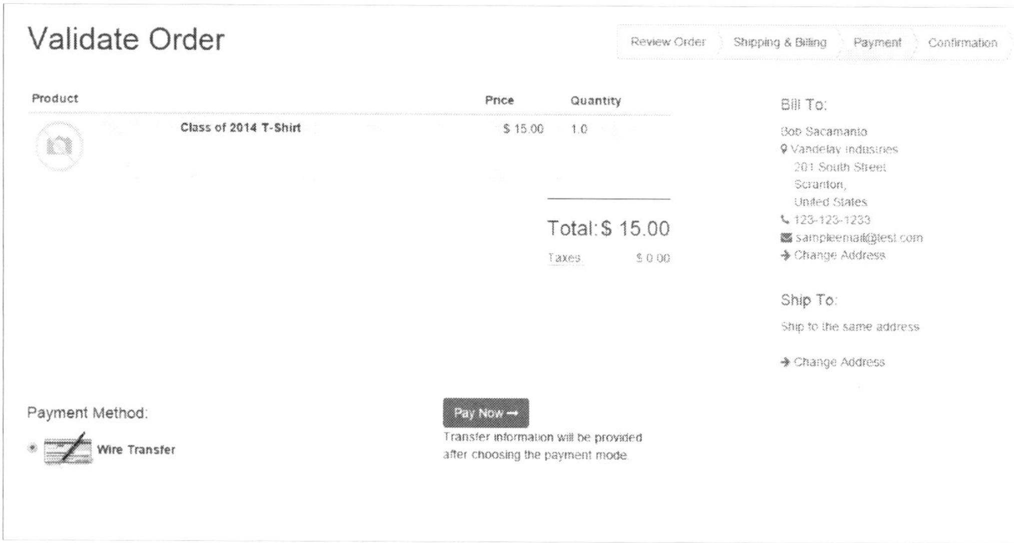

Now that we have reached this point, the remainder of the process is just like any other e-commerce system. You will notice, however, that the only payment method that is available is a **Wire Transfer**. Next, we will see how we can add PayPal as a payment processor.

Adding PayPal as a payment processor

While Odoo, by default, only includes wire transfer, the framework is modular and can be extended with additional payment methods. One of the most popular e-commerce payment processors, PayPal can be quickly installed and integrated into your Odoo e-commerce system.

We install the PayPal payment processor a little differently because it is a module, not a full application. You still go to settings and local apps, but you will want to uncheck the **Apps** filter from the search.

After clearing the **Apps** filter, simply type in `PayPal`, and you will see the standard **Install** button:

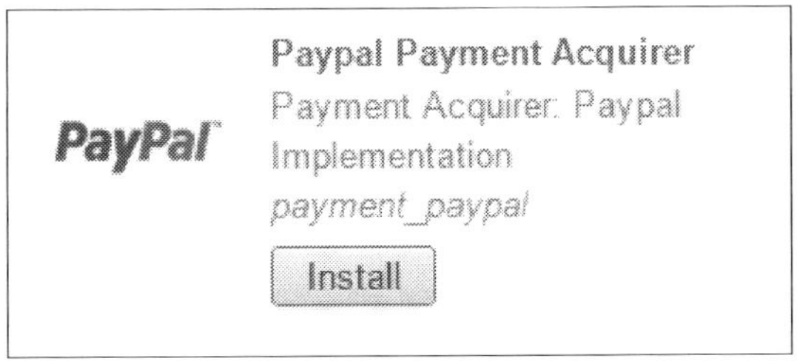

Once you click on **Install**, the screen will refresh and you will be left on the **Local Modules** screen with the **Apps** filter back in place. We now need to go under the **Payments** menu and choose the **Payment Acquires** option to bring up the list of payment acquires. You will see the **PayPal** provider in that list.

Click on **PayPal** to open the form and see the available options:

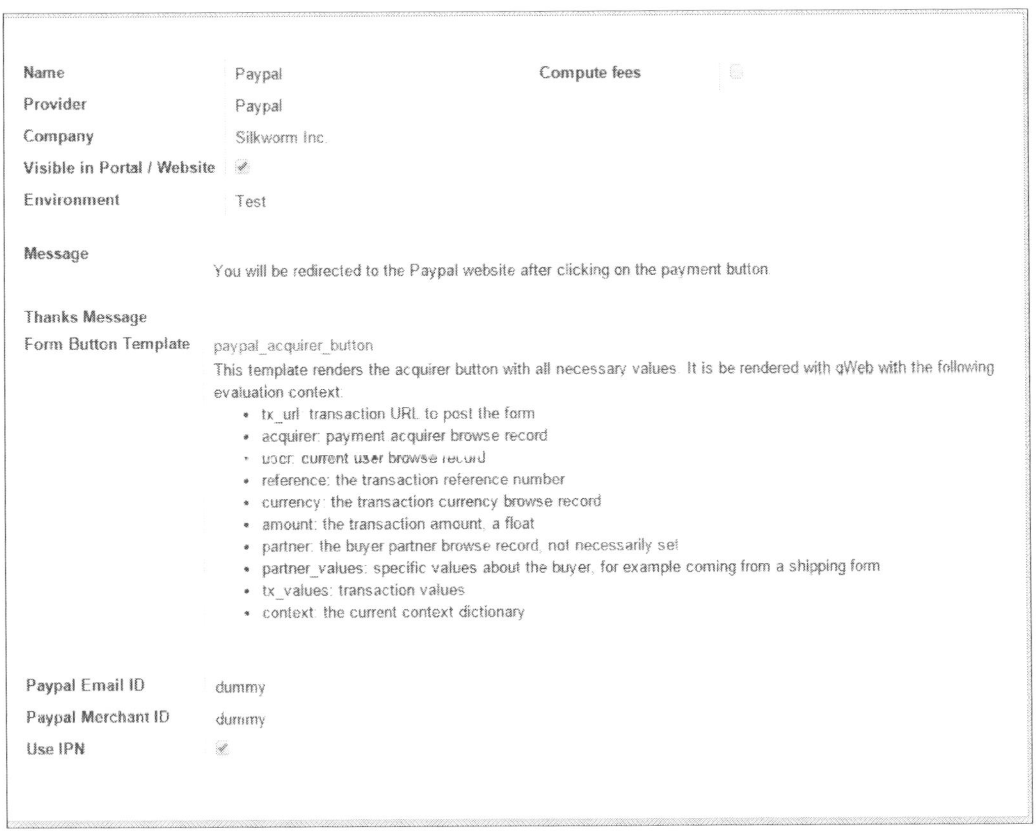

Under the **Environment** option, you will see that we default to the **Test** environment, which PayPal calls the sandbox. This allows you to configure your **Paypal Email ID** and **PayPal Merchant ID** at the bottom and begin testing your store. Once you have everything worked out, you can turn the environment from Test to Production.

Naturally, you will need to setup a PayPal account and use the credentials they give you to fill out the form.

Summary

In this chapter, you learned how Odoo e-commerce fits in with the website builder, how to get it installed, and the basic configuration options. Next, we looked at product variants and how they could be used to make it easier to present products that come in multiple styles.

You spent a little time learning about the advanced product options Odoo offers, such as alternative products, accessories, and defining multiple categories. After looking at the checkout process, you learned how to add an additional payment processor, PayPal, and where you need to go to set the options required to make it all work.

In the next chapter, we will look at one of the most exciting aspects of working with Odoo—how to use the Odoo developer mode to add additional fields to your models and modify views to customize Odoo to fit the requirements of your business.

13

Customizing Odoo for Your Business

In this chapter, we will cover one of the greatest advantages of Odoo—the ability to customize the software to meet the unique needs of your business. Fortunately, Odoo provides a great deal of flexibility in which you can customize Odoo without writing any code or developing a module. We will begin by learning how to activate the Odoo developer mode and then back up our database. This is a very important practice when customizing Odoo. Next, we will learn how to add fields to our database and display them on forms and views. Note that customizing Odoo is a very broad topic that would take many chapters to describe. You might consider this to be an introduction to customization.

The following topics are covered in this chapter:

- Entering and exiting the developer mode
- Backing up our database
- Restoring data from a backup
- Appending custom fields to models
- Displaying our newly added fields upon forms and list views

Activating the developer mode

To customize Odoo, the first step is to activate the developer mode. Once you enter this mode, Odoo will provide you with a lot more onscreen information as you navigate through the interface. This mode also allows you to make changes to the database and store that information in a file.

To activate the developer mode, go to the menu in the top-right corner of the screen. This menu will have the label of the user you are currently logged in as. In our case, this is the **Administrator** menu. Choose **About Odoo** from the menu:

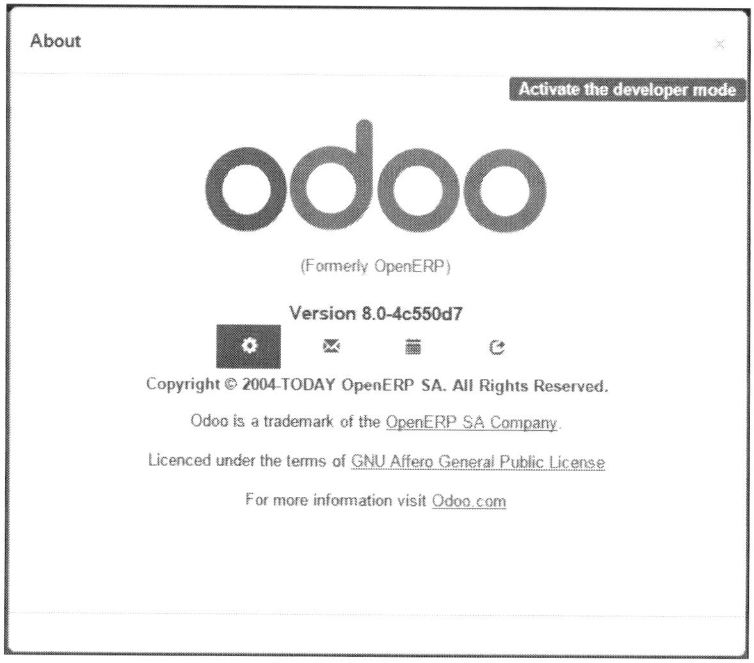

Once you have entered this screen, you can click on **Activate the developer mode** to begin customizing Odoo.

Odoo recognizes that you are in the developer mode by adding `&debug=#` to the URL in your web browser. Additionally, Odoo changes the information that is provided when you hover over various fields in the interface. For example, when viewing a sales order record while in the developer mode, you can move the cursor over the **Date** field to reveal details about how that field is represented internally in Odoo.

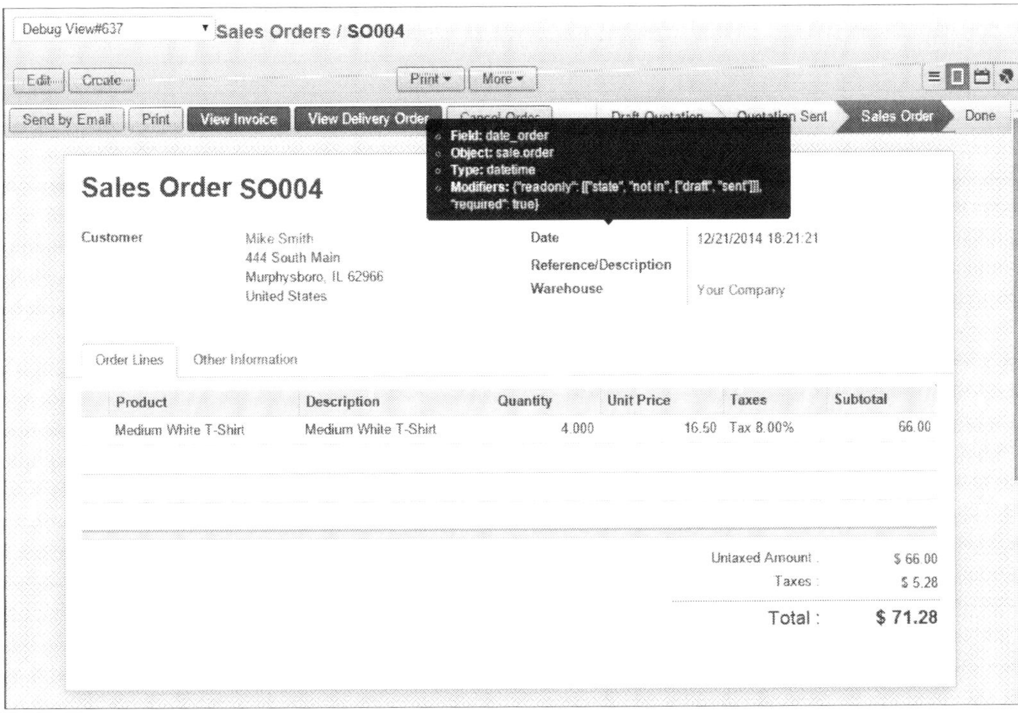

The preceding screenshot demonstrates how Odoo displays information while you are in the developer mode. In this example, we can see that the **Date** field is named `date_order` and that the field belongs to the `sale.order` object. Additionally, we can see the field type is `date` and there are modifiers assigned to the field. This type of information will be of great value as you continue to customize Odoo.

Getting out of the developer mode

Now that you are in the developer mode, there will come a time when you want to exit the developer mode and work with Odoo as you normally would. To exit the developer mode, simply remove `debug=#` from the URL string in your browser:

Make sure you leave the `&` symbol in place when you remove the debug tag from the URL. If you get any errors or other unusual behavior after removing `debug=#` from your URL, you can typically use your browser's back button. If this also fails, you can always restart the browser and log back in to Odoo.

Backing up your database

When you make changes while in the developer mode, those changes are written into the database associated with the company. One of the major advantages of this approach is that you do not have to write code in Python or create a custom module to implement simple customizations. One of the major disadvantages, however, is that there is the potential that you could make a change that is undesirable and perhaps difficult to reverse.

Therefore, it is very important and highly recommended that you make backups of your database both before and after you make any customization through the developer mode.

> **Do not skip this step!**
>
> It is always a good idea to frequently back up your database. However, it is absolutely imperative that you back up your database before undertaking any customization.

To back up your database, you must first log out of Odoo. After you have successfully logged out, click on the **Manage Databases** link on the login form. From this screen, you click on the **Backup** link in the top-left corner of the **Database Management** menu:

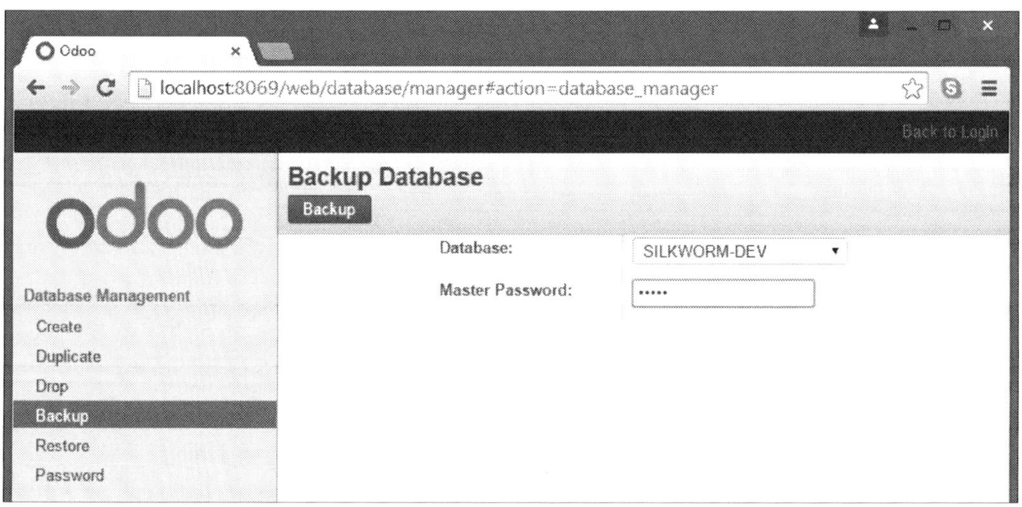

To back up your database, select the database from the pop-up menu and enter the master password for the Odoo installation (by default, **Master Password** will be `admin`). Next, click on the **Backup** button.

After you click on the **Backup** button, Odoo will then save your database to your local drive. Depending on the browser you are using and the settings in your browser, the prompt you will get to save your file will vary. The default filename will end with the `.dump` extension.

After you save your file, Odoo will download it into the directory you have specified. If this is the first time you have backed up your database, you should also take the time to verify that you can successfully restore the database. While this may seem like an unnecessary exercise, it is important to remember that a backup is only as good as your ability to successfully restore it.

Restoring a database in Odoo

To restore a database in Odoo, click on the **Restore** option in the **Database Management** menu:

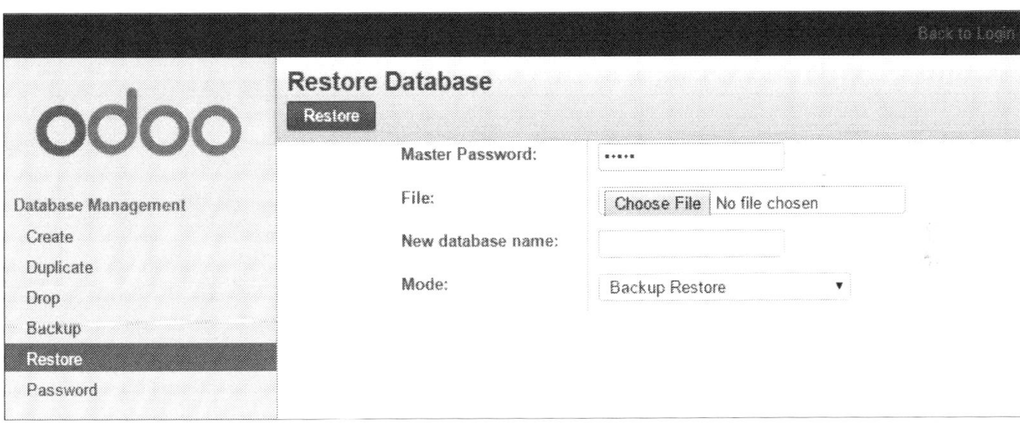

To restore your database, you need to provide three pieces of information—the backup **File** you want to restore, **Master Password** of Odoo, and **New database name**. Clicking on the **Browse...** button in the file selection area will prompt you to select the `.dump` file that was created when you performed the backup.

After you have specified the file and the other required fields, click on **Restore** to begin restoring the database. A small progress bar at the bottom left of the browser will update you on the progress of the restore. Once the restore is complete, log in to the database to make sure everything is working as expected.

Now with a successful backup and restoration, you are ready to begin customizing Odoo. If something goes wrong, you will have the ability to restore your backup. While customizing Odoo, remember to back up the database frequently and test the restore process often.

Adding a custom field to Odoo

One of the most common reasons for customizing Odoo is to collect additional information that is specific to your company. If you are running an insurance company, perhaps you want to specify the policy number on your sales order. If you are working in property management, perhaps you would like to store the date in which the lease agreement will expire.

For our working example, we will be adding fields that will help us better manage the data and processes for our silkscreen company. Specifically, we will be adding the following fields to the sales order header:

Field name	Label	Field type	Purpose
`x_daterequired`	**Date Required**	`Date`	In the screen printing industry, deadlines drive when the production must begin and when the product should be delivered to the customer.
`x_rush`	**Rush Order**	`Boolean`	The necessity to flag some sales orders as rush orders is related to **Date Required**. A **Rush Order** label can then be prioritized and given expedited treatment.

Custom field names in Odoo should be preceded by `x_`. This is so that field names in future Odoo versions and standard updates will not accidentally conflict with the custom fields you have added.

The easiest way to add a custom field to a form is by using a menu that appears on that form. In this case, we will be adding the fields to the **Sales Order** form. To begin adding a field, navigate to **Sales | Sales Orders**, open an order in the form view, and choose **Manage Views** from the developer's pop-up menu in the top-left corner of the form. The developer's menu does not have a label but displays `Debug View#` as its first option.

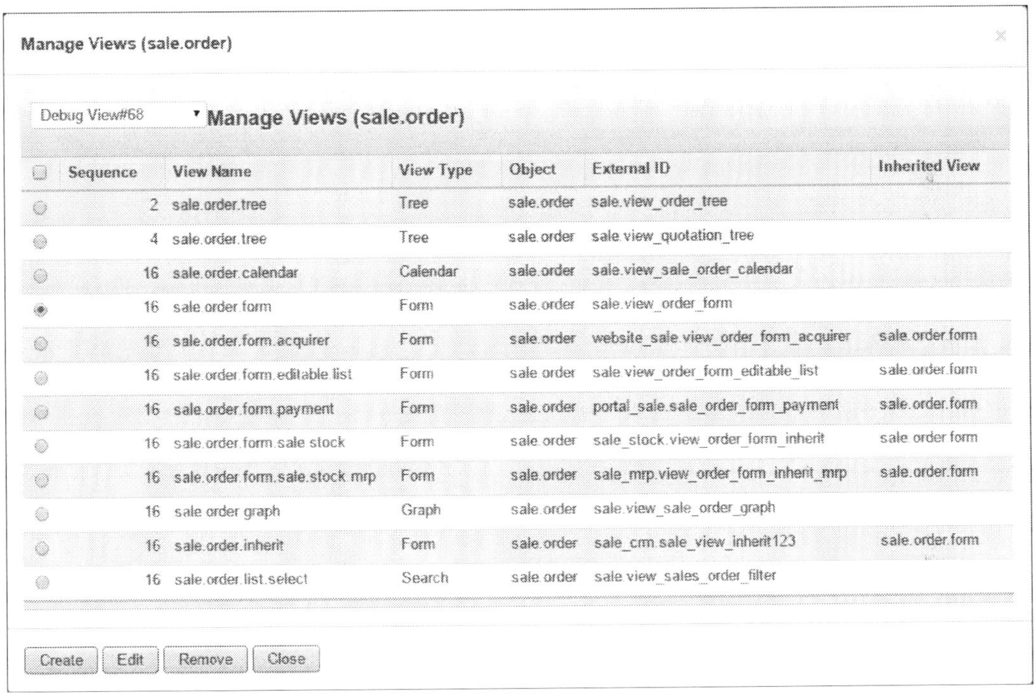

By default, Odoo will select the view that you were on when you chose the **Manage Views** option from the menu. In this case, the view currently selected is the **sale.order.form** view. (For now, ignore other values such as **External ID** and **Inherited View**.) Click on the **Edit** button to modify the **sale.order.form** view.

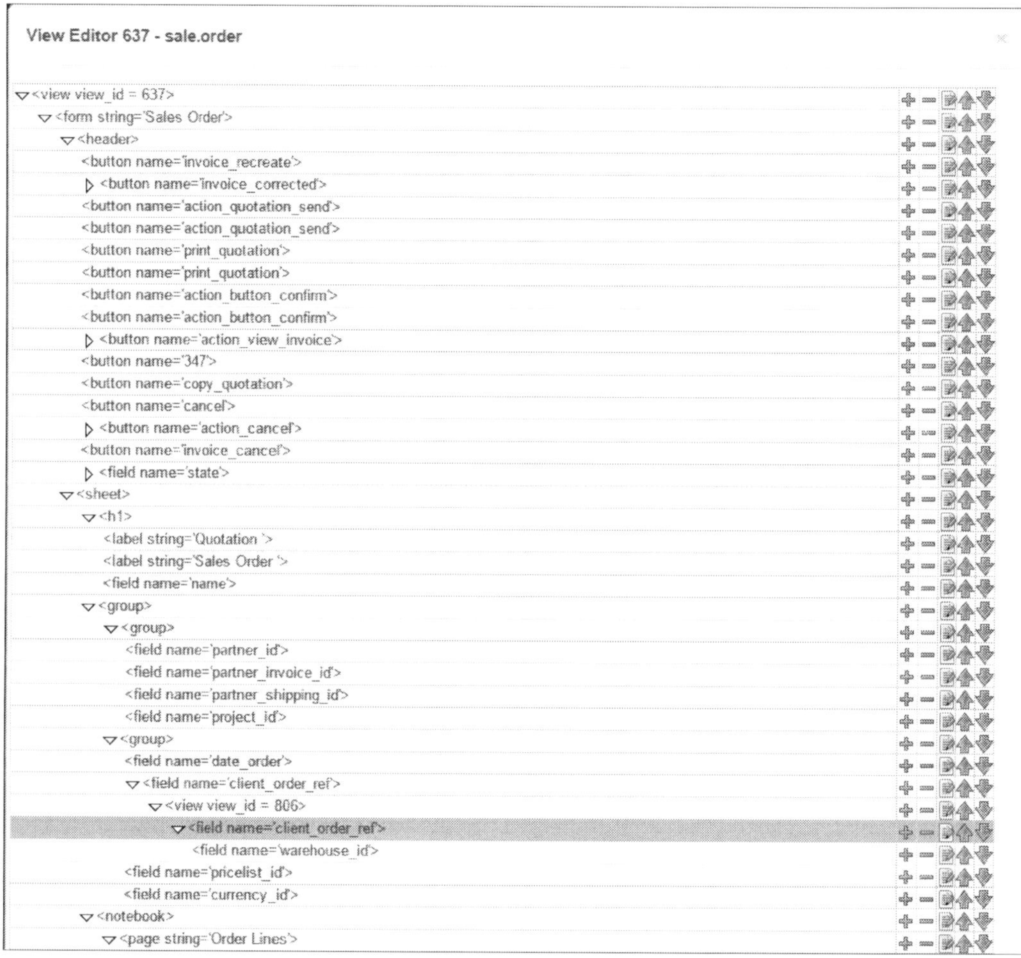

After clicking on **Edit,** you will be presented with **View Editor**. This form allows you to add, delete, and modify the fields that are displayed in the view. At first, this form can be a bit overwhelming in its complexity, but it will get easier after using it a few times. In the wide column on the left, you will see the field names of the view organized in a hierarchical tree format. By default, all of the tags and fields of the view are expanded, but you can use the small triangles to the far left to collapse the levels.

Scroll down until you find the field name `client_order_ref`. It is selected in the preceding screenshot and labeled **View Editor 637 - sale.order**.

Now, click on the small blue plus (+) icon among the set of buttons on the far right. This tells Odoo that you want to add a field at that specific location in the view.

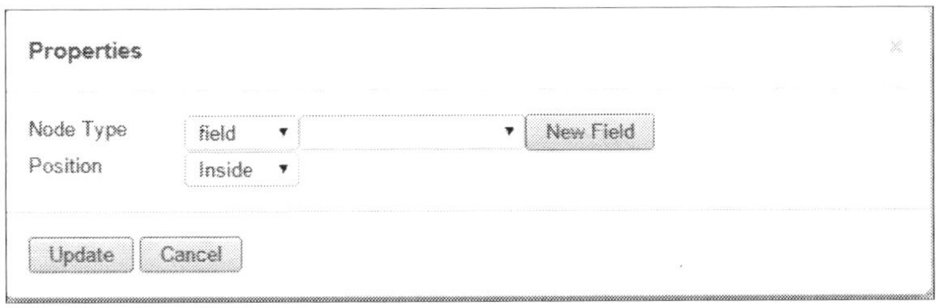

After clicking on the plus (+) icon, you are presented with a **Properties** form. The **Node Type** field is prepopulated with `field`, which is the value that we need to add our field to the form. Set the **Position** field to `AfterA`, which tells Odoo that we wish to add our new field after the `client_order_ref` field on the form view.

If the field we wish to display already existed in the `sale.order` model, we could simply select it from the pop-up menu next to **field**, and it would be displayed on the form view. Instead, click on the **New Field** button to add our brand new field to the **Sales Order** form.

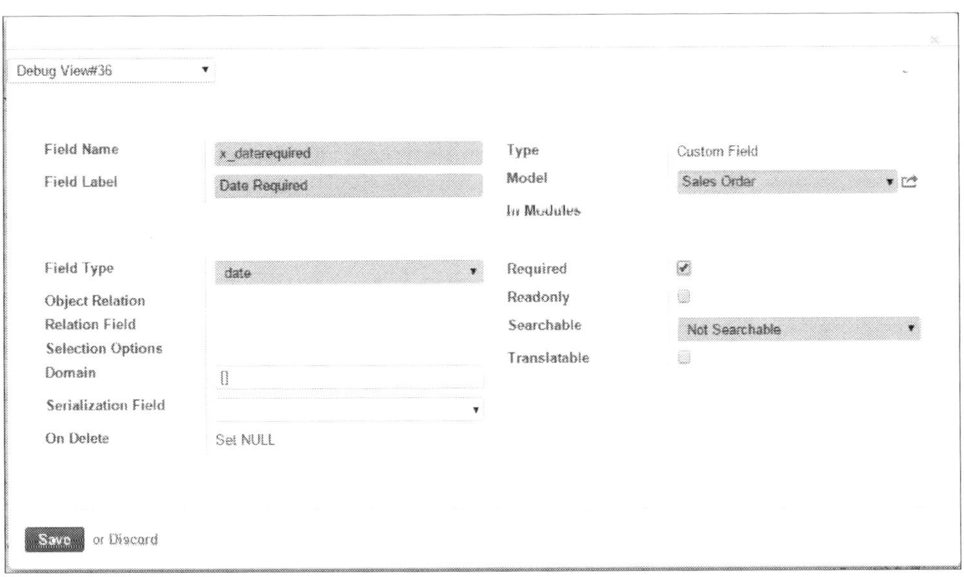

Now you will be presented with a field editor form, as depicted in the preceding screenshot.

The `x_` prefix is already specified in the **Field Name** field by default, in order to encourage the use of good naming conventions. We have filled in the other data required for the field, including setting the **Field Name** field to `x_daterequired`, the **Field Label** field to `Date Required`, and the **Field Type** field to **date**. Additionally, we have clicked on the **Required** checkbox so that the user will be required to specify this value when entering a sales order. For this example, we will leave the rest of the form as it is.

Click on **Save** to finish adding our new field to the `sale.order` model.

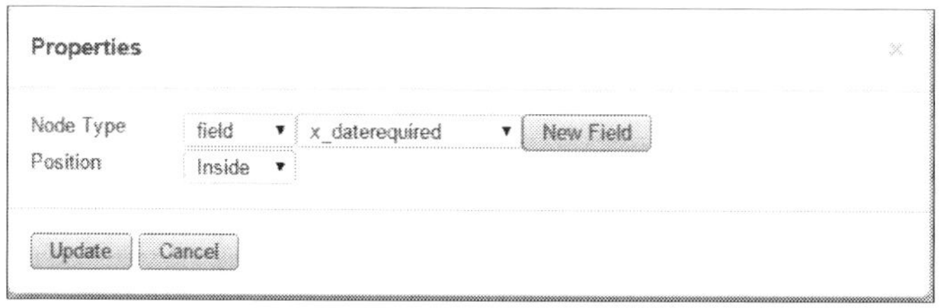

Odoo will automatically select **x_daterequired** in the pop-up list. At this point, the field has been added to the `sale.order` model in the database. We are now ready to add this field to our **Sales Order** form.

Click on **Update** to proceed:

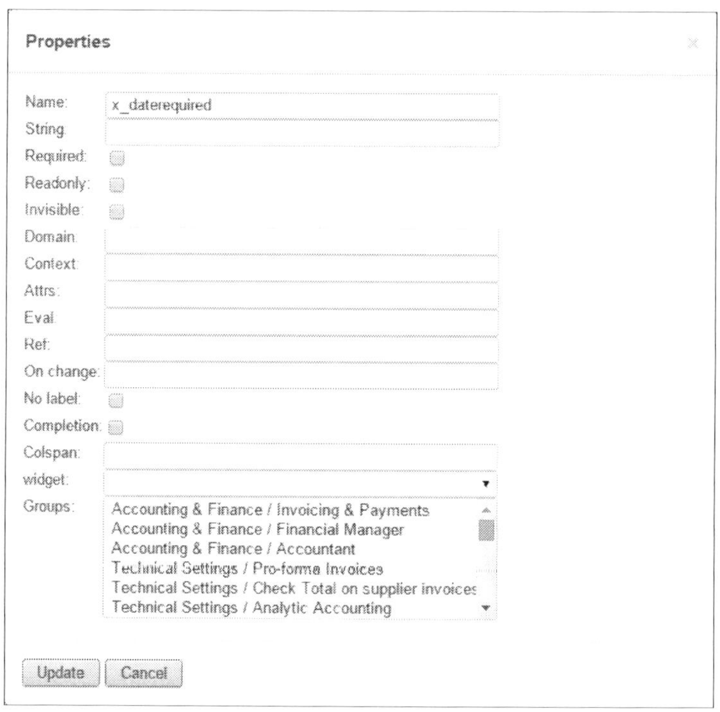

In this **Properties** form, we can specify how we wish the field to appear on the form. For example, we could override the field label we set in the field properties by specifying a different value in the **String** field on this form.

> A **Name** field might contain a maximum of 64 alphanumeric characters and underscores but no other special characters and spaces. The name might often appear cryptic, but end users of Odoo typically do not need to ever see these names. The **String** field, however, will be seen as it is used as a label on forms to prompt for user input. A **String** field can contain up to 256 characters including spaces and special characters.

Here, it is also possible to restrict the field to specific user groups using the **Groups** list at the bottom. For now, we will accept all the defaults and click on **Update** to close this screen. Next, click on **Close** on the **View Editor** window and again click on **Close** on the **Manage Views** window.

Odoo will automatically refresh the **Sales Orders** form, allowing you to see the **Date Required** field you have just added:

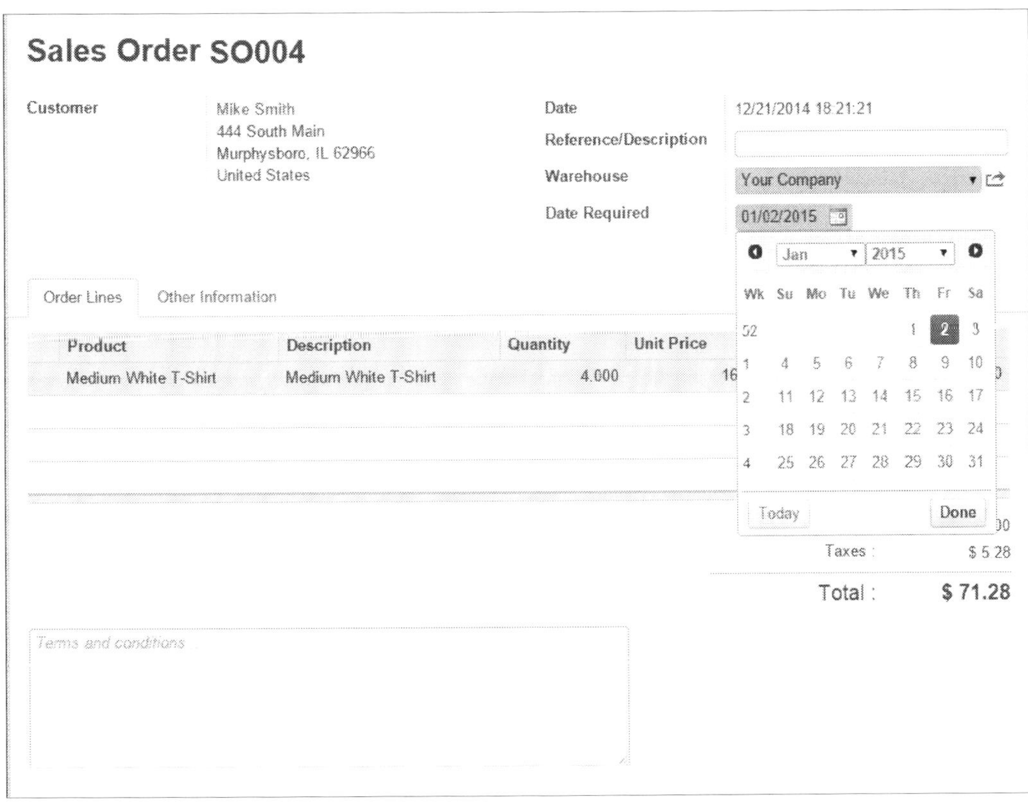

Adding another field to the sales order form

Following the same procedure, let's add the **Rush Order** checkbox to the **Sales Order** form. If you get lost, simply refer to the procedure for adding the **Date Required** field to the form.

Here is a summary of the process:

1. Select **Manage Views** from the pop-up menu on the top-left corner of the form.
2. Click on the **Edit** button to modify the view.
3. Scroll down and click on the **+** icon to the right of the **x_daterequired** field that we just added.
4. Click on **New Field** on the **Properties** form.
5. Fill out the form using `x_rush` for **Field Name**, `Rush Order` for **Field Label**, and `Boolean` for **Field Type**. Do *not* check the **Required** field for this field as we want the ability to not have the **Rush Order** option checked.
6. Click on **Save** to store your new settings for the field.
7. Click on **Update** to tell Odoo to add the new field to the view.
8. Click on **Update** again to accept the default values for the field view.
9. Click on **Close** to exit the **View Editor**.
10. Click on **Close** again to exit the **Manage Views** form.

If you have followed the preceding steps, you should now have the **Rush Order** checkbox added to the **Sales Order** form.

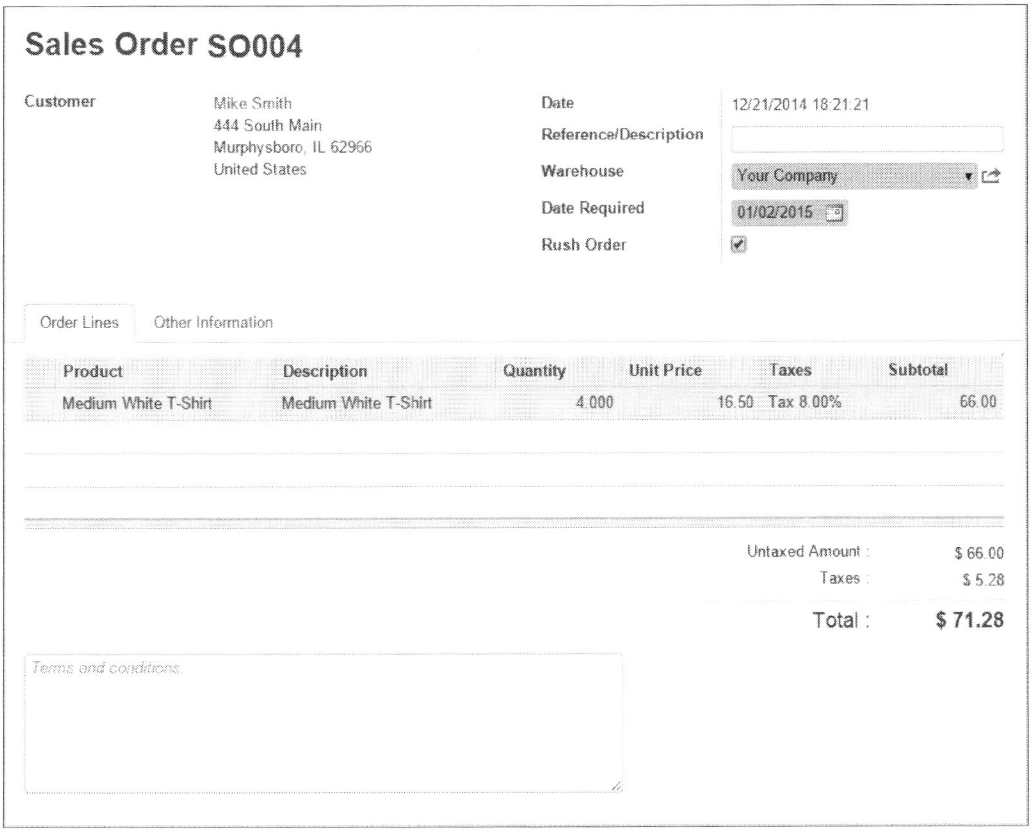

Using the same method, you can add fields to almost any form within Odoo.

Adding a field to an existing view

After adding our fields to the `sale.order` model and displaying them on the **Sales Order** form, it would be nice to include these fields in our sales order listing. This way, users can see at a glance when orders are due and know whether they are rush orders.

We begin by going to the **Sales Order** list view and choosing **Manage Views**. Next, click on **Edit** to bring up the **View Editor** for the sales order list:

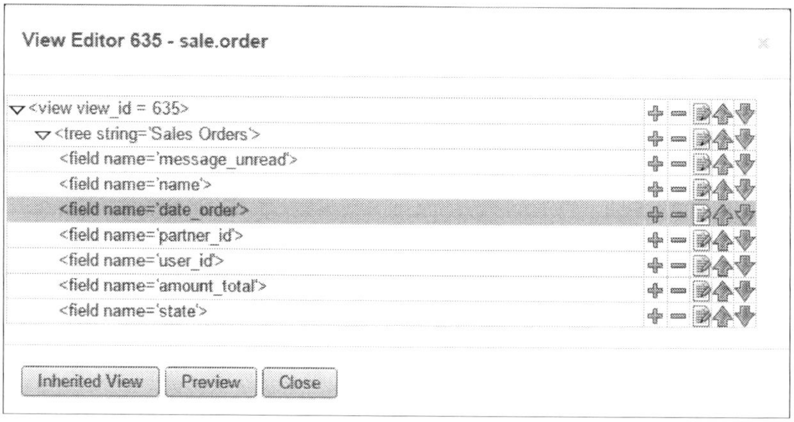

You will notice that this list is far less complex than the one for the **Order Sales** form view. This is simply because a list view (also known as a tree view) has much fewer options and fields on it than a form that edits and manages the data for just one record at a time.

Click on the **+** to the right of the `date_order` field. This will pop open the **Properties** window:

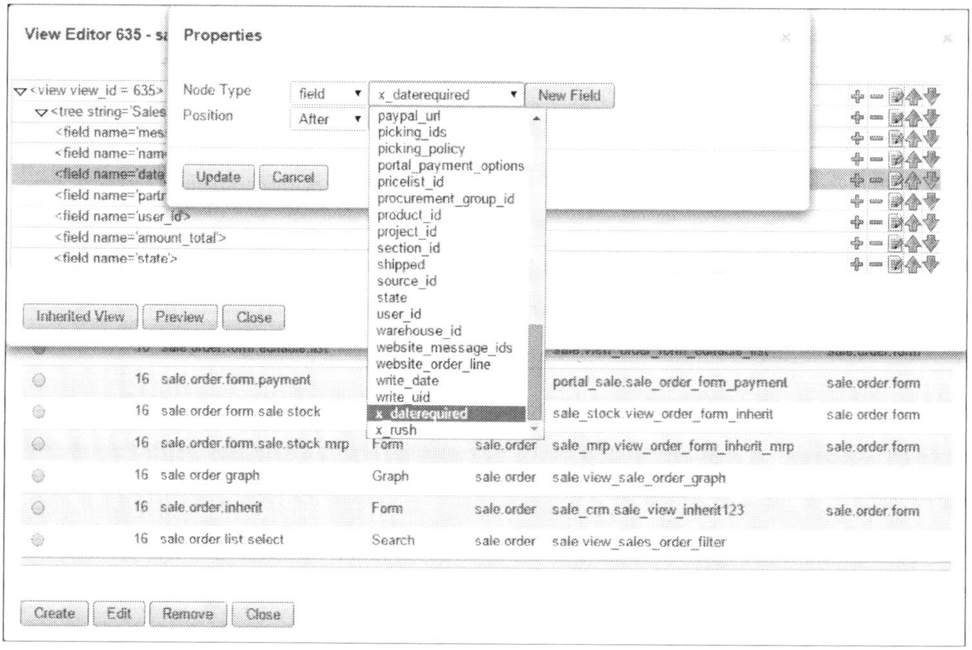

After selecting **x_daterequired** in the list, click on the two **Update** buttons. Then, you can follow the same process to add the **x_rush** field to the list view. Finally, click on the **Close** buttons to shut the **View Editor** as well as the **Manage Views** form.

The screen will refresh, and you will see our two new fields in the **Sales Order** list view.

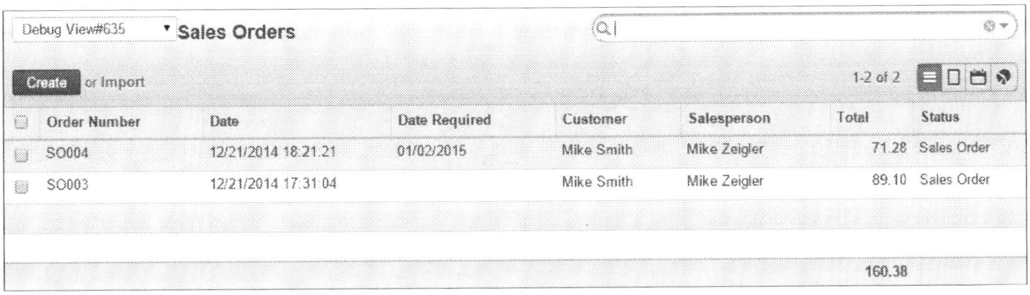

As you can see, it is pretty easy to create new fields and then add those fields to views and forms.

Customizing search operations in Odoo

In addition to having the ability to modify the forms and list views in Odoo, you can also customize searching in Odoo to better fit the needs of your organization. For example, when customers place orders, it is common in a business-to-business scenario that you will be provided a purchase order or another source document that the customer references internally.

By default, Odoo does not include the source document field in your search. You must use the **Advanced Search** function each and every time, in order to look up a customer's order by the source document that they have provided to you. As in much of this book, this example comes from a real case scenario. When customers call, often they might not have an invoice number or sales order number from your company; instead, they might only have their internal source document. Let's see how we can customize Odoo to more easily search on the **Source Document** field in the sales order.

Specifying additional fields you wish for Odoo to use in the search

One of the greatest features of Odoo's developer tools is that you can hover over any field in a form and see important information about that field. For our example, we are going to hover over the **Source Document** field to learn how this field is represented within Odoo's database.

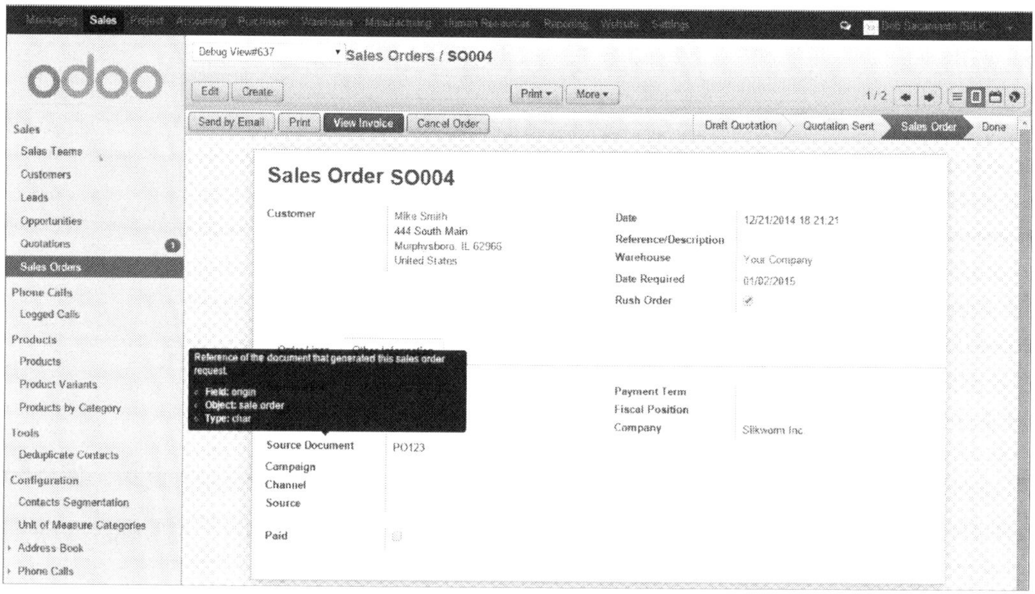

As you can see, the field name for the **Source Document** field in the sales order is **origin**. We can also verify that this field belongs to the `sale.order` object and it is of **Type char**.

We will use this information to modify the search view so that we can add the ability to search for the source document in our list view without using the advanced search.

Editing the search view

You edit the search view by navigating to the list for the search you wish to modify. In this case, we will simply click on **Sales Orders** under the main **Sales** menu. Then, under the **Debug View** menu, choose **Edit SearchView**.

The XML for the search view, as shown here, will appear for you to edit:

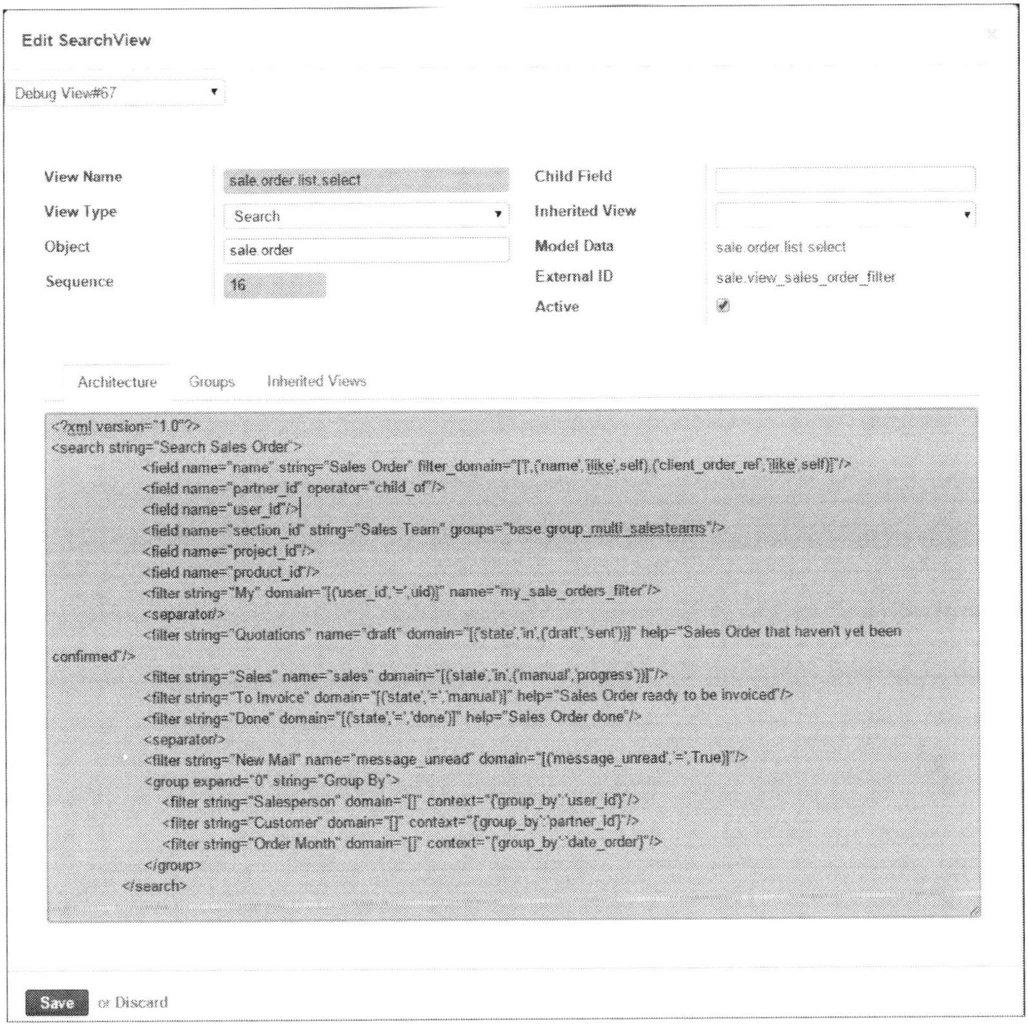

Take a little time to look at the structure of this form. You will see that many tags start with `<field name="`. Each of these fields defines what search fields are available in the list's search box.

To search in our Source Document, we only need to add a `field` tag for the `origin` field to the list. Here, you can see we have added it under the `project_id` field:

```
<?xml version="1.0"?>
<search string="Search Sales Order">
        <field name="name" string="Sales Order" filter_domain="['|',('name','ilike',self),('client_order_ref','ilike',self)]"/>
        <field name="partner_id" operator="child_of"/>
        <field name="user_id"/>
        <field name="section_id" string="Sales Team" groups="base.group_multi_salesteams"/>
        <field name="project_id"/>
        <field name="origin"/>
        <field name="product_id"/>
        <filter string="My" domain="[('user_id','=',uid)]" name="my_sale_orders_filter"/>
        <separator/>
        <filter string="Quotations" name="draft" domain="[('state','in',('draft','sent'))]" help="Sales Order that haven't yet been confirmed"/>
        <filter string="Sales" name="sales" domain="[('state','in',('manual','progress'))]"/>
        <filter string="To Invoice" domain="[('state','=','manual')]" help="Sales Order ready to be invoiced"/>
        <filter string="Done" domain="[('state','=','done')]" help="Sales Order done"/>
        <separator/>
```

After you save the form, refresh the page. If you begin typing in the search box, you will now see **Source Document** available in the search list.

> When making changes here in these forms, all of the previous warnings apply. Make sure you do not make changes in live systems, and make sure you have good backups.

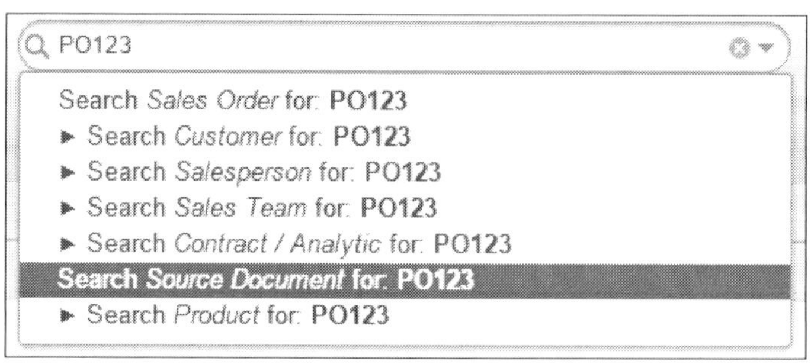

As you can see, the **Source Document** field is added to the search under **Contract / Analytic**, which is the description associated with the `project_id` field in Odoo.

Examining the models in Odoo

Using the developer mode in Odoo to locate the names of fields can save you a great deal of time while customizing Odoo. There are some times, however, that you would like to look through the Odoo models and see a full catalogue of all the fields available within a given model. To view this information, go to the **Settings** menu and under the **Database Structure** submenu choose **Models**.

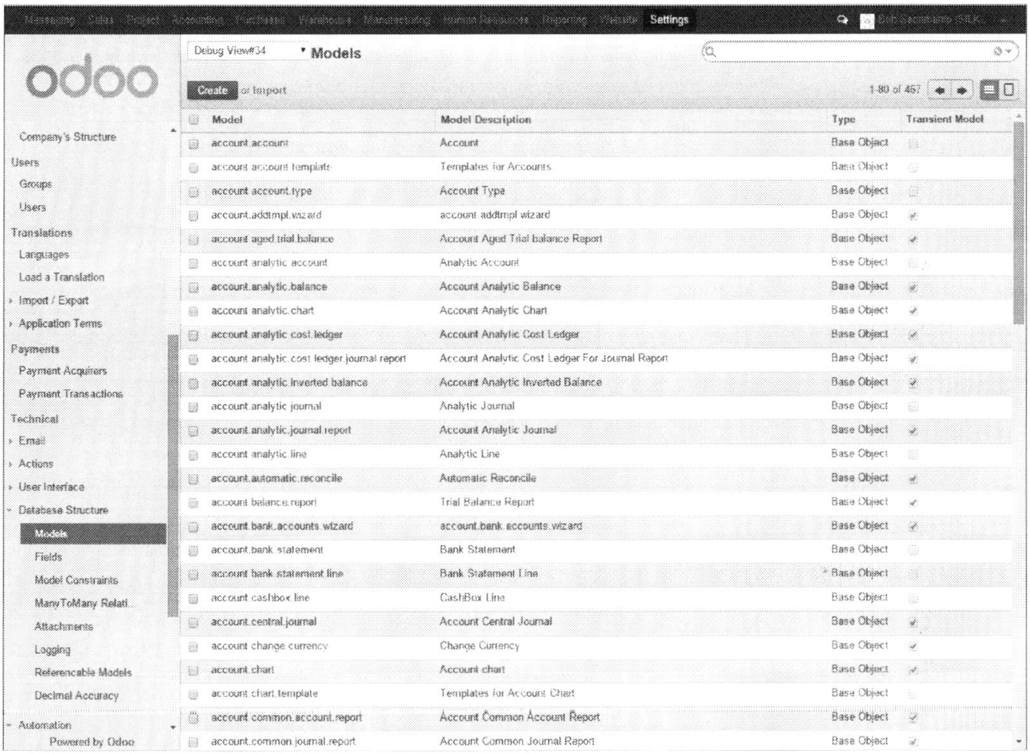

Now, you can see a list of all the models that Odoo has within in the system. You can use the search function to find the model you wish to examine, and then, click on the record to bring up the fields in the model. In the following example, we have located the `sales.order` model and clicked on it to display the fields:

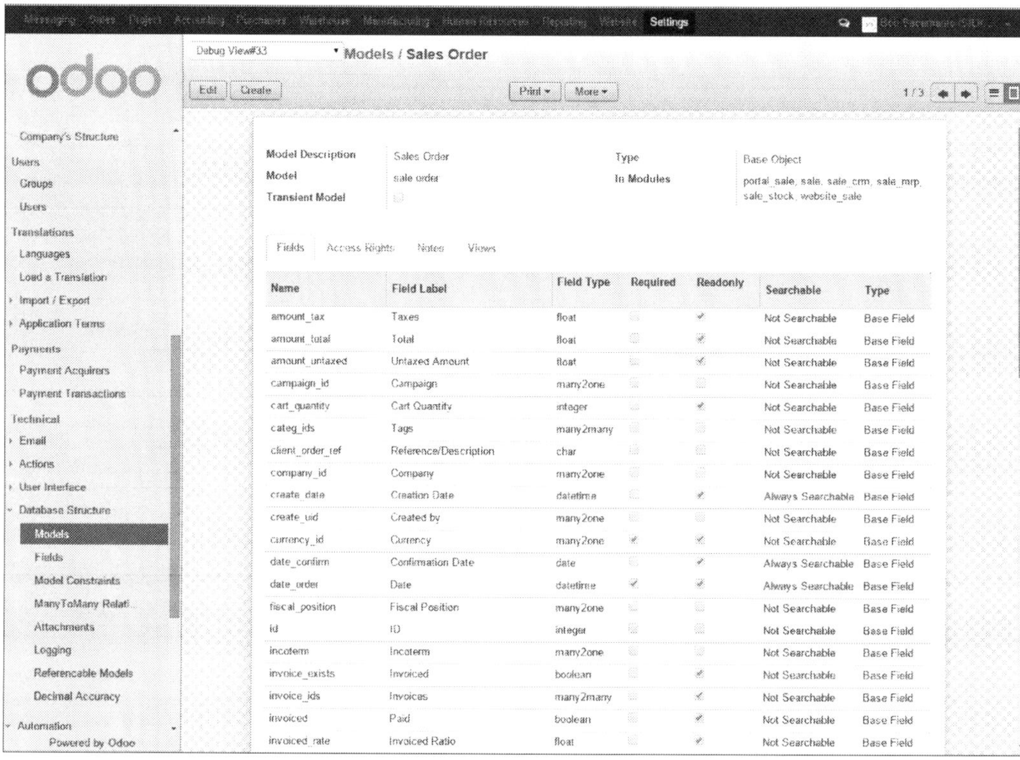

Here, you will notice that at the top right, we can see all the modules that use the `sale.order` model. For each field, we can see the name, the description or label for the field, and the field type as well as whether it is required or not.

Additionally, if the field is read only, there will be a checkbox in that column, and also, you can determine whether the field is in fact searchable. As you will see in this example, the type is often **Base Field**. If you scroll to the bottom and check the fields we added earlier in the chapter, you will see they are of the **Custom Field** type.

Summary

In this chapter, we started by discussing how to activate the Odoo developer mode. Next, we walked through how to make a backup of the Odoo database and how to restore that database using the manage database tools in Odoo. It was emphasized how important it is to back up databases prior to performing any customization in Odoo. Next, we went step by step through how to customize Odoo by adding fields to the database and ultimately to your forms and views. This is by no means a comprehensive guide on Odoo customization; it is merely an introduction to common ways to easily customize forms, lists, and searches.

In the next chapter, we will explore how to use the Odoo report designer to customize reports and export data from Odoo. We will begin by looking at how to customize our company headers and footers that will appear on our standard documents. With Odoo, we can use dynamic fields to automatically fill in values from our database into our reports. Using the new Web template language, we will have a great deal of power and flexibility while building reports that integrate well with Odoo.

14
Modifying Documents and Reports

Regardless of how great the built-in reports are in any ERP system, it is inevitable that most companies will need to make some custom modifications to the standard documents and reports. Of course, Odoo is no exception. The goal of this chapter is to give the reader a solid introduction to the Odoo reporting framework.

In this chapter, we will cover:

- How to make simple changes to headers and footers of your reports in RML
- The basic framework of how Odoo organizes reports and forms
- How to modify and make changes to reports using the new Odoo 8 reporting framework and the QWeb template language

Within Odoo, it is possible to make some changes without modifying the documents themselves. For example, you can change the headers and footers that appear on all your reports throughout the company.

In addition to the older RML format, Odoo 8 includes an all new reporting framework that allows for a lot more flexibility and support for mobile devices as compared to the previous reporting framework. A powerful template language called QWeb allows you to integrate data from Odoo into your reports. This chapter walks you through these steps and shows you how to modify existing Odoo reports.

> Like in other areas of Odoo development, make frequent backups of your databases. In some of the examples, we will change the database in ways that can make it difficult to recover if something goes wrong.

Getting the skills required to modify reports

In my experience, many end users believe that with perhaps an hour or two of training, they will be able to create their own reports. This is not just an Odoo issue; it is a common perception that many end users have when working with an ERP system. Unfortunately, creating or modifying reports is often not easy and should be considered more of a developer task than an end user task. Be prepared to spend considerable time to acquire the skills required to make significant changes to the documents and reports in Odoo.

Furthermore, reporting has changed dramatically in the past several years. Previously, many companies were dependent on paper reports and Excel sheets to properly communicate information through the company. Very often in Odoo, what was previously a physical report, can be better managed through filtering and grouping views properly or using the business intelligence features built into Odoo. Be sure to carefully consider your report options from many different angles.

> Scope creep refers to projects that continue to grow in complexity beyond the original design. Pay special attention to report requests, as it can be an area in which you can end up with many additional requirements that you did not anticipate.

Company report configuration

When Odoo is first installed, you will be presented with a default template that will appear on many of the standard reports. Even if you don't plan to make a lot of major changes to the standard reports in Odoo, it is very likely you will want to modify the headers and footers and other parts of your report template to be more specific for your company.

To begin editing Odoo headers and footers, log in as an Odoo administrator. Navigate to the **Settings** menu on the far right and select **Companies** in the **Companies** submenu. Click on the **Report Configuration** tab and you will see the XML markup that is used to create the template for your company reports. The following screenshot is of the **Report Configuration** tab in the company settings:

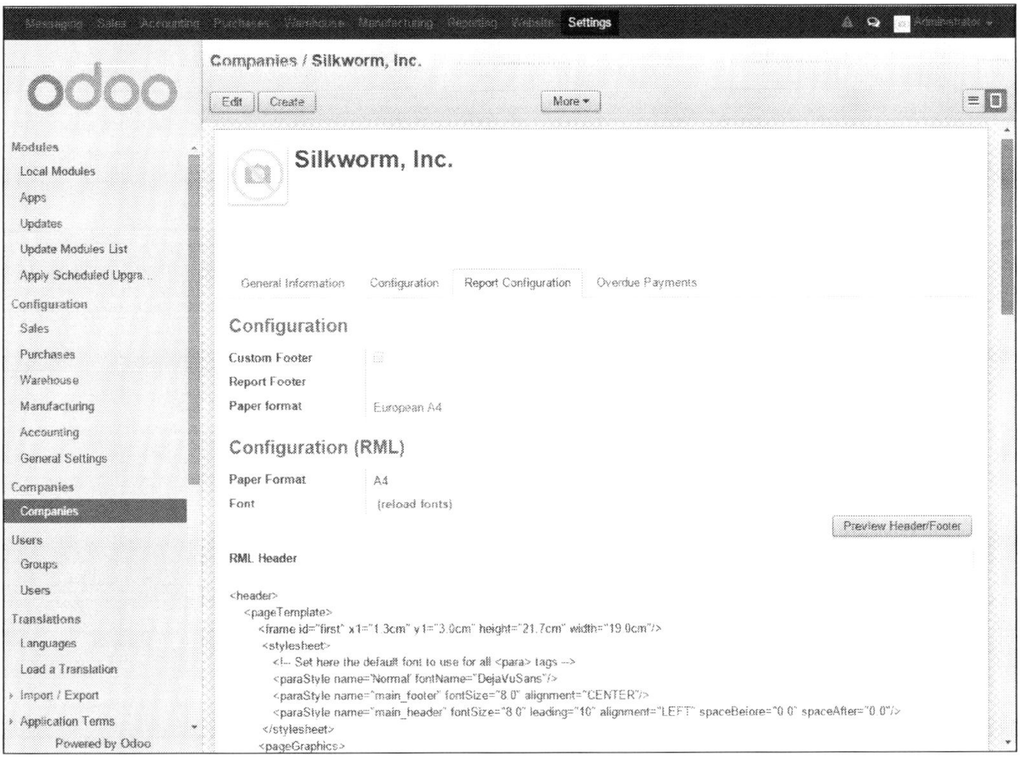

Once you select the **Report Configuration** tab, you will be brought to a screen that has several sections to help you define your reports.

Determining your report configuration

In the Report **Configuration** section, Odoo allows you to define a custom footer and select **Paper Format** and **Font** for your report. By default, Odoo will automatically create a footer for you but once you click on the checkbox, an edit box will appear to let you define your own report footer.

Examining the configuration

For those familiar with RML or XML in general, this code is likely to look familiar and much less intimidating. If you are new to XML, you can expect to spend some time looking at other resources that will aid you in making changes to the report template in Odoo.

Report Markup Language

In previous versions of Odoo, nearly all of the documents were built in **Report Markup Language** (**RML**). While Odoo has adapted an entirely new reporting template language, QWeb, which is to create a more common platform for mobile websites and reporting, there are some areas in Odoo that still use RML. This includes the report header and the report footer on the company page.

RML is a flexible markup language created by ReportLab Europe Ltd. One of the primary features of this language is to produce PDF files. Adobe's PDF format is widely accepted; it is an open standard and is commonly recognized as a legal document format in many countries. Odoo utilizes this format as the primary method of providing documents to the Odoo end user.

RML provides the template that Odoo requires to produce the required document. By modifying the RML, you can customize reports to your liking. For further information on RML, review the documentation at `http://www.reportlab.com/docs/rml2pdf-ds.pdf`.

Modifying the RML header

Odoo exposes the report template within the company settings because this will be one of the most frequent changes a company will require. There are three template segments that you can modify:

- The templates for documents that will typically be seen externally
- The template for documents and reports that will typically be distributed internally
- The template used for landscape documents

The header and footer information are all within the same text box. The header and footer sections are commented within the code so that you know where each section begins and ends.

The RML for the company header

Let's look at the RML for the company header. The following is a screenshot of the RML used for the company header:

```
<!– page header –>
<lines>1.3cm 27.7cm 20cm 27.7cm</lines>
<drawRightString x="20cm" y="27.8cm">[[ company.rml_header1 ]]</drawRightString>
<drawString x="1.3cm" y="27.3cm">[[ company.partner_id.name ]]</drawString>
<place x="1.3cm" y="25.3cm" height="1.8cm" width="15.0cm">
   <para style="main_header">[[ display_address(company.partner_id) or '' ]]</para>
</place>
<drawString x="1.3cm" y="25.0cm">Phone:</drawString>
<drawRightString x="7cm" y="25.0cm">[[ company.partner_id.phone or '' ]]</drawRightString>
<drawString x="1.3cm" y="24.6cm">Mail:</drawString>
<drawRightString x="7cm" y="24.6cm">[[ company.partner_id.email or '' ]]</drawRightString>
<lines>1.3cm 24.5cm 7cm 24.5cm</lines>
```

Take special notice of the `<!–page header -->` tag at the very top. It identifies that this segment of RML is utilized to produce the header on the reports. In RML, any text that is wrapped between a `<!--` tag at the beginning and a `-->` tag at the end are considered comments. These will help you identify where you need to make the desired changes.

Making our first simple change

You have to start somewhere. When modifying reports, the best approach is to start simple and test each and every change as you make it. Do not expect to go in and make a dozen changes to the RML header and then click on **Save**; not until you have a lot of experience.

For our change, notice that in the default header, Odoo labels the e-mail address tab **Mail:**.

To see the header and how it will look on a real report, you can use the **Preview Header/Footer** button and you will get a PDF example of your header. The following screenshot shows the default **Mail:** label used in the company header:

While this is not a big deal, it would be more appropriate to have the e-mail address labeled as `Email Address:` in our company header.

To make this change, we only need to change `Mail:` to `Email Address:` in the header section of the RML and save the record. The following screenshot shows the changed label in the company header:

```
<drawString x="1.3cm" y="25.0cm">Phone:</drawString>
<drawRightString x="7cm" y="25.0cm">[[ company.partner_id.phone or '' ]]</drawRightString>
<drawString x="1.3cm" y="24.6cm">Email Address:</drawString>
<drawRightString x="7cm" y="24.6cm">[[ company.partner_id.email or '' ]]</drawRightString>
<lines>1.3cm 24.5cm 7cm 24.5cm</lines>
```

After you have saved the changes, you can produce the print PDF of another sales order to see the change. The following screenshot shows the changed label in the company header:

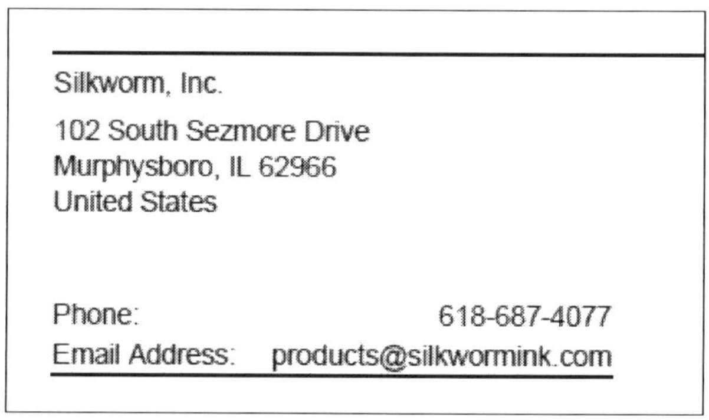

As you can see, it is possible to make small changes to the company header quickly, without a great deal of concern for all the complex parts of the RML that you might not understand. But do be aware, there are references such as `company.parnter_id.email` and other scripting in the RML that, if broken, might render the report unusable.

The RML for the company footer

Now, let's take a look at the RML for the company footer. The following screenshot shows the RML used for the company footer:

```
<!–page bottom–>
<lines>1.2cm 2.65cm 19.9cm 2.65cm</lines>
<place x="1.3cm" y="0cm" height="2.55cm" width="19.0cm">
    <para style="main_footer">[[ company.rml_footer ]]</para>
    <para style="main_footer">Contact : [[ user.name ]] - Page: <pageNumber/></para>
</place>
```

This <!–page bottom --> comment tag identifies that the code following it is what will be used to display the company footer on the report.

Understanding dynamic fields in your reports

When RML is processed, the text that is between brackets, [[" and "]], is processed dynamically. This means that the report will not show exactly what is in between the brackets, but instead will fill that data from within Odoo. In our company footer, for example, the text [[user.name]] tells the reporting engine to replace that text with the user's name. Take a few minutes to look through the RML and identify where there is information contained in these brackets.

Additionally, this dynamic syntax can call custom Python methods as well. For example, [[display_address(company.partner_id)]] calls a Python method to correctly format the address for the company header.

Learning how Odoo organizes reports

Unfortunately, the ability to edit the header and footer of the company information does not get you very far. If you spend time with Odoo, it is inevitable that a time will come when you need to make changes to specific Odoo documents. For example, a company might need to customize their quotation or sales order to make it more visually attractive to their customers. Perhaps, a company would like to change the appearance of their invoice or the picking tickets that they use to pull products from the inventory.

However, before you can begin going in and modifying reports or adding new reports, it is important that you have an overall understanding of how reports are organized within Odoo. You can get access to the reports within Odoo by going to the **Settings** menu, then in the **Technical** settings further down in the menu, you will find the **Reports** section. Clicking on it will list the reports in Odoo:

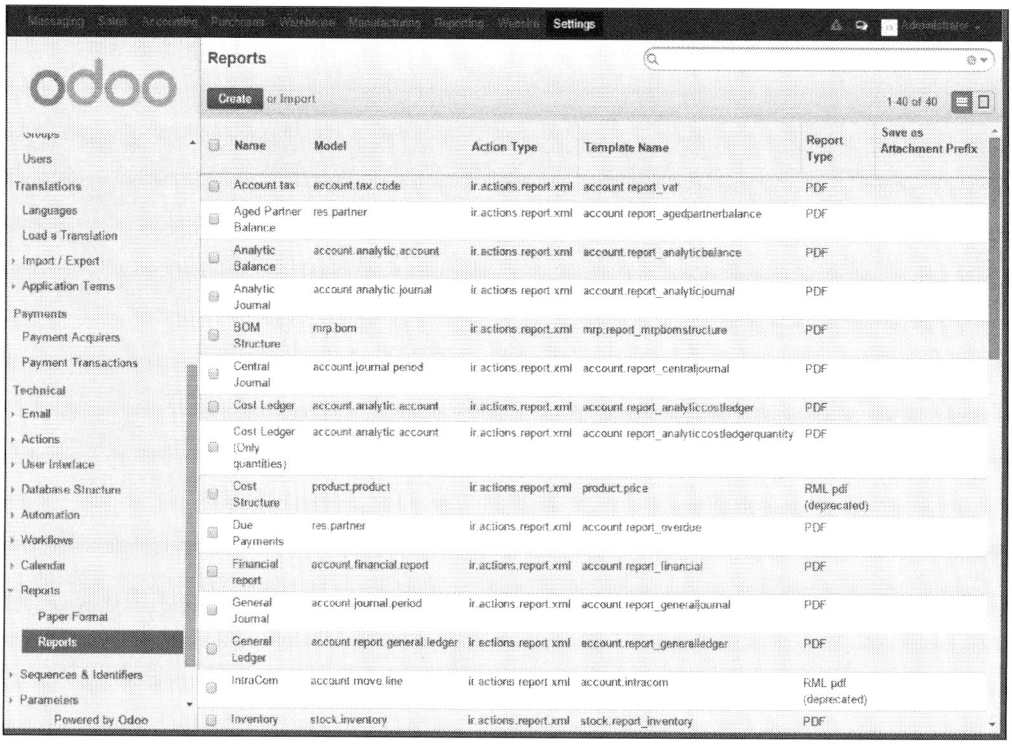

In the preceding screenshot, you can see the list of reports with critical information that tells you which model or main set of information the report is associated with, the type of action used to trigger that report, the template for the report, and the report type.

> The **Save as Attachment Prefix** option can be used to append a prefix to the beginning of the report name when it is saved.

Understanding the report types

Each of the past few major upgrades to Odoo has brought with it upgrades and new improvements to the reporting engine. Odoo 8 is no different and many of the old reports are gone. However, Odoo still provides support for those older types of reports. In the previous screenshot, when you see a report type of RML PDF (depreciated), that is a report that is still using the old reporting mechanism. You can still open up those older reports and make changes to them. However, most of the reports now use Odoo's new Odoo report framework, QWeb templates.

What is the QWeb template framework?

The QWeb template framework is actually far more useful than just for basic reports. The QWeb template is also the main way that all of the Website Builder and new CMS generates the HTML to create the page. In reports, QWeb works in exactly the same way but instead, directs the output into a PDF file.

The great part about this is once you learn how to modify reports in QWeb, that same skill will allow you to create dynamic web pages that can tie directly into Odoo.

Looking at the definition for the sales order form

As with other examples in this book, we are going to choose a very common business requirement for this example. Most companies are not going to want to use the default sales order. In fact, after involvement in hundreds of Accounting and ERP systems, I cannot recall any system implementation that involves sales orders that were not customized at some point.

Using what you have learned in previous chapters, you might want to bring up a quotation or a sales order and have it ready to print, so that you can see your changes as they happen. Any changes you make will modify both the quotation and the sales order as they share the same QWeb template.

> Odoo is quite friendly at allowing you to use more than one tab in your browser for most operations. I often keep one tab open on the document I want to print and then keep another tab open with the report I am editing.

When you are ready to edit the sales order, scroll down the report list and find the **Quotation / Order** field, and then click on it. It is also the only report in the default list of Odoo reports that is built on the `sale.order` model.

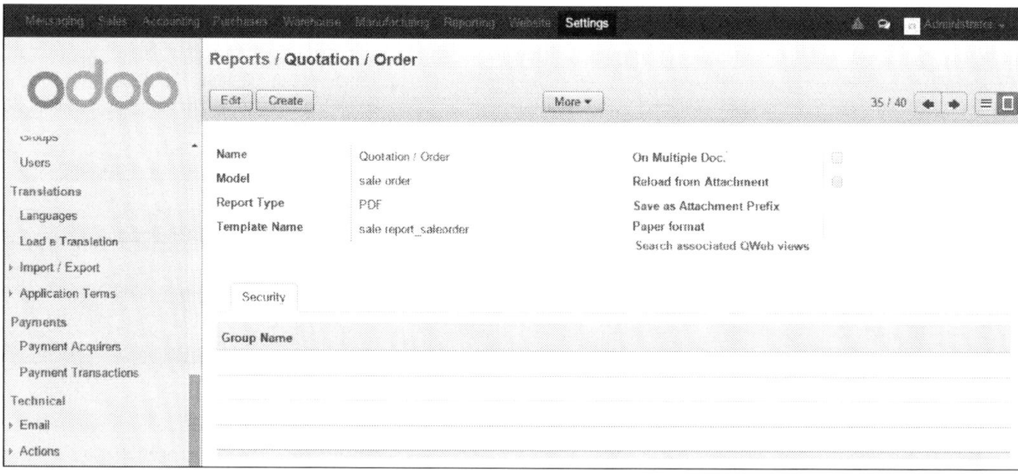

You will notice there is some basic information at the top of the page and then a **Security** tab at the bottom of the report, which is empty. You can use this tab to put additional restrictions on the report beyond what has already been specified in the `sale.order` model.

The previous screen is primarily the configuration of the report. The actual report itself can be found by clicking on **Search associated QWeb views**:

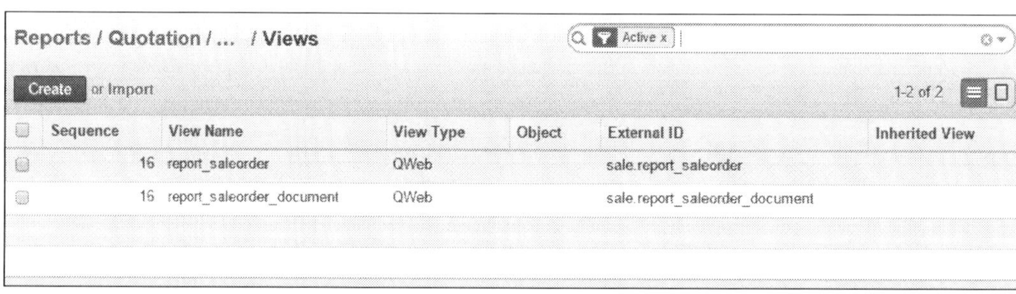

This brings up all the QWeb views associated with the report. While there are two views listed, the one we are interested in is **report_saleorder_document**. The other view is basically a container that holds the content of the document view and you would rarely need to modify that unless you were an experienced Odoo Developer.

Click on the **report_saleorder_document** view to open the view:

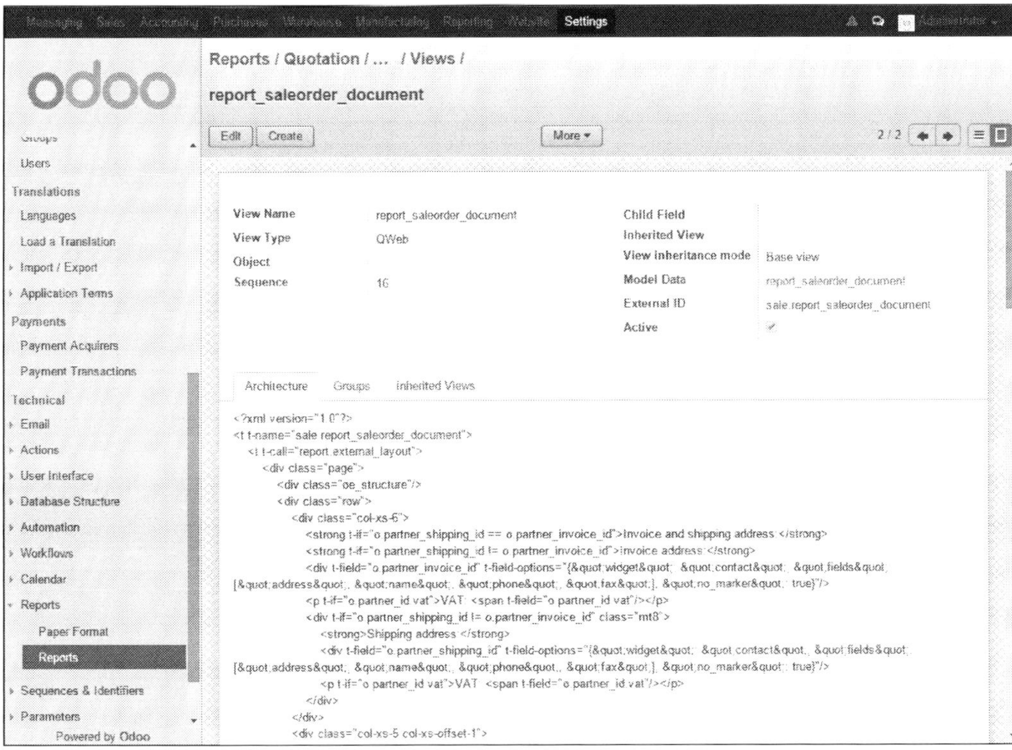

So we are finally here! You have to drill down a little bit to get to them but after you have done it a few times, it really is pretty easy. Now we are looking at the actual QWeb report template. Odoo calls these templates views when they are associated with Odoo reports.

If you look through the architecture, you should quickly find elements within it that compare directly to the standard quotation or sales order report.

Here is a sample quotation that was produced using the default QWeb template we are viewing:

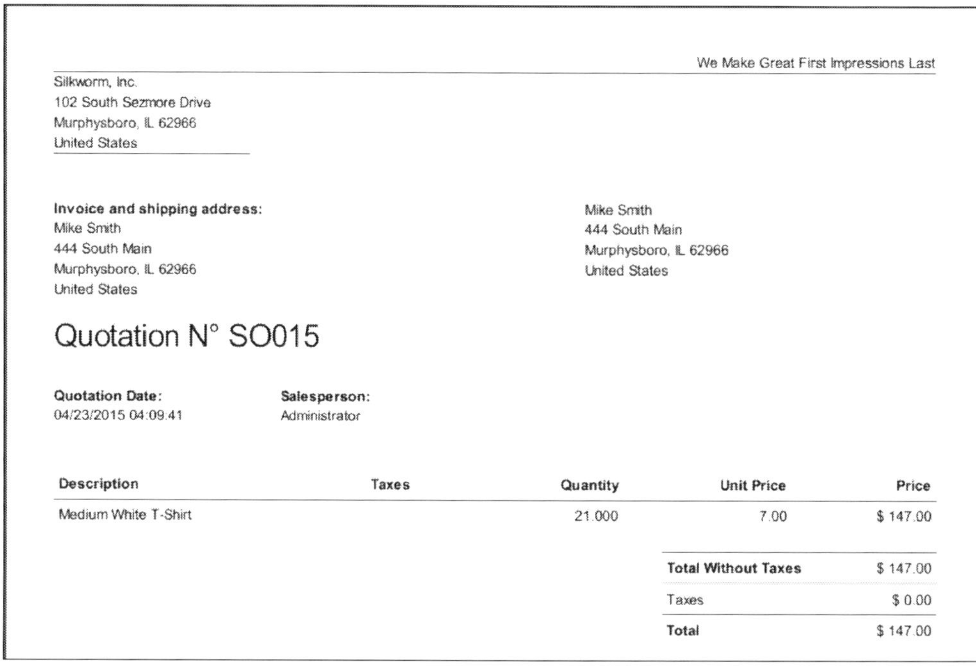

We Make Great First Impressions Last

Silkworm, Inc.
102 South Sezmore Drive
Murphysboro, IL 62966
United States

Invoice and shipping address:
Mike Smith
444 South Main
Murphysboro, IL 62966
United States

Mike Smith
444 South Main
Murphysboro, IL 62966
United States

Quotation N° SO015

Quotation Date: 04/23/2015 04:09:41

Salesperson: Administrator

Description	Taxes	Quantity	Unit Price	Price
Medium White T-Shirt		21.000	7.00	$ 147.00

Total Without Taxes	$ 147.00
Taxes	$ 0.00
Total	$ 147.00

So as we should always do, let's make a small change and see the result. I cannot emphasize enough how important it is to create a backup frequently and make small changes when you are first getting started.

Once again, we will use a real business requirement that would be a common request. You will notice that quotation number uses N°, which depending on localization, might not be what is desirable. So, let's assume for this change that we want to have **Quote #:** instead of **Quotation N°** on our report.

This is relatively simple. Click on **Edit**, as you would on any Odoo form, to edit the template. Then, scroll down into the template until you find `Quotation N°`:

```
<h2>
    <span t-if="o.state not in ['draft','sent']">Order N° </span>
    <span t-if="o.state in ['draft','sent']">Quotation N° </span>
    <span t-field="o.name"/>
</h2>
```

Replace the selected text you see in the preceding screenshot, `Quotation N°`, with `Quote #`, and then save the document. Be very careful with the changes you make until you understand XML. A less common but worst-case scenario is that perhaps, the mistake you make will still allow the document to save, but it will be broken.

> Because the XML is represented with ordinary text, a little trick you can use is to copy and paste the XML into a text editor to have a quick backup, in case you make a mistake or do not get the results you expected.

After you have saved the document, you should be able to print the document and see your change when you print the quotation again.

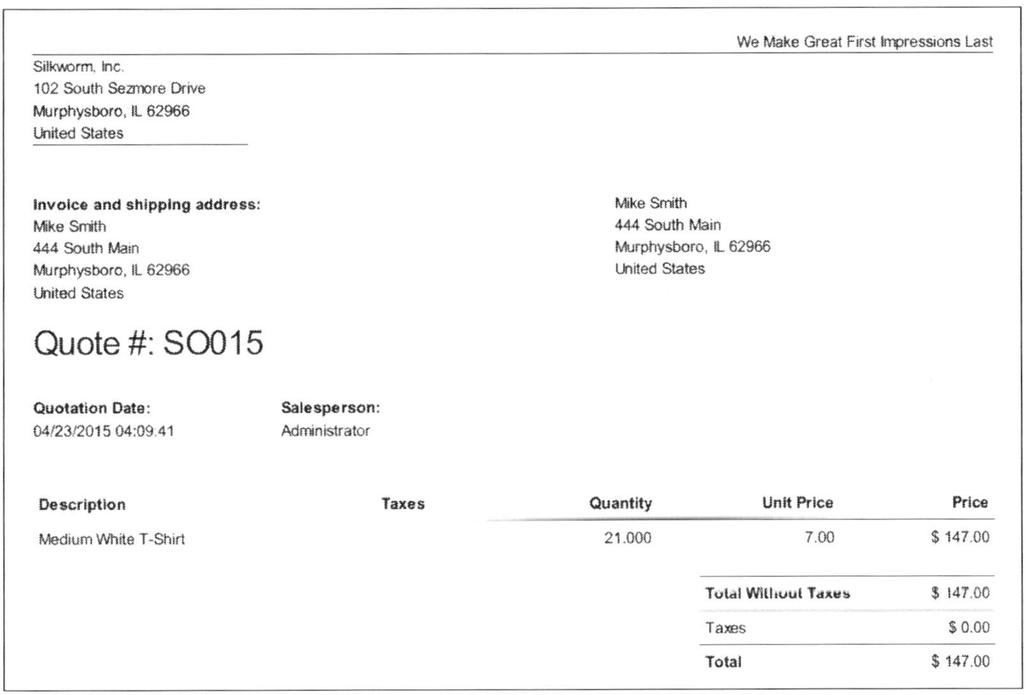

We Make Great First Impressions Last

Silkworm, Inc.
102 South Sezmore Drive
Murphysboro, IL 62966
United States

Invoice and shipping address:
Mike Smith
444 South Main
Murphysboro, IL 62966
United States

Mike Smith
444 South Main
Murphysboro, IL 62966
United States

Quote #: SO015

Quotation Date: 04/23/2015 04:09:41

Salesperson: Administrator

Description	Taxes	Quantity	Unit Price	Price
Medium White T-Shirt		21.000	7.00	$ 147.00

Total Without Taxes	$ 147.00
Taxes	$ 0.00
Total	$ 147.00

We have made that small change successfully and changed it. But even just knowing how to do this will allow you to often add many things you need to a report.

Learning more about the power of QWeb templates

Now that you have learned to make that small change, let's look a little closer at how Odoo is able to use the exact same template for both the quotation and the sales order. In fact, you might have already figured out how Odoo is doing this from looking a little bit around the code we just modified.

One of the best things you can do to learn how to modify reports is to look at existing reports within Odoo and see how they accomplish what you might want to accomplish. When trying to solve a problem, see if you can find another report in Odoo that is already doing something similar to what you want.

> Often, it can be a lot easier to copy and paste a part of the template you need and then change it, rather than trying to get all the `<./?>` syntax straight and just right. It's easier if you are working from a reference point.

Using a T-IF in a QWeb template report

Much of the power of QWeb allows you to conditionally show information depending on various fields and information within the document. In this case, Odoo is looking at the status of the order to determine whether the template should have a label for quotation or for sales order. Let's take a close look at the syntax so that we can understand exactly what it means.

If you don't understand at least some basic XML, now would be a good time to look at some of the available resources we have listed in the *Appendix, Locating Additional Odoo Resources* or do a simple Google search on the XML tutorial:

```
<span t-if="o.state not in ['draft','sent']">Order N° </span>
<span t-if="o.state in ['draft','sent']">Quote #:</span>
```

You will notice that each section is wrapped in its own set of `<span>` tags. Then right after the first span tag starts, we have the `t-if=` condition. Everything between the double quotes is the condition that will determine whether what is included between the span tags will print.

In this specific case, `o` represents the order. We use the period or dot notation to specify which field we want to check. In this case, it is the state field. Even if you are not a programmer, if you read it out and ignore the confusing syntax and punctuation, it should start to make sense. The only difference between each of these `t-if=` statements is the word `not` just following `o.state`. When the state of the order is not in the drafts or sent tab, then it is an order. When the state of the order is in the drafts or sent tab, then we have a quotation.

If XML and programming is very new to you, some of this could be a bit confusing. However, if you take some time to look at existing reports and use some of the resources in *Appendix, Locating Additional Odoo Resources* to learn more, you will be customizing Odoo reports in no time.

Summary

In this chapter, we started by walking through how to change the templates on company reports through Odoo to modify the header of your report. Next, you learned about Odoo's reporting system and how reports are organized within Odoo. Finally, you learned how to use the powerful QWeb template language to make changes to reports.

In the next chapter, we will explore how we can use the Odoo workflow editor to customize Odoo to adapt to the demands of your business processes. For our example, we will be extending the standard Odoo workflow so that sales orders can only be confirmed once the artwork for that order has been approved.

15
Understanding Workflows

One of the key objectives of an ERP system is to organize information as it passes through business processes in the company. As operations grow in complexity, companies typically attempt to better define their processes by diagramming and creating formal workflows. While there are a variety of workflow methodologies, the primary goal is the same—to provide clear documentation of the processes that make up the core operations of the business. The better these processes are defined and executed, the better the company can manage their operations.

In this chapter, we will:

- Take a look at Odoo's business-friendly view of a workflow
- Use the Odoo graphical workflow editor to examine the sales order workflow
- Study how activities and transitions can be used to manage the state of a document in Odoo
- Learn how to modify workflows with a real-world example that requires an art-approval process before the sales order can be confirmed

Odoo facilitates the ability to map business processes to Odoo by providing a workflow designer. This designer is utilized for many of the major Odoo applications including sales, purchasing, and invoicing. Odoo provides both a high-level view of the workflow processes as well as a developer mode that gives an experienced Odoo developer the ability to alter the default workflows in Odoo.

> Modifying workflows should only be attempted by experienced Odoo developers. While Odoo offers a visual interface for modifying workflows, there is a real risk that you could break existing workflows. Before modifying any workflows, make sure it is on a nonproduction version of Odoo and that you have a viable backup.

Planning the changes to our workflow

One of the most common changes in a workflow is to create an additional step required in a process. For example, a company might want to have an extra layer of approval if a purchase order is over a certain amount. Another example would be a quality assurance process that would be performed before a delivery order can be shipped.

When deciding how you want to modify your workflow, make sure you have considered all of the possibilities on how you could configure Odoo without changes in workflow. If you don't thoroughly understand all of the options available to you in Odoo, it is quite possible that you will end up unnecessarily complicating your implementation by modifying workflows.

For our real world example, for some orders we are going to require that a customer must approve the artwork for an order before it can be confirmed for production. However, before we can begin modifying the workflow, it is important that we take the time to look at the standard sales order workflow in Odoo.

An example of the Odoo workflow

When you have been putting in quotations and converting them to sales orders, behind the scenes, Odoo has been following a default workflow for that process. Let's take a look at the Odoo default sales order workflow.

> The end user process flow diagrams that were available in OpenERP/Odoo 7 were removed in Odoo 8 because they were considered obsolete and unmaintained.

Activating the developer mode

As in the previous chapter, we will need to activate the developer mode to back up our database and access the workflows in Odoo.

Choose **About Odoo** from the menu in the top-right corner and click on **Activate the developer mode**. For more detailed instructions, see the *Activating the developer mode* and *Backing up your database* sections of *Chapter 13, Customizing Odoo for Your Business*.

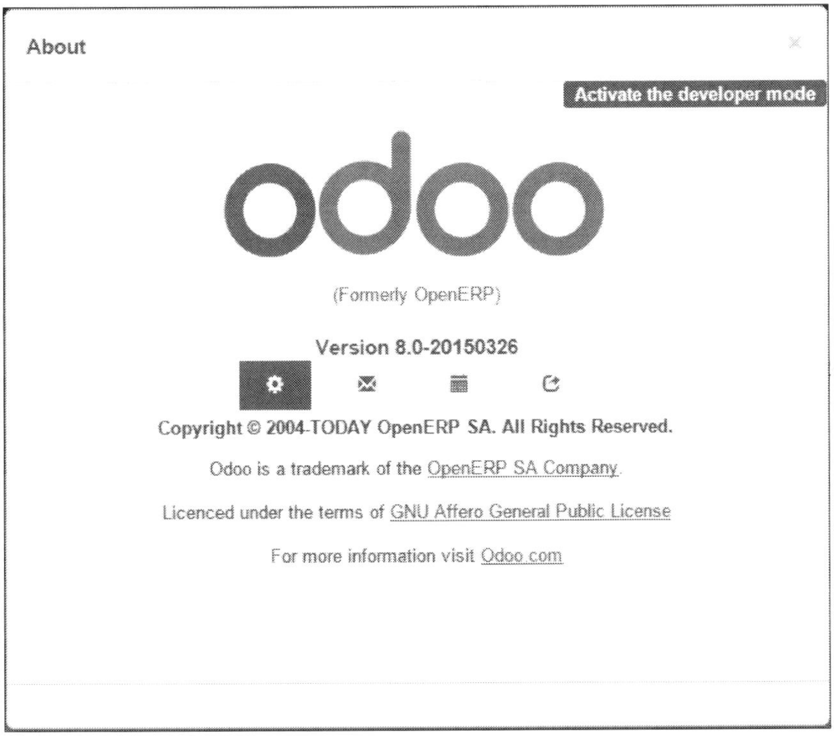

Looking at the Odoo workflow in detail

The developer view of the workflow describes the conditions to determine the various document states and how each process should be handled. To understand a workflow, it is important to recognize exactly what a workflow can accomplish in Odoo.

In Odoo, a workflow can:

- Modify the states or stages that a document is currently in
- Determine what conditions or states in a document are required to execute a process
- Make process decisions based on user roles and access privileges
- Create subflows to encapsulate complexity

Odoo also provides a very nice visual workflow designer that allows you to both analyze workflows, as well as make some limited modifications. I am specifically stating limited modifications as you are likely to need to have at least some experience in Odoo development if you are going to make anything but minor changes to workflows.

Looking at the sales orders workflow inside the workflow designer

To access the visual workflow designer for the **Sales Orders** workflow, go to the **Sales** screen and choose **Edit Workflow** from the developer **Debug** drop-down menu on the top left of the form. Here in the following screenshot, we are selecting **Edit Workflow** from the developer menu:

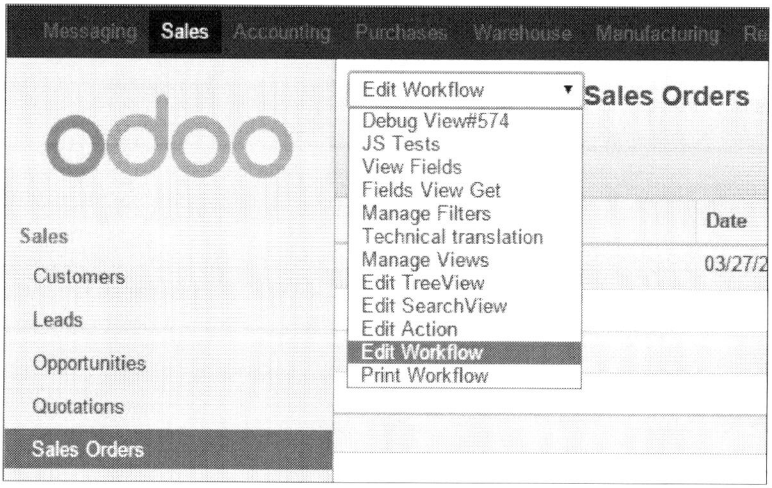

After you have clicked on **Edit Workflow**, Odoo will bring up the workflow in a list format. Click on the **Diagram view** icon on the far right to view the workflow visually:

Once you have selected the diagram view, you will be presented with a screen that will look similar to the workflow in the following screenshot:

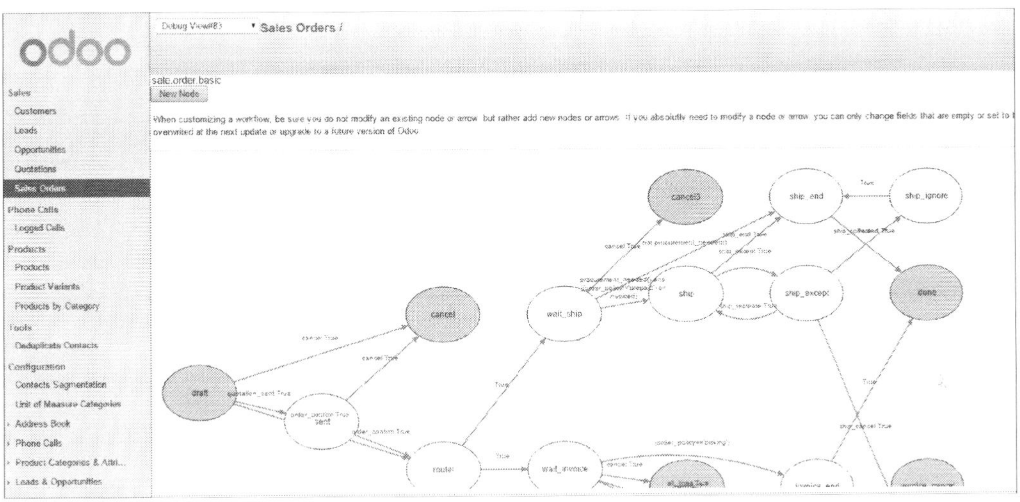

At first, this sales order workflow is going to look very intimidating. Honestly, it is a rather intimidating workflow altogether. While Odoo certainly makes it possible to modify workflows, this is often best left until after you understand Odoo workflows thoroughly. This chapter will help get you started, but be prepared to spend a great deal of time studying Odoo workflows if you intend to make extensive modifications with any degree of success.

> Your first goal should be to gain a solid understanding of how the workflow functions before attempting to make any changes to it. Also, it cannot be stressed often enough—make sure you back up your database before making any changes to an Odoo workflow.

Workflow nodes

In the diagram view of the workflow, the oval symbols are the workflow nodes. Each node can act on documents and execute processes. Nodes that are shaded in gray indicate that the node begins or ends the workflow. For example, **draft** is a beginning workflow node. This, of course, corresponds to the state in which sales orders start when they are first created.

Looking closer at the sales order workflow

We are going to examine in depth just a small part of the sales order workflow. Primarily, we will study the initial nodes where we create a draft sales order and then either send, cancel, or confirm that sales order. The following screenshot focuses on the initial steps of the sales order process:

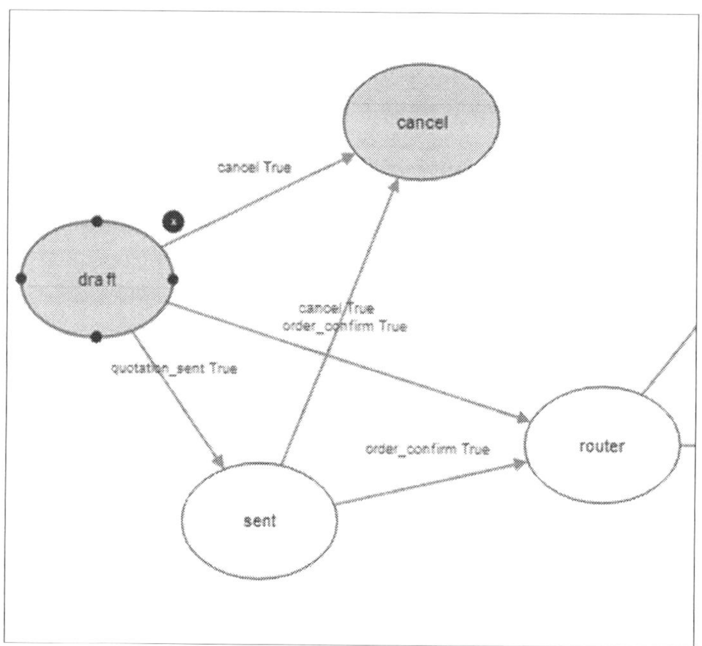

Take a look at the draft node. We can see from the preceding figure that there are three potential pathways out of the draft node in this workflow. One of the arrows goes to the **sent** node, another to the **cancel** node, and finally one goes to the **router** node. The option to send, cancel, or confirm a sales order directly acts on the draft node in the workflow.

A quick look at the options we have when we create a sales order will help us demonstrate how these functions map to the workflow.

The following screenshot shows the commands that are available when our sales order is in a draft state:

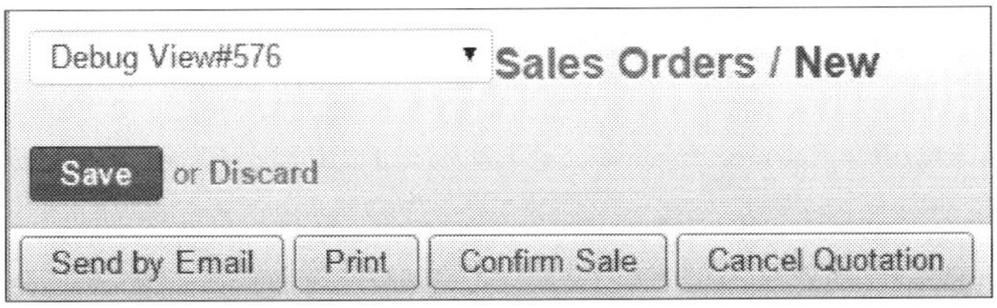

The commands shown in the preceding screenshot are as follows:

- **Send by Email**: This button will trigger **quotation_sent** and proceed to the **sent** node
- **Confirm Sale**: This button will trigger **order_confirm** and proceed to the **router** node
- **Cancel Quotation**: This button will proceed to the **cancel** node

A question or two might now come to mind. Why are there only three available transitions out of the **draft** node? What about **Save**? What about **Print**? Workflows primarily determine the state of the document. In this case, Odoo doesn't care to have a printed process in the workflow. You can print the document, but it has no effect whatsoever on the workflow. You can also **Save** the document, but saving that document does not inherently impact Odoo's workflow. However, when we actually send a document by e-mail, Odoo has implemented a workflow process (**quotation_sent**) that allows us to see the sales order as being sent to the customer via e-mail.

Examining a workflow node in detail

Now, let's further examine the **draft** workflow node by double-clicking on the node. Here, we can see the **Activity** screen for the draft state:

Naturally, the name of this node is `draft`. We can also see that it is tied to the **Workflow** field, which is named as `sale.order.basic`. This node's oval was shaded gray because **Flow Start** is checked. It is the beginning of the sales orders workflow. Workflows can only have one start, but they can have multiple stops.

Click on the **Transitions** page to see how this node functions.

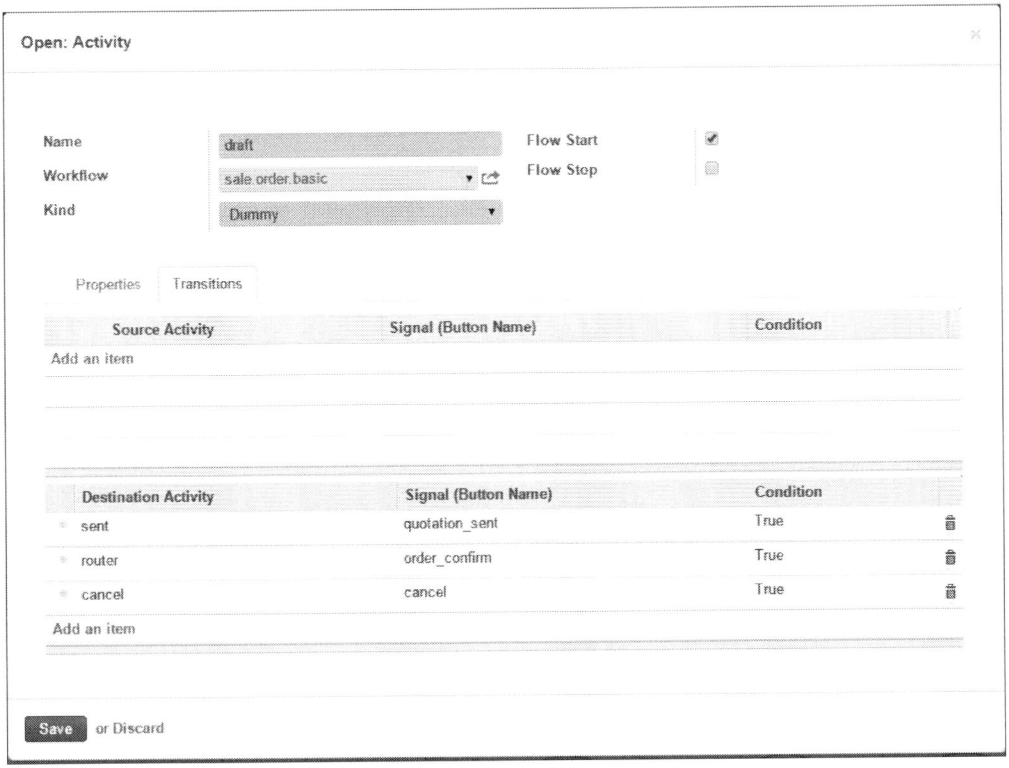

The **Destination Activity** column is what ties this node to the other nodes in the workflow figure. So, for example, when you click on the **Send by Email** button to send a quotation, this node receives the **quotation_sent** signal and then routes the sales order document to the sent node. If you click on the **Cancel Order** button, the **cancel** signal is sent to the cancel node.

Take a minute to compare the preceding three destination activities to the workflow figure. It is critical that you understand, for example, why the sales order will never go to the sent node in the workflow if you have not clicked on the **Send by Email** button in the sales order form.

Transitions in workflows

Transitions between the nodes are what literally hold the workflow together. You can see the transition from a different perspective by double-clicking on the transition in the workflow designer. Let's take a look at the cancel transition by double-clicking on the arrow connecting the draft node to the cancel node in the following screenshot:

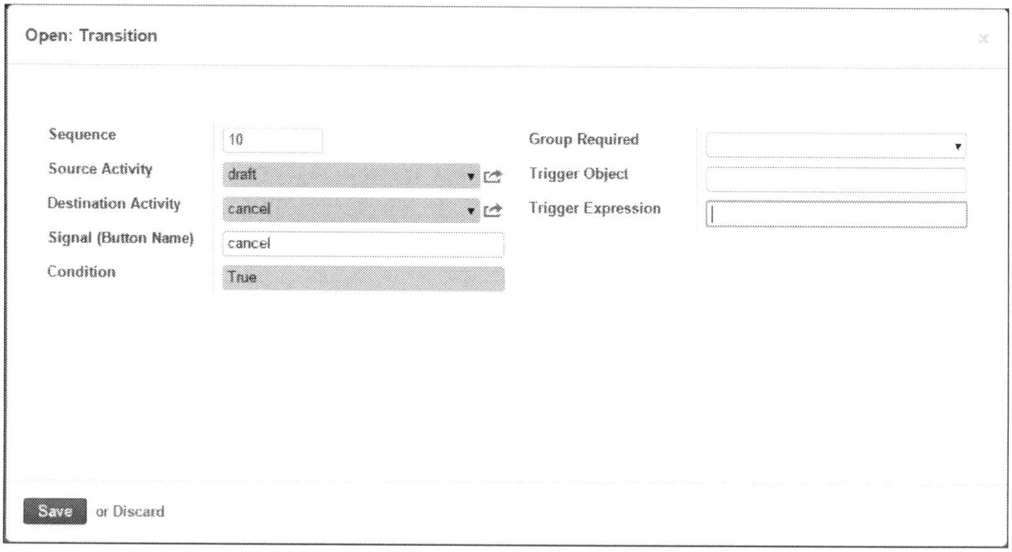

The **Source Activity** is clearly labeled as the draft node and the **Destination Activity** is field clearly labeled as the cancel node. This data is the same data as we viewed in the draft node under the **Transitions** page.

For this example, we have intentionally picked a very simple transition. If the user clicks on the **Cancel Order** button, the cancel transition just goes right on to the cancel node in the workflow. The condition is always **True**, meaning that we are not examining anything in the sales order or requesting any other input from the user. For example, if you only wanted certain user groups to be able to cancel a draft sales order, you could assign the group under the **Group Required** field in the form.

Ending a workflow

Every workflow needs to have a beginning and, of course, an ending. A document in Odoo can end in a variety of ways. Most often the conventions are done or canceled depending on the outcome of the workflow. Following our simple draft sales order example, we are going to look at the cancel node and see how we define the ending of an Odoo workflow.

Double-click on the cancel node to bring up the details:

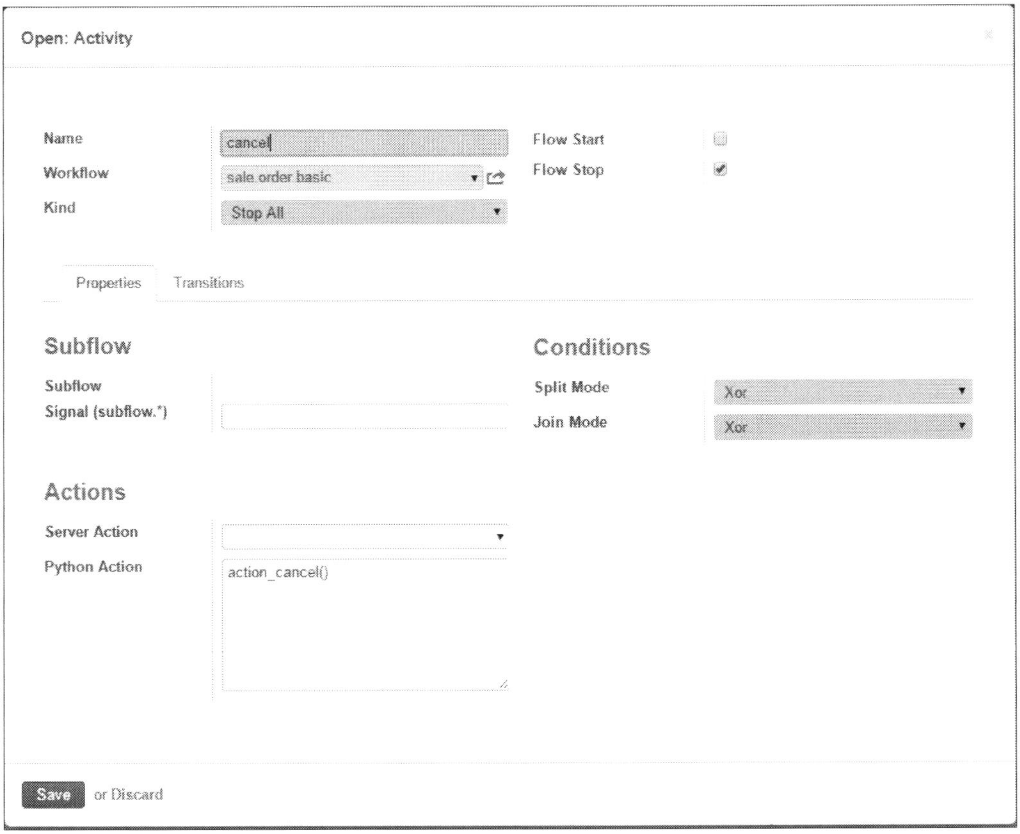

On the right, we can see that **Flow Stop** is checked. Additionally, the **Kind** field is set to **Stop All**. These settings tell Odoo that this workflow has ended. Many Odoo nodes are also tied directly to Python actions. In this example, you can see that the `action_cancel()` method is called during this step in the workflow. Combining the flexibility of workflows and Python scripts allows an experienced Odoo developer to create customized industry solutions.

Modifying workflows

The first step to modify workflows is to have a complete understanding of the existing workflow. Next, you need determine exactly how you want the updated workflow to function. In this chapter, we will make a modification using the visual editor and modifying views through the developer tools.

Changing workflows is not something that is for novice Odoo users. It is very possible, and quite likely, that when experimenting with modifying workflows, you will break something. Make backups and make sure that you can successfully restore those backups. Only after you fully understand how the exiting workflows function and you have solid backups should you even consider modifying workflows in Odoo. Never modify a workflow on a live production system.

Try to complete your modifications one at a time and test them thoroughly so that you don't create an unexpected state in your workflow.

Adding a step into the workflow for art approval

In our real world workflow, it is critical that the right artwork is designed and used for the T-shirt order to be accurate. This art approval step is so important that we do not want a sales order confirmed and put into production until the artwork for that order has been approved. There is an extra step we need to add to the workflow that will make sure a sales order cannot be confirmed unless the art approval process is complete.

Editing the sales order workflow

If you are not already in the developer mode, enter it now. Navigate to the sales application and pull up any sales order. Click on the **Developer** menu in the upper-left corner and choose **Edit Workflow**. Next, click on the small diagram icon on the far right to view the sales order workflow.

Now, you should see the familiar sales order workflow that we will modify to include a step for art approval.

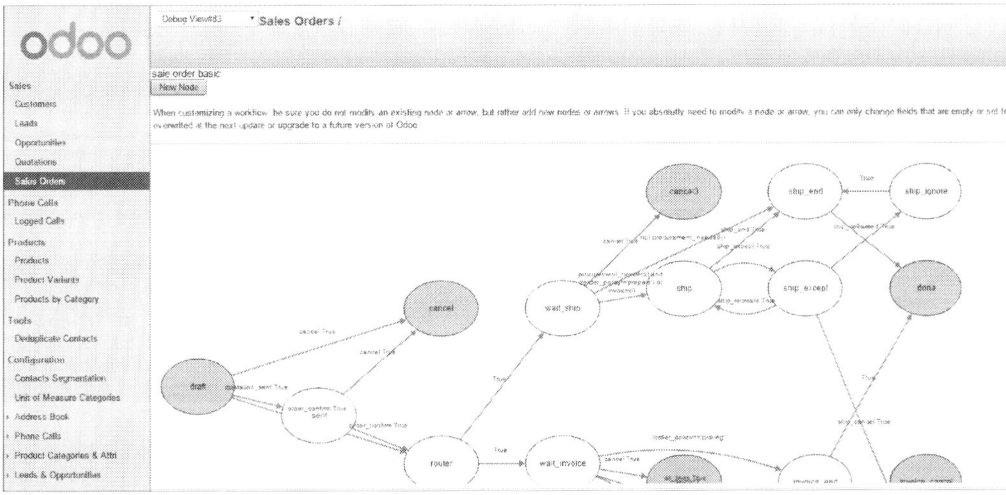

We will now add an additional activity to the workflow that will require the art to be approved before we can process the order.

> Once we begin modifying this workflow, the operation of the sales order module will be changed. It is highly recommended that you perform all of these steps on an instance of Odoo that is disposable.

Summary of the steps to changing the workflow

Modifying a workflow will typically involve several steps. It is important to outline them before we begin.

> The goal is that before a sales order is confirmed, the art must first be approved.

The steps are as follows:

1. Add a new activity to the workflow to handle the art approval.
2. Modify the transitions in the workflow to allow the art approval activity.
3. Add a button to the sales order form to **Approve Art**.
4. Modify the **Confirm Order** button, so it is only active once the art has been approved.

Adding a new activity node to a workflow

We add a new activity node to the workflow by clicking on the **New Node** button, which is located in the upper-left corner of the workflow editor. The following screenshot is of the **New Node** button in the workflow editor:

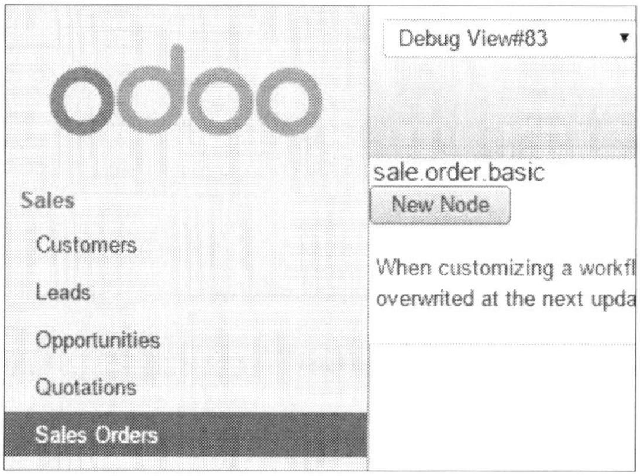

After you have clicked on the **New Node** button, a form will pop up that will allow you to define the activity for the art approval process:

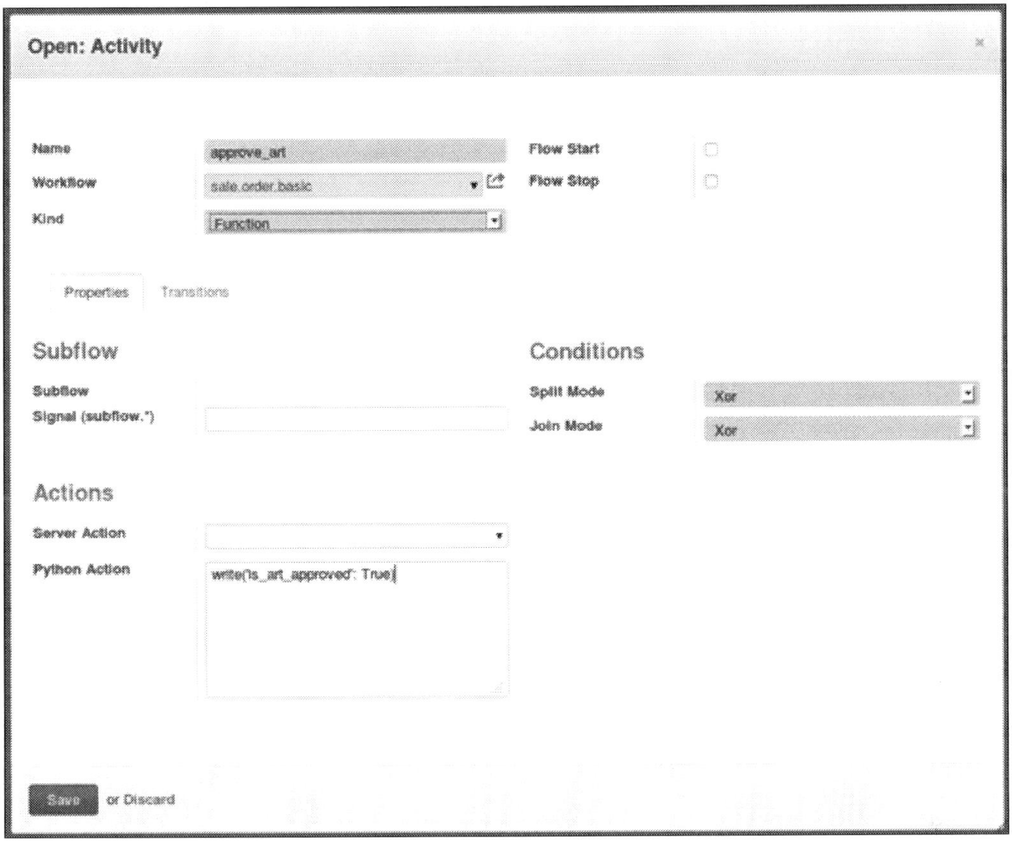

We have named the activity as `approve_art`. This will let us identify it easily in the workflow. The **Workflow** field is already defined for us as `sale.order.basic`. Under **Kind**, we have changed the default setting of **Dummy** to `Function`. With `Function` selected, Odoo will execute the code provided in the **Python Action** setting at the bottom of the form.

Modifying the sales order state in the activity

The entire purpose of this `approve_art` activity is to set the state of the sales order document to `art_approved`. This state will then be a prerequisite for displaying the **Confirm Order** button on the sales order. After you have filled out the form to create the new activity, make sure you click on **Save** to commit your changes. Next, we will create the transition that will trigger this activity.

Modifying the transitions to include art approval

Adding the activity will leave an oval named `approve_art` floating in your workflow. This is because we have not attached the activity to any transitions. Let's begin by hooking up the `approve_art` activity to the draft node with a transition. As long as the sales order document is in a `draft` state, we want the ability to trigger the `approve_art` activity.

To create the transition, click on the `draft` node. Then, using one of the four black handles on the node, drag it to the `approve_art` activity. Do not click on the dark circle with the small **x**, as this is used to delete the entire `draft` node. The following screenshot is of the draft node selected before being dragged to the **approve_art** node:

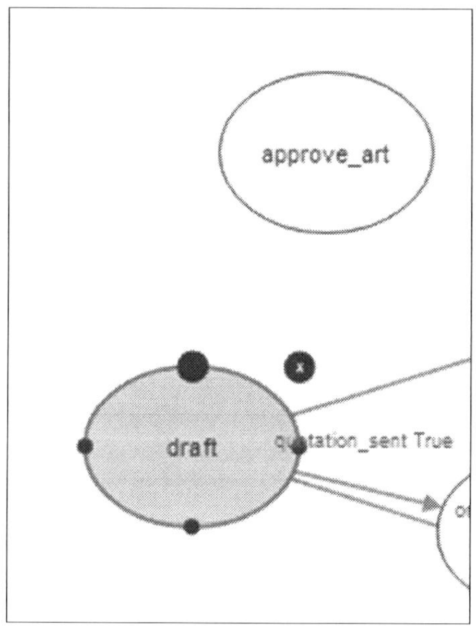

Dragging the draft node to the `approve_art` node will create the transition. The following is a screenshot of the draft node connected to the **approve_art** node to add a transition:

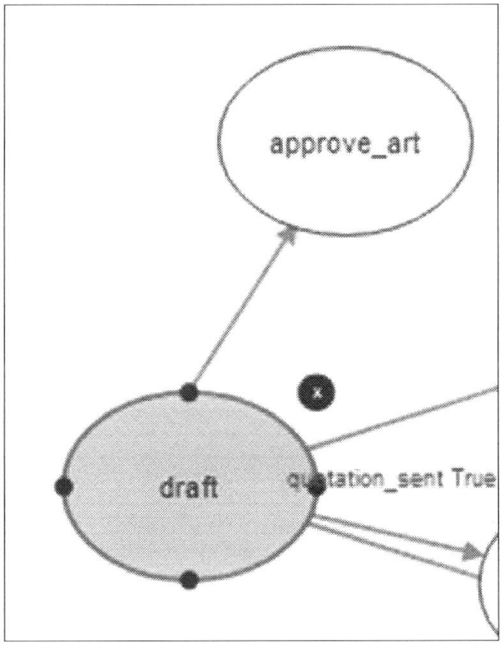

After you drag the draft node to the `approve_art` node and release your mouse button, the transition editor will appear.

Defining a transition

We will now define our transition to call the `approve_art` activity and set the state of our sales order to `art_approved`. So, what is the trigger? A button we will create on the sales order form will provide the necessary signal to call the `approve_art` activity. We will define this transition as follows:

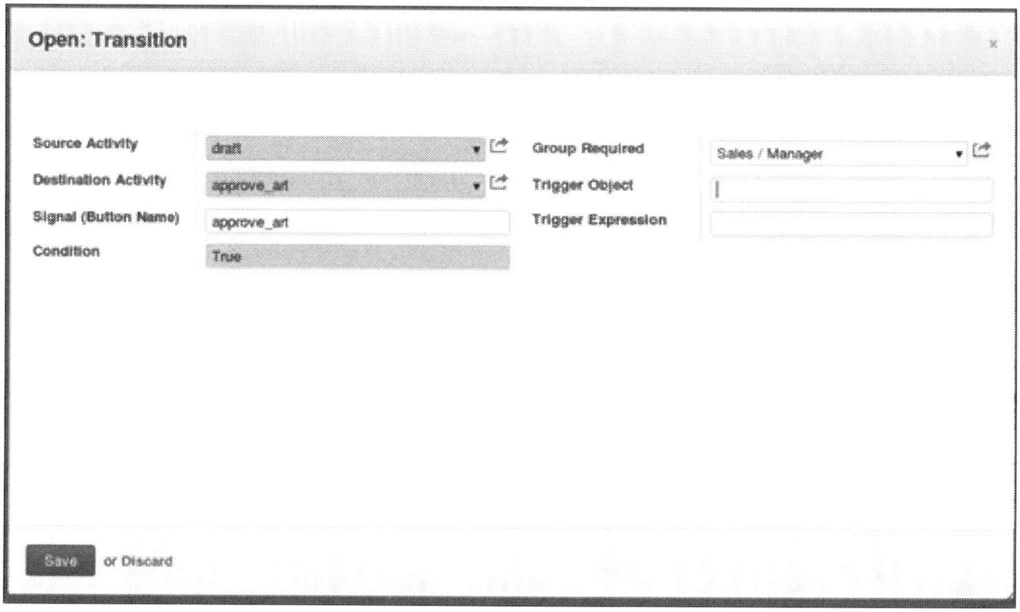

When you drag between the two nodes to create the transition, the source and destination activity are filled in automatically. We then set **Signal (Button Name)** to `approve_art`. This means for this workflow to be functional and for the `approve_art` activity to be called, we must create a button named `approve_art` on our order form.

Once we click on this new `approve_art` button, the `approve_art` activity will be called. That activity will then set the state of the sales order to `art_approved`.

Restricting the art approval to the sales manager

In defining our transition, we have set the group required to **Sales / Manager**. This means that in order for the art to be approved, the user must be part of the sales manager group who has communicated with the customer and given the go-ahead for the artwork.

Once you have clicked on **Save**, our `approve_art` activity is hooked into the `draft` node. However, we still have not defined where the workflow should go from there. We must now wire the `approve_art` activity into the workflow so that we can confirm the order and continue processing the sales order. The following is a screenshot of the workflow with the `approve_art` activity connected to the draft activity:

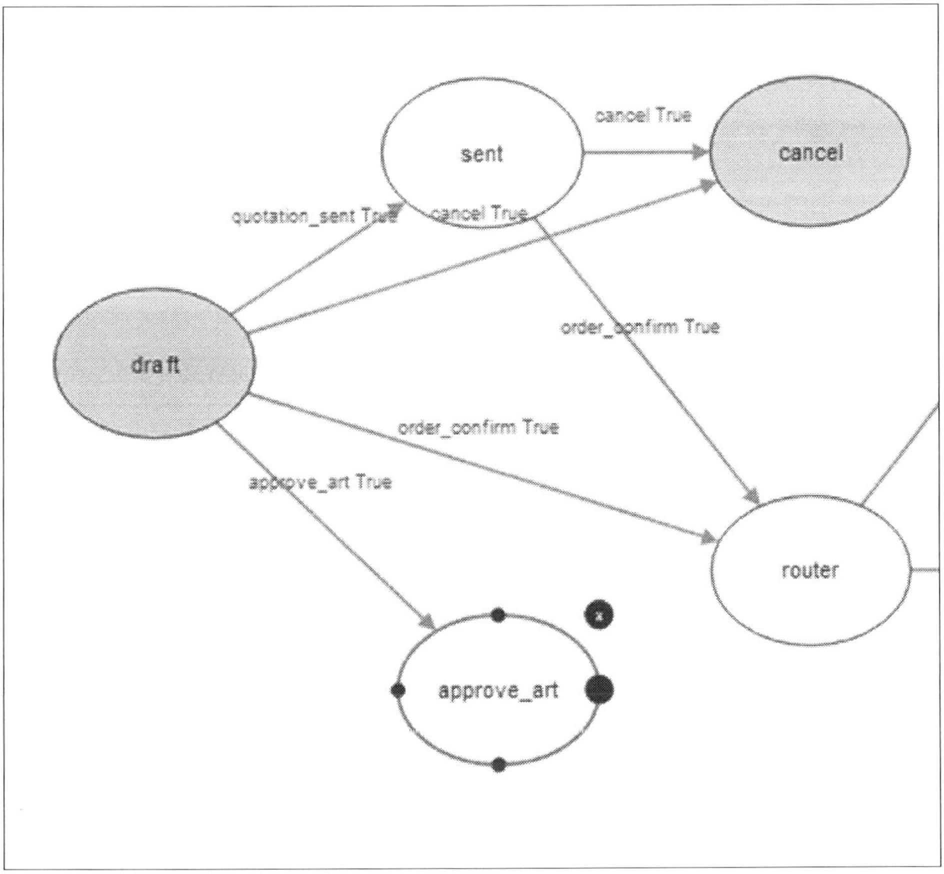

To connect the `approve_art` activity to the `router` activity, select the `approve_art` node, then click and drag one of the four dark circle handles and drag that to the `router` activity. You will then get a dialog for you to specify the transition between the two activities.

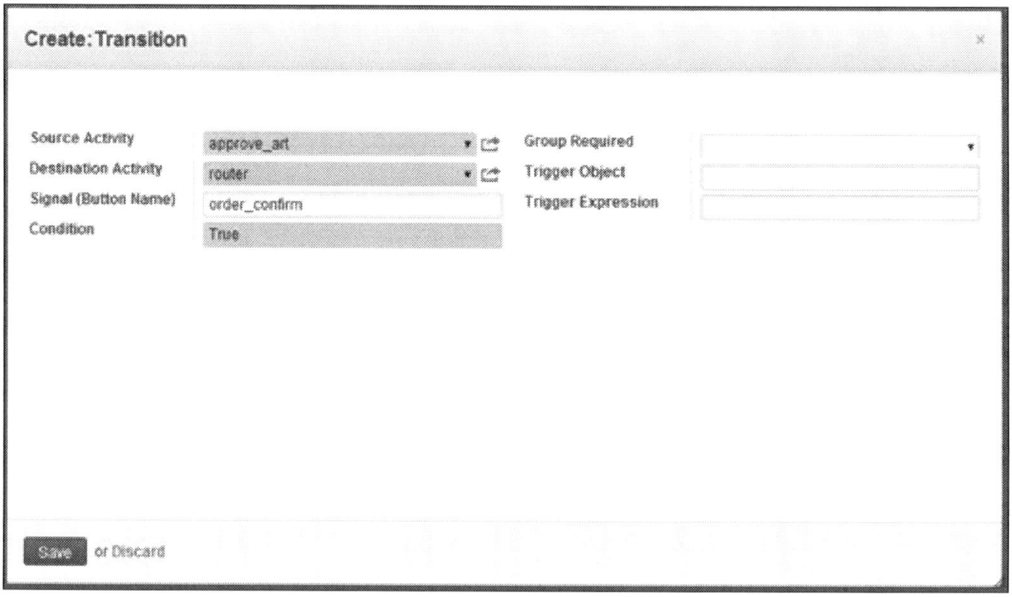

Like in the previous transition we created, the source and destination is filled in automatically. Our **Signal (Button Name)** field is set to `order_confirm`. Why `order_confirm`? Because we are going to change the `order_confirm` button to only be available once the document is in the `art_approved` state. When the art has not been approved, the **Confirm Order** button will not appear on the screen.

Modifying the other transitions in the workflow

While we have been successful in putting in the `art_approval` activity and wiring it to the router so that the sales order can be processed, we must also modify other transitions. We can begin by deleting the transition that goes directly from the draft activity to the router activity.

Simply click on the transition between the two activities, and then click on the dark circle with the small **x** to delete the transition.

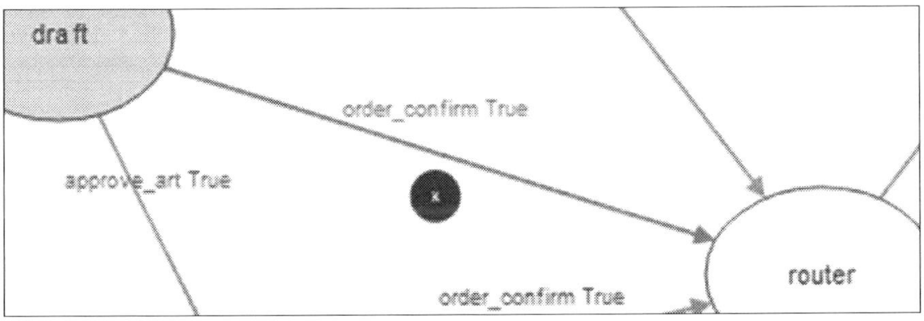

We must make another change concerning the sent activity. If you look at the sales order workflow, you will notice that once you have sent a quote, the sent activity allows you to directly confirm the order. We don't want that. We always want to make sure that the art is approved before we can confirm the order.

Let us change the transition from the sent activity, so that it can also respond to the **approve_art** button instead of the confirm button. To modify the transition, double-click on the transition (line) between the sent activity and the router activity.

Then, modify the transition so that it is properly connected to the **art_approval** activity and the signal is the **approve_art** button, instead of the order confirm button.

> I have mentioned the **router** activity several times, but this chapter will not cover the remainder of the activities contained in this workflow. You might still be wondering, *what does the router node do?* Depending on the configuration settings for Sales Order, the router decides whether the sales order will be shipped before invoicing, shipped after the invoice is paid, or shipped and invoiced *on demand*, meaning, in no particular order.

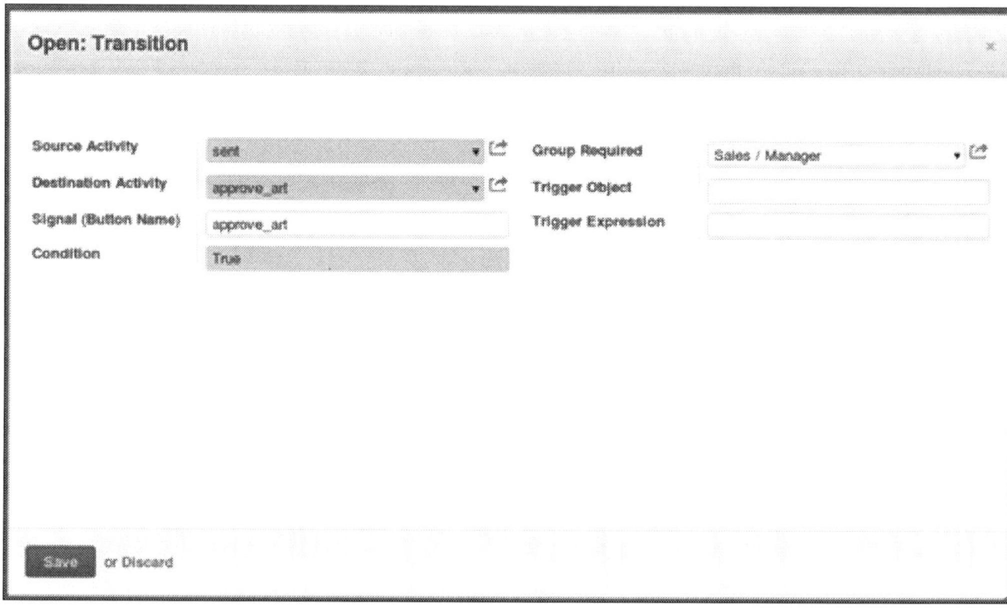

As you can see from this transition, we still have the **Source Activity** field as **sent**. However, we have now changed the destination to **approve_art** and the **Signal (Button Name)** field to get there is now `approve_art`. We have also specified the **Group Required** field as **Sales / Manager**, so they are the only ones that can approve the art and prepare the order to be confirmed.

With these changes, the workflow will not let us confirm a sales order unless we first approve the art for that order.

This is the modified sales order workflow up to this point:

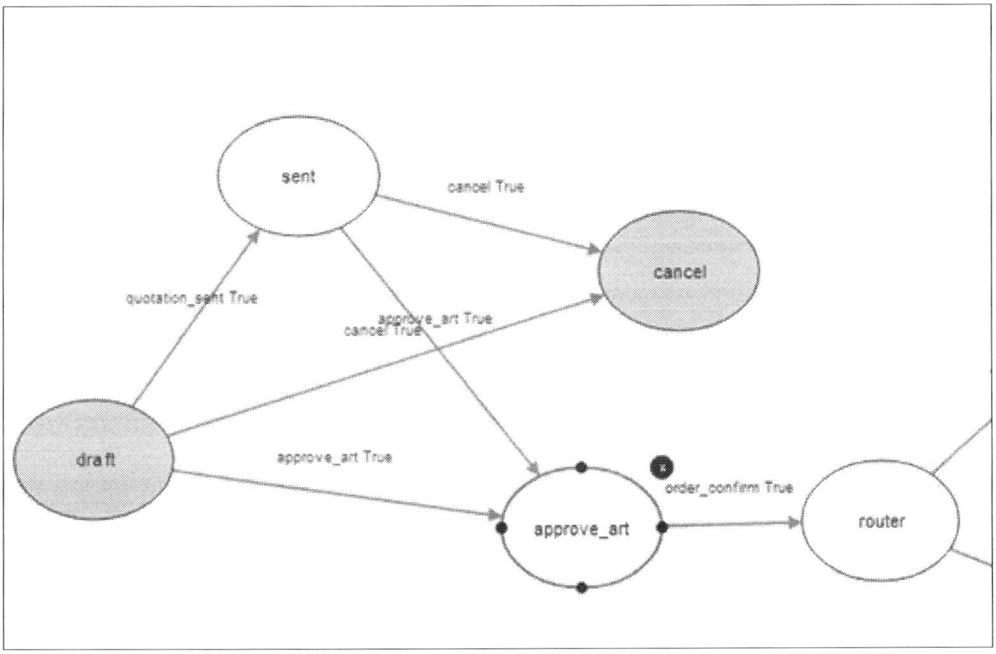

This workflow gets us very close to the behavior we desire. Notice how while we are in the draft mode, we can send a quotation, approve the art, or cancel the order. Once we have sent the sales order, we can approve the art or cancel the order. Once we are at the **approve_art** activity, we can confirm the sales order. There is one transition missing to make the workflow complete. Can you see what it is?

What happens when we are sitting in the **approve_art** state, once the art has been approved? We can confirm the order. Unfortunately, without another transition, we have no way to cancel the order. Let's add the final transition to the workflow to cancel the order.

Using the free black handle at the top of the **approve_art** activity node, drag to the cancel activity to create the transition that we need to cancel the order.

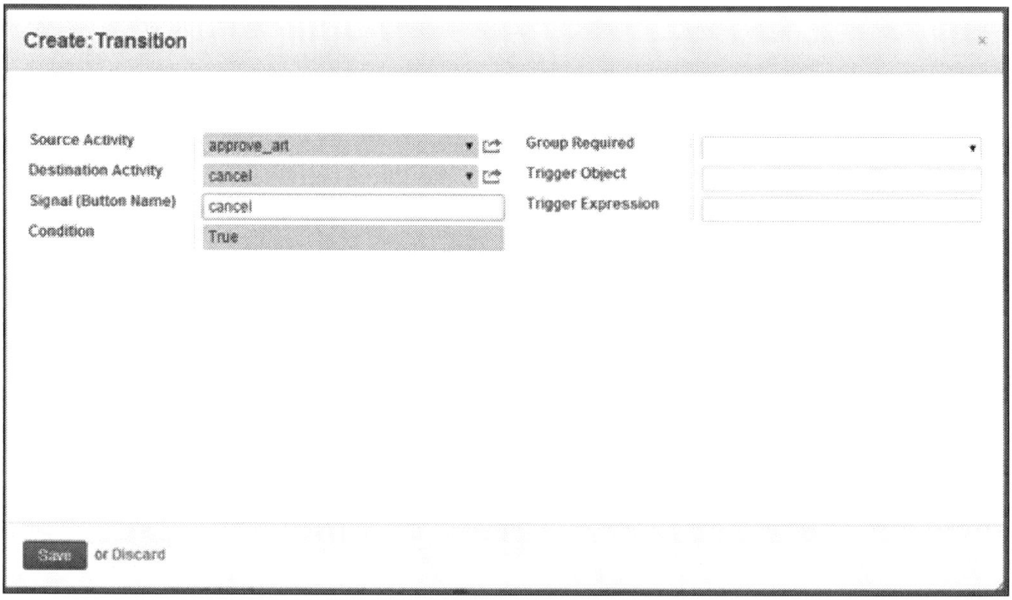

Once you save this transition, we can now cancel the quotation after the art has been approved. Our work in the workflow designer is now complete.

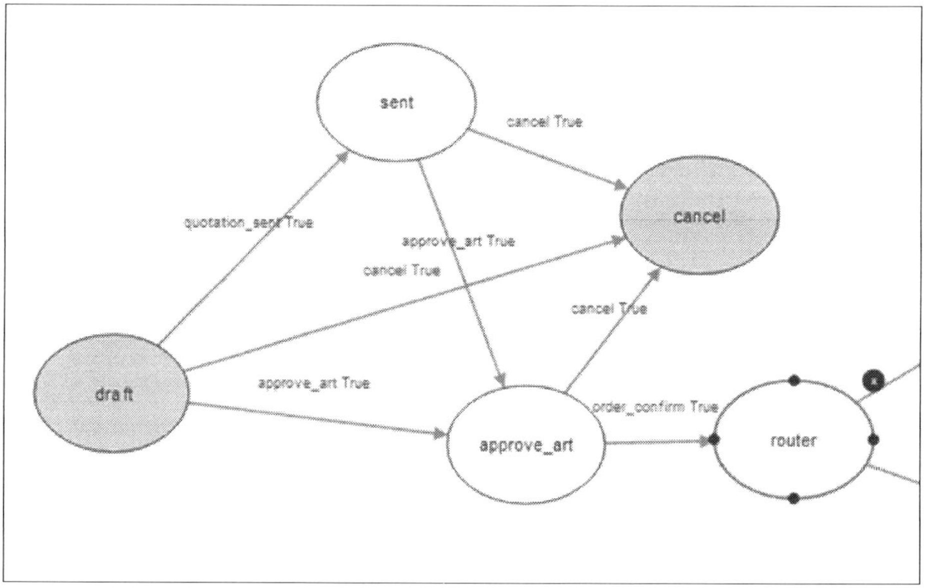

In *Chapter 16, Discovering Custom Odoo Modules*, we will expand on this workflow and create the necessary custom Odoo module that will be required to specify the **art_approved** state inside our sales order model, as well as add the **Approve Art** button to our sales order form.

Summary

In this chapter, you learned about high-level Odoo workflow views and how they can be used to better understand the processes in Odoo. Next, we looked at the developer view of the workflow designer and how you can visually analyze and modify the document workflows in Odoo. After covering the basic sales order workflow, we modified the workflow to create an approval process for the art designs in our real world project.

In the next chapter, we will dive into creating our own custom modules in Odoo. With custom modules, we can extend Odoo with additional fields, automate processes, and better integrate Odoo for an enterprise operation. Even better, Odoo's design approach means you will not be making any changes to the Odoo source code. Instead, you will learn how to extend Odoo with a module that you will build from the ground up!

16
Discovering Custom Odoo Modules

While Odoo has a lot of built-in and community modules, it is inevitable that there will be quite a few businesses that will have requirements that will be difficult to achieve with the currently available modules. The Odoo framework offers developers the capability of extending Odoo to accomplish business objectives and (hopefully) make Odoo fit in better with the workflow of the company. It is important, however, before attempting to write custom Odoo modules that you completely understand the functionality of Odoo and the various modules that are available in the community.

In this chapter, we will cover:

- Learning the basic structure of an Odoo module
- Using a module to add additional fields to your Odoo system
- Extending the views in your Odoo instance to include new fields
- Making changes to the available states to use in an Odoo workflow

Through careful configuration, many business objectives can be achieved without writing custom modules. It is important that before you go down the path of writing custom Odoo modules you make absolutely sure that the business requirements are clear and you have thoroughly explored all the options available inside Odoo. There are many settings that provide additional functionality to the Odoo system. You don't want to spend days, weeks, or even months building an Odoo module to then find out that much of that functionality was already available.

The goal of this chapter is to introduce you to custom module development in Odoo. Even if you are a beginning developer and don't know much about programming, you should be able to follow along and build a module in Odoo. If you don't know Python or XML, you are likely to find some aspects of this chapter a little more challenging. Fortunately, there are many resources in the Odoo community that can help you on your path to Odoo development.

Exploring the Odoo application and module directory

In addition to the built-in Odoo modules and the various settings that can change the way Odoo functions, there is also a growing collection of custom Odoo modules written by the community. When you find a business requirement in which you believe you might need to make some custom module development, take the time to go to the Odoo application repository and search for modules that could perhaps fit the purpose. Even if the module is not exactly what you are looking for, there can often be a lot of valuable code in those modules that can help you with your own module development.

You can find the Odoo application and module repository at `https://www.odoo.com/apps`.

Building our first Odoo module

One of the best features of the Odoo framework is that we can extend Odoo and write our own modules without having to modify any of the Odoo source code. Instead, the changes we make are all contained in their own directory and within their own files.

The primary advantage to this point is that when Odoo modifies their source code with patches or bug fixes, we do not have to worry about our changes being overwritten. Also, while we might still need to modify our code, if Odoo makes a dramatic change to their source code, there is a reasonable chance the changes required will be minimal.

> Like in other areas of Odoo development, make frequent backups of your databases. Some of the examples we will show make changes to the database that can be difficult to undo.

Each module in Odoo has basic requirements for it to be properly recognized by the Odoo framework and installed. Once we successfully install our module, then the framework will extend Odoo with the appropriate functionality.

Specifying a custom directory to hold our Odoo modules

We will begin by creating a directory to hold our Odoo module. We have two options of how we can create the directory to hold our module. With our first option, we could create our directory in the `addons` folder, where all the rest of the add-ons for Odoo are stored. This method is easy and allows Odoo to see our module simply by restarting the Odoo server.

Alternatively, we could create a separate folder to hold our add-ons. This method has the advantage that we keep our modules separate from the standard Odoo modules. However, to use this method, we must change the Odoo configuration to see the alterative directory.

To specify an alternative directory to store our modules, include the following line in the Odoo configuration file:

```
addons_path = /home/Odoo/server/addons,/home/mymodules
```

With the preceding `addons_path` specified, we could then have a directory `mymodules` within our `home` directory to store our custom Odoo modules.

After you have decided on the approach you want to take, create a directory to contain your module. For our example, we will create a directory named `silkworm` and include it in the standard Odoo `addons` directory.

The contents of your module directory

Within our module directory, `silkworm`, we will create two files that are required in every Odoo module. These two files must always be named the same:

- `__init__.py`
- `__Odoo__.py`

Although it is difficult to tell, in both cases, there are two underscores together at the beginning and then another two underscores just before the file extension. You must name these files exactly this way to have a valid Odoo module.

These are Python files and can be edited with any text editor. We will begin by defining these two required files.

Creating and editing the files

Depending on your operating system of choice, there are a variety of editors you could use to create and edit the files for your module. In Windows, you could use something as simple as Notepad. In Ubuntu, there are also several choices including Nano, Vi, or Vim.

The __init__.py file

The purpose of the `__init__.py` file is to specify the Python files you want to include in your module. You will usually have one Python file but could have more or less, depending on the complexity of the module you are developing. If you were to have a Python file with your code and that file was named `codexample.py`, you would have `import codexample` inside the `__init__.py` file. You will notice you don't have to include the `.py` extension inside the `__init__.py` file.

For our example, the `__init__.py` file will contain one line that specifies the name of the file in which we will be placing the Python code for our module:

```
import silkworm
```

The __Odoo__.py file

The `__Odoo__.py` file is essentially a manifest for your Odoo module. It describes the necessary attributes of your module to the Odoo framework. Sometimes, this file is also called the module descriptor file. The structure in the file is what is called a dictionary in Python:

```
{
    'name': 'Screen Printing',
    'version': '1.0',
    'description': """
    This module adds functionality for
         screen printing companies
    """,
    'author': 'Greg Moss',
    'depends': ['base','sale'],
    'data': ['silkworm_view.xml'],
    'demo': [],
    'installable': True,
    'auto_install': False,
}
```

This is how the `__Odoo__.py` file appears when edited in Nano.

The `__Odoo__.py` file contains a single Python dictionary. Even if you don't know Python, the syntax is simple if you have had even a little experience in programming. When you install a module in Odoo, this file describes the details the framework needs to properly configure your module.

name

The `name` entry is what will appear in the module's listing inside Odoo.

version

The `version` entry allows you to specify a version number for your module. This is valuable as you extend the functionality of your module and need to keep a track of the various releases.

description

The `description` entry will appear when you prepare to install the module in Odoo. It should clearly describe the purpose of the module to someone who might be unfamiliar with it. You should take the time to fill out this entry. Even this little bit of documentation can help someone who is trying to utilize the module in the future.

> In this example, notice the triple double-quotes before and after the description value. Python uses this syntax to allow you to continue a string on multiple lines.

author

Providing the name of the author of your module is also important, as it could help future users track down the main person who can provide assistance.

depends

The preceding elements were pretty self-explanatory and are mostly for documentation purposes. This entry, however, tells the framework what other modules your module will build upon. At minimum, you will need to include `base` as one of your module dependences. In our example, we will be extending the sales order system, so we have also included `sale` as one of the module dependencies.

data

The `data` item specifies the XML view files you want to include in your module. We will cover view files in depth later in the chapter. If you plan to change something in Odoo's forms or user interface, it is likely to involve creating a view file. Other types of data files can be specified here, such as files containing initial data or access rights, but for our example, we have named only the file `silkworm_view.xml`.

demo

Odoo provides a rather convenient method of including demonstration data with your module. When you create your database, you have the option to include demonstration data with that Odoo instance. We have left this blank for our example, but if we wished to make demonstration data available when the module is installed, we could fill in this entry.

installable

You might use the `installable` entry to temporarily disable a module for installation. Most often, it will be `True` because you want the ability to install the module in an Odoo instance.

auto_install

When the `auto_install` entry is set to `True`, Odoo will then automatically install this module when it finds that all the dependency modules are installed. If you have no dependencies, this means that it will be automatically installed when you create a new database. Given Odoo's modular application approach, you typically would not want to have the `auto_install` flag set to true for most module development.

Extending an Odoo model in silkworm.py

Next, we create another file named `silkworm.py`. We will begin by creating a module that performs the same customizations we performed through the developer mode in *Chapter 13, Customizing Odoo for Your Business*.

Why would we want to put our customization into a module, rather than just using developer mode?

First off, changes made through the developer mode are isolated within that instance of Odoo. If you decide that you want to create a new database, you will have to make all the developer changes by hand, again. More importantly, when you make the changes in a module, you have much more control over the final results.

> The developer mode is very powerful for quickly looking at views, analyzing fields on forms, and understanding more about the Odoo framework. However, it is typically far better to make any actual changes by creating a module rather than modifying the views or models in the developer mode.

Using a module to add custom fields to a model

In *Chapter 13, Customizing Odoo for Your Business*, we added **Date Required** and **Rush Order** to our `sales.order` model. Now let's see how we can do exactly the same thing in our module.

In our `__init__.py` file, we only had one line, the `import silkworm` command.

To add the **Date Required** and **Rush Order** fields to our sales order, we can place the following code in the `silkworm.py` file:

```
from osv import osv, fields


class silkworm_sale_order(osv.Model):
    _inherit = 'sale.order'

    _columns = {
        'x_daterequired': fields.date('Date Required'),
        'x_rush': fields.boolean('Rush Order'),
      }
```

> In Python, the `from` command allows you to specify which libraries you wish to utilize in your custom classes. For our simple example, we are only pulling in `osv` and `fields`.

Inheriting from the sales order module in Odoo

In our `class` statement, we specify the class `silkworm_sale_order`, and it has the parameter `osv.Model`. Remember that when learning the Odoo framework, it will take a bit of time to get familiar to the syntax. For now, you don't have to understand why you are specifying `osv.Model`; just understand that it is required with most classes:

```
_inherit= 'sale.order'
```

For those new to object-oriented programming in general, the `_inherit` statement essentially makes the functionality of the Odoo sales order module available to your class.

Next, we can extend the Odoo sales order module with our two custom fields:

```
    _columns = {
        'x_daterequired': fields.date('Date Required',
required=True),
        'x_rush': fields.boolean('Rush Order'),
        }
```

Once again, this is a Python dictionary. We specify the names of the fields on the left followed by a colon. You will notice in the syntax that we also specify the data types and provide the labels we want to display in the views inside Odoo. Notice that we have also set `required=True` for the `x_daterequired` field so that the user will have to provide this data when they create a sales order record.

Python conventions

Unlike many programming languages, Python takes white space very seriously. In fact, you must exactly indent your code or the Python compiler will generate an error. For example, the `_inherit` attribute and the `_columns` dictionary are indented exactly four spaces over from the `class` command.

Adding the fields to our sales order view

Now that we have specified the fields, we want to add our sales order model; we must now create our view file that will display the fields in the sales order header. We have specified the name of this file inside of `__Odoo__.py` within the `data` entry. For our example, the file name is `silkworm_view.xml`.

Using your editor of choice, create the `silkworm_view.xml` file. In this file, place the following code:

```
<?xml version="1.0" encoding="utf-8"?>

<Odoo>
    <data>
       <record id="sale_view_order_form" model="ir.ui.view">
         <field name="model">sale.order</field>
         <field name="inherit_id" ref="sale.view_order_form"/>
         <field name="arch" type="xml">
           <field name="client_order_ref" position="after">
             <field name="x_daterequired"/>
             <field name="x_rush"/>
```

```
            </field>
        </record>
    </data>
</Odoo>
```

Odoo specifies views using the XML syntax. The first line in the file is the standard element that you will find at the top of many XML files, specifying the version and type of encoding used.

Next, Odoo view files contain beginning and ending `Odoo` tags. Inside these tags, there are matching opening and closing `data` tags. To modify or add views in your custom Odoo module, you add `record` tags.

Each record must have an `id` tag. In this case, we also have a `model` tag that is specified as `ir.ui.view`:

```
<record id="sale_view_order_form" model="ir.ui.view">
```

This is a framework convention, and you will learn about other models that are available as you continue to study Odoo development.

Next, we must specify the base `model` with which this view interacts. For our example, this is `sale.order`. This relates directly to the fact that we have added the fields to the `sale.order` model in our Python file:

```
<field name="model">sale.order</field>
```

If, instead, you were adding additional fields to the purchase order header, you would specify `purchase.order`.

> Use the developer mode in Odoo to hover over fields and determine which models they relate to. To find the view names you need to use, go into **Manage Views** in the developer mode. This can save you a great deal of time when developing in Odoo.

Next, let's look at the line that contains `inherit_id`:

```
<field name="inherit_id" ref="sale.view_order_form"/>
```

Much like we had to inherit from `sale.model` when we create our `silkworm_sale_order` class, we must inherit from the `sale.view_order_form` view so that we can add the additional fields. One big trick in finding the value you require for `ref` is to use **Manage Views** while in the developer mode.

For this example, while on a sales order in Odoo, choose **Manage Views** from the developer menu on the left. You will then get taken to the form that shows you exactly the **External ID** field you need to add fields to the form.

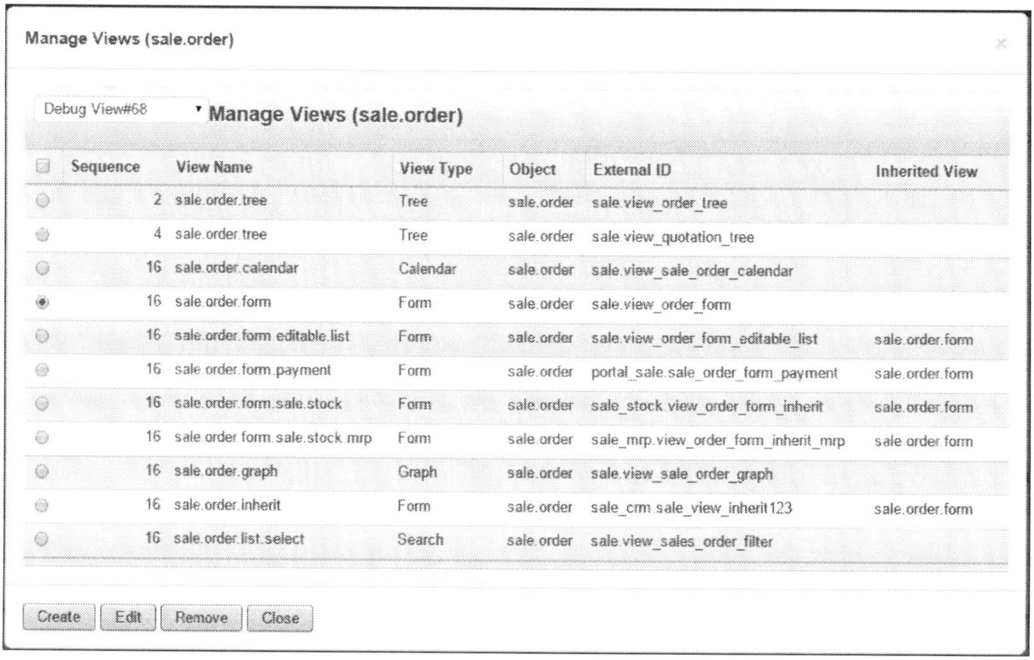

The **Manage Views** screen shown here is available in the developer mode menu.

This screen can be a very handy reference for you to find the information to reference the base form that you wish to update. Essentially, you place the value from the **External ID** field into the `ref` attribute for the `_inherit` entry:

```
<field name="inherit_id" ref="sale.view_order_form"/>
```

The next entry in the list is required for all view changes:

```
<field name="arch" type="xml">
```

Like other aspects of the framework, you don't need to know exactly why this syntax is used. Just use it.

Now we are ready to get to the segments that specify exactly where we wish to place our new custom fields on the form:

```
<field name="client_order_ref" position="after">
```

When you are adding fields to a form, it is important for Odoo to have the information it requires to determine exactly where the fields should go. In this example, we are telling the Odoo framework that we want to first find the field named `client_order_ref`. Next, we use `position="after"` to specify that we want the fields to appear after `client_order_ref`.

> In addition to `after`, the position attribute can be specified as `position="before"` to place a field before that element or `position="replace"` to replace an element. If, instead of `after` you used `replace`, the `client_order_ref` field would be replaced by the new field we add next.

Once again, we can use the developer mode to visually find the field name we require. Here, we have moved the mouse over the **Customer Reference** field to reveal details about that field.

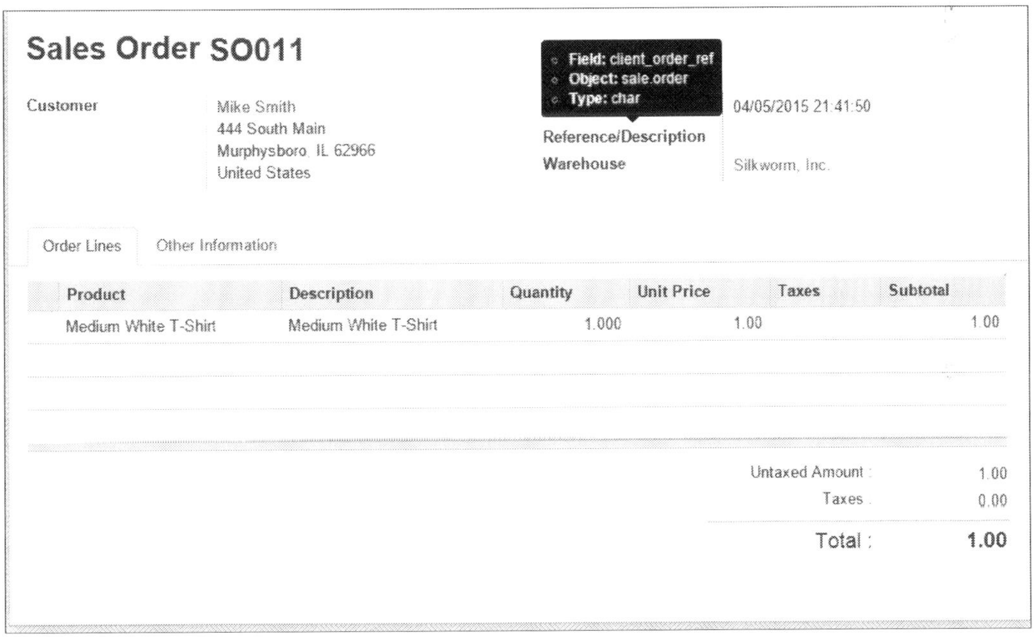

Now that we know where to add our fields, we can specify custom fields to display:

```
<field name="x_daterequired"/>
<field name="x_rush"/>
```

Getting ready to install our module

Right now, our module is very simple and just adds two fields to our sales order form. Still, we should quickly review the files that you should have in your module directory:

- `__init__.py`
- `__Odoo__.py`
- `silkworm.py`
- `silkworm_view.py`

To install the module, you must restart your server. If you don't restart your server, then Odoo will not see your module. If you have put the module folder in the Odoo `addons` directory, where the rest of the modules reside, and all of your syntax is correct in the files, there is a good chance that you are ready to install the module.

In the top menu, click on **Settings** and choose **Update Modules List** from the menus on the left:

On the **Module Update** screen, click on the **Update** button. Once you have clicked on **Update**, Odoo will refresh the available list of add-ons.

Next, we will install the module. Click on **Installed Modules** from the menu on the left.

> When you create a custom module, do not use the **Apps** option under the **Modules** menu section. This will only show you the modules and applications that are available on the Odoo app repository or are part of the standard Odoo installation.

Remove the **Installed** filter from the search box. Yes, this entire process is somewhat counter-intuitive. Just think of the **Installed Modules** section as the place that truly holds all the available modules including your custom modules. Once you take off the **Installed** filter you can search for `silk` to locate your module for installation.

Click on the **Install** button to begin the installation process.

After a few seconds, the screen will refresh. You can now pull up a sales order and see the fields added to your form.

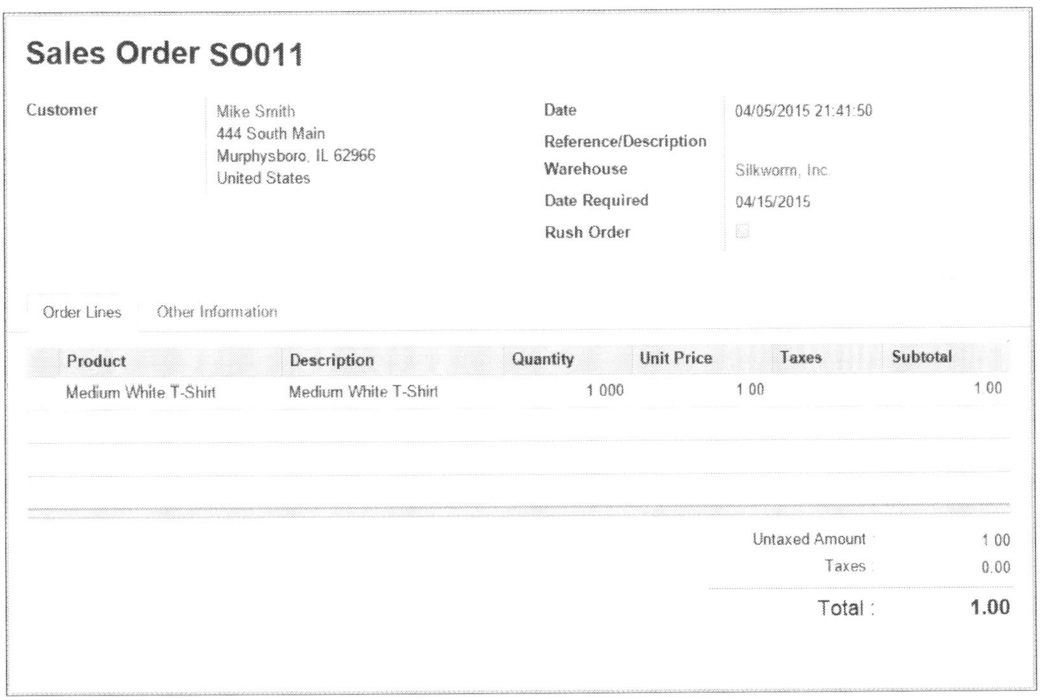

This screenshot of a sales order shows the custom fields added in our module.

> When developing, it is inevitable that a module will not install correctly or after installing you will have an error that will prevent you from logging into Odoo. If you find yourself unable to resolve the error, one workaround to get Odoo back up and running again is to rename the module directory. This prevents Odoo from locating the module to be installed.

Extending our module to customize the sales order workflow

In the workflow chapter (*Chapter 15, Understanding Workflows*), we created a workflow that would require art to be approved before a sales order could be confirmed. Now, we will extend our custom module to integrate with that workflow and implement the required business process. When modifying workflows, you are frequently working with the state of the document. As a business process is executed, the system manages the flow of that process by setting the state of the documents involved.

The standard Odoo workflow allows you three primary options when you create a draft sales order: confirm the draft sales order, send the draft order to a customer by e-mail, or cancel the draft sales order. Depending on your business requirements, there are quite a few other steps involved than what the default workflow provides. For our business example, we wish to have an **Approve Art** stage that must be completed before a sales order can be confirmed.

Adding the button to the sales order

In order to approve the artwork, we will need to add a button to the sales order form. This button is then the trigger to set the state of the document to `art-approved`. While it is possible to add a button to your form by going through the developer mode, it is far better to put your code into a module.

Let's look at the code for `silkworm_view.xml` after we have included the code required to add this button to the sales order:

```
<?xml version="1.0" encoding="utf-8"?>

<Odoo>
    <data>
        <record id="sale_view_order_form" model="ir.ui.view">
          <field name="model">sale.order</field>
          <field name="inherit_id" ref="sale.view_order_form"/>
```

```
            <field name="arch" type="xml">

              <button name="print_quotation" position="after">
                   <button name="approve_art" string="Approve Art"
                   states="draft,sent" groups="base.group_user"/>
              </button>

              <field name="client_order_ref" position="after">
                <field name="x_daterequired"/>
                <field name="x_rush"/>
              </field>
            </field>
          </record>
       </data>
   </Odoo>
```

Just like when we added the **Date Required** and **Rush Order** fields to the form, we can add a button to the form in a similar manner:

```
<button name="print_quotation" position="after">
```

This tells Odoo that we want to position our **Approve Art** button after the **Print_Quotation** button. Between the open and closing button tags, we place the code for our new button:

```
<button name="approve_art" string="Approve Art"
states="draft,sent" groups="base.group_user"/>
```

We have named our button `approve_art`. In our workflow, we specified `approve_art` as the trigger. Let's look again at how that trigger is specified in the workflow:

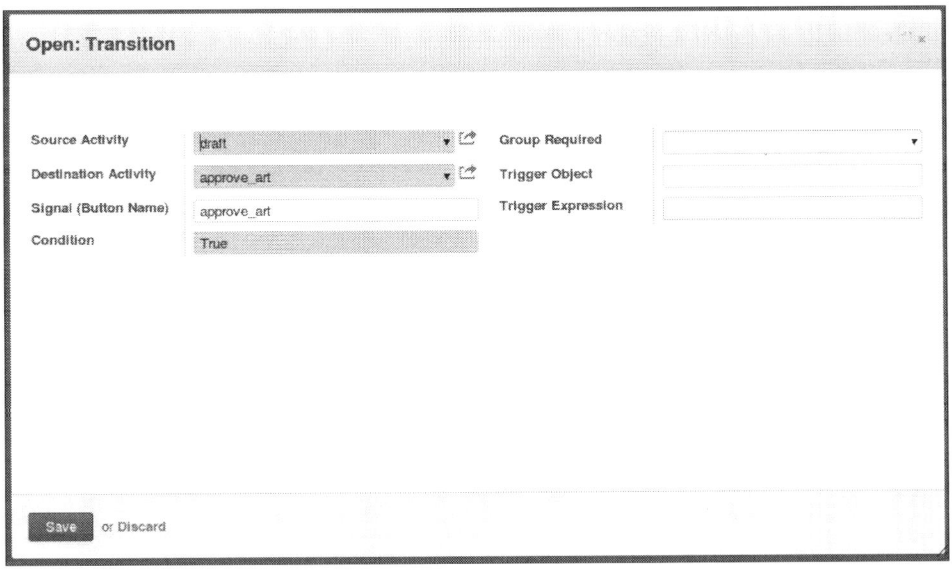

This screenshot depicts the workflow transition from `draft` to `approved_art`.

By adding the button in our form view, we now have the ability to transition from the `draft` node to the `approve_art` node in our workflow. The **Signal (Button Name)** value matches the `name` attribute of the button in our module.

Notice also that the **Source Activity** option of the transition is `draft`. In the button code, we have included the attribute `states="draft,sent"`. Odoo buttons include a `states` attribute that lets you specify in what states the button will be active.

> You will need to always make sure that you set the states attribute of your button to match the corresponding **Source Activity** in your workflow.

For our example, we have specified `draft` and `sent` because those are the states in which we wish the **Approve Art** button to be active.

Modifying the available states of the sales order model

Next, we need to update our sales order model to add the `art_approved` state as one of the potential states of the sales order. When we override the list of available states in the sales order, we are going to be required to specify all of the potential states.

While there are better, more sophisticated designs you would use for a production system, for this example, we are going to get the available states from the Odoo sales order module and then add the state we need to this list. When building your module in Odoo, it is vital to become familiar with the base modules you are extending. Since we are extending the sales order module, let's open up the base sales order code and find the `state` column in that class.

Finding your way around the base Odoo modules

Odoo modules and applications are all stored in the same folder, `addons`. Each module has its own folder and are generally well-named and easy to associate with the functionality in Odoo.

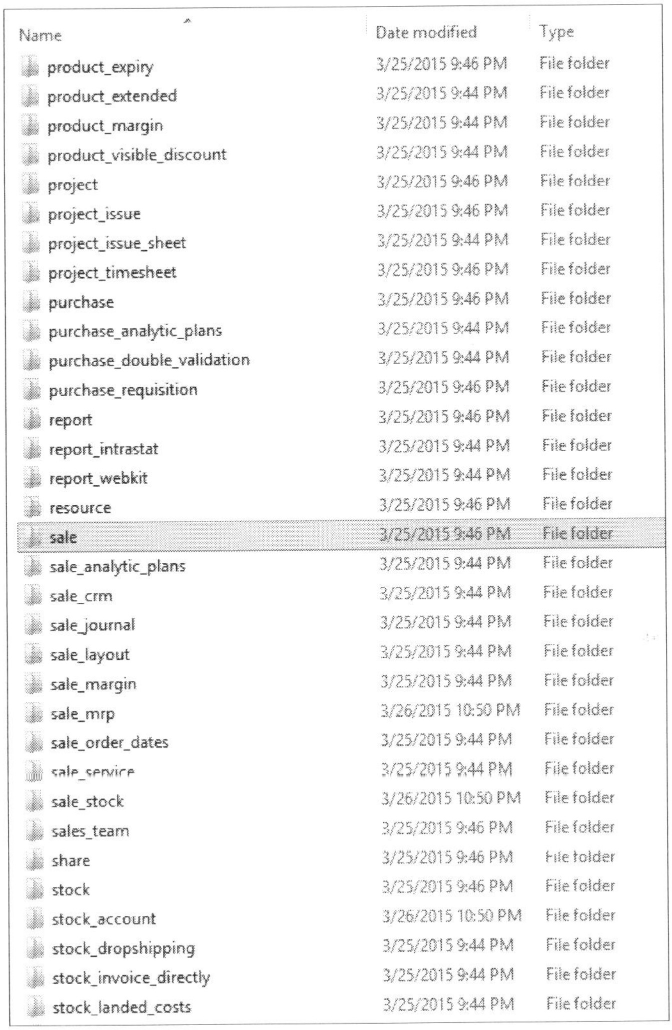

Since we are working in the sales order module, we need to look in the `sale` directory for the code file. Odoo is also pretty consistent about naming the primary module code the same as the directory, only with a python extension (`.py`).

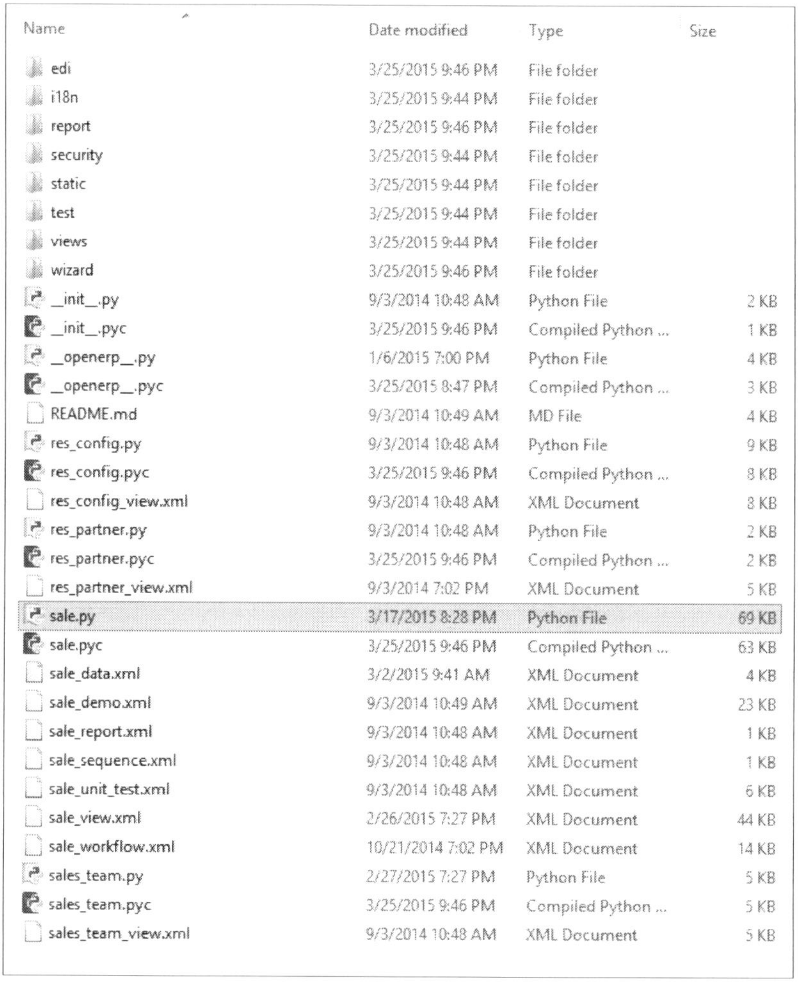

After we open up our file in the text editor, we want to find the `sale_order` class. This is the same class from which we inherited our module. Next, after finding that class, we want to find the column that determines the values for the state. After you have explored a few of the Odoo classes, it will be easier for you to find where the columns are defined.

Here is the code in `sale.py` that interests us:

```
'discount': fields.float('Discount (%)', digits_compute=
dp.get_precision('Discount'), readonly=True,
states={'draft': [('readonly', False)]}),
'th_weight': fields.float('Weight', readonly=True,
states={'draft': [('readonly', False)]}),

'state': fields.selection([('cancel', 'Cancelled'),('draft',
'Draft'),('confirmed', 'Confirmed'),('exception',
'Exception'),('done', 'Done')], 'Status', required=True,
readonly=True,
        help='* The \'Draft\' status is set when the related
        sales order in draft status. \
            \n* The \'Confirmed\' status is set when the
            related sales order is confirmed. \
            \n* The \'Exception\' status is set when the
            related sales order is set as exception. \
            \n* The \'Done\' status is set when the sales
            order line has been picked. \
            \n* The \'Cancelled\' status is set when a user
            cancel the sales order related.'),

'order_partner_id': fields.related('order_id',
'partner_id', type='many2one', relation='res.partner',
store=True, string='Customer'),
'salesman_id':fields.related('order_id', 'user_id',
type='many2one', relation='res.users', store=True,
string='Salesperson'),
```

The `state` column in our model is what we need to extend with our `art approved` state option. Here, you can see the other states that are already available in sales order:

- `cancel`
- `draft`
- `confirmed`
- `exception`
- `done`

We will then copy the `state` column from `sale.py` and paste it into our module. Next, we extend the available states with `art_approve`.

Updating the other buttons for the workflow

If you are ambitious and went ahead and rebuilt your module and ran it, you would quickly find that more work needs to be done. Even though we have added our button to the form and can now actually accept that button into our workflow, we must adjust the `states` attribute of the other buttons so that they are active at the appropriate times. For example, we do not want the **Confirm Sale** button available on the screen until the art is approved.

Modifying the attributes of the confirm button

By default, the **Confirm Sale** button is available when the sales order is in a draft state. Adding the following code to our XML view tells OpenERP to modify the attribute of the **Confirm Sale** button so that it is only available after the art has been approved:

```
<button name="action_button_confirm" position="attributes">
      <attribute name="states">art_approved</attribute>
</button>
```

In this example, we have used the `position="attributes"` attribute (yes, that is a bit confusing) to modify the `states` attribute of the `action_button_confirm` button in the default sales order workflow. The **Confirm Sale** button will no longer be available while the sales order is in the `draft` state. The sales order must be in the `art_approved` state for the **Confirm Sale** button to be visible on the form.

Modifying the attributes of the print and cancel buttons

Modifying workflows will often require you to carefully consider when you want buttons to appear, and when you do not want buttons to appear. For our example, while we are waiting to approve the art, we still want to be able to print the order and cancel the order. With the default **Sales Order** module buttons, these buttons will not be visible when the state of the sales order is in `art_approved`. Therefore, we must update the attributes of these buttons so that they will be visible once the art has been approved:

```
<button name="print_quotation" position="attributes">
     <attribute name="states">draft,sent,art_approved</attribute>
</button>

<button name="cancel" position="attributes">
     <attribute name="states">draft,sent,art_approved</attribute>
</button>
```

For each button, we have modified the states attributes to include the `art_approved` date. It is also important that we include all the other states we want to have these buttons visible as well. We are completely replacing the default states with the states from our module.

> Modifying workflows and states can have unpredictable consequences on existing documents. Make sure that you back up your database. Test your modified workflows carefully and ensure data integrity when modifying workflows in live production systems.

Seeing it all come together

Now after you save, restart the server, and run your module, the workflow for the sales order will be modified so that you can only confirm orders that have had their art approved.

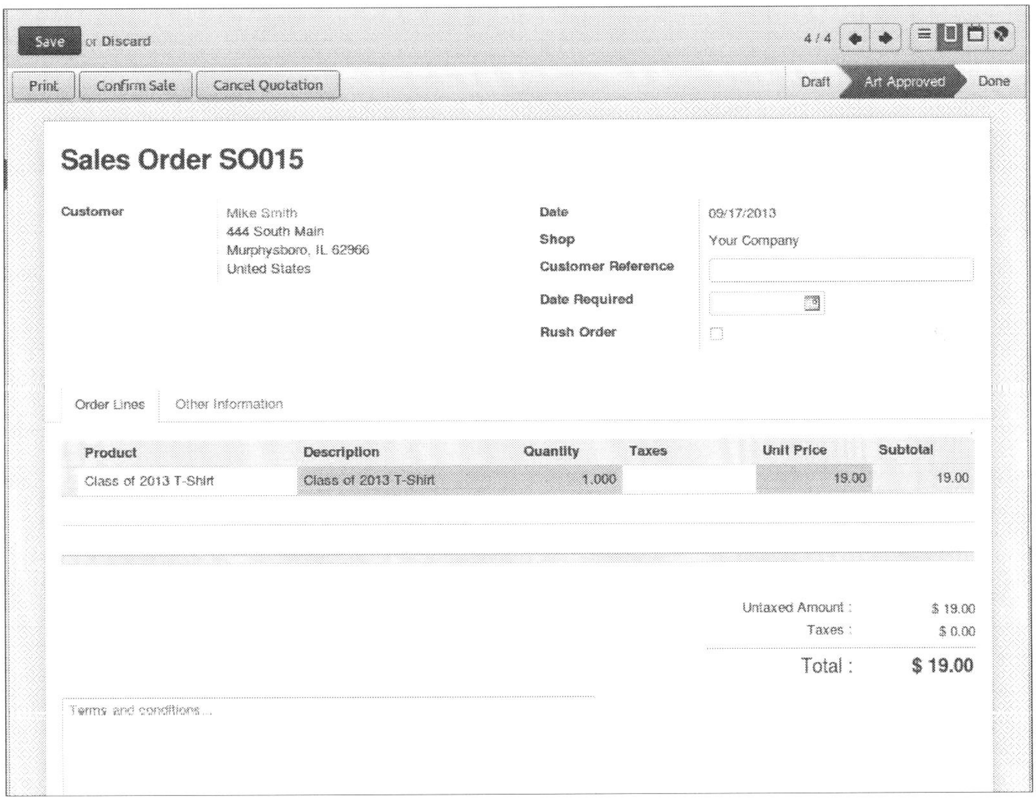

You will see that not only do the buttons now properly behave with our workflow, the **Art Approved** state is now displayed in the upper-right corner. The user is getting clear feedback that the art has been approved, and the sales order is now ready to be confirmed.

Using a module to add a filter to a search view

One very nice feature of Odoo is the flexible but easy-to-use search functionality that is provided on every list view. With a module, you can add additional filter options that make it easier for users to find the information they are looking for. In our real-world example, we have placed an importance on rush orders. Therefore, it would be desirable to have a filter option on our sales order view that will limit our listing to only display rush orders.

Here is how the final search filter view will appear after we implement the module changes:

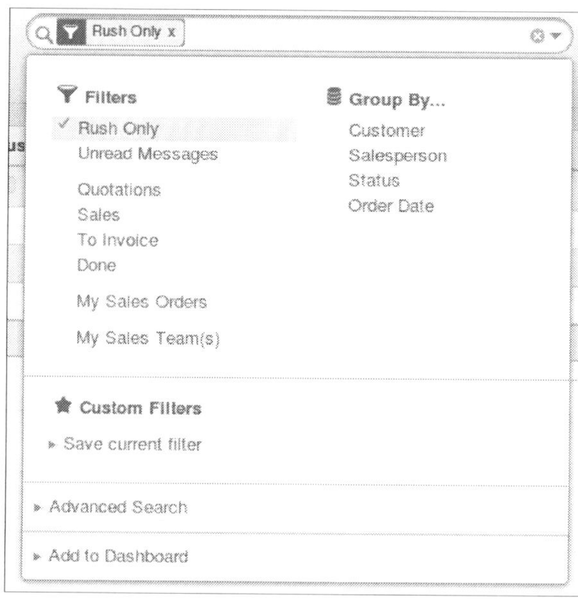

When **Rush Order** is checked, the sales order list view will limit the orders to only those orders that are specified as rush orders. Quickly, users can now locate rush orders without creating custom filters. This is an example of how a small change can have significant real-world benefits to usability. Best of all, with Odoo, you are making these changes without modifying any of the base Odoo source code.

Adding the code to create the rush order filter

The code segment will naturally be added to the `silkworm_view.xml` file. It will have the same record structure as our other modification. Adding this code segment and updating the module will implement the change we desire:

```
<record id="sale_view_sales_order_filter" model="ir.ui.view">
      <field name="name">sale.order.search</field>
     <field name="model">sale.order</field>
     <field name="inherit_id" ref="sale.view_sales_order_filter"/>
     <field name="arch" type="xml">
        <field name="name" position="after">
        <filter name="rush" string="Rush Only" domain="[('x_
rush','=',True)]"/>
        </field>
      </field>
     </record>
```

Let's look at some of the more important elements of this code segment. It follows a similar structure as the modification that added fields to our form. When looking at the code in any module, it is most important to identify the `inherit_id` field's `ref` value. This is what ties your view modifications to the view in the base module.

In this case, our `inherit_id` is `sale.view_sales_order_filter`.

> Use the developer mode to lookup the view name from inside Odoo. Navigate to the view you want to work with and in the developer menu; you can choose **Manage View** to see the external ID of the view. You can also use the developer mode to quickly look at the syntax of views and use them to help you determine how your filters should be structured.

Creating the filter

The filter is specified by one line of XML code:

```
<filter name="rush" string="Rush Only"
domain="[('x_rush','=',True)]"/>
```

In this code, we specify the name of our filter and the string we wish to display in the search view. The filter is applied with the domain parameter. We specify the field from our sales order model and that it must equal `true` in order for this filter to be valid.

The technical name for this syntax in Python is a **Tuple**. It is possible to include multiple filters in the domain. For example, we can also specify that we only want sales orders that are confirmed by specifying an additional condition in our filter:

```
<filter name="rush" string="Rush Only"
domain="[('x_rush','=',True),('state','=','progress')]"/>
```

Odoo considers a confirmed sales order to be in the state specified as progress. With this change, our rush only filter will also limit the sales orders to only those that are confirmed.

Summary

In this chapter, you learned about the basic Odoo structure for modules. Files must be named in exactly the way the Odoo framework expects, and you must follow the structure for your module to properly load into Odoo. We explored how to extend Odoo with additional fields and display them on forms. Next, we extended our custom module with a workflow example. This allowed us to see how we can peek into existing Odoo modules to assist us with developing our own module.

Locating Additional Odoo Resources

Odoo is built using a variety of open source technologies and components. This appendix includes a list of resources that can extend your knowledge in supporting an Odoo installation.

Locating the essential Odoo documentation

If you are looking for the official Odoo documentation, this is the link for you `https://www.odoo.com/documentation`.

This documentation currently automatically directs you to the latest Odoo version and provides direct access to the fundamental technical documentation.

Visiting the Official Odoo help forum

When you run into issues with your Odoo installation or you have questions about specific features, one of the best resources available is the official Odoo help forum. The site is simple, in that you can search for questions and if you can't find your specific question been addressed, you can then ask your own questions at `http://help.Odoo.com`.

The Odoo Community Association

The **Odoo Community Association**, or **OCA**, is a nonprofit organization whose mission is to support the collaborative development of Odoo features and promote its widespread use. The OCA is committed to providing resources and legal support to the Odoo community and ensuring that Odoo remains both open source and maintained for the public benefit. You can visit OCA at `https://odoo-community.org/`.

Finding Odoo applications and modules

Odoo 8.0 is typically downloaded in a format that already comes with many modules that are available for installation. However, there are many more modules in the online repository. If you are thinking about making any customizations in Odoo, check this link to make sure someone else has not already done the work for you: `https://apps.Odoo.com/`.

Getting the latest Odoo 8 release notes

While it is kind of buried and has a funny URL, this is a good resource for changes in Odoo 8, `https://www.odoo.com/blog/odoo-news-5/post/odoo-8-release-notes-186`.

Downloading Odoo from GitHub

Odoo branches are maintained on GitHub. The primary Odoo project is located at: `https://github.com/odoo/odoo`.

Locating resources on Ubuntu

While you can certainly work with Odoo under the Windows environment, most of the community is in agreement that it is better to run your Odoo server under Ubuntu. Here are some resources that can help you get started with Ubuntu.

The official Ubuntu website

If you are planning on working with Odoo and Ubuntu, you will want to begin by getting familiar with the official Ubuntu website at `http://www.ubuntu.com/`.

Directly download Ubuntu server or desktop

Resources for downloading Ubuntu in various formats and configurations are available at `http://www.ubuntu.com/download`.

The official Ubuntu documentation

The official Ubuntu website has a comprehensive set of documentation that is a great reference for troubleshooting your Odoo installation, which is available at `https://help.ubuntu.com/`.

Getting access to additional developer documentation

The Odoo framework provides a lot of power, but also comes with a fairly steep learning curve. While *Chapter 16, Discovering Customer Odoo Modules*, will help get you started, if you are serious about developing for Odoo, you will find the resources listed here in valuable in your pursuit.

Getting quick access to Odoo installations using Odoo Runbot

Wouldn't it be great if you could try out a variety of Odoo builds and installations quickly and easily, without going through all the time and complexity of an Odoo installation? Well, fortunately, the Odoo Runbot provides you with many different Odoo branches that you can connect to and actually review the build for yourself.

This resource divides the installations by version, build, and age of the version. Even better, you can get immediate access to the branches right on GitHub, which is available at `http://runbot.Odoo.com/`.

Finding the Postgres resources

Along with supporting any ERP system, it is important to understand the underlying database architecture. Odoo 8.0 requires Postgres 9.1 or later as the backend database. Here is a list of resources that can help you maintain your Postgres server.

The official Postgres website

While Odoo handles many of the complex database management tasks you would have with other ERP systems, there will be times when the official Postgres website will be useful in maintaining your Odoo installation, which is available at `http://www.postgresql.org/`.

Downloading Postgres

The following are links for downloading Postgres in various configurations:

- `http://www.postgresql.org/download/`
- `http://www.postgresql.org/download/linux/ubuntu/`

The Postgres documentation

The standard Postgres documentation will be useful when you need to perform operations on your Odoo database, which is available at `http://www.postgresql.org/docs/9.3`.

Locating the Python resources

Odoo modules are created in Python, a free and powerful programming language. Most module development will require you to at least become familiar with the basics of Python. Odoo requires Python version 2.7 or higher.

The official Python website

The link to the official website for Python is `http://www.python.org/`.

Downloading Python

Depending on the platform you plan to install Odoo on to, you might need to download Python before you can install Odoo from `http://www.python.org/download/`.

The Python documentation

Writing modules or applications in Odoo requires a basic knowledge of Python. The official Python documentation can be located at `http://docs.python.org/2/`.

Finding the XML resources

Odoo views are designed and maintained in XML, which is short for Extensible Markup Language. A basic understanding of XML will help you in customizing views, modifying search criteria, and managing workflows. Here is a list of XML resources.

The World Wide Web Consortium XML resource page

This is the official page for the XML specification, `http://www.w3.org/XML/`.

The XML tutorials and documentation

If you are just beginning to learn XML, make sure that you visit this excellent collection of tutorials and documentation at `http://www.w3schools.com/xml/`.

Locating the RML resources

RML or Report Markup Language is a specialized XML format utilized for reporting. Odoo uses RML for most forms and simple reports inside of Odoo. Understanding RML basics will help you in designing reports or modifying headers and footers of reports, which are available at `http://www.reportlab.com/docs/rml-for-idiots.pdf`.

Alternative reporting solutions

Many companies will want more reporting options that are currently not available in Odoo. Like many other ERP systems, companies will typically utilize and integrate alternative reporting platforms. Here are a few that are popular in the Odoo community.

Aeroo reports

Aeroo reports is a reporting engine for Odoo that is based on the Aeroo library. Report templates are created in **Open Document Format** (**ODF**) and were considered a very popular alternative to RML reports in Odoo 7. This is still a perfectly viable reporting solution with an Odoo 8 version that you can download from the Odoo application store, which is available at `https://apps.openerp.com/apps/modules/8.0/report_aeroo/`.

Jaspersoft reports

Jaspersoft offers a variety of both open source and licensed reporting solutions. There is a report server as well as has a very nice graphical report editor available.

The community edition of the Jasper reports server

The community edition of Jasper reports server is available at `http://community.jaspersoft.com/project/jasperreports-server`.

The community edition of the Ireport designer

The server software provides report access and processing. To design reports graphically, you will need to download the Ireport designer for the operating system of your choice, which is available at `http://community.jaspersoft.com/project/ireport-designer`.

Pentaho/Kettle

Pentaho, which is also known as Kettle, is a very useful tool for data translations and for reporting to Excel or other formats. It doesn't provide the extensive reporting tools of Jasper but is very robust integrating Odoo with other systems and creating automated data exports. Depending on your needs, Pentaho might help. You can download it from `http://kettle.pentaho.com/`.

Index

Symbols

A

B

C

D

E

F

G

H

I

J

K

L

M

O

P

Q

R

S

X

Y

[PACKT] open source
community experience distilled
PUBLISHING

Thank you for buying
Working with Odoo

About Packt Publishing

Packt, pronounced 'packed', published its first book, *Mastering phpMyAdmin for Effective MySQL Management*, in April 2004, and subsequently continued to specialize in publishing highly focused books on specific technologies and solutions.

Our books and publications share the experiences of your fellow IT professionals in adapting and customizing today's systems, applications, and frameworks. Our solution-based books give you the knowledge and power to customize the software and technologies you're using to get the job done. Packt books are more specific and less general than the IT books you have seen in the past. Our unique business model allows us to bring you more focused information, giving you more of what you need to know, and less of what you don't.

Packt is a modern yet unique publishing company that focuses on producing quality, cutting-edge books for communities of developers, administrators, and newbies alike. For more information, please visit our website at `www.packtpub.com`.

About Packt Open Source

In 2010, Packt launched two new brands, Packt Open Source and Packt Enterprise, in order to continue its focus on specialization. This book is part of the Packt Open Source brand, home to books published on software built around open source licenses, and offering information to anybody from advanced developers to budding web designers. The Open Source brand also runs Packt's Open Source Royalty Scheme, by which Packt gives a royalty to each open source project about whose software a book is sold.

Writing for Packt

We welcome all inquiries from people who are interested in authoring. Book proposals should be sent to `author@packtpub.com`. If your book idea is still at an early stage and you would like to discuss it first before writing a formal book proposal, then please contact us; one of our commissioning editors will get in touch with you.

We're not just looking for published authors; if you have strong technical skills but no writing experience, our experienced editors can help you develop a writing career, or simply get some additional reward for your expertise.